"Rarely has a book so amply fulfilled the promise of its title! Steven Sabat's unique ability to interpret the life worlds of his patients, his scholarly grasp of the research literature, and his vivid case histories set a new standard in understanding the experience of Alzheimer's Disease. In an age of neuroscience and genetic determinism, his book is a timely reminder that mental disorder, even in cases of obvious 'brain disease', may be a product as much of dysfunctional treatments as of dysfunctional brains." **Bill Fulford, Editor,** *Philosophy, Psychiatry, Psychology*

"This is truly a humane and scholarly treatise on the lived experience of Alzheimer's Disease. Sabat guides us beyond the shattered biomedical world of patients diagnosed with dementia to reveal them still as people with intact capabilities. A 'must read' for anyone involved in the assessment, diagnosis, and treatment of AD." **Phyllis Braudy Harris, Professor of Sociology, John Carroll University and co-editor of** *Dementia: The International Journal of Social Research and Practice*

"Steven Sabat's book points the way to a soundly based and eminently humane approach to dealing with the problems of language and communication that are encountered in Alzheimer's Disease. Linguists and psycholinguists could learn a great deal from him." **Roy Harris, Editor,** *Language and Communication*

"This is the finest book thus far written about the experience of Alzheimer's Disease. Readers will be deeply impressed by Sabat's many detailed observations and interpretations of the psychological needs of persons with dementia, and with his case examples of how responding to these needs can be beneficial. This book is an immediate classic." **Stephen G. Post, Center for Biomedical Ethics, Case Western Reserve University**

"In his deep commitment to discovering and honoring the experience of selfhood, Sabat has penetrated the tangled veil of Alzheimer's to reveal with illuminating scholarship, uncommon empathy, and profoundly skilled listening the enduring humanity of persons with the disease." **Lisa Snyder, Alzheimer's Disease Research Center, University of California, San Diego**

To my father, *Gabriel,* and to the memory of my mother, *Edythe*, members of "the greatest generation," who encouraged me to find my own path, define my own good, and to give to others,

To the memory of my nana, *Gussie Bloom Chester*, who taught me that dignity and sweet love remain alive despite old age and illness to the body,

To my daughter, *Deborah*, who brings unimaginable love and joy to my life; may she find her own path, define her own good, and give to others,

And,

To the memory of my beloved aunt, *Helen Billie Chester*, without whose shining, vibrant, loving presence, and untimely, tragic death, this book never would have been written.

STEVEN R. SABAT

The Experience of Alzheimer's Disease

Life Through a Tangled Veil

The right of Steven R. Sabat to be identified as author
of this work has been asserted in accordance with
the Copyright, Designs and Patents Act 1988

First published 2001

2 4 6 8 10 9 7 5 3 1

Blackwell Publishers Ltd
108 Cowley Road
Oxford OX4 1JF
UK

Blackwell Publishers Inc.
350 Main Street
Malden, Massachusetts 02148
USA

British Library Cataloguing in Publication Data

A CIP catalogue record for this book is available from the
British Library.

Library of Congress Cataloging-in-Publication Data
is available for this book.

ISBN 0631 216650 (hbk)
ISBN 0631 216669 (pbk)

Typeset in 10.5 on 13 pt Galliard
by Graphicraft Limited, Hong Kong
Printed in Great Britain by MPG Books, Bodmin, Cornwall

This book is printed on acid-free paper

Contents

Preface

"It's a tidal wave lurking in the ocean of our future."

A few years ago, while addressing caregivers of people afflicted with Alzheimer's disease (AD), I heard myself say these words. Anyone who has experienced living with this disease as a caregiver or as one who has the disease knows that its effects are devastating. Lives are turned upside down, long-held plans for the future become wistful musings over what might have been, the long-anticipated "golden years" become tarnished with pain, sadness, and irreversible, inexorable loss. At present more than four million people in North America alone have been diagnosed as having "probable" Alzheimer's disease and, in the coming decades, barring a cure and preventive measures, that number will triple. The psychological and financial demands placed on caregivers and on society will be daunting to say the very least, affecting tens of millions of people directly and indirectly, for the disease produces irreversible brain damage which affects a variety of abilities, ultimately leaving the afflicted person incapable of living independently and, in many cases, incapable of being cared for at home by loved ones.

But how the afflicted and those who care for them cope with the disease's effects depends upon our understanding of not only the defects caused by the disease, but also the abilities which remain intact and how those abilities can be recognized and supported by others. Thus, the book you are about to read is not about Alzheimer's disease as a medical entity, but rather about a number of people who have had the disease, the ways in which their experience of the world and of themselves was affected as a result, and the remaining intact abilities that they demonstrated despite their brain injuries. As Oliver Sacks has noted, it is one thing to talk about the disease a person has, but quite another to talk about the person the disease has. Although the nature of the brain damage caused by Alzheimer's disease is by definition similar from person to person, the way in which the disease manifests itself can vary greatly from person to person and the afflicted person's behavior is affected also by the behavior of those in the social world in which he or she lives as well as by the sufferer's own reactions to the disease.

The extent to which the afflicted person's independence and well-being can be maintained will have profound effects upon the extent and types of resources that society will have to bring to bear in the process of caregiving. How we view the sufferer – as a human being whose sense of self, whose dignity, dispositions, pride, and whose ability to understand the meaning of situations and to act meaningfully, remain intact to some degree on the one hand, or as a "demented", defective, helpless and confused patient lacking a self, on the other – will affect the ways in which we treat that person, which, in turn, will affect how that person behaves. In order to discover the extent to which the afflicted person can still manifest intact mental and behavioral functions, it is necessary to gain more than a snapshot of the individual in question. Such a snapshot is usually taken in the hospital clinic, nursing home, or day care center through the use of a battery of standardized tests, and focuses primarily on the afflicted person's deficits, which are then given technical names such as *apraxia* (inability to organize a sequence of movements correctly), *aphasia* (difficulties in the use of language), *agnosia* (disorder of perception), and so on. Thus the afflicted person becomes "understood" primarily in terms of what he or she cannot do.

As a complement to such a snapshot, one can observe and interact with the afflicted person on a day-to-day basis in natural social settings, the very settings in which we live most of our lives. Instead of searching for and then highlighting the defects manifested in the necessarily limited range of abilities sampled by standard tests, which are then represented by "objective" numbers and the interpretations of what the numbers mean, we can approach the person as an individual engaged in a valiant, ongoing attempt to navigate through the social world to the best of his or her ability and take note of the successful attempts, and the circumstances in which they occur, as well as those in which failure seems to occur. We can try to understand the sufferers' present behavior in the context of their own personal histories and their own personal relationships with others, as they engage what will be the final battle of their earthly lives.

In some ways, this book represents a paradigm shift in that the afflicted person is seen as the *subject* of study rather than as an *object* of study. Indeed, in the vast majority of studies in the literature, we never come to know any particular person with AD at all but, rather, we learn about the deficits of the "average Alzheimer's disease (AD) sufferer," as if there was, in fact, such a person. There is no such thing as "the average person." There are only statistical averages. I make no pretense at any grand generalizations in this volume. What is true for the AD sufferers you will meet in the pages to follow may be true of many, many more, and this is something that only time and further research will establish. However, what is presented herein is and was true for these particular AD sufferers.

I will present in the following pages, for your consideration, findings that emerged from my long-term, person-to-person relationships with AD sufferers – relationships that were distinctly different from patient-physician or patient-researcher relationships in terms of the social dynamics and the duration involved. The primary point of my encounters with AD sufferers was neither to study their disease, nor to study them, but to be with and share time with them, to provide them with a non-anxious partner in conversation, to learn from them, and perhaps to give some unexpected meaning to their lives by engaging them as people who, despite their irreversible illness, had something potentially valuable to share with the world.

So the book in your hands has multiple facets, including an understanding of the effects of the disease from the point of view of the person who is afflicted as seen in his or her discourse, and the cognitive and social abilities which remain intact despite a variety of losses. In addition, I will explore the ways in which a Social Constructionist approach can help us to understand the "excess disabilities" (disabilities not attributable to brain injury) which result from dysfunctional treatment of afflicted persons. We will see how such dysfunctional treatment can be identified and its effects ameliorated, and the ways in which the remaining abilities of those afflicted can reveal intact aspects of selfhood, their humanity, and the continuum of human experience.

This book is thus an attempt to bring to life the world, the intact abilities, and the selfhood of people with AD through their own words and actions in the natural everyday social world. My life has been enriched immeasurably by the courage, sensitivity, and humanity of these individuals and their caregivers, and I will forever be in their debt. Their voices need to be heard. We all need to listen. These pages are their instrument.

Steven R. Sabat

Acknowledgments

A book about heroic people owes a great deal to many humane beings. I have been blessed by the presence of some exceptional people on the long and winding road to writing this book.

First, I wish to acknowledge my teachers. They imparted to me a sense of wonder and an excitement about learning through the example of their own cultivated humanity and love of learning. They insisted that each of us could make the world a better place by improving ourselves, by questioning the status quo, by caring about the larger community of which we were a part, and by reaching for the stars. They gave the best of themselves to me and did so with abiding honor and commitment. Some of them have since died, some have not, but regardless, they are all still very much alive in me and I often find myself speaking their words to my own students. So, in the order of their appearance in my life, to Etta H. Markowitz, Rose P. Modica, E. Patricia Burns, John J. Marcatante, Lucille DiBiase, Rosemary Fleming, Richard A. Kaye, James Landes, Raymond Cocoros, Jack Kirman, Michael Wreszin, Daniel N. Robinson, W.S. Battersby, Jack Orbach, and Mitchell L. Kietzman, I offer my eternal gratitude and the hope that this book might please them.

Norman J. Finkel, my colleague and friend, has provided me not only with many, many hours of enlightening conversation and feedback concerning a wide range of issues which I take up in the pages that follow, but with a great deal of encouragement as well. I will always appreciate his clear insights into clinical and legal issues as well as his abiding, caring, friendship. James T. Lamiell read and reacted to a number of chapters, provided me with a great deal of encouragement, and introduced me to the work of William Stern. Jim has been a colleague in the best sense of the word and a good friend throughout.

Acknowledgments

Rom Harré has offered some of his seemingly boundless energy in commenting on some of the chapters and discussing with me various aspects of Social Construction Theory, which he is always eager to expand upon and modify as is required by the data of life as it is lived. His enthusiasm for this project, his collaboration with me on others, and his ever-present generosity of spirit, have been of tremendous value and I am deeply grateful for his insightful, enlivening presence.

The Directors and staff of the Holy Cross Hospital Adult Day Care Center in Silver Spring, Maryland have been not only helpful and generous in allowing me to become part of the social community at the Center, but have been actively interested in the fruits of the time I have spent with the participants there since 1984. Jim MacRae was the Director when I first appeared at the Center, and he was refreshingly open in allowing me to integrate myself into the community there. I am particularly grateful to the late Bob Grossman, Activities Coordinator and then Director, whose love of people and enthusiasm for life remain present at the Center. Even though he was a devoted Washington Redskins football fan, Bob was a wonderful friend, an extraordinarily giving member of the community, and his laughter and humor brought out the best in others. He remains alive in my heart and mind and I treasure the time we shared in common purpose. Beth Shapiro, L.C.S.W., presently the Director of the Center, has been kind, caring, generously helpful, full of insight, and ever cooperative with me and with my students (even though she is a devoted fan of the Baltimore Orioles). She has been ever conscientious in her efforts to improve the lives of the participants at the Center and has been a source of insight and support for me.

Stephanie Sarnoff, whom I have known since our undergraduate days together, and who is presently the Director of the Scarsdale, N.Y. Public Library, has not only helped me tremendously by tracking down obscure references in what seemed to be nanoseconds, but has been steadfast in her support of my efforts and heartfelt in her interest in this book from the beginning. She has listened and reacted with discernment to many sections and her honest intellectual appraisals, abiding social conscience, and loving, devoted friendship have been sources of tremendous strength for me. Neala S. Schwartzberg, my dear friend since our days in graduate school together, and an insightful, wonderful writer, provided me with great encouragement to write this book long before I shaped the first words, and continued

xii

to express her interest and support for this effort throughout, "goading" me, never letting me forget that this book was in me to write.

Martin Davies, my first editor at Blackwell, was tremendously enthusiastic about this book from our first meeting and conversation about the topic. His belief in the idea of the book and in me were of signal importance from the start. Janey Fisher approached the task of copy-editing with uncommon conscientiousness and devotion and, in doing so, called my attention to numerous points and helped make the book better than it would have been otherwise. It was a pleasure to work with her, and to benefit from her careful, considered feedback. Ally Dunnett, Deputy Managing Editor at Blackwell, generously provided me with answers to what must have seemed like a veritable blizzard of questions, helping me to navigate unfamiliar terrain. Sarah Bird, Associate Commissioning Editor for Psychology at Blackwell, has likewise helped me with sundry details about which I asked her. In all, my experience with the people at Blackwell has been wonderful and I shall be grateful always for the care and devotion they've extended to me.

Finally, I would like to thank the people suffering from Alzheimer's disease, whose stories you will encounter in the pages that follow, for their heroic, unstinting efforts in working with me. Their generosity and warmth in the face of unremitting difficulties was and is astounding, and the time we shared will ever be a source of great meaning in my life. I should also like to express my deep gratitude to their families, who gave me their time, generous cooperation and who allowed me to become part of their lives during an episode that was harsh, to say the least, in many ways. I will always be grateful for their presence in my life. In struggling each day with what Luria called "the tenacity of the damned," these exceptional people, those who had Alzheimer's and those who cared for them, embodied the human spirit at its best.

Chapter 1

Ways of Understanding the Effects of the Disease

Some years ago I administered a battery of neuropsychological tests to a warm, kindly grandmother who had been diagnosed with probable Alzheimer's disease (AD). She made numerous errors on questions about the present day of the week, the date, the season, the year, and many other test items in the areas of language, calculation, perception, and memory which she would have answered perfectly at an earlier, healthier time in her life. Although she evinced clear embarrassment about her performance, she and I seemed to have made contact with one another as persons, exchanged some genuine humor and shared much warmth in the process. The final test item required her to write a sentence about anything she chose. Before writing her sentence, she asked, "Are you a doctor?" Not wanting to make the issue more complicated than necessary (I have a Ph.D. but not an M.D.), I said, "Yes." She then wrote: "It is good to hear the doctor." Later that day, in a clinical conference involving specialists such as psychiatrists, neurologists, psychologists, pharmacologists, nurses, and the like, her case and test results were being discussed. The above sentence was analyzed by one of the physicians present as containing a *paraphasia*, an unintended linguistic error, in that, he opined, what she really meant to say was, "It is good to *see* the doctor." Of course, the latter locution is spoken and heard more frequently, and we do often say, "I have to see the doctor," or "It's good to see you." So it would seem logical that she had indeed made an error due to the presence of AD, and I myself had wondered about that sentence when I first saw what she had written. After all, it is quite common to note that AD affects linguistic skills negatively, so her use of the word "hear" easily could have been interpreted as being an error.

1

In conversations with her adult daughter, who was the woman's primary caregiver, I discovered among other things that the lovely, sweet grandmother whom I had tested had been a very kind and nurturing mother, was a relatively recent widow, that she had been married to her husband for more than 45 years, and that the marriage had been a stormy one primarily owing to the fact that her husband had been verbally abusive toward her fairly consistently throughout the marriage. My thoughts immediately flashed back to that sentence she wrote. During the testing session, she and I did, indeed, make a human connection that could be characterized by words such as warm, sweet, endearing, understanding, sympathetic. Could it have been the case that, because of the verbal abuse she had endured throughout her marriage, she was especially sensitive to the ways in which she was addressed by others and that the very evident warmth and good humor that we shared in the testing session led her quite logically to write, "It is good to hear the doctor?" Could it have been the case that what might easily be interpreted as a symptom of AD was really not a symptom of the disease at all but, rather, given the context of her life and her history, a perfectly reasonable and "correct" statement?

A series of related questions immediately follows: Might this be but one example of many instances in which seemingly aberrant behavior is not really a symptom of AD, but more properly understood as appropriate and meaningful given the afflicted person's life and experience, past and present? Might such innocent errors of interpretation help to create, in the minds of caregivers, further negative expectations about the afflicted? Might those incorrect negative expectations then have an untoward effect on the afflicted person's interaction with others in the social world, thereby exacerbating the effects of the brain damage produced by the disease? Are there other examples of normal, intact psychological abilities which might go unnoticed in similar ways and, if so, what might they be? How might the correct recognition and support of such intact abilities affect the life and behavior of the afflicted person and thereby help caregivers in their efforts?

There is, at present, no medical intervention which can prevent or stop the progress of the brain damage produced by Alzheimer's disease. If, on the other hand, we can identify problems whose origin is not the disease itself, but can be found in dysfunctional social interactions

2

which are fueled by incorrect assumptions about the afflicted person, it may be possible to minimize those dysfunctional interactions and thereby improve the lives of the afflicted and caregivers alike. These are some of the issues which I will address in this book. A good place to begin is to examine the methods which have been employed in the attempt to understand the effects of the disease, for such methods themselves affect how we understand AD sufferers in terms of what we can learn and what we cannot learn about them.

Classical and Romantic Science

The brief example above serves to begin an exploration of how we go about trying to understand the effects of Alzheimer's disease on a person's psychological and behavioral abilities. Just as a carpenter has different tools with which to go about his or her job, physicians, psychologists, and social workers have different tools as well. In the business of scientific investigation there are two fundamental approaches which the legendary A.R. Luria discussed again and again in his own work, and referred to as Classical Science and Romantic Science. Each has its assets and limitations, and it would seem that each serves as a complement to the other even though the former has been employed far more extensively than the latter.

Classical Science

According to Luria (1987a),

> Classical scholars are those who look upon events in terms of their constituent parts. Step by step they single out important units and elements until they can formulate abstract, general laws. One outcome of this approach is the reduction of living reality with all its richness of detail to abstract schemas. The properties of the living whole are lost, which provoked Goethe to pen, "Gray is every theory, but ever green is the tree of life." (p. x.)

Following the model of Classical Science, many of those who study the mental and behavioral dysfunctions which accompany AD do so

3

by means of breaking down psychological life into certain components, such as the cognitive component, and then breaking that component down further into elements such as memory, language functions, calculation, attention, general intelligence, the organization of movement, orientation to time and place, and the like. Thus this approach is often called "Reductionistic." Each of the elements is examined separately through the use of standardized tests in a setting such as the hospital clinic. AD sufferers' scores are then aggregated and a group average or median (50th percentile) score is calculated, and these averages (or medians) are then compared to those of age-matched normal subjects who have taken the same tests. The averages and variance scores for the normal and AD groups are subjected to statistical analyses, and the areas in which the AD sufferers' scores are found to be significantly different from those of the normal subjects define the "constellation" of defective symptoms of Alzheimer's disease.

Thus, the symptoms are defined on the basis of the average "group" performance in an attempt to understand what is true of AD sufferers "in general" and thereby "generalizations" are made about the nature of AD. For example, as described by Ogden (1996), "Other cognitive functions usually become impaired after the memory problems are established. Speech and language are almost always affected to a lesser or greater degree, and speech content may become impoverished and concrete; the patient may find it difficult to stay on the topic being discussed. . . . In the middle stages . . . abstract thinking gradually becomes difficult . . ." (p. 218). This strategy is often used and can have great value in the context of studies in which the efficacy of certain drugs is being investigated as well as in the clinical diagnosis of the disease as will be discussed below.

Neuropathology: A basic introduction

Another area in which the approach of Classical Science has borne some fruit is that of our understanding of the neuropathological aspects of the disease, though even here there is, as will become clear, room for pause. The general approach and interpretation adopted by many researchers in the twentieth century is that psychological and behavioral dysfunctions which accompany AD are due to some failure in brain function – an organic mental disorder. Thus, the various symptoms can be understood in terms of (reduced to) abnormalities in the brain. Although first described by Alois Alzheimer in 1906, among the definitive contemporary studies in the field of the neuropathology of dementia of the Alzheimer's type are those of Blessed et al. (1968) and Tomlinson et al. (1970) which involved a post-mortem examination comparing the brains of those who had been deemed healthy to those who were assessed as being "demented" based upon the results of clinically administered standard tests. The main findings included the presence of senile plaques composed of beta-amyloid tissue, an abnormal protein, and neurofibrillary tangles (strands of axonal material that displace normal neurons) in the cerebral cortex which were believed to result from, or as being a concomitant of, the degeneration named after Alzheimer. The mean (average) plaque count of the group of those diagnosed as being "demented" was significantly higher than that of those who were not diagnosed as such. The pathological process results in the degeneration of neurons such that they cannot receive (dendritic and cell body degeneration) and send (axonal and terminal bouton degeneration) neural impulses as they would if they were intact, and this pathology has a profound effect on information-processing and behavior.

In addition, there has been observed to be other evidence of brain atrophy as seen in the enlargement of the cerebral ventricles, which contain cerebrospinal fluid, along with neurofibrillary tangles in the hippocampus, which is important for certain memory functions such as explicit recall of information. Although the cortex becomes atrophied, losing as much as a third of its volume as the disease progresses, there are some areas of the cortex which are relatively spared. The importance of aspects of this latter finding will be addressed in subsequent chapters. The extent and location of brain atrophy is shown in Figure 1.1 (page 6) which shows a lateral and a medial view of the human brain.

Figure 1.1 is a composite of many AD sufferers' brains, and is described by Brun (1983) as being representative of the "average AD case." The darker the shading, the more severe is the degeneration. It should thus be clear that the primary sensory (especially the visual and somatosensory) and the motor areas of the cortex, are relatively spared. This means that the afflicted person's ability to see and to feel bodily sensations and to move body parts *per se* are relatively normal. The frontal "association" areas, important for planning ahead, and other "executive" functioning, are less affected than are the posterior "association" areas of the parietal, temporal, and occipital lobes (Brun,

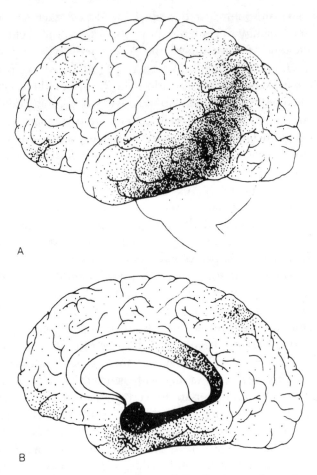

Figure 1.1 Schematic representation of distribution and severity of degeneration on (A) lateral and (B) medial aspect of the brain in an average Alzheimer's case. The darker the area, the more pronounced the degeneration. White areas are spared, with only basic change discernible. (After Brun, 1983.) Reprinted with the permission of The Free Press, a Division of Simon & Schuster, Inc., from *Alzheimer's Disease: The Standard Reference*, edited by Barry Reisberg, M.D. Copyright © 1983 by Barry Reisberg, M.D.

1983). Damage to the posterior association areas can result in a variety of problems in such functions as: the organization of visual input which is required for naming objects and identifying others by sight alone in the case of occipital association area damage;

distinguishing right from left, identifying objects by touch alone, organizing sequences of complex movement such as that required in tieing one's shoes, for example, in the case of parietal association area damage; and linguistic abilities in speech, reading, writing, and understanding the spoken word in the case of damage to the left hemisphere's temporal, parietal, and visual association areas. In the medial view of the brain, one can see that there is marked degeneration in the hippocampus and adjacent areas. Damage to the hippocampus can result in a variety of problems related to explicit memory – such that a person might have great difficulty in recalling events that have taken place in the relatively recent past.

In addition to the degeneration of neurons, there have been found to be marked reductions in many chemical transmitter substances (Carlsson, 1983) – the chemicals which allow for communication among and between neurons in the Central Nervous System. Specifically, in the above study, there were found to be reductions of about 50 percent in dopamine, serotonin, and acetylcholine, and 25 percent in norepinephrine. The reduction in acetylcholine levels has been related to the loss of cells in the Nucleus Basalis of Meynert – cells which are important in the synthesis of acetylcholine. Although normal, age-matched persons also show reductions in levels of transmitter substances, AD sufferers show greater reductions than do normals in two or more transmitter systems.

It is also the case that dementia of the Alzheimer's type is more common among women than among men, whereas dementia of the multi-infarct type (due to a series of small strokes) is more common among men than women (Gurland et al., 1983). Of all the forms of "progressive dementing illnesses," AD is the most common in older adults (Breteler et al., 1992) and its prevalence in the population has been found to increase with advancing age, going from 10 percent among those over age 65, to approximately 47 percent of those over the age of 85 (Evans et al., 1989).

Diagnosis

Still, there is no specific test which can provide for a definitive diagnosis of AD, save for biopsy and post-mortem examination of brain tissue, and at present the diagnosis of "possible," "probable," and "definite" AD is made on the basis of exclusion of some possible factors and the presence of others (McKhann et al., 1984). Specifically, thus far, a diagnosis of "definite" AD can be made only on the basis of histopathological evidence obtained from a biopsy or autopsy, when viewed in conjunction with clinical evidence. Such clinical evidence includes the absence of any other systematic disorders or brain diseases (history of hypertension, strokes, other neurological disorders, endocrine disease, metabolic imbalances, vascular degeneration, drug use, etc.) which, themselves, could account for the dysfunctions in memory and other cognitive abilities. A complete psychiatric evaluation must be made in order to exclude the possibility of various psychiatric disorders.

The criteria for "probable" AD include a progressive worsening of memory and other cognitive functions, a diagnosis of dementia arrived at via clinical examination and documented by the Mini-Mental State Test (Folstein et al., 1975) or a similar examination, and confirmed by the results of standard neuropsychological tests which reveal deficits in two or more areas of cognition. Such deficits may include problems with language (*aphasia*), motor skills (*apraxia*) and perception (*agnosia*). An onset of the of the symptoms between the ages of 40 and 90, most often after the age of 65, impaired activities of daily living, and evidence of cerebral atrophy on CT-scans, increased slow-wave activity in the EEG, associated symptoms of depression, insomnia, delusions, hallucinations, catastrophic verbal emotional outbursts, and plateaus in the progression of the illness are also considered consistent with the diagnosis of probable AD (McKhann et al., 1984).

Problematic issues

However, as I stated at the outset of this section, there is room for pause in the above data. First, in the data presented by Blessed et al. (1968) and by Tomlinson et al. (1968, 1970), there is considerable overlap between the characteristics of the brains of those diagnosed as being "demented" and those of the normal control group. Specifically, 40 percent of the former group show no cerebral atrophy (controls 46 percent), 16 percent showed no senile plaques (controls 21 percent), 28 percent showed no neurofibrillary tangles (controls 39 percent). Thus, it is surmised that it is the combination of these indicators that is key to AD, and the authors claimed that these indicators were present to a greater degree in the "demented" subjects' brains than in the brains of control subjects in 16 of 25 cases. In addition, some authors (Collerton and Fairbairn, 1985) have reported that AD has been demonstrated without observable damage to the hippocampus, and as Kitwood (1988) pointed out, moderate or severe dementia, as assessed by standard clinical tests, can accompany widely varying degrees of brain damage. For example, it has been shown that cerebral atrophy is present in many, but not all, cases of dementia (Albert et al., 1984). Thus, the brain-state of some people who had been diagnosed as having been demented was well within the range of age-matched normal subjects, a fact that adds serious complications to a strictly neurophysiological understanding of AD and its symptoms.

Added to this problem is the fact that the symptoms demonstrated by AD sufferers vary considerably from person to person, such that there is no true "typical" or "average" AD sufferer even though there are statistical averages in existence. Thus, although various types of dementia, and AD specifically, involve brain damage, it is clear that there remain questions not only about the exact nature of the damage as well as its cause, but also about whether the myriad dysfunctions observed in AD sufferers are due to brain pathology alone. This latter issue was clear from the early, and perhaps less technically rigorous, work of Rothschild and Sharp (1941), whose case studies revealed three people who were severely demented, but whose brains showed only mild neuropathology upon autopsy. In the same study, the authors reported two cases in which the subjects' cognitive functions had been largely intact despite severe neuropathological changes in their brains.

It is, perhaps, ironic that the various assets of the Classical approach also contribute to our thinking that the dysfunctions observed in AD sufferers are due solely to the effects of the disease itself. For, in addition to the issues raised above on the neuropathological level, there are similar issues which inhere in the way in which standard test scores are interpreted by researchers. For example, beyond the initial diagnosis, researchers attempt to analyze the cognitive abilities of those afflicted by using a variety of tests and measurements to chart the progress of the disease. The test scores and the performance of the afflicted on a variety of measures are compared to those of healthy people of similar age, education, and gender who have taken the identical tests, and we note the areas in which the AD sufferers' average scores are significantly, in a statistical sense, lower than those of the normal group. The only difference between the groups is that one group has been diagnosed with "probable" AD and the other has not been so diagnosed, and thus we attribute the difference in scores to the presence of the disease. On this basis, we can easily come to think of any person with AD as an instance of the "stereotypic" AD sufferer who is then treated accordingly. We will come to see that such an assumption and the nature of the interaction between the afflicted and the healthy which occurs as a result, will have potentially profound effects on the behavior of the afflicted.

In summary, then, from a Classical Science point of view, the behavioral and psychological dysfunctions we observe in AD sufferers are due principally to the presence of the disease, and are understood objectively via the use of standard tests. Thus, the picture that is painted of the AD sufferer is one which embodies, in the tradition of one contemporary medical approach to understanding a disease, what Oliver Sacks has called a "defectological" view, in that the afflicted person is defined principally in terms of his or her cata-logued dysfunctions. Such a picture can help to create a stereotype which is defined in *Webster's Third New International Dictionary*, (unabridged, 1986) as "something conforming to a fixed or general pattern and lacking individual distinguishing marks or qualities; a standardized mental picture held in common by members of a group and representing an oversimplified opinion, affective attitude, or uncritical judgment (as of a person, a race, an issue, or an event)" (p. 2238). In the case of AD, the stereotype is clearly based on defects, dysfunctions.

It is important to note, however, that such methods of analysis have other consequential limitations which must be understood. One limitation is the fact that through the above approaches, one never comes to understand any particular AD sufferer in his or her totality as a person living in the world; we come to know only the scores on certain standardized tests of particular abstract cognitive functions and the dysfunctions that are thereby revealed. In a real sense, then, what is being investigated in this way is how the disease affects a series of "functions" as opposed to how it affects persons living in the world. Persons cannot be understood simply as being the sum total of an arbitrary list of measured cognitive functions any more than they can be understood as being simply the sum of certain anatomical parts, chemical components, or neurophysiological mechanisms and events. From a profile of test scores, it would be virtually impossible to understand what it would be like to engage an AD sufferer in a conversation, for example. Furthermore, just as there is no American family which actually has 2.3 children, or 1.7 automobiles (character-istics of the "average" family), what is described by statistical averages may not be true of any individual person who is afflicted with AD. As Heschel (1965) noted in *Who Is Man?*,

> Generalization, by means of which theories evolve, fails in trying to understand man. For in dealing with a particular man, I do not come upon a generality but an individuality, a person. It is precisely the exclusive application of generalities to human situations that accounts for many of our failures. . . . No man is an average man. The ordinary, typical man . . . is the homunculus of statistics. In real life there is no ordinary, undistinguished man unless man resigns himself to be drowned in indifference and commonness. Spiritual suicide is within everybody's reach. (pp. 37–8.)

Another limitation of the Classical approach of using standard tests to assess cognitive function is that the elements of cognitive function are defined rather arbitrarily and examined separately, one at a time. Thus there are individual tests for aspects of language function (naming, repeating, spelling, writing, and so on), memory function, attention, perception, and the like. This approach has the advantage of being translatable into quantitative scores, and such scores can be useful to researchers involved in the attempt to analyze the effects of drugs on specific symptoms of the disease, as well as in their attempts to com-pare different subjects tested similarly in different places. However, it is also the case that these elements of cognitive function are not engaged separately, independently of one another, in natural everyday life. Rather, in the course of daily social experience and interaction, a whole panoply of cognitive functions is called upon more or less simultaneously, each "separate" elementary function thus interacting with others. It is not inappropriate, I think, to use the analogy of chemistry to understand the problem here: just as it is true that a compound such as water is made of the elements hydrogen and oxygen, it is also true that when two atoms of hydrogen and one of

11

oxygen are combined, the result is qualitatively different in nature from either hydrogen or oxygen taken individually. Thus, there may be striking differences between cognitive function as measured by tests and that revealed in day-to-day life.

It should be apparent from the above that the scores stemming from such an approach would not give us any insight into how a particular AD sufferer would respond to seeing a loved one, or to a compliment, a joke, another's need for help, or to being patronized, shunned, or embarrassed. Yet, although these reactions are surely part of psychological, cognitive life, requiring a high level of brain function, there are no standard tests with which they can be measured. The fact that there are no standard tests geared to assess such aspects of life is not a reason either to omit them from our consideration, or to relegate them to a less relevant, less meaningful status captured by the words, "subjective" or "qualitative." As the renowned neurologist, Macdonald Critchley (1953) noted, not all aspects of behavioral change following brain injury can be understood through the use of quantitative methods – numbers do not capture many aspects of what persons do, how they do what they do, and the reasons behind their behavior. The Classical approach can easily be conducive to our focusing mainly upon "functions," brain structures, and the neuropathology which accompanies AD, to seeing afflicted persons as organisms manifesting deficits in the aforementioned neurophysiological and cognitive functions. As informative and potentially useful as such an approach has been and might be, it discloses little of the experiential human reality which confronts the afflicted. This issue forms the basis for Stephen Post's (1998) warnings against what he calls a "hyper-cognitive culture" which shapes personhood theories of ethics – a culture which defines cognition in terms of the status of specific, limited mental functions and, by so doing, comes to view those who "lack certain empowering cognitive capacities" as nonpersons. Such a "hypercognitive culture" pays little attention to what Post calls "the emotional, relational, aesthetic, and spiritual aspects of well-being" (p. 72) which are open to those who are deeply forgetful, even in advanced stages of AD.

Related to Post's concerns are those of Tom Kitwood with regard to the way in which we "frame" dementia. From Kitwood's point of view (1988), there are two general ways in which one might understand dementia: the technical and the personal. The technical,

12

which I have described as being a result of the Classical Science method of study, includes the neuropathological, neurophysiological approaches and leads to an understanding that the immediate cause of AD and its symptoms is to be found in extra-personal issues in spite of evidence (Bird et al., 1986) which showed that one of the neuropathological markers of dementia, ventricular enlargement, was found to have a significant relationship to the recent loss of a spouse. Analysis of the technical data indicates, to Kitwood, that "it seems more likely that psychology is involved to some extent in the proximal causation of dementia . . . dementia in old age is not solely attributable to malfunction of the hardware, but to faulty software as well" (p. 172). Psychological (personal) factors might include loss of loved ones and other important social connections, other changes in life, such as disempowerment through the various effects of retirement, loss of one's role as a worker-producer, reduction of income and of mobility and the inability to adapt to such changes in life. To lose connections with contexts in which one is valued and accepted and in which one's experiences are shared, argues Kitwood, may affect psychological as well as physical well-being. If there are, indeed, compelling reasons to understand and include personal, psychological factors in the etiology of dementia, it would seem logical that psychological factors might also be involved in continuing, or even exacerbating, the downward spiral that characterizes various abilities of those afflicted. In the absence of medical interventions which can halt the progress of the disease, it would seem advantageous to understand more deeply the social and psychological problems that confront the sufferer and thereby affect his or her experience and behavior.

How, then, can we come to a more detailed, richer understanding of the experience of persons afflicted with AD as they go about the task of living with and among others? That is, how can we see the afflicted as persons who have their own desires, hopes, fears, loves, identify the nature of those aspects of their lives, and thereby see them as being defined and understandable in terms of characteristics beyond their "presenting symptoms"?

Romantic Science

Luria (1987b) offers another approach to scientific investigation, which he called Romantic Science:

Romantic scholars' traits, attitudes, and strategies are just the opposite. They do not follow the path of reductionism, which is the leading philosophy of the classical group. Romantics in science want neither to split living reality into its elementary components nor to represent the wealth of life's concrete events in abstract models that lose the properties of the phenomena themselves. It is of utmost importance to romantics to preserve the wealth of living reality, and they aspire to a science that retains this richness. (p. 6.)

Part of the "wealth of living reality" of which Luria wrote, and which is tacitly omitted from the Classical approach to studying AD, includes the quality of the afflicted person's abilities in interacting with others in the social fabric of everyday life. From Aristotle's observation that human beings are social creatures, to many more recent commentaries (Aronson, 1980, for example) it is clear that most of our business in this world involves our interactions with others. Even the interaction of an AD sufferer with a health professional during tests in the hospital clinic is a social situation of a specific kind. Unfortunately, one unspoken assumption made by those administering tests is that the test items measure "pure" isolated cognitive functions that are not "confounded" by social situations which may provide a backdrop or context and might, thereby, "falsely enhance" the performance of the test-taker on the items at hand. To assume that a social situation, such as the testing situation for example, is not itself a context and that it has little or no effect on persons is to be blind to a fundamental fact of human life. This issue has been addressed specifically by Jerome Bruner in his introduction to Luria's (1987b) *Mind of a Mnemonist*: "Explanation of any human condition is so bound to context, so complexly interpretive at so many levels, that it cannot be achieved by considering isolated segments of life in vitro, and it can never be, even at its best, brought to a final conclusion beyond the shadow of human doubt" (p. xii).

In speaking about his wife who had been diagnosed with AD, a deeply devoted caregiver commented that he encountered a problem with her when the visiting nurse came to help his wife bathe. I asked about the nature of the problem, and he explained that when the nurse arrives, his wife begins to cry, that he cannot stop her from crying, and that this must be another of the problems that is caused by the disease. Indeed, it is not uncommon to hear reports of AD sufferers who cry inconsolably. Frequently, such behavior is labelled in technical terms such as "emotionally labile" and sometimes described as a "catastrophic reaction," both of which carry a connotation of dysfunction and are seen as symptoms of the disease. In exploring this situation with him, I proposed the following alternative interpretation: Given his and his wife's ages and the social climate in which they grew up, it seemed to me that bathing might be seen by his wife as an extremely private activity. Thus, to have a "stranger" involved in such intimate contact with her, might be terribly embarrassing. Furthermore, she might well recognize that she is powerless to avoid such a situation, might be deeply saddened as a result, and also saddened because she is no longer capable of tending to herself as she did for most of her life. He gave this possibility some thought and found, given what he knew of his wife of many decades, that it contained a great deal of merit, for it was clear to him that "she still knew things."

Taking the above into account, from a Romantic Science point of view, the behavior of the afflicted cannot be understood solely in terms of the effects of neuropathology, but must also include the effects of (a) the behavior of others in the afflicted person's social world, (b) the afflicted person's reactions, both positive and negative, to the behavior of others, and (c) the afflicted person's reactions to the effects of the disease on his or her abilities. Interestingly, this view is mirrored in spirit in the words of Lipowski (1969) who noted, with regard to the broad concept of disease as defined in the *British Medical Dictionary* (MacNalty, 1963), that a disease is not to be understood as being separate from the afflicted person, and that a person encompasses not only a biological organism but also the world of:

> ... feeling and symbolic activities in thought and language. Furthermore, he is a member of a social group with which he interacts. A concept of disease is incomplete unless it takes cognizance of these facts. How a person experiences the pathological process, what it means to him, and how this meaning influences his behaviour and interaction with others are all integral components of disease as viewed as a total human response. (p. 1198.)

The recent theoretical approaches of Social Constructionism and Positioning Theory can be used to analyze and illustrate a number of these factors, and it is to these that we now turn. Although specific and more detailed applications of these approaches to AD sufferers will be found in later chapters, I will present an introduction here.

An introduction to Social Constructionist Theory and Positioning Theory

A goal of Romantic Science is to "preserve the wealth of living reality" of the phenomena to be investigated and explained. Part of the living reality of AD is the subjective experience of the afflicted and the quality of the interaction between him or her and others in the social world. From a Social Constructionist point of view, also referred to as Discursive Psychology (Harré and van Langenhove, 1999), the social world of persons can be understood in terms of discursive practices, that is, conversational and other symbolic exchanges, institutional practices, and the use of social rhetorics. It is within conversations that social acts occur. Thus, one way to investigate the effects of AD and still preserve the "wealth of living reality" of the AD sufferer is to examine the conversations and other symbolic exchanges which occur between the afflicted and the healthy in the social situations of everyday life.

In the title of their 1986 book, *The Loss of Self*, Cohen and Eisdorfer offer an example of one of the defects which is alleged to stem from the neuropathological process of AD, and Kitwood (1988) theorized that a loss of self, as understood as a fragmentation of the "continuing thread of 'I am' experience that gives unity to autobiography, an enduring sense of identity" may be part of the personal problem of AD sufferers. If one were to assume that AD does, indeed, result in such a loss, such an assumption itself would surely have an effect on the ways in which one would look upon, think about, and treat the afflicted. That is, if I assumed that an AD sufferer had lost his or her sense of self, I would necessarily treat him or her differently than I would if I had not made such an assumption, and that treatment might have a powerful effect on the behavior of the afflicted. But exactly what does it mean to have lost one's self? Could one, in fact, sustain such a loss and, if so, how would it happen?

Aspects of Social Constructionist Theory (Coulter, 1981; Harré, 1983, 1991; Mulhausler and Harré, 1993) can be used as a heuristic device in order to explore and analyze the issues involved in these questions, especially those pertaining to the predicaments of selfhood which face those who suffer from AD. Although this will be a topic of a subsequent chapter, I will introduce briefly some of the terms involved and provide some examples which will allow us to proceed.

Aspects of selfhood

From the Constructionist point of view, one's selfhood can be manifested outwardly in a variety of ways, and we can call these manifestations Self 1, Self 2, and Self 3. *Self 1* is the self of personal identity which is experienced as the continuity of one's own singular point of view from which one perceives, and acts in, the world. That is, each of us, barring psychopathology as in the case of multiple-personality disorder for example, experiences him or herself as one and the same person from moment to moment relative to the environment, as well as relative to time past, time present, and time future. This aspect of selfhood is expressed discursively through the use of personal pronouns such as "I," "Me," and adjectives such as "My," "Mine." By using such pronouns, we index, or locate in the psycho-social world, our expressions of belief, doubt, interest, responsibility, sadness, as being our own. In principle, one could be amnesic with regard to one's name and yet still demonstrate an intact Self 1 by saying such things as, "I wish I could recall my name."

In addition to our experience of the world from a continuous point of view, each of us has a unique set of mental and physical attributes that render us different to some extent from any other person. Some of those attributes may be relatively stable or constant over time, others may change. Thus, being a six-foot tall caucasian adult male would be an example of a stable attribute, whereas being an undergraduate student might be a current attribute but one which will change upon graduation. Being a college graduate would then become part of one's stable attributes. Such mental and physical attributes as we have at present, and have had over the course of a lifetime, along with our beliefs about those attributes, are part of what can be called *Self 2*. Among our mental attributes are our beliefs. Some of those beliefs may be rather stable over decades, others may change. For example, one can be a life-long believer in Christian charity, while at the same time change one's view about the role of the US in foreign policy or the role of government in education.

Therefore, holding an advanced degree and having been diagnosed as having "probable" AD would be part of a person's Self 2, as would be one's belief that AD is an anathema, worthy of sadness and a harbinger of negative things to come.

Finally, there are the ways in which one presents oneself in the world, the displays of one's personality and character. Such displays are part of one's *Self 3*. The emphasis here is on the plural, as there are many different social personae which any one person may manifest. For example, one and the same person can be a loving parent, a demanding professor, a helpful neighbor, a delightfully humorous friend, and a devoted, romantic, loving spouse, to name but a few. Each of these personae is manifested in distinct types of behavior, and any one may be especially dominant in a particular social situation. It might be, therefore, that the same person is seen quite differently through the eyes of his or her students as opposed to his or her child, spouse, friends, because the person would have clearly different social relations, and display different behaviors, with each. There is an aspect of Self 3 that is crucial and which differentiates it further from Self 1 and Self 2: in order to manifest one or another Self 3 persona, the cooperation of others in the social world is required. For example, in order for a person to manifest the persona of romantic, loving, husband or wife, that person's spouse must cooperate; a person cannot manifest, or construct, the persona of "authoritative professor" if students do not recognize him or her as their teacher and behave accordingly. Therefore, because successful manifestations, or constructions, of Self 3 require, for their very existence, interpersonal interaction and the social recognition given by others, they can be especially vulnerable.

Positioning Theory and Alzheimer's disease sufferers

It was immediately following a talk I had given to caregivers that an intelligent and sensitive caregiver, and her spouse who was an AD sufferer, approached me with a few questions and comments. She began by thanking me for the lecture, and introduced herself. She then introduced her husband who was standing to her side and slightly behind her, by saying, "This is my husband; he's the patient." In this situation, the spouse of the speaker was positioned immediately as an Alzheimer's sufferer.

Within a dynamic social situation and through conversation, individuals can be positioned by others or can position themselves in terms of what Harré and van Langenhove (1999) call "fluid parts or roles that make a person's actions intelligible and relatively determinate as social acts." Such parts or social roles can include, but are not limited to, being "powerful or powerless, confident or apologetic, dominant or submissive, definitive or tentative, authorized or unauthorized." In the above example one can see that, via the terms of the introduction, the caregiver was positioning herself as healthy, perhaps powerful and dominant, and her husband as ill, perhaps tentative and submissive, and whatever other relatively negative attributes are connoted by AD. Positioning is understood to be part of a larger personal storyline or narrative. The larger narrative has the purpose of explaining, giving reasons for, the behavior of oneself and others in the natural social world – such as, for example, their presence at the caregiver education series of which my lecture was a part. In this instance, the caregiver was there to listen to, and perhaps learn from, a lecture about AD. Her spouse, the AD sufferer, was there because she didn't want to leave him alone at home while she attended the lecture.

In another situation, a different caregiver-spouse had arrived to pick up her husband, an AD sufferer, from the adult day care center where he had spent the day while she was at work. As they were departing from the day care center, he said to her, "Okay, what are we going to do now?" She responded by saying, "What would you like to do now?" When I asked her at a later time why she responded to his question that way, she commented that she didn't want him to become accustomed to being told what he was going to do, where he was going to go and the like. Instead, she wanted him to feel that he had a say in what they would do, where they would go, that his wishes and desires were important to her. In this case, she was not going to allow herself to engage in behavior which would result in what we can call the positioning of her husband as being passive and submissive, and thus feeling that his motives and desires were of less import than her own.

If we return to the situation I described at the outset of this chapter, that of the grandmother who wrote, "It is good to hear the doctor," once again we can see the dynamic of positioning at work. Her locution was interpreted as being a *paraphasia*, an error, principally

19

on the basis of the fact that she had been diagnosed with probable AD. Positioned as ill, and given her numerous errors on other test items, the construction of her sentence was likewise interpreted immediately as another sign of dysfunction. Speaking more generally, her diagnosis of probable AD became the principle basis of a storyline or narrative being constructed about her which served to explain her behavior.

The initial positioning of a person can lead not only to explanations of that person's behavior consistent with that positioning, but also to the development of expectations about and interpretations of that person's subsequent behavior. This is a subtle, but important, point. If I position someone as being ill, and dysfunctional as a result, it is more likely that in future situations in which a variety of explanations of behavior is possible, I will opt for the explanation based upon the initial positioning and the expectations which follow in its wake. In many cases, we see what we expect to see; we interpret the meaning of our experience in light of our prior expectations (Tanner and Swets, 1954).

One can see from the above and the earlier examples of AD sufferers that there can be a relationship between the process of positioning, certain Self 2 attributes, and the construction and manifestation of Self 3 personae. Specifically, the ability of an individual to gain the cooperation of others in the process of constructing one or another Self 3 persona, will depend in part upon the way in which the individual is positioned by others and the extent to which the individual accepts that positioning. It is not necessary that a person accept being positioned in a particular way by someone else. However, in the case of an AD sufferer, the ability to reject undesired forms of positioning may be compromised to some degree. Thus, the AD sufferer's ability to construct a Self 3 other than that of "the dysfunctional, possibly confused patient," which is based upon his or her present Self 2 attribute of having been diagnosed with probable Alzheimer's disease, is at great risk.

Let us take, for example, an AD sufferer who has spent his or her vocational life as an academic person, having earned advanced degrees. Although the person in question is presently retired from academic life, he or she still possesses Self 2 attributes that include past cherished educational and vocational achievements, knowledge, and dispositions. Such a person might well prefer to be viewed as an

20

intellectual and treated with the respect and dignity which he or she has earned and enjoyed for many decades. However, this AD sufferer may not be able to construct the Self 3 of "intellectual" or "professor" because others have positioned him or her principally on the basis of a particular current (Self 2) attribute, namely, the diagnosis of AD, and will thus not cooperate in the construction of the more valued Self 3 persona. And, if the afflicted makes repeated attempts to construct the more valued persona, it is not uncommon to hear healthy others comment either that the afflicted is "denying his or her illness" or that the afflicted "still thinks he's (she's) a professor." Both interpretations carry negative, dysfunctional connotations. Imagine, if you will, how frustrating it might be to be positioned in such a way – essentially being held prisoner of others' thoughts about you when those very thoughts focus on Self 2 attributes which are, themselves, anathema to you.

Positioning and normal aging: What does senile mean?

Another aspect of positioning can be seen in the ways in which normal aging itself has been viewed as a cause of inevitable decline and defect. For example, a great deal of research in the area of language has treated aging mainly in terms of the the decrements noticed in the elderly speakers studied (Coupland et al., 1991), and it has been argued that there are many sources of prejudice that threaten the feeling of self-worth as well as the quality of life of many elderly people (Coupland and Coupland, 1999). Often, older people are treated in negative stereotypic ways which are rooted in social creations as opposed to the facts of natural biological aging (Scrutton, 1990) and such stereotypes "restrict the social role and status of older people, structure their expectations of themselves, prevent them from achieving their potential and deny them equal opportunity" (p. 13).

The negative positioning of the elderly can be found as well in the changing definition of the word, "senile" as seen in its usage. According to the *Oxford English Dictionary* (2nd edn 1989), senile means "[b]elonging to, suited for or incident to old age. Now only of diseases." If we look back to 1661, however, we find that the word was used thus: "Boyle 'Style of Script . . . A person in whom Nature, Education, and Time have happily Match'd a Senile Maturity of Judgement with a Youthful Vigour of Phansie." The next entry reads, "1797 Jefferson 'Writ.' (1859) IV. 192 To exchange the roar and tumult of bulls and bears, for the prattle of my grand-children and senile rest." Yet, in the twentieth century, we find the more familiar association between senile and decay, as the former is so very often used to connote the latter. That is, when we hear the comment "He's getting senile," we don't think immediately that the speaker means "He's getting old," or "He's growing wiser" (as a result of age). The association between senility (old age) and decay can be seen as a result of the use of the word, senile, in medically related ways to describe various illnesses occurring in elderly people, such as "senile dementia." An example is that found in Kraepelin's *Clinical Psychiatry* viii. 273 cited in *OED* 1989: "Senile dementia includes those forms of mental disease appearing in the period of involution." In this brief sketch we can see how, through our very language and over the course of time, elderly people have been positioned in a negative way. To be old and also to be afflicted with AD can be seen, in this light, as being doubly damned.

Summary

From the foregoing, we can see that

1   The methods we employ to study AD and its effects reveal very different aspects of the ways in which AD affects the individual from the anatomical and neurochemical levels to the cognitive and social levels.
2   The methods of Classical Science are geared to uncover certain generalities and yield theories regarding the disease's causes and effects, can be useful for purposes of diagnosis and testing the efficacy of drug-based interventions, and for the examination of certain individual elements of cognitive function.
3   Such methods in and of themselves are, however, not appropriate to the exhaustive study of the variety of ways in which the disease affects the experience of any particular individual as he or she attempts to navigate through a world of dynamic social interaction.
4   The methods of Romantic Science, though not geared to unearthing generalities, are more appropriate to the examination

of the living reality of the individual AD sufferer's cognitive and social experience of the world and the quality of interactions between the afflicted and the healthy.

5   The discursive practices of those in the social world of the AD sufferer can have powerful effects upon the ways in which the afflicted is perceived and engaged and, by extension, upon the experience of the afflicted.

6   These same discursive practices can exert similar effects upon the elderly who are healthy.

7   The discourse of individual AD sufferers can be revealing of the ways in which they experience others as well as the disease and its effects.

The Subjects of Study

In the chapters that follow I will explore how, in social situations, aspects of the afflicted person's experience and remaining abilities are revealed in discourse. However, you will not come to know about some "generic" afflicted person, but instead meet specific people with AD with whom I enjoyed long-term associations. Each of the afflicted people you will encounter in these pages had his or her own individual history, proclivities, hopes, ways of coping with the effects of the disease, and reactions to others. Some were highly educated, others were not. Some attended adult day care centers, others did not. Each had been diagnosed with probable AD according to NINCDS-ADRDA criteria (McKhann et al., 1984) years before our association began; each was considered to be in the "moderate" to "severe" stages of the disease (Reisberg et al., 1982); and this Self 2 attribute was, perhaps, the only one they shared universally. In other words, each person had his or her own life story into which was then written the tangled chapter called Alzheimer's disease.

Chapter 2

Language and
Communication

Dr. B: "Things get jumbled and Alzheimer's gives me fragments."

The Case of Dr. B

The above sentence is clearly well formed, was spoken fluently, and gave me my first insight into Dr. B's experience of AD. He said this to me on the occasion of the first of many meetings that spelled our association. As time passed, I came to learn that, as a result of AD, he had frequent word-finding problems, he mispronounced words, and his sentences were at times ill-formed and often punctuated with long pauses between words. Yet, in spite of such problems, he was able to communicate a great deal to me about his experience of the disease as well as about himself as a human being. But here I get ahead of myself, for this story is not simply about outcomes or results, but about a human relationship and the process of communication between one healthy person and one who was diagnosed with AD.

I had heard about Dr. B often from the social worker at the adult day care center which he attended two to three days each week while his wife was at work. Finally, I was to meet him. I walked into the day care center, down the ramp built to accommodate those in wheel-chairs, and said hello to a few people who were standing in the hall. One of those people was a rather tall, distinguished-looking man, well-dressed in casual clothes, whom I had never before encountered. We exchanged a few pleasantries of the day and after about two minutes I excused myself and proceeded to the social worker's office. After a minute or two of conversation with her, she said, "Why don't we go find Dr. B?" We walked into the hall, she looked to her left and said, "Oh, there he is . . ." and she called his name. He turned around and she continued, "Have you met Dr. Sabat?"

I realized that that was the man with whom I'd just spoken, and although I was tempted to interject and answer her question in the affirmative, I held my tongue, stood there silently, heard him say, "No I haven't," and allowed myself to be introduced formally to the man I with whom I had just chatted a few moments ago. I had "held my tongue" because I knew that the social worker had not asked the question of me, but of him, and that she didn't know that I had just spoken with him. She then led us into an empty room where she told him that I was the neuropsychologist about whom she had spoken to him, that I was the person who was interested in understanding the effects of AD. Thus began my association with a man who, although he had been diagnosed with probable AD years earlier, would enrich my life with his presence.

Although he did grope for words at times, the tone and meaning of his sentences were clear. "How long have you been doing this work?" he asked. Suddenly, I was in the position of explaining myself to him. So I recounted to him a short history of how I came to work with AD sufferers. He asked about where I attended graduate school and when I graduated. The questions did not come fluently, for he had clear difficulty in finding the right words to use, and this resulted in protracted pauses between his words from time to time. He noted such instances by saying, "Bear with me." Often, about five minutes after I had answered a particular question, he asked the same question again and, once again, I answered. I told him that I was interested in learning about the remaining abilities of AD sufferers and that "If I can work with you, maybe the results will be helpful to people." And so began a nine-month odyssey of cooperative research which soon became known, in his words, as "The Project." We met twice each week, for approximately two hours each day, and our conversations were tape-recorded and transcribed. I have made no attempt, in any of the transcriptions that follow, to correct any mispronounced words or poorly formed sentences.

A snapshot

I came to know that he was 68 years old and had been diagnosed four years earlier. According to standardized tests, he was considered moderately (Stage 4 on the Global Deterioration Scale [Reisberg et al., 1983]) to severely afflicted (score of 5 on the Mini-Mental State test [Folstein et al., 1975]). He held a Ph.D. degree, was a scientist whose interests spanned ecology to zoology, was a student of music and of art, and I learned that he told his daughter, when she was a child, that he could fix anything except teeth and balloons. His family was central to him. At the time of our association, he was unable to drive, had great difficulty dressing himself, had significant problems in the areas of word-finding (naming), spelling, reading, and auditory comprehension, as seen on standard tests such as the Boston Diagnostic Aphasia Examination, could not recall the day of the week, the month, the year, and couldn't copy a simple drawing, nor could he perform simple calculations. Often, he had difficulty recalling the names of particular staff members at the day care center as well as the center's location. There was great variability in his signature and he had great difficulty with writing in general. Toward the middle months of our association, when he was at home and dusk approached, his wife reported that he insisted upon carrying a flashlight with him. Thus we have a snapshot of the symptoms, the defects, of AD as manifested in Dr. B, but in our conversations he revealed a great deal more about his cognitive and communicative ability and the ways in which AD manifested itself in him via his use of language.

A methodological issue

It should be noted that there are few studies concerned with the pragmatic ability of AD sufferers, that is, their ability to use language in conversation. This is due primarily, I think, to a combination of two facts: first, that researchers have made significant choices about the need to use standardized measures to study language function in general and conversation is one aspect of language function, and second, that conversation by definition involves the "free exchange of thoughts or views" (*Webster's Third New International Dictionary*, unabridged, 1986). The very nature of conversation involves the interlocutors' mutual agreement about the subjects to be discussed. It is, indeed, difficult to have a free exchange of thoughts about mutually agreed upon topics when one uses standard, or scripted materials for "mock" conversation in which the topics are unilaterally imposed upon AD sufferers. The topics are quite limited and superficial and can often be of little interest to the AD sufferer.

For example, on the Verbal Expression Test, which is modelled after part of the Illinois Test of Psycholinguistic Abilities, and which is purported to measure the "creative use of speech," the subjects are asked to tell everything they can about an envelope, a nail, a button, and a marble, and on the Boston Diagnostic Aphasia Examination (BDAE) the subject is asked to describe what is occurring in a line drawing (the well-known "Cookie Theft Picture"). In addition, on the BDAE, in the section called, "Conversational and Expository Speech," the afflicted is asked questions such as, "How are you today?", "Have you ever been in this hospital before?", "Do you think we can help you?". In the instructions to a sub-section called, "Open-ended conversation," "it is suggested that the examiner begin with familiar topics such as, 'What kind of work were you doing before you became ill?', 'Tell me what happened to bring you to the hospital.'" The examiner is instructed to "encourage the patient to speak for at least ten minutes."

To infer anything about AD sufferers' conversational abilities from such approaches involves a daunting problem of validity, for there is nothing in the test situations that remotely resembles the definition of conversation. Often, the test materials and topics are quite trivial and short-lived (for examples, see Bayles, 1982; Hutchinson and Jensen, 1980), these are hardly of interest to those who have AD, and the testing situation is anxiety-provoking to some, if not many. It is difficult at best for healthy individuals to engage in a conversation about a topic that is meaningless or trivial, and even if they could, their behavior in such a situation could hardly be considered reflective of their conversational ability in general. There is no reason to assume that AD sufferers would react to such a situation any differently. Finally, and this is not an insignificant point, in much of the reported research, the interlocutors are virtual strangers and spend comparatively brief periods of time together.

Yet, Appell et al. (1982) commented that AD sufferers showed a "breakdown of language as a tool: for conveying or obtaining information, for directing actions, either or oneself or of others . . . ;" Obler (1981) wrote, "Indeed, the abilities to initiate speech, to maintain speech, and to appropriately stop speech . . . may all be impaired in the language of dementing individuals" and Hier et al. (1985)

concluded that we see, in "dementia subjects," a ". . . failure to use language to convey information." In addition, Flicker et al. (1987) commented that AD sufferers' word-finding difficulty "detracts significantly from their ability to communicate, and consequently from their capacity to interact socially and function independently." These comments reflect "the belief that the kinds of communication asked for and allowed in a testing situation are similar to those obtained in natural, truly spontaneous speech between partners in conversation" (Sabat, 1994a). We will see, in this chapter, how Dr. B and other AD sufferers were able to convey a great deal of information, maintain their speech about issues that were of concern to them, and interact well socially, when engaged in natural, spontaneous conversation by an interested and supportive interlocutor with whom they had developed a person-to-person relationship.

His experience of and reaction to the disease

During our first meeting, after I explained my purpose, the following exchange took place:

Dr. B: When the hell are we going to start this project?

SRS: Right now.

Dr. B: I am going back and picking up information that is useless. What is it that you're looking for? I get information in static things. My wife will talk to me and I will get information, but in a little while, I realize it is useless information.

SRS: Useless in what sense?

Dr. B: Ah, well, mostly in the fact that I think about Alzheimer's. Things get jumbled and Alzheimer's gives me fragments.

SRS: So when you think about Alzheimer's, what's the first thing you think?

Dr. B: Um, mad as hell . . . constantly on my mind . . . which may or may not screw up your project.

For Dr. B, the constant flow of daily experience would often come in fragments, some clear and retained, others lost. He was clearly aware of the effects of the disease and admitted that he was preoccupied with and angry about his being afflicted. Yet, in the last line of the above extract, he indicates his concern about the possibility that his difficulties might "screw up" the project. One must wonder if, as a result of such a logical preoccupation with the effects of the disease, the afflicted person's attention is effectively divided, thus adding to the difficulty in acquiring and storing new information and then retrieving it from memory. From Dr. B's experience, it would seem that this is very much a possibility:

SRS: Does it happen that sometimes you're in the middle of doing something and you think about Alzheimer's and then forget about what it is that you were just doing?

Dr. B: Oh, I get that quite a bit. Now what does that mean? I don't know.

SRS: Do you think about Alzheimer's a lot?

Dr. B: Yes.

It would become clear, however, that there were chunks of new information that remained with him for days, even weeks and longer, despite this situation.

For example, during our first week of meetings, he asked that I give him a piece of paper with my name and phone numbers so that he would be able to help himself should he fail to recall my name, and I did so. Actually, I also tried to connect my name with something familiar – the name of the late President of Egypt, Anwar Sadat. Ironically in my eyes, from that day on, he referred to me as "Sadat." A week after our first meetings, one of my students took a walk with him, introducing herself as my student, and he responded by saying, "Oh yes, that guy. I have a piece of paper." On that same occasion, after asking the student's name and repeating it a number of times he told her, "Excuse me if I forget, but I've got this problem. Sometimes I go in small ways, but don't be alarmed. I have Alzheimer's."

I found it interesting that Dr. B would explain his situation to her, for he had not done so with me after our first meeting and I had seen him a number of times since. His behavior thus implicitly indicated that he had long-term memory of my knowledge about his condition (because he never repeated it), and that he recognized that he had not met the student before.

There is yet another significant dimension, taken from Discursive Psychology, in terms of which we can analyze his comment to the student, and this involves Austin's (1961) distinction between the *illocutionary force* and the *perlocutionary force* of an utterance. The illocutionary force of a speech act is understood as being what is achieved *in* saying something (such as a promise, a warning, an apology, a command) and the perlocutionary force is what is achieved *by* saying something. For example, congratulating someone would be the illocutionary force of a comment, while pleasing the recipient would be the perlocutionary force. In the above comment, we see the illocutionary force of what Dr. B said to the student as being a warning about and an apology for, possible subsequent deviations or abnormalities in his behavior, as well as his concern for her feelings ("...don't be alarmed..."). Likewise, we see the perlocutionary force of his comment as being an attempt to put his interlocutor at ease. In both cases, it is apparent that, even though Dr. B manifested striking problems as measured by standard tests of language functions, he was still sufficiently in command of the use of speech acts to interact in a socially graceful, concerned way with his interlocutor. The existence of such behavior, and the ability to gauge the social situation accurately, implies the existence of intact brain systems which would allow for the assessment of the situation and the related behavior in kind.

His reaction to the disease was a subject which he addressed many times. In the following extract, I have included, in parentheses, the length of the pauses (in seconds) that occurred while he was speaking. Thus the reader can gain some sense of the rhythm of his speech. In what follows, rather than being untroubled by the effects of AD (as has often been alleged of the afflicted), Dr. B was quite clear in saying:

> *Dr. B:* Well, I uh, [*4.0 sec.*] oh but, my everything that dominates me now is Alzheimer's [*2.5 sec.*]. No question about it.
> *SRS:* What is it that you think about?
> *Dr. B:* What do I think about?
> *SRS:* Um hum.
> *Dr. B:* I think about, uh, the delumition [diminution], you know, of what I've been able to do and what and what I [*2.6 sec.*] may, may never do.
> *SRS:* Um hum.
> *Dr. B:* Uh, and I know prominently [*2.3 sec.*] that I have Alzheimer's and I can't, can't stop it.
> *SRS:* That must be very frustrating.

Dr. B: Ya, and [*3.1 sec.*] not to be able to do anything about it, anything.

SRS: You feel trapped?

Dr. B: Yeah, yeah, I feel that I don't have a full family now. Uh [*5 sec.*] I, I take a lot of [*3.1 sec.*] things [*2.9 sec.*] that I feel are [*5.6 sec.*], uh, there fear, there are, been, things that I would, should do, you know, but it doesn't, it hasn't ever, you know, come through. I don't know, I don't know what I'm talking about.

SRS: Oh yes – I think you do. I think I know. May I try to tell you what I think you're talking about?

Dr. B: What.

SRS: You're saying that you feel there are things you should be able to do,

Dr. B: Yeah,

SRS: and you don't seem to be able to do them.

Dr. B: Yeah.

SRS: What sorts of things?

Dr. B: What the things are? Uh, I have, uh, demunition of what [*2.5 sec.*], what I could read [*2.1 sec.*], uh, and that's very important to me, and, and [*2.2 sec.*] my wife is an absolute doll and uh, so [*3.4 sec.*] it doesn't, uh, so like I have times when I can't, I can't get up in terms of, um, that I sort of gone fooey sometimes. And then I don't think I, uh, I know that I am slowing down. I don't know how to put an end, and a quarter or a thirty of something. But, but I do works [*4.4 sec.*] I, I can't work for that I used to do, that I used to do. And then, on the other hand, I get a spurt.

SRS: Um hum.

Dr. B: I get a spurt and it, uh, [*2.3 sec.*] I have, I have, uh [*2.5 sec.*], a good time but, uh, it doesn't, doesn't hold.

SRS: It doesn't last very long?

Dr. B: No. And [*4.6 sec.*] I, you know, love, I love my wife very much and she works her tooshie off because she, I have, I have to give her, you know, and uh . . .

SRS: How do you feel about that?

Dr. B: No thing you can do. Wife and, uh [*3.1 sec.*] I pray for Alzheimer's things, you know. [*4.8 sec.*] What do I do? What do I do? [*laughs*] I don't have any more.

31

SRS: Do you feel sometimes that you're almost a fraction of the person . . . [*Dr. B interrupts*]

Dr. B: Oh, I do that almost every day! What, what does it mean? It doesn't mean anything, though. I've, I've hard, hard work and I have to *schlep* [carry, haul, in Yiddish] stuff sometimes now for, for my wife, and sometimes it works okay and sometimes it doesn't. Now I don't have it constantly . . . Well [*6.3 sec.*], I get wisps of [*2.1 sec.*] people, of thoughts, that [*3.5 sec.*] show me that Alzheimer's is right on top of me. And, uh, that there's nothing I can do about it . . . Well uh, I'm, and I'm, something has knocked me down [*3.5 sec.*], something's knocked me down and I can't do anything about it.

Such a feeling is captured by Martin Seligman's notion (1975) of learned helplessness and the related form of depression that arises as a result of the individual perceiving that there is nothing that can be done to alleviate conditions that are harmful, painful, and/or detrimental. That is, depression can be a reaction to a perceived sense of the loss of control over situations, and Dr. B certainly expresses quite clearly his sense of loss and lack of control ("I can't do anything about it") as well as his awareness of the effects of the disease. He even goes so far as to evidence his realization that the losses he's experiencing will affect the quality of his life in the future (". . . the delumition . . . of what I may never do . . ."). And again, in another conversation:

Dr. B: Look – even if I get eliminated, eliminated with Alzheimer's – I don't give a shit whatever else does is, you know, I have had with this Alzheimer's is enough to break my back.

SRS: This is enough to, uh, drive you crazy, isn't it?

Dr. B: Oh ya . . . it has given me a lot of turmoil.

Although his comment above is poorly formed, the illocutionary force of his statement is clear: AD is enough to "break my back," it drives him crazy, gives him "a lot of turmoil." And even a few months before his death, just before he entered a nursing home:

SRS: Did you ever feel like banging your fist against the wall?

Dr. B: Oh, I've done it, I've done it.

SRS: Have you ever been so frustrated in your life?

Dr. B: Well, some people will go ahead and, and just, uh, kill themselves.

SRS: Um hum. But you're not that type?

Dr. B: No, I don't think so. The thing, the worst thing is that I'm just wrung out and wrung out.

His sense of loss with regard to reading

Dr. B initiated the following conversation by telling me that he and his wife went to a large bookstore and that he bought two books, one of which was about a former President:

Dr. B: And, and I was looking for an article about, you know who was it that failed to get the – he, he wasn't, he, you know, his wife – he has a wonderful wife, was a wonderful nife, and he was, but he was um, doing, he ran for the privy.

SRS: President? [Those with word-finding problems are often correct about the initial sounds of the word being sought, so given that he said, "ran for the", I guessed "presidency".]

Dr. B: President.

SRS: He ran for president.

Dr. B: Yes, yes, you got it.

SRS: Was he elected president?

Dr. B: No, he didn't make it.

SRS: Okay, let's figure out who it is.

Dr. B: Yeah!

SRS: Is it Adlai Stevenson?

Dr. B: Not Adlai, but you're very close to it.

SRS: Hubert Humphrey?

Dr. B: No.

SRS: Tom Dewey?

Dr. B: No.

SRS: Mike Dukakis?

Dr. B: No.

SRS: Was it Mondale?

Dr. B: No – oh Jesus!

SRS: Carter?

Dr. B: No. Then he put out some books. His name, he had.

SRS: Nixon?

Dr. B: No, not Nixon, good grife [*pronounced greye-ff*]!

SRS: Was this . . .

Dr. B: Only recently. The book, there were books.

SRS: McGovern?

Dr. B: No. He uh,

SRS: This is a guy who ran for president and didn't make it.

Dr. B: He didn't make it. Um, ya, and he wrote a book. He wrote a book and it was a wonderful book and I've been reading it myself.

SRS: Is this a Democrat?

Dr. B: Yes!

SRS: Wasn't Mondale.

Dr. B: No.

SRS: And it wasn't Dukakis.

Dr. B: No. Oh, this is getting stupid.

SRS: Johnson?

Dr. B: No. He had a wonderful wife. He and his wife were very adoring.

SRS: Not Jimmy Carter?

Dr. B: Jimmy Carter – right.

SRS: And his wife, Rosalyn.

Dr. B: Yes. And I bought a book. And it was very, very good. It was very difficult for them. And he ran for the, the person.

SRS: President?

Dr. B: Yeah.

SRS: He ran against Reagan.

Dr. B: Yeah and he lost.

SRS: You must have looked at that and shook your head. Reagan was elected twice. You knew him as an actor for many years.

Dr. B: And he was *still* a schmuck!

It was not as difficult to do this as might be thought by looking at the many lines involved. It was more like playing "20 questions." I knew that he would be able to recognize the name if he heard it. The first time I mentioned "Carter" he responded in the negative, but when I said "Jimmy Carter" he recognized it immediately. I came back to the name again, as I did with others, because I was aware of the possibility that Dr. B may not have been completely focused on

34

what I was saying, for in his previous comment (just before I said "Carter"), he evinced frustration at not being able to recall the name, saying, "No – oh, Jesus!" Another reason for my sticking this out with him was that I wanted the conversation to continue, given that he brought up the subject. As it happened, this was a good idea because he then explained to me not only his reasons for wanting to go to the bookstore, but his estimation of the types of books that were there and how that indicated to him something about his own condition at present.

Dr. B: I told my wife that I'm not getting the material that I had just a little year, just a little year before.

SRS: You weren't reading as much,

Dr. B: Right.

SRS: and you felt a need to – that you wanted to do more of that.

Dr. B: Yes, yes. It was *me* that I, that I went out and I said.

SRS: It was wonderful that you did that.

Dr. B: Ya. Now there are other, two other, this gets all crazy . . . Because I told my wife I was losing my, what was going on, my wanting to have this material.

SRS: You felt that?

Dr. B: Ya, oh ya, I knew I wasn't, I wasn't good on it.

SRS: Have you, in your life, been a very avid reader?

Dr. B: Um, a long time ago, ya, everything was fine. But in this there was not doing it. I am sure, I am positive, I am positive you will look at these books and these are not magnificent, sophisticated, you know, other things, and uh, *I lost so much, I realized how much* from the sophisticated, nothing big, big, and wow, gee, I was getting way out . . . falling out . . . it is *not* the Reader's Digest, it is *not* the Reader's Digest.

SRS: You wouldn't read that would you?

Dr. B: No! I didn't.

SRS: If you had to pick a word to describe the Reader's Digest, what would you call it?

Dr. B: Jerky [*chuckles*].

One of the wonderful aspects of the relationship between Dr. B and his wife was that she at no time dismissed him as a result of the obvious problems he was having. She encouraged him to choose things that he wanted to do and this adventure of going to the bookstore was one example. He recognized that it was *his* will that was being expressed ("It was *me*."). Also evident still was his ability to discriminate between books meant for the sophisticated as opposed to the lay reader and the difference in his own reading ability at present, when compared to times past.

He had great difficulty in reading, yet at times he could read some things well. He began reading Jimmy Carter's book and told me of the deep sadness that accompanied Carter on the night of his defeat by Reagan. In the process, he recognized that this book was not terribly sophisticated by his high academic standards, yet he was having trouble, and this told him just how much his ability had declined. Although he expressed no outward emotion about this issue, it was deeply troubling to him as he would indicate in another conversation, in which I asked Dr. B if he had read any more of the book:

Dr. B: Well, the book that I bought?

SRS: Yes.

Dr. B: I've got – this is a problem. This is it, sorta silly [*chuckles*]. We bought the book, we bought two books, and um, for a week or so I was being able to, to, to do the very much, you know, I can write and stuff like that. So it was, it was grandeur, but um, it uh, it didn't, I was tensed, you know, as to is it mine, is it still mine?

SRS: With the book that you were reading,

Dr. B: Well, you know, the two books that I told you about. And um, it's, it's, I listened to about two or three daw, uh, pages and uh, it, it was difficulty, it had some difficulty. I think the difficulty is that I really was not on a rhythm, there was not, there was not a rhythm of that kind of thing. And I get all over the place. So that's it . . . I bought the two books, I have the two books, and I thought, you know, it was, it was pretty good. Uh, and I think I was getting some good, um, also the Alzheimer's is uh, tears me apart on it. It comes to the point of how to read, for me. I try keeping notes, but frequently it's not.

SRS: It doesn't work?

Dr. B: It doesn't work for me and um, I fell a lot of antagonize to myself.

SRS: You get annoyed with yourself?
Dr. B: Yeah, pissed off.

One can note in the above conversations, that he is aware of his losses, that AD "tears me apart", that for a time, he found some success in reading (". . . it was grandeur . . ."), but then became worried as to whether it would last (". . . I was tensed . . . is it still mine?"). We also see some linguistic difficulties in his use of "privy" and "person" for President, his use of "fell a lot of antagonize to" for "felt a lot of annoyance with" himself in not being able to read something that he knows to be rather simple material. Despite word-finding problems and some poorly formed sentences, the illocutionary force of his statements is quite clear.

It had been apparent from the outset of our association that Dr. B had serious word-finding problems. Such problems as seen on standard tests of language function have been duly noted in the literature as one type of linguistic deficit stemming from AD (Irigaray, 1973; Gardner, 1974; Schwartz et al., 1979; Bayles, 1979, 1982; Obler, 1981; Appell et al., 1982; Martin and Fedio, 1983; Kempler, 1984; Nebes et al., 1984; Hier et al., 1985; Huff et al., 1986; Flicker et al., 1987; Murdoch et al., 1987; Huff et al., 1988; Shuttleworth and Huber, 1988), in addition to object naming, conveying information, and comprehension (Appell et al., 1982).

Often, he would say things that I did not understand clearly and immediately, but I assumed that he was trying to tell me something and so at times I would pursue the meaning first by letting him know that I was having trouble understanding him. At other times, as in the above extracts, I would guess as to his meaning and ask him. Making the assumption that he was, indeed, trying to tell me something is akin to what Dennett (1990) calls, "*taking the intentional stance*" toward another. In other words, I was positioning Dr. B as someone who was trying to convey something intelligible, and placed at least some of the responsibility for understanding him on myself, which is clearly related to Rommetveit's (1974) notion of anticipatory comprehension, or the listener's readiness to understand. Dr. B expressed his satisfaction with this approach quite clearly to one of my students when he said, "Your mentor, when he doesn't see what I say, he says so and I appreciate that."

A note on interpersonal dynamics

Imagine, if you will, what it would be like if someone seemed to understand what you, an AD sufferer, were saying, but really did not, and simply said, "Okay, okay" or "Um-hum" in response to what you said. And suppose further that you were trying to tell the other person that he or she was standing on your foot, that it hurt, and were asking the person to move. Given that you were told, "okay," you would have every right to expect that the person understood the meaning of your request and would then move so as to ease your discomfort. However, your interlocutor did not understand, and so remains standing on your foot, and you become annoyed, agitated, repeating your request ever more loudly. You, however, do not realize that you aren't being understood, and the other person interprets your anger and exasperation as being a symptom of AD rather than a justifiable annoyance.

You have now become a prisoner not only of the disease that disrupts your ability to use words with facility and of being positioned as the "ill person," but you are also confined by the less than honest responses of your interlocutor. I do not wish to imply, by saying "less than honest," that the problem in this scenario is that the healthy interlocutor is being a liar. It is quite common for people to feel uncomfortable about pointing out to an AD sufferer that the latter is not being clear in his or her speech. It is easily understandable that one could cause the afflicted consternation by calling attention to such a problem and, in many cases, especially in the clinical testing situation, this is quite true. However, in the course of social interaction, it is a well established part of conversation and social grace to admit to not understanding what is being said by another, and to work cooperatively to achieve clarity in conversational exchanges. There is a difference between saying, "You're not being clear" and "I'm having trouble understanding what you're trying to tell me."

Taking the intentional stance and thereby positioning the AD sufferer as one who has something meaningful to say and is, indeed, trying to communicate, can easily lead to the use of an effective, facilitative speech act called *indirect repair* (Sabat, 1991a, 1999) on the part of the healthy partner. Indirect repair refers to inquiring about the intention of the speaker, through the use of questions marked not by interrogatives but by intonation patterns, to the use of rephrasing what you think the speaker said and checking to see if you understood his or her meaning correctly. Thus, the responsibility for effective communication between people lies with the listener as well as with the speaker. Such use of "cooperative strategies" is discussed by many authors (Rommetveit, 1974; Goodwin, 1980; de Bleser and Weisman, 1986; Goodwin and Heritage, 1990) and it is clear that it is important to keep the perspective of the other person in mind (Tannen, 1984).

The use of indirect repair can be seen to have been effective in the dialogue above as well as in the following extract of conversation in which Dr. B was describing his experience of the effects of AD when he is distracted while in the middle of thinking and trying to say something.

> *Dr. B:* When I leave something with hiatus I think maybe I get, I wouldn't say disturbed, but it, it, it, screws up the rhythm.
>
> *SRS:* Oh, so if you're in the middle of thinking about something . . .
>
> *Dr. B:* Uh-huh.
>
> *SRS:* And you get distracted . . .
>
> *Dr. B:* Yeah.
>
> *SRS:* Then you lose what you wanted to say?
>
> *Dr. B:* Yeah, but um, I can, uh, wait for a little while.
>
> *SRS:* Um-hum.
>
> *Dr. B:* And uh, I get, and uh, I get rejuvenation, and uh, up it comes.
>
> *SRS:* So there are times when you get distracted and you lose track of what you wanted to say, but if you wait a little while, it comes back?
>
> *Dr. B:* Ya, it'll sort of creeps in.
>
> *SRS:* That's really good-it's helpful to know that.
>
> *Dr. B:* What does it mean?
>
> *SRS:* It means that you . . . [*he interrupts*]
>
> *Dr. B:* Is this of any value?
>
> *SRS:* Are you kidding? [*said in a gentle, supportive tone*] Let me tell you why it's of value to me.

Before I could go on, he interrupted to assure me, in all sincerity, "I'm not playing with games, every so often I........go ahead."

In this extract, we see not only how the use of indirect repair (repairing the listener's understanding) helped me to understand Dr. B's point clearly, but we also see something that I will take up in detail in Chapter 5: his question, "Is this of any value?" Here, he has already become a collaborator with me in the "project" and is interested in knowing if there is value in what he said. That is, he wants to know if what he has reported has any significant meaning in the context of the research. But let us first return to the meaning, the value, of his earlier comments above:

1   If I know that sometimes, when an AD sufferer is distracted while in the midst of a conversation, he or she might lose track of the present thought, and
2   If I know that the afflicted person might be able to retrieve the thought after a short while,
3   I would know not to interrupt the pauses during which the afflicted person was trying to retrieve the thread of conversation because
4   The interruption would serve only as yet another distraction that would exacerbate the problem, and therefore,
5   I would know that I should give my afflicted interlocutor more time to think before I interrupted the thought process even with so much of a question as, "What did you want to say?"

This knowledge accompanied me in all subsequent conversations with Dr. B as well as with other AD sufferers. There would often be pauses, as noted in one of the above extracts, between words or sentences, in the order of anywhere between two and seven seconds. For many reasons, perhaps, people are often uncomfortable when there are protracted moments of silence during conversations, and when such moments occur they feel the urge to fill those moments with talk, even if it means interrupting the speaker's turn at talking. In fact, there is a point of view called "the simplest systematics" which is held by some researchers in the field of Psycholinguistics (Sacks et al., 1974), and these researchers propose that certain rules must be observed in order for a conversation to be successful. One such rule is that long pauses, beyond a few seconds within a conversation, make that conversation, by definition, unsuccessful. The rules must be, in the view of the authors, context-free and immune to aspects of "situatedness, identities, particularities of content or context" (p. 699). However, other authors (Rommetveit, 1974; O'Connell et al., 1990) point out that part of the implicit social "contract" that characterizes every conversation includes factors such as who the interlocutors happen to be, the purpose of the conversation, the time available, and the location of the conversation. Hence, the duration of gaps or pauses, be they long or short, do not alone determine the success or failure of a conversation, and to the extent that the purposes of the interlocutors are fulfilled, the length of the pauses are instrumental in the success of the interchange. This surely seems to be the case when the interlocutors include an AD sufferer who may need the longer silences in order to frame his or her thoughts well (Sabat, 1991b). Not only does the afflicted person need more time to frame thoughts, to find words, but he or she also may have a need for others to speak more slowly. Dr. B made this clear in talking about the director of the day care center, whom he liked very much:

> *Dr. B:* I find, trying to get the Alzheimer's block, I find him, that he's talking very much, very fast, very going, and uh, you know, he's got his job.
> *SRS:* Does he speak too quickly for you?
> *Dr. B:* In the main, yes.
> *SRS:* He talks too quickly?
> *Dr. B:* Yeah.
> *SRS:* If he speaks too quickly, maybe you should tell him to slow down.
> *Dr. B:* I think I've done that; I'm not sure.

In a subsequent conversation with Mrs. B, I learned that Dr. B had not only retained the advice I gave him, but applied it to another situation when he answered the telephone. She observed that he listened and suddenly said, "Excuse me, I have Alzheimer's. Could you speak slower please?" From this, it would seem that a good strategy to employ in conversation with an afflicted person is for the healthy interlocutor to speak at a pace that mimics the afflicted speaker's pace. We will return to this issue for further exploration in Chapter 3.

Implicit memory

In addition, in this episode, we see the existence of his intact "implicit memory." Implicit memory is defined as a change in behavior that occurs as a result of previous experience, and has been shown to exist in cases of severe anterograde amnesia in which a person has no explicit recall of having had the previous experience (Graf et al., 1984; Squire, 1986; Heindel et al., 1989; Schacter, 1996). On our first few walks outside together, whenever we reached the mailbox, Dr. B would point to it and indicate to me that he knew where we were relative to the day care center. After the first few walks, he no longer did this, as if to show that he had already made his point and didn't have to do so any longer. This could be viewed as an instance of intact implicit memory because at first, he had to show that he could, indeed, navigate on his own, but having proved that he could, he no longer needed to do so. If he had no memory whatsoever of having shown me that he could use the landmark and orient himself, he would have continued to do so each time we went for a walk.

Another example of his intact implicit memory was revealed when, one morning, the social worker told me that Dr. B had become upset with some people earlier that day. It seemed that a group of people from the hospital with which the day care center is affiliated decided to hold a meeting that morning in the room in which Dr. B and I had our meeting two days earlier. He was insisting that they not use that room because that was the room we would be using for our meeting. This particular room was not the one in which we met most often, but had used for the first time two days earlier because it was quiet, away from the noise of the social programs and activities of the center's main rooms.

Nowhere in the moments of everyday life would such a situation cause me to feel delight. Nowhere, that is, except in my attempts to understand the experience of a person with Alzheimer's disease from his or her point of view. Despite recent research, it is all too common to assume that if a person has Alzheimer's, the person either has lost memory functions or will lose those functions in the not-too-distant future. To be sure there are losses, but such losses are far from complete. Thus, upon hearing about Dr. B's encounter with the hospital personnel, I was delighted in that he had held onto the memory, for two days, of where we had previously met. Now would he remember that he remembered and, if so, what would be his explanation for his ability to store that experience in, and retrieve it from, long-term memory?

Those questions could be answered only by Dr. B and so I went to meet him.

SRS: This past Tuesday, on the sixth, we used a different room, remember? We started out in the room we're usually in and it was noisy and then we went down the hall, and

Dr. B: Ya.

SRS: went into another room.

Dr. B: That's right.

SRS: It was the first time we ever used that room.

Dr. B: Um hum.

SRS: Today,

Dr. B: Um hum,

SRS: two days later,

Dr. B: Ya,

SRS: you saw some people in that room

Dr. B: Um hum

SRS: and it bothered you that there were people in that room because that was our room?

Dr. B: Ya, ya.

SRS: You remembered!

Dr. B: Ya.

SRS: This is two days later.

Dr. B: That's right.

SRS: So what I'm trying to point out to you is that you had held on to that information.

Dr. B: Oh yes! Oh yes! It came in and it stayed there for some period of time.

SRS: Two days – now that's long-term memory.

Dr. B: Is it?

SRS: Yes it is.

Dr. B: And that's what it is. I, uh, all I can say is, uh, the material is, uh, was the same, was okay, and then even a couple of things while I was doing in the evening, I think it was in the evening, um, and I was getting retrievals. I'm gonna call them retrievals.

43

And I had on some time I was retrieving material that I never should, I shouldn't have been able to pull it in.

SRS: Why do you say that you shouldn't have been able to?

Dr. B: Well, uh, well maybe because it shouldn't have been out of step or something like that. Are we doing something?

SRS: Yes! I think that what you're noticing is that sometimes pieces of information elude you – you can't retrieve it sometimes.

Dr. B: Ya, that's fair. It's, it's but I'm relaxed I was able to pull out some things.

SRS: So this is telling us that when you're relaxed you have an easier time retrieving information.

Dr. B: Yes that's right, but not all the time. See there's loss, loss, loss, but not systematically . . . So I wish the heck I had, you know, a machine and could do it. Course I was doing it the other night. All this is night stuff.

SRS: Um hum.

Dr. B: And I still held on, and I still held onto it, um, material that I wanted. I fought like hell.

And a week later when I brought up this very same subject, and said that it was terrific that he had held on to that information, he said, "Well, it was uh, terrifically important to me."

We have here a phenomenon (wanting the hospital staff people to leave that room) that is itself suggestive of the presence of his memory for having used that room. In other words, Dr. B had passed by many other rooms at the day care center and never once tried to have the occupants leave. On this occasion, having had, two days earlier, the experience of working with me in that room, he now tried to hasten the staff's departure. If one were to have asked Dr. B directly, "Which room did you use last time you saw Dr. Sabat?", he would have had great difficulty in answering if he could have answered at all. However, in that particular moment, his behavior itself reflected his intact memory of the significance of that room to him. In recent years, there have been increasing reports of intact implicit, or procedural, memory among those with Alzheimer's, and here in a natural setting, we have still another piece.

What this means, along with Dr. B's comment about getting retrievals, is that the AD sufferer (even when having great difficulty with words or with recall memory function) is, in this case and perhaps in many others, able to hold onto information in memory far longer than much research on explicit recall memory has suggested. In addition, it means that although retrieval from memory may not be possible at one time, it is at another, and the forms of retrieval we must look at must include overt verbal and nonverbal behavior in natural settings. Further, it is clear from his own words that Dr. B had greater success in retrieving information that was important to him especially when he was relaxed. This information can serve to inform not only those who depend solely upon formal testing situations for their assessment of the cognitive abilities of AD sufferers, but also caregivers of many different stripes. If we understand that being relaxed can help the AD sufferer retrieve information from memory, then providing that person with a non-anxious presence in conversation would be a significant facilitative strategy.

His need of and gratitude for "therapeutic" conversation

The extracts of conversation that follow began with Dr. B asking me about my daughter. In responding to him, I commented that I felt grateful for her presence and he then went on discuss his wife as well as an upcoming trip that they would be taking to visit a sick, elderly relative. The prospect of the trip was apparently a source of anxiety and he needed to talk.

Dr. B: I'm uh, fortunate.

SRS: You are?

Dr. B: I'm fortunate. I'm fortunate, you know if it wasn't for my wife and, and, uh, all that, you know I'd be like that [*makes "phttt" sound*].

SRS: It's true, it's true, you really are very lucky . . . because you obviously work very well together – you and your wife.

Dr. B: Oh sure, oh ya. We uh, my wife's the boss [*chuckles*]. My wife's the boss [*in a sing-song, kidding voice*]. That's the way it were.

SRS: Has she always been the boss?

Dr. B: Uh, no we really come together. I think is the Alzheimer's is the thing that gave us, um, the first start of *tsouris* [Yiddish word for "grief"], you know, with Alzheimer's,

SRS: Ya, ya,

45

Dr. B: and that knocked the shit out of me.

SRS: How did that change things with your wife? Did that make a real difference in your marriage?

Dr. B: Well, ah, my wife then had to, uh, take – maybe overtake a lot of work, a lot of work. And, uh, so everything juh, jumped on, you know, was on her. And she had some things that she wanted to do. Fortunately, we have four children that are, um, very, very good. Each one of them is a prime [prize?].

SRS: Just a moment ago, you said your wife had to take over a lot of things. Was that frustrating for you?

Dr. B: Well, we we have a lot of things that we don't. Right now, my wife takes up the slack.

SRS: Um hum.

Dr. B: And she has a powerful project [she has an important job], you know, in her own, so um, that's that really really, you know, okeedoke!

SRS: I got a message that you may have to be out of town some time . . .

Dr. B: Ya,

SRS: I'm not sure what it was.

Dr. B: Ya, my uh, not my daughter, my wife – Oh Jesus Christ!

Here, he became terribly frustrated as a result of not being able to identify the relative whom he and his wife would be visiting. I assumed that he realized that it was a relative because he first mentioned his daughter, then his wife, both of whom are, of course, relatives. His problem seemed to be one of *recalling* the sought-for noun, and I tried to provide him with possibilities so that he might be able to *recognize* the identity of that relative upon hearing it:

SRS: It's a relative, huh?

Dr. B: A relative, ya, who is getting elderly.

SRS: Is it somebody in your wife's family?

Dr. B: Ya.

SRS: Is it her mother?

Dr. B: No, uh, and you know, she's, she's done very well, and she's been in the hospital and she's also in Oklahoma and we're going over.

SRS: I see. Is this an aunt, maybe? [Actually it was his wife's sister – an aunt to their children.]

Dr. B: Yes, it's an aunt, it's an aunt. She's very old.

SRS: Bless her heart!

Dr. B: In Oklahoma they live long! [Here he interjected some humor, as he chuckled while speaking.]

SRS: Not like in New York! All that clean air.

Although I didn't realize that this would be an extended conversation, he apparently wanted to speak at length and so, before he began, he indicated his concern for the amount of time I might have, wondering if I had to leave soon.

Dr. B: Now are we constrained here in terms of, do you have to run off?

SRS: No, plenty of time. Do you think you'll drive out to . . . ?

Dr. B: Oh no, we're gonna fly.

SRS: Oh, that will be a thrill a minute for you! As I remember, you're not exactly a big fan of flying.

Dr. B: Well, it's a very long trip. Well, what gives either for you or for me, or something?

SRS: Well, you want to go first and tell me what gives for you?

Dr. B: Well, we've been spending a lot of time as to how to do the situation right now in Oklahoma, so we have to go to Oklahoma, because she's very ill. When it comes it comes. It's a real *schlep* . . . Now here's another problem. The problem is, here I am Alzheimer's and we will have to fly. Now which leaves me some nervous [used the Yiddish word].

SRS: So you feel nervous?

Dr. B: From Alzheimer's.

SRS: Well do you think that's going to bother you?

Dr. B: Ah, we'll have to find out [*laughs*]. We're just gonna have to find out.

SRS: I'm glad to hear you say that.

Dr. B: Why, because I have to go?

SRS: Well, I'm glad to hear you say "we'll have to find out." You're not anticipating that it's going to be terrible, you're not doing that and that's good.

47

Dr. B: My wife was thinking that maybe one of our sons would go instead of me going. Um, but I think I got, I loosened up. I figure I got to do it anyway. You see, it's the Alzheimer's that gives me, "Oh my G-d! Look at all the things I have to do! How do I know what I have to do?"

SRS: Ya, all of a sudden there's a whole list of things, and you want to keep things straight in your mind.

Dr. B: Fortunately, my wife is, has a very steady head, and um, she has, she's, she's able to do a lot of things.

SRS: She seems like an incredible person.

Dr. B: Ya, she is. Oh she is, ya . . . But I keep thinking, what am I doing this? I have Alzheimer's and I got a, another *tsuris* and so I almost, I was very, very nervous for Alzheimer's and I don't know what the hell Alzheimer's is now, who the hell knows it? But I'm gonna take it anyway. [I took this to mean that he'd take the trip nonetheless.]

SRS: I'm glad.

Dr. B: You are? Why?

SRS: I'm glad because sometimes people almost make invalids out of themselves. They underestimate themselves and withdraw,

Dr. B: You're right.

SRS: and withdraw from things,

Dr. B: Yeah, and they get scared as shit. It's, it's ironic if you want to think about it, of who ah, who wears the pants. Uh, not that I lose the pants or anything, but it's she uh, she really does it very, very, takes, takes charge in using the head.

SRS: You're very lucky because there are some people who could never,

Dr. B: Ah, ah! (mimicking my comment, as if to sound completely overwhelmed by responsibility.) Plus the fact that I was able to understand some of the things that you and I are talking about. And so she, uh, she's the one, she, she, she takes charge of paperwork on many things, um, which helps her. So we decided we would do. So there [*exhales deeply*]. Okay, this is approximately what I was coming to. *Well, her sister is very old.* How old can she stay? She's a piss and vinegar too.

SRS: A lot of spunk?

Dr. B: Oh ya – "what did you come here for? What are you doing here? Go home!" [*mimicking her tone, attitude*].

SRS: That's the attitude she'll have!

Dr. B: I still need bucking up, and uh, I think my wife prods me every so often and she's right and she pushes me and pushes me, "you can do it, you can do it."

SRS: That is wonderful. Sometimes we all need encouragement.

Dr. B: So I think I'll be okay. I think I'll make it . . . So many times when I think about what you and I have talked about, um, and my wife and I, and I say "Gee whiz, where is that guy? I need that guy!"

SRS: You can call me anytime.

Dr. B: You've got enough telephone numbers. [Months earlier I gave him three numbers he could use to reach me.] You know, sometimes I have the fear of the telephone.

SRS: Fear?

Dr. B: I get, I get prustrated, frustrated with the telephone because, uh, it's sorta serious, stupid. I don't, I don't want to Alzheimer's and, but nevertheless I get very very jerky about the whole thing.

SRS: You mean nervous?

Dr. B: Yeah nervous and about going into the yonder.

SRS: Oh, in the airplane? ["wild blue yonder", from the US Air Force Song, is the clue here].

Dr. B: Ya.

SRS: Well, you've always been that way haven't you? [He always had a distaste for flying.]

Dr. B: Ya. Well I sure do . . . really glad, you know, you let me ventilate. Were you here in the time? I mean did did you come out purposely for you, for me to work?

SRS: Yes.

Dr. B: That's very good, very kind.

SRS: You're very important to me.

Dr. B: I'm delighted to keep talking, but you have your own.

SRS: Well, I still have time.

Dr. B: You do? You want to take a walk?

SRS: Sure.

Dr. B: Let's take a walk.

In spite of his many linguistic problems as revealed by standard tests, this conversation revealed some important themes relative to

49

Dr. B's experience of AD and the illocutionary force of his speech acts: his frustration about not being able to identify the relative he was going to visit, his awareness that his wife had to take on many of the responsibilities that were his in the past ("she takes charge in using the head"), his upcoming trip and the anxiety he felt about it and all the related details involved, his frustration concerning the use of the telephone, his need for encouragement, his recognition of and gratitude for my having come to work with him and giving him an opportunity to "ventilate," and finally, toward the end of this extract, he expressed his concern for my schedule and any constraints that might exist regarding the remaining time I had to spend with him. Throughout, I was providing him with a non-anxious partner in conversation, giving him room to speak, checking to see that I understood him correctly, letting him know that I wanted to understand and would work to do so. I believe that this approach was at least partly behind his comment, "Gee whiz, where is that guy? I need that guy!"

Within the conversation, he experienced a number of word-finding problems and the way in which we tried to find the right words could be instructive to caregivers. At the outset of the conversation concerning his upcoming trip, he couldn't find the word to describe the relative who was ill and whom he and his wife were going to visit. Here, we see that the problem was really a recall memory problem, because he was able to answer correctly to the multiple-choice format (use of recognition memory): he knew quite clearly that the person was in his wife's family, but not his wife's mother. The clue to the fact that the person was in his family was that at first he referred to the person as his daughter, then his wife, and in both cases corrected himself. I asked if the person was an aunt and he said she was – and she was, for it was his sister-in-law who is an aunt to his children. It should be noted that later in the conversation (see italicized words) Dr. B referred immediately to the person as his wife's sister. This is important for several reasons. First, it shows that he had more difficulty finding those words when confronted, that is, when I asked him point blank to discuss his trip – rather than during the natural flow of the conversation when he later found those words quite easily. Second, it shows the great variability in Dr. B's success in finding the words for which he is searching. There may, at times, be a causal connection between the first and second points. In other words, the act of confronting the afflicted person with a point-blank question whose answer requires recall of a specific piece of information, may contribute to the person's anxiety and thus have a negative impact on the retrieval process.

That Dr. B was nervous about flying was not connected only to the fact of his present condition, for he always felt uncomfortable about it even though he had been a pilot in the military. Without knowing this background information, one could arrive at the erroneous conclusion that such discomfort was due exclusively to the problems caused by Alzheimer's. Clinicians must be relentless in uncovering background information regarding the dispositions and attitudes of brain-injured people lest they mistakenly attribute aspects of the person's present behavior to the effects of disease alone. Dr. B's frustration concerning the telephone was, indeed, connected to the effects of Alzheimer's because the disease made him less efficient in processing information, especially the spoken word. He was often reluctant to explain to people on the other end of the phone that he had Alzheimer's, and that is, I think, understandable. He did learn, however, to say simply, "please slow down."

When talking about the telephone and his nervousness, he suddenly switched the subject to his nervousness about flying. As I indicated in the body of the dialogue, the key to understanding that shift was his use of the phrase "going into the yonder." It is very important that family members and other caregivers be extremely attentive to the person's use of words, to look past the surface structure, and to use the context of the conversation as a guide in the process of "translating" what the afflicted person is trying to say. Without such an approach, the person can easily and mistakenly be construed as, positioned as, being tremendously confused and then treated as if that were true.

The effect of distraction on conversation

Earlier, I discussed the possible distracting, disruptive effects of interrupting the AD sufferer in the middle of his or her turn at talking. It is also possible for the afflicted person to be distracted by something other than the healthy interlocutor, and for such a distraction to have a powerful effect on conversational coherence. This next extract occurred on the heels of my attempt to discover what it was that gave

51

him the first sign that something was wrong with him years earlier. He said that he knew something was wrong with him before he knew that it was called Alzheimer's, but he didn't seem to be able to say exactly what it was. However, in the process of trying to speak about the subject, he spoke about his oldest son and then his daughter (this made sense as there were troubling episodes which involved both adult children and which they recounted to me in my interviews with them). When he began to talk about his daughter, I noticed that his eyes moved from looking at me and he began to scan a folder that was on the nearby chair, a folder that contained information about Alzheimer's disease. This is what transpired:

> *Dr. B:* I think my daughter is very, very sophisticated herself [*here he looks at the folder*]. She doesn't, well, she uh, she doesn't, relist. Um, and it'd be in the system. I think, I think it could be system. What I'm doing, I don't know. I think I'm going batty on this thing.
>
> *SRS:* I think you've got a lot of thoughts in your head,
>
> *Dr. B:* Ya,
>
> *SRS:* and you're going from one thing to the other to the other.
>
> *Dr. B:* Yes!
>
> *SRS:* And they're getting mixed up like a stew.
>
> *Dr. B:* It is! And I don't even know if I have any, doing it.
>
> *SRS:* Well, what we need to do is block things off a bit.
>
> *Dr. B:* Right.
>
> *SRS:* You know what happened? Let me show you what happened. We were talking about your daughter,
>
> *Dr. B:* Ya,
>
> *SRS:* You looked at this folder,
>
> *Dr. B:* Um hum,
>
> *SRS:* and you immediately started thinking about all this Alzheimer's stuff,
>
> *Dr. B:* Ya,
>
> *SRS:* in the middle of talking about your daughter, and it seemed like the two subjects were coming together. It was almost as if you were speaking one word from Alzheimer's business that you had thoughts about, and another word about your daughter and what she's up to,
>
> *Dr. B:* Ya, and, and, and it sounded like a mish-mosh.

52

SRS: But you knew that.

Dr. B: But I knew that. I knew, oh yeah, I knew it. I knew that it was inevitable of these two melds.

A number of points must be noted here, for this incident can provide insights for caregivers and researchers alike:

(1) If I hadn't noticed the shift of Dr. B's eyes while he was beginning to speak about his daughter, and if I had not been aware of exactly what he was glancing at during those few moments, I might have thought his discourse to be bizarre at the very least. I might have agreed with him that he was going batty, and my treatment and expectations of him might have been negatively affected in that I might have positioned him as being incoherent.

(2) Because I was cognizant of where he was looking and the nature of the material in his view as well as what that material meant to him, I was able to understand immediately that his discourse was not an example of "empty speech" or another linguistic defect *per se*. Rather, this was a case of divided attention in which two different thoughts were gaining access to his awareness simultaneously and his speech production suffered as a result.

(3) His comments that "I think I'm going batty on this thing", and ". . . it sounded like a mish-mosh", indicates his ability to reflect upon and have insight into the fact that he was having a problem expressing himself.

Recent research (Freed et al., 1989) has indicated that some AD sufferers have deficits in selective attention. It is one thing not to be able to attend to something for a period of time and thus be deficient in processing whatever information had just been made available. It is another thing to be unable to inhibit the processing of other sources of information, so that when two different things are coming into awareness simultaneously, one cannot then process either source of input effectively. This is a different type of attentional problem.

In a sense, attention implies inhibition – when we attend to the voice on the telephone, we inhibit other sources of sensory input to a large degree. Likewise, as we speak we often have other thoughts occurring simultaneously, but we can inhibit our attention to those other thoughts, continue with the present point, and then come back to those other thoughts and discuss them if we wish. Dr. B was being confronted with two very potent thoughts: one concerning his daughter and the other the material about Alzheimer's in the folder before him. Both gained representation simultaneously and successively in his speech because he could not inhibit the processing of, and his reaction to, the second source of information (the folder). One could also interpret this as his being very "stimulus bound," with the folder being so potent. But what is helpful here thus far is that what happened and why it happened may not indicate anything more than the effects of divided attention. The importance of this for clinicians and caregivers is great, for it is quite tempting to make incorrect inferences about thinking and about language skills from such behavior and thereby create lists of symptoms on the basis of those inferences.

From the point of view of Dr. B, and perhaps others who suffer the effects of Alzheimer's, the observational ability and understanding of the healthy person in the conversation is extremely important. In this case, his immediate interpretation of what happened was that he was going "batty." Such interpretations are common in cases of other forms of brain injury (the effects of hemi-spatial neglect, for example, wherein owing to parietal lobe damage, the person seems to ignore the half of the body and extrapersonal space opposite the side of brain damage) as well. Yet, the truth of the matter is that Dr. B was not going batty and he should not have had to labor under such a misapprehension. Thus, I immediately attempted to show him exactly what had happened, and he made the connection quite well.

(4)   Again from the point of view of Dr. B, he knew that what he said did not make sense. He knew this immediately and later understood why his discourse suffered. His ability to reflect immediately on what had happened indicates his ability to discriminate, from his own point of view, those occasions on which he is mixing thoughts together from those occasions on which he is not. It should be noted that one possible effect of thinking that "I'm going batty" is that the person may become angry, anxious, frustrated, or depressed, all or any of which can serve to cause further problems in interacting with others.

54

At the end of that part of our meeting, in a moment that struck me as being ironic as well as poignant, Dr. B said, "I don't know if I'm boring you." I cannot imagine that this man would have thought, at any other time in his life, that there was a possibility that he was boring someone else. Perhaps it is a measure of his estimation of how much he felt he had lost to the ravages of Alzheimer's that he could make such a statement to me. I don't know. However, the truth of the matter is that he never bored me in the least, and I responded by telling him as much:

> *Dr. B:* I don't know if I'm boring you.
> *SRS:* Never. You never bore me, are you kidding? Never, not for a minute.
> *Dr. B:* Okay.
> *SRS:* So many things that you say, you probably would say "What's the big deal" about,
> *Dr. B:* Ya.
> *SRS:* but from my point of view, a lot of this is a big deal.
> *Dr. B:* Um, but your daughter has a, um, you have to do with your daughter.
> *SRS:* I still have plenty of time.

His expressions of concern for me

Here again, in the second to the last of the above lines, he knew that after our meetings I would go to pick up my daughter at her school, and he was always conscious of that fact. This was important to him in that he was recognizing my responsibility to her – for that responsibility would be of great concern to him if he were in my position. In that sense, he was making my cause his cause. He thus showed an obvious concern for the needs of another person – this was the illocutionary force of his statement, and it is surely a highly valued and highly complex form of cognitive ability.

I find it fascinating that even when so many elements of cognitive ability are in some form of decline, there are still others remaining intact – others that, in their complexity, seem to require the presence of the very abilities which, when measured alone, are defective. In other words, expressing one's concern for the needs of another person as in the above example, would require that the person exhibiting that quality be able to pay attention, to retrieve from memory information about the cared-for person's needs, to be able to use language to communicate that concern, to understand the context of the situation, to name but a few abilities. Yet, taken one at a time, Dr. B's abilities in the areas of attention, memory, and his use of elements of language function, could all be measured as being defective on standardized tests.

He again expressed his concern for me when, one day, I was late for my meeting with him because I had a recurrence of an old hip injury that made walking an adventure. When Dr. B saw me limp into the day care center and I told him what happened, he was completely supportive of and concerned for me. This was made clear in the first few moments of our conversation in which he began by expressing his sense that there was no time to talk:

> *Dr. B:* I think it collapsed.
> *SRS:* Oh – really?
> *Dr. B:* Well, it's, it's three o'clock.
> *SRS:* Ya, but I think we'll have some time to talk anyway. I'm going to take some aspirins or something to get rid of this.
> *Dr. B:* Look – you're a good friend, you know, but you're a schmuck! Stop it!
> *SRS:* I shouldn't hurt myself, right?
> *Dr. B:* Well yeah! What are you, crazy?
> *SRS:* I have to be more careful.
> *Dr. B:* And it's not going to go away fast.
> *SRS:* No, I just have to rest.
> *Dr. B:* That I'll buy, that I'll buy. Well unfortunately my, we have our own things, and uh, we had not intimitated, we, we, were not red, ready for something like, like uh, like this. [Notice here he corrected himself for "intimitated" – he was going for "anticipated" given the form of his self-correction – "we . . . were not red, ready for something . . ."]
> *SRS:* You mean my getting hurt?
> *Dr. B:* You getting hurt.

Interestingly, his use of "we . . . were not red, ready for something," could be viewed as a type of defect called a "circumlocution" in that he was trying to say "anticipated" and then used these other words instead. Thinking of his behavior as an example of a defect would add to positioning him as "defective." It is just as logical to refer to his circumlocution in a positive way – he was seeking a word, could not find that word and used others instead to convey his thought successfully.

The flashlight and the light of his life

Approximately eight years after the first sign of difficulty with his memory, and four years since the diagnosis, Dr. B had experienced incontinence at the day care center, and evinced great embarrassment in its wake. Increasingly, he experienced bouts of great anxiety, and would become obsessed with trivial things:

> *SRS:* Does this happen – that something preys on your mind – like the pants?
> *Dr. B:* Well, you mean like in, in, ignifiscance thing [insignificant thing]?
> *SRS:* Yes, an insignificant thing.
> *Dr. B:* Right!
> *SRS:* You become obsessed with something insignificant?
> *Dr. B:* Right . . . but that damn sta, that thing in me, I don't understand. I'm, I'm trying to analyze why, why this is, why this shitty thing is obsess, assessed.

At the same time, he also found it more and more difficult to focus his attention, so as to inhibit the interference, the intrusions of surrounding, irrelevant sights and sounds. Whereas earlier in our association while sitting in the day care center office, he would say, "there are too many stimuli in here," now he would begin to cry, shut his eyes and cover his ears when in the same situation. Frequently, he experienced anxiety around dusk, and had taken to carrying a flashlight with him at that time of day. As he told me about it, and the reaction of his wife, he also showed evidence of ironic humor:

> *Dr. B:* Oh – I, I, I must tell you something. I have, I have had a tube. My wife talked to me, "ha, ha, ha" why do you, you know? This is like a f-f-fedding.
> *SRS:* A flashlight?

Dr. B: A flashlight. And I kept that like that. Like that, and it, it, it was in an area, ya. And uh, we uh, start again. [Here he seemed to have lost the thought, and asked me to go back to the beginning: "start again".]

SRS: You have a flashlight.

Dr. B: My wife talked to her and it was a uh, you know,

SRS: Okay, your wife is always kidding you about the flashlight?

Dr. B: Right. And she said, "what are you doing, this is only a piece of something and don't, don't worry about it." And I go up the stairs and my wife doesn't, doesn't like, was not liking, and so uh, finally my wife said, "look, uh you, you've left it or felled it someplace that we and so she poo-pooed. She poopooed it very hard and, uh, as to where it would go.

SRS: And so she was saying, "what do you need this for? What's the big deal?"

Dr. B: Yeah, what's the big deal.

SRS: But something happened huh? Did something happen in the past few days that sort of vindicated you and the flashlight? [There was an electrical storm and a power failure.]

Dr. B: Oh yes, yes, yes! The lights went out! The lights went out and uh, I told my wife, "well, you know, look what happened." And she was, and I, I won!

SRS: There was a storm and the lights went out and you had a flashlight!

Dr. B: I had this tube. I call it the tube. I call it, I call it the tube.

SRS: Well, it looks like a tube.

Dr. B: [*laughing*] Now I don't even know where it is.

SRS: I guess you had the last laugh.

There was something so ironic, so funny, about this episode that we both laughed a good laugh. He asked about the time repeatedly, wanting the hours to fly by so that he could be with his wife. Later, he came back to the subject and I asked,

SRS: So it was a good thing that you had that flashlight?

Dr. B: Yes! And I teased my wife and she realized that it was a tough, it was a good cushion, or whatever you want to call it.

SRS: Yes, I think cushion is a very good word for it, because it provided, it was sort of a soft landing.

Dr. B: That's right.

Again, we have the use of a word, in this case "cushion," to indicate not the common noun, but more of an abstract meaning in terms of the effect that it can provide. On some accounts this word, when used initially by Dr. B, would signal something bizarre. However, having spent a great deal of time with him, it seemed clear to me how he was using the word and I sought to confirm my suspicion via indirect repair. His wife never made an issue about the flashlight, even allowing him to take it along with him when they went to see a show for she knew it provided him with some sense of security. She expressed trepidation about the possibility that he might use it when the lights in the theater would be dimmed but, as it happened, he was drawn so much to the show that he never employed it at all.

When Dr. B mentioned being with his wife a number of times, I wanted to know what he thought about marriage. I knew from his children and from his wife that this was a very good marriage, and so I asked about the subject. In this case, I was putting Dr. B in a senior position *vis-à-vis* myself in that I was treating him as the expert.

SRS: So would you say that in most marriages you have your squabbles sometimes?

Dr. B: Of course, of course! If anybody, if anybody says, you know, "it's beautiful, it's beautiful," that's a bunch of crap. Every so often, you know, every so often, you get a, you get, you get something like that.

SRS: So you'd say it's kind of normal, even in the best of marriages,

Dr. B: Of course!

SRS: to have some squabbles here and there.

Dr. B: Oh sure, oh heavens yes.

SRS: So you're really serious – if anybody says in a really good marriage you never have an argument, that's nonsense.

Dr. B: Of course, of course, ya.

SRS: How do you make up once you have a squabble?

Dr. B: Things just, just meld out. That's all I can say.

SRS: You don't hold grudges then?

Dr. B: No, no, I don't, we would never have like that.

And when I asked him, "What makes you happy these days?",

> *Dr. B:* Well, number one is the light of my life. So that's one thing. Um, and then, uh, the rest of my life is the uh, my children, about three or four.
>
> *SRS:* So your wife and your children are sources of happiness for you?
>
> *Dr. B:* Sure, sure. Oh, ya! So the world to me still lives.

Here, just a few months before his death, when more and more of his speech became difficult to understand and his anxiety came in torrents, and the number of "defects" in his abilities could be listed in a striking manner, he was still quite clear about what was important to him. Interestingly, although he was deep in the throes of AD, the central focus of his life was his family, as it always had been. We will return to other aspects of Dr. B's story in chapters to follow. Now, however, let us turn to another person diagnosed with AD and listen to her voice as she reveals aspects of her experience.

The Case of Dr. M

"Yes, and oh, do you know how awful it is to try to talk, and have an idea and it goes away?" This was spoken by the woman who, at the age of 15, wrote the following:

> Often in the midst of work I meditate, then sigh,
> And ask the puzzling question of "why?"
> What cause is there for all I do as days and years go by?
> What makes us act as we all act? And why?
> Is there an explanation now for all twixt earth and sky,
> How did it all begin at first and why?
> What will happen when I'm gone,
> Now who can prophesy?
> How will people live and think, and why?
> What is the reason for our wish to live and not to die,
> Why am I on this endless quest of "why?"

It was two days before Dr. B's death that I met Dr. M for the first time. That meeting, and virtually all those which followed were at her home, where she lived with her husband of fifty years. It was almost a year to the day since I had first met Dr. B and, much as it was the year before, I, in my hard ignorance, had no idea of just how much I was about to learn under the tutelage of a person afflicted with AD. Our first meeting began in a way that was chillingly similar to my first meeting with Dr. B, in that she began by questioning me about the work I did, with whom, and how often. There was a palpable intelligence in her manner, her rhythm of speaking, her tone of voice, the look in her eyes. I told her of my work with people at the day care center. All this led, in the first few minutes of conversation, to her spelling out the fundamental issue on her mind with regard to me:

> *Dr. M:* Well, you're given me several kinds of peoples that, uh, have come there and how, how do you, uh, show me how he uses that, that person, uh, with the, with, with what you have noted.
>
> *SRS:* Ah, now I'm not sure I understand what you're getting at here.
>
> *Dr. M:* Yeah, I'm not s-s-s-s too. Uh, I want, t, to know is how do you do, *could* do something that would be useful for me,
>
> *SRS:* Ah!
>
> *Dr. M:* because it's, how do we put those two together?

A snapshot

When our association began, Dr. M was 75 years old. She had a seven-year history of word-finding problems and began experiencing memory problems at the age of 66. Four years after the onset of the word-finding problems, she had become fearful of driving ("What if I pushed the gas pedal instead of the brake?"). Two years before our association began, she underwent a battery of neuropsychological tests which indicated decrements in memory, abstraction, concept formation, and word-finding which were consistent with a diagnosis of probable AD. She "tended to be concrete in her understanding of verbal relationships between things and ideas . . . her interpretation of proverbs was concrete" and she had "not adjusted well to the change" in her abilities. On tests of language function, including the Boston Naming Test and the Boston Diagnostic Aphasia Examination, she made "numerous errors of both the semantic and phonemic

61

type . . . frequently used circumlocution which made the quality of her speech stilted." She evidenced great difficulty in dressing herself, was unable to use eating utensils, had become incontinent, and also had great difficulty with spelling, writing, and reading. On the Geriatric Depression Scale, Dr. M's responses, two years before our conversations began, indicated mild depression. At the time of our association, she could no longer sign her name. She held a Ph.D. degree and had taught at university level. She also earned an M.S.W. degree at the age of 67, although while earning that degree she first began to notice problems with her memory. She was described by her husband as someone who had always been "fiercely independent," and had enjoyed a life-long love affair with words. Indeed, some of the poetry she wrote at age ten had been noticed and published in her home-town newspaper (it was a relatively large city), and she had written an autobiography at the age of 15, one year before she moved out of her parents' home and began college. Thus, there was a tragic irony to her word-finding and other linguistic problems and these became uppermost among her concerns as they affected many aspects of her life. Despite all her linguistic and other cognitive difficulties, as documented via her performance on standard tests, she was able to communicate a great deal about her experience of AD and of herself as a human being.

Her experience of and reaction to the disease

I had told her that I wanted to be able to understand AD from her point of view and she then gave me the first of many insights into her own experience, especially that of the word-finding problems which were of paramount importance to her:

> *Dr. M:* Sure. I, uh, I can handle myself when I try to not let myself be presented as an Alcazheimer's, I'm very different.
> *SRS:* Oh, you mean in a social situation?
> *Dr. M:* Um hum. I mean that if I'm if, wherever I am, and I want to keep myself, uh, somewhat not involved,
> *SRS:* Um hum,
> *Dr. M:* uh, I am different from the time when I feel all, all clear.
> *SRS:* Um hum, um hum. So you have ways of staying out of situations,

Dr. M: Um hum,
SRS: that, when you feel like you're not quite able to deal with what's . . . [*she interrupts*]
Dr. M: That's right.
SRS: going on.

This was her first mention of the idea that she had developed strategies in order to cope with situations which were difficult for her. Note that the use of indirect repair helped to elucidate this aspect of her behavior ("So you have ways of staying out of situations . . ."). She would return to this idea later in this same conversation, and present me with a piece of information that I had never expected to hear.

I was providing Dr. M with an example of how there are times when the the person with AD tries to find a word, but uses another word instead, and how the type of mistake can provide a clue to the listener as to the identity of the desired word. (The person says "adventurous" a number of times but is clearly not comfortable with that word. After a few repetitions, the person says "advantageous," which was the desired word all along. In this case, the first few letters and the ending of the word initially used and those of the word actually desired are the same.) Having provided Dr. M with this example, she began to speak:

Dr. M: I say, in ca, cases like that, um, let's, ya have, I tend to, I don't know how I do this way, I tend to, if I get stuck, I get uh, speaking and getting the person off the track,
SRS: Um hum.
Dr. M: a little, he comes up or she comes out [she is saying this as she would in the situation she just described – she will divert her interlocutor's attention to something else] and I say, can you say it differently to me?
SRS: Um hum.
Dr. M: But that's pr, pr, protecting myself.

In this revelation, there are at least two strategies described by Dr. M as her means of self-protection when she cannot find the word she desires to use during a conversation. The first is that she will get the person "off the track" by saying something that does not relate to the present conversation. This may be a way of buying time for herself, but it can have a very different result in the mind of the person with whom she is speaking. Her interlocutor, having experienced Dr. M do this a number of times, may conclude that, because of AD, she cannot stay on the subject, that her ability to converse is compromised. In other words, the person with whom she is speaking may easily view her behavior not as a logical means of her protecting herself from the embarrassment of being unable to find a word, but instead as a sign of her confusion. This latter interpretation could also be applied to her "second strategy," asking her interlocutor to "say it differently to me?" In this case, the logical interpretation would be that her auditory comprehension or attentional focus is compromised.

In both instances, her strategy can easily lead to misunderstandings, on the part of others, of her own ability to understand and to keep the subject of conversation in focus. She can become positioned as confused when, in fact, she is not. And, if she is viewed in such a way, others may then refrain from engaging her in conversation, and the process of social isolation begins. People who are afflicted with AD and who have severe word-finding problems must be encouraged to adopt different strategies so as to avoid the possibility of being misunderstood in such a way. One possible strategy would be simply to say "I'm having trouble finding the word I want to use. Please give me a moment," or something along those lines. In this way, the afflicted person may be able to establish at least *some* control over the situation.

There is yet another side to this story, an aspect which Mr. M shed light upon during the course of this meeting. Often, we understand "word-finding problems" to mean that the person is somehow unable to retrieve the desired word and cannot go on with his or her part of the conversation as a result. Mr. M pointed out, however, "It's possible that there is also, in terms of getting the wrong word, a choice between two words, one of which is best, and the other of which is not completely inappropriate." Mr. M then applied this notion to his wife:

> One of her problems is not being able to use a second or third or fourth best word, because she wants the *best* word. And that goes all the way back to childhood, when she was encouraged to be special. And so she has to have the special word and so she freezes if she can't say something in real educated, fancy, esoteric, language and not just simple language.

64

Thus, in the case of Dr. M, there were times when her word-finding problems were made more severe because she was one who wanted to paint with words rather than simply utter them, and so the search for the *mot juste* was more difficult than that for the more common synonym. In one of our conversations, she corroborated this interpretation: "I, I can't get the words, but it has to do with a word I like to use and I can't find."

> *SRS:* You're not just any ordinary person who has some problems finding words. You're a person for whom words, words to you are kind of like a musical instrument.
>
> *Dr. M:* Um hum, um hum. That's exactly right.
>
> *SRS:* And so the kind of frustration you feel would be greater than for a person whose focus in life was not so literary. That could give you cause for a lot of grief.
>
> *Dr. M:* I think the issue is, that is, for me maybe especially this day for some reason or other, but for last, maybe four years, that I am not satisfied with myself because what I want isn't here. I've, uh, thinking of it and it makes me angry as well as, that is part of the . . . and I guess that is what is happening now. Don't you think?

Often, word-finding problems can pose a severe problem for those who are trying to understand the afflicted person's spoken thoughts. In such cases, it is important to try not to attend to the instances of difficulty but, rather, to listen for the deeper meaning instead, also taking note of the speaker's emotional tone. Having done that, one can then try, through the use of indirect repair, to corroborate one's understanding of what the afflicted person has said. In the following example, I had inquired about Dr. M's childhood and adolescence so as to have an idea of the person behind the disease, and used indirect repair to check my understanding of what she was saying:

> *Dr. M:* But we went to the family, got to, uh, being a one child family, uh, we uh, they, I was the most important, fab, thing. And uh, and I was 16 about that and when I got through, when I got just that much, that seemed fine. But then when I didn't want to have the, uh, of the child of a family, but my own family, I left my own family. Uh, I went. Do you know?

65

SRS: You decided at some point that you wanted to be on your own.

Dr. M: Um hum. That's right.

SRS: And you left home.

Dr. M: Um hum.

SRS: And you were pretty young.

Dr. M: Um hum, ya, I was 16.

SRS: Wow, pretty courageous . . . no?

Dr. M: That – I didn't seem coura – I mean, why is it courageous?

SRS: Well, a woman of 16, now that had to have been a bunch of years ago, not to comment on your age!

Dr. M: Um hum [*laughs*].

SRS: But it seems to me that at the time you were 16 it was probably not very common for a young woman to leave

Dr. M: Um hum,

SRS: home before she was married.

Dr. M: Um hum, ya, that's true.

SRS: And so it seems to me that in order to do that, you had to be going against a certain social norm.

Dr. M: Um hum, ya, but I had always done that . . . that's really true, I told you.

SRS: Well, to me it was courageous and to you it was a way of life! [*both of us laugh*].

The conversation went on, but not before Dr. M asked about the point of all of this background about herself. Here, she is again interrogating me as to my purpose. Following my answer to her question, she returned, without my prompting, to the subject of her leaving home. In this conversation we find, at the outset, an example of her desire to understand what I was learning from the conversation about her life and also an example of a word-finding problem and how the error is related to the sought-after word:

Dr. M: Ya, uh huh. So now what are you getting out of that? What's it going to do in talking about what we're going to sa, talk about more, about who I am?

SRS: Well you're just telling me things about yourself and I'm hearing it. It's important for me to know about you, the kind of person you are, what things appeal to you. I want to see you at your best, you know, so that I know how to communicate well with you. It seems to me that if I pulled out paper and pencil tests, I'd see one aspect of you,

Dr. M: Um hum.

SRS: and I would rather, at this point, I would rather have it be just natural.

Dr. M: Um hum.

SRS: Natural flow of conversation and see what you do. And you're conveying some things to me that are important about you. You went to college and then you went to graduate school.

Dr. M: Well I got, ya, but then I, I . . . then, then after I, I didn't. I think this would be interesting. I, I went and didn't, I, I went far, not very far away to my parents because they had, that's that's the only place they were had. And I got a place for my own, and I said I, I want it to be mine – not theirs – and I, and then I said that I wanted to be with them sometime, but I didn't want to be with them all the time [*chuckles*].

SRS: How did they take it?

Dr. M: Well, my mother tried to get two kids, uh, who, who had, that she would take into the house in view, view of, of me. Not, not in *view* – that's not the WORD! [*voice grows louder and louder*].

SRS: No – I know! And I know what the word is. It sounds like view and it's a French word. The "u" part is right.

Dr. M: Ya!

SRS: The beginning letter is not a "v", it's a different letter and it's a French word. I'll betcha.

Dr. M: I don't know, tell me.

SRS: In "LIEU"

Dr. M: In lieu of!

SRS: Right?

Dr. M: Yup! [*laughs*] Very good!

SRS: Okay, see? All right!

Dr. M: But I didn't get that, you did.

SRS: Well, ya, I did. But you see, the only way I could get that is if you were talking, you see, in the context of the sentence it made sense to me. I knew what you were going for. So they wanted to have two young people come into the home instead of you – in lieu of you.

> *Dr. M:* Uh huh, but the kids didn't like my mother [*we both laugh*]. I was really sorry for her.

In this instance, Dr. M learned that her erroneous choice was not random at all, but clearly related to the word she wanted to use, that if she truly didn't know the word, she would not have been able to recognize it upon hearing it, and she wouldn't have used a word that rhymed with the desired word in the first place.

As our conversation continued, Dr. M revealed still another insight into others' reactions:

> *SRS:* You were looking for the expression "in lieu of" and you said "in view of." So you had the first letter wrong but the rest of the word [you used] was the same sound [as the one you wanted to use].
>
> *Dr. M:* Trouble is that you know too much about words because anybody else would just go along with [*chuckles*].

It has been my experience as well that others will "go along" with the afflicted person's errors instead of showing the person, in some easy going way as I did with Dr. M, that there is a certain logic to the error, and that he or she can be understood and helped. But for the person with AD, the thought that there is no logic at all to the error can itself be a cause of great anxiety and that anxiety can, in turn, have an adverse effect on subsequent behavior. That is, the anxiety can have a disruptive effect and lead to the person being positioned further "as an Alzheimer's" and thus not seen in light of other, more positive characteristics that still remain intact.

Interestingly enough, the afflicted person's realization that "that's not the word (I want, or meant)" indicates the ability to reflect on the preceding behavior in a completely appropriate way. Such reflective ability should be noted by caregivers to indicate an active evaluative thought process which can affect the afflicted person's self-image. An example of this idea follows:

> *SRS:* That's wonderful when you find somebody who kind of knows what you want.
>
> *Dr. M:* Ya, but, but does every, are the other people who you work with, uh, doing, taking the uh, possible . . . things. [*Now in*

a harsh-like, but joking whisper] THINGS! I never says "things"
[*laughs*].
SRS: [*laughs*] I knew that too!

Dr. M was indeed correct. Her love of and respect for language would never permit her to use the word "thing" or "things" instead of the proper word or words. Indeed, the very fact that she would do so now would serve only to indicate to her just how badly the disease had affected her. To go from eloquent grace in the use of words to such a pedestrian (for her) level leads to a deep sense of dissatisfaction, annoyance, impatience, anxiety, and low self-esteem to the point that she would hesitate to speak in other social situations such as the support group she attended.

Caregivers must be aware of this issue, for it is indeed possible that the afflicted person has such feelings but does not discuss them. Such feelings would, however, have an effect on behavior nonetheless. Fortunately, even in this first meeting, Dr. M had enough trust in me to allow the above to emerge and then, a bit later, was far more direct:

Dr. M: You know what? Because I don't speak like I used to be, it seems to me that I don't have *any* good way of speaking.
SRS: Well. I think you speak rather well. Now maybe you don't speak as well as you did at another time, and maybe you're dissatisfied with that.
Dr. M: Ya, I am.

I went on to explain to Dr. M that the problem of finding the right word, especially a noun when she says "thing," is compounded by the dissatisfaction and anxiety that arises when the word is not readily available. The reactive anxiety then becomes a focus of attention, and attention is not given as much to finding the word as it is to the emotional reaction to the initial failure. If the anxiety can be kept to a minimum, then the chances are greater that she will find the word. She picked up on this idea and indicated that it should be communicated to others and also that another emotional reaction was important for her as well:

Dr. M: Do other people talk like you're doing in using that kind of . . . ?

69

SRS: Not that I know of.

Dr. M: Well, you mean, you ought to tell them!

SRS: I'm trying.

Dr. M: I don't know whether the, uh, some of my not working well is that being, I'm being angry with myself.

SRS: Ah-there's another thing that I think is very important and I'm very happy that you said that . . . it's hard to retrieve information when you are angry with yourself,

Dr. M: Um hum.

SRS: because you're devoting so much attention to . . . [*she interrupts*]

Dr. M: That's, ya, that's a real important thing as far as for myself, because I want, I want to be able to do that and I, I hate not.

It is patently clear that she was deeply troubled, frustrated, angry about, and embarrassed by, her inability to use the language with *elan* such as she had for virtually all her life.

Her concern about the value of our meetings

Dr. M: Now then, I want to tell you something, uh, that has some – I hope you're getting something out of this.

SRS: Oh yes! Oh yes! No question about it!

Dr. M: Because I, I feel, I don't want to, to use your time.

SRS: You're worried that maybe my coming here might be wasting my time?

Dr. M: Yes, exactly!

SRS: Well, I'm assuring you that you're not.

Dr. M: Okay! I think I know, we have, uh, it's connected to my saying that the person who is in the pro, has, has the problem has something very much that others can't have because they haven't the opportunity to get there.

SRS: That is, other people can't quite understand what it's like to have the problem because they

Dr. M: Yes.

SRS: don't have it.

Dr. M: They don't know. But you, apparently, may get it.

One of the "defects" which was attributed to her on the basis of her performance on the neuropsychological test battery was that she was deficient in the area of concept formation. Clearly, however, from the first of her comments above, she was in possession of the concept of fairness, for she wanted to be sure that my working with her wasn't a waste of my time. Again, in the above extract, we see the facilitative effect of the use of indirect repair in helping to understand her point about how others don't understand what it's like to have AD. In addition, we also see that she is able to reflect on the notion that many others who are healthy aren't able to understand what it is like to have AD, but that I "apparently, may get it." She has come to this conclusion, it would seem, on the basis of my having reached out to her overtly in an attempt to be empathetic, to understand what she is going through.

A means of coping with the effect of divided attention

We were in the middle of a conversation and she couldn't recall what she was trying to convey when she said:

Dr. M: Ooh, this would be good but I'm not, I don't, get ready. I can't say it now, but it, it is, let me think and not look at you. [*Some time then transpired.*]

SRS: Is that something that is helpful to you – not to have to look at the other person? Does that put pressure on you when you look at the other person or is it a distraction?

Dr. M: Now, well, I'll tell you about that [*chuckles*]. Um, I, uh, was looking at you and have been and I, I only about three, no, about half a – a very small time, I suddenly got what I was trying to see when I look at you. I have been looking at you all the time because you look like somebody I know.

SRS: Oh really?

Dr. M: And I, I couldn't know who it was. And uh, and it was important because there was something about that person. Now I don't know where it's gone – I, I do know where it's gone. And then, I thought, that it's not how you looked like, it's uh, something other about that man. And it turned out to be just only, only about three minutes ago, that it's uh, my, my, um, son – one of 'em – I have three. You have so many things like

71

him, and so I, I've been looking and say, what? What's – he doesn't absolutely look like him, there's something in it. And so I was thinking, "What's that guy got that that's got?" I don't know that that's helpful. It's, it's, but that's a connection.

SRS: This is interesting, because the thought of my resemblance to your son was competing with your trying to find the thread of our conversation. So your attention was divided and you said, "Let me not look at him," which was a wonderful way to try to direct your attention to what you really wanted to find.

As with Dr. B, when his attention was drawn to the folder which contained information about AD, we see here the effect of divided attention on Dr. M's ability to remain focused on a subject. In this case, the source of distraction was Dr. M's silent association about the resemblance between myself and one of her sons, and then her attempt to pinpoint the source of that resemblance.

Without the knowledge that the afflicted person may be distracted by his or her own competing thoughts, we can see the effect of positioning on our construction of the behavior displayed by the person with AD. Specifically, the afflicted person is seen primarily as cognitively deficient and so his or her aberrant behavior indicates an inability to stay on the topic of conversation, or a failure in linguistic function, not listening when spoken to, the inability to think clearly or something of that ilk. In fact, the behavior in question was due to the afflicted person experiencing the internal competition between two thoughts and the inability to inhibit one of them for the moment. It is ironic that the reason for the AD sufferer's difficulty here was not that she couldn't think, but that she had too many potent, meaningful thoughts occurring simultaneously. In such moments, it can be profitable for all concerned if the healthy interlocutor inquires as to what is happening, for a reasonable explanation may be forthcoming and a sense of connection and trust between the AD sufferer and his or her partner in conversation can be solidified.

Reducing anxiety, planning ahead, and being understood

Dr. M and her husband were planning a holiday trip and there would be a little more than two weeks' time until our next meeting. During this last meeting before her trip, I showed her how to breathe diaphragmatically, deeply, whenever she felt anxiety.

> *SRS:* I have to try to understand how you experience
> *Dr. M:* Um hum.
> *SRS:* things in the world. That is, I have to know that you get frustrated, angry with yourself. It's important to know because maybe we can do things to help you calm down.
> *Dr. M:* Uh huh, maybe because – what could you, how can make, how could you say?
> *SRS:* How could I get you to calm down?
> *Dr. M:* Yes!
> *SRS:* I'll show you.

At this point I showed Dr. M a technique called diaphragmatic breathing in which one must concentrate upon inhaling from the diaphragm instead of from the thoracic area of the chest. Slow, deep, rhythmic, diaphragmatic breathing can help to bring about relaxation. Anxiety, anger, and the like results in short breaths from the thoracic area (upper chest) which serve to prevent relaxation. The concentration then goes to breathing deeply and away from the churning, emotional thoughts. Thus, I told her that whenever she feels frustrated, angry about not being able to find a word, she should begin diaphragmatic breathing for a few minutes to dissipate the tension and relax. It is possible that the thoughts that eluded her before could be retrieved during the period of deep breathing or in the following minutes. I went on to explain that the disease itself is a formidable battle to fight, but that if she is angry with herself as well, that constitutes still another battle that she doesn't need in addition. One battle is enough.

As I was about to leave,

> *Dr. M:* Now what do, do you want to give me, a, a uh, I'm going to be away. I appreciate learning about what I could do without you.
> *SRS:* Oh – oh, you want homework!
> *Dr. M:* Yes! – Yes! Yes! [*laughing heartily and joyfully*].

I couldn't help but feel, as she responded, that Dr. M's sense of delight was, to some extent, due to the fact that I understood what she meant even though she hadn't been able to find and use the word, "homework." She wanted to be able to do something beneficial to her during the time we would not be meeting. Put in the language of a teacher, that meant, "homework." Her delight at being understood was poignant, for it was not common in her experience as a person with AD to be understood easily by someone so new in her life as was I. Reactions of this kind occurred many times during the course of our association and in another instance, she added a rather touching thought that underscored a source of her frustration and sadness:

> *SRS:* You may have trouble finding the word, "physician," and so you'll say, "the person who takes care of me when I'm having any problem physically." Okay, okay, I understood what you meant.
> *Dr. M:* Ya, but there aren't very many yous, and many people that I would uh, free myself to put, uh, the way we were talking.

Here she notes rather clearly a sense of isolation that she feels, as there aren't many people with whom she would as feel free to express herself as she felt with me. Also seen above is her desire to plan ahead, as it were, regarding "homework," which indicated intact frontal lobe function, as those who have damage to that area of the brain are quite clearly deficient in their ability to think ahead and plan accordingly.

Her loss of connection with others

Dr. M and her husband had taken a holiday for two weeks that involved a long ride on a train. The social situation on the train was one which she had enjoyed at other times in her life but now her diminished ability to speak fluently and her associated anguish had a profound effect:

> *Dr. M:* My talking is very much worse. Really wo, wo, very wo, um hum.
> *SRS:* Really – you do think it's worse.
> *Dr. M:* Oh ya, maybe you will tell me otherwise.
> *SRS:* What makes you think that it's worse?

Dr. M: Um, it ta, ta, becau, the, I was in another area and uh, the connection with people was different as with here . . . if I were going on a, a, let's use the time thing. If I were twenty years away from and had done that [taken the train ride] that would be a fun thing,

SRS: Uh huh, I understand.

Dr. M: and even with people whom I have no feeling that I'd like to keep on talking to them, it would, it would have been good.

SRS: Um hum.

Dr. M: My connection with people was, was not there. And that's, I think that, I think that I should say this very much uh, I can't speak as well – that's what the thing is.

SRS: Um hum.

Dr. M: And apparently, since I was a child uh, I was a good talker. And that is and also I, that's because that, and now it's different because among the may [many] important things, I can't talk to people. Now to some I can do a little thing, and make a joke and and then I feel very good. And now there's not, uh, that.

And, in reflecting further upon her diminished ability to interact gracefully with others via the sharp, warm wit, refined language, and sense of humor that characterized most of her life, she said, ". . . the way I have organized my li, self all the time . . . but I can't get it . . . but see, those are most of the moments in my life now and I don't want that."

She was accustomed to being able to engage people, to initiate conversation, to draw them out, and now, owing to the effects of AD, she felt that she was no longer able to do that and it clearly plagued and embarrassed her into relative silence – a style that was, itself, anathema to her and caused her further anguish. The depth of that anguish affected her in many ways, an example of which follows. Also in the following extract, I have indicated, in parentheses, the length of her pauses between words and between conversational turns between us to provide the reader with some idea of the pace of her speech. It might be of value to use a stopwatch here so as to experience the time gaps fully.

SRS: What can you do pretty well? What do you feel good about? [*22.1 sec.*]

Dr. M: I hadn't been thinking that way for a while.

SRS: Ah well . . .

Dr. M: That's nice. [Here her comment about my question was something of a compliment and reflected her training as a social worker.]

SRS: Let's see, let's look at the part of the glass that's half full.

Dr. M: All right! [*4.0 sec.*] Well I'm [*10.9 sec.*] I don't usually talk this way do I?

SRS: Talk about what's good, you mean?

Dr. M: I think I feel [*43 sec.*]

SRS: Maybe I can rephrase the question, okay?

Dr. M: You probably should-could.

SRS: Thank you for your confidence!

Dr. M: I did – that popped out [*laughter*] and apparently that was something that I wanted to think about.

SRS: Well, instead of what's good, let's say what things do you – they may be things that you take for granted, but,

Dr. M: That's true, I know I have many of those.

SRS: Um hum, so . . .

Dr. M: But the most things that I'm, that's [*5.6 sec.*] that I uh keep my eye on or notice is not for the best.

SRS: Well, that's pretty normal, I'd say, it's really easy to notice the things you can't do.

Dr. M: Um hum.

SRS: Or the things you have trouble doing. I think that's very normal. You must feel annoyed, or disappointed with yourself at times, impatient with yourself,

Dr. M: It's moreso now, uh huh.

Her insight into an aspect of her deep sadness

It was clear that she was being dominated, as was Dr. B, by her thoughts of and emotional reactions to her diminished abilities. Such thoughts and reactions could, and often did, have deleterious effects upon her behavior and we proceeded to a discussion of this:

SRS: The whole point of this is to try to achieve a certain balance. The glass is half empty or half full. I think knowing that if you become anxious or frustrated, it just hinders you,

Dr. M: Um hum.

SRS: It detracts from the abilities that you have.

Dr. M: Um hum.

SRS: So from my point of view I would want to work on not focusing solely, not focusing only, on what doesn't work.

Dr. M: Either one or the other.

SRS: Right – not to say everything is roses and not to say that everything is garbage.

Dr. M: That's nicely said.

SRS: Thank you! But it's easy to say that everything is garbage because,

Dr. M: No, no, no, no, Oh yes! I do! You're right. I, I treating things that they're garbage.

SRS: Because there are some things that are important to you and you can't do them and so everything is terrible, and I'm trying to say that there are some things that are important to you,

Dr. M: Well, I tell you, I think I'm, uh, I'm causing that myself. You see, there are very important things that I cannot change. And uh, I thought it in this way: I happened to have a, a visit to my uh [*2.4 sec.*] uh [*12.5 sec.*], the person who takes care of me when I have any problem physically.

SRS: A dentist?

Dr. M: No, not in this case.

SRS: It's not a mailman?

Dr. M: No, it's a female person [*laughs*].

SRS: A physician?

Dr. M: Yes! I asked her a number of things. One of them was, um, what's the, do we have any notion about how long this is going to go on? And uh I said, because you see if it's a long time I would do different things than I would do if it wasn't in a long time. And she nodded, ya, that's true. Uh, but she says I can't answer you, I can't answer for myself. Because I didn't know these things that uh, that uh, that we can [*9.5 sec. and then she knocks once on the table*], that's [*referring to her knock on the table*] a . . . [*3.0 sec.*]

SRS: Period [*signifying that she's ending her turn speaking*].

Dr. M: Ya.

Identifying priorities

Up to this point in our conversation, as she had in previous conversations, Dr. M had discussed many of her reactions to AD – her anger, sadness, and frustration in reaction to the losses she experienced as a result of the disease. She seemed to reflect what Dr. B had said about the disease when he commented that there was nothing he could do about it, that it gave him turmoil, as well as the accompanying reactive depression. In the above extract, she again shows that her word-finding problems have to do with her ability to *recall* words (she is able to recognize the sought-after word) and also that she is able to think in terms of the future – that there would be a difference in what she would do if the disease were to go on for a long time as opposed to a short time. In addition, she came to the realization that, with regard to most things, she was "...treating things that they're garbage ...," and that "...I'm causing that myself," that essentially, she was seeing all the negatives and not seeing anything positive in her life. Such an insight, which is often considered admirable in people who have incurred no brain damage whatsoever, led to my presenting her with a hypothetical answer to the question she posed to her physician. From that point, we proceeded to a discussion of priorities:

SRS: Okay, suppose the physician said, "yeah, this is going to go on for a long time." What would you do?

Dr. M: I'd say what do you mean by that?

SRS: Ten years.

Dr. M: [*7.0 sec.*] Well, I would, I think, go through it in a more [*8.5 sec.*] from various ones of the faculties that I have. But I felt, I said to her it would be very important because it would be a very different thing. Um, and I had, there were a number of things that I had hopen to do and I wondered what, which ones I could, uh [*4.1 sec.*] and uh she, uh, that was what.

SRS: If I knew I had two years to live, maybe I would do things differently than I would if I had 52 more years to live. And maybe I wouldn't. Maybe there are things in my life that I would keep doing because I love to do them anyway. But we never know how much time we have

Dr. M: Um hum.

SRS: so sometimes people will say, because you don't know, why
not do things that are important to you now? Do them!

Dr. M: [*11.8 sec.*] It's a good idea.

SRS: So if you have some priorities, then I think it's very important that you act on them.

Dr. M: All right, um hum, that's a good thing.

She proceeded then to identify a particular project that she had post-
poned for quite some time:

Dr. M: I have, up in the attic, I have papers that are of interest
to a lot of people perhaps, if I use it right, and I guess I'm a lot
like the person you mentioned [who always put things off
until tomorrow and tomorrow never came] you know. But, you
see, now but now I, I can break it down to here is the more
important and the least and that kind of stuff. That's a good
idea.

SRS: You know what? If you have some priorities, if you have,

Dr. M: Um hum,

SRS: then I think it's very important that you act on them.

Dr. M: All right, that's a good thing.

SRS: Nobody knows what you know. No one else can know
what you know. I don't mean about the color of a banana, but
you have contributions to make and you have to do them, even
now. It may take a lot more work than it might have 15 years
ago, but it would give you something that you could sink your
teeth into,

Dr. M: That's good. I'll do it.

Having been caught up in her reactions to the problems posed by
Alzheimer's, Dr. M had left undone some things that were important
to her. Wondering how long the problems would last, and thinking a
great deal of the time about the negative aspects of her being, she
had lost track of some of those things which she could do, their
importance to her, the fleeting passage of time and the uncertainty of
how many days lie ahead. During this conversation, she came to some
realizations through the use of "if . . . then" thinking – a type of
hypothetical thinking which requires the function of frontal association areas of the brain.

After thinking about these various ideas, she made a decision to act and charted out her own course regarding the important papers in the attic – papers that only decades of productive life could create. It seemed that some university librarians were interested in some of her papers, and the task was to sort through them. This project gave her something into which she could pour her great energy, into which she could "sink her teeth." This, then, could be the focus of energy otherwise devoted to thoughts of frustration, anger, dissatisfaction, lack of control, despair. This project also gave her a feeling of having control over something that was "her baby."

The effect of encouragement

Dr. B had commented that he needed "bucking up," encouragement, and Dr. M was no different in that respect. After helping her to identify a project in which she could engage her energies and see through to its end with the help of her husband, I encouraged her further and she then made clear to me the effect all this had on her mood:

Dr. M: This was a good session, don't you think?
SRS: I think so. It was wonderful.
Dr. M: Gee, we're almost through.
SRS: We are, we are.
Dr. M: Um, I'm not the fir, the first, the real person that came out when you, before when you,
SRS: first.
Dr. M: came on this uh, on this day, is different. Thank you very much. [I took her comment above to mean something akin to "I'm a different person than the one who greeted you when you first came here today."]
SRS: Well, let me tell you, it's a great pleasure, it's a great pleasure to talk with you.
Dr. M: Now that I know where, where . . . I, I, I need to find for myself [*4.5 sec.*] what are the real important things in uh, one person's life and see how that . . . we have to see how it works out.
SRS: One thing that we can do, is we can set goals.
Dr. M: I was going to say exactly that. I knew where they are – the papers right up there [*pointing upward to the ceiling*].

SRS: In the attic?

Dr. M: Um hum.

SRS: Well, I'll tell you what – by next Thursday,

Dr. M: I think there's something happening next Thursday, [*goes to look at the calendar*]

SRS: Ah – let's find out.

Dr. M: and I forgot what it is and as you know, I forget.

SRS: But you didn't forget that there was something happening!

Dr. M: [*warm laughter*].

SRS: You said you had some papers upstairs, two groups. How about getting one of the groups together for next week?

Dr. M: Only one?

SRS: Start on one and do two!

Dr. M: I'm playing!

This conversation began with Dr. M saying, sadly, that the things she keeps her eye on or notices most, are not for the best. Toward the end of the conversation, she allowed that she is not the same person who greeted me when I first arrived and thanked me. She came to the conclusion that she needed to decide for herself what the truly important things in life are for her. When she commented that she thought there was something happening on the next Thursday, but that she forgot what it was (". . . as you know, I forget"), I immediately pointed out to her that she hadn't forgotten that something was, indeed, happening. It is surely possible to dwell on the adverse effects of recall problems, but the fact remained that she hadn't forgotten everything – which, when pointed out to her, became still another form of encouragement that followed simply from observing and acknowledging what was true. When I suggested that we set goals, I was speaking what she was thinking in that moment, and when I suggested one goal she came back quickly with an extension of that goal in a witty way ("Only one?"). She was, in her own word, "playing."

Going from despair to "playing" is quite a journey in an hour and a half. In between, there were issues to be addressed. Annoyance, frustration, and self deprecation had to be replaced with a combination of positive, attainable goals and some self-worth built upon compassion, encouragement, and humor. Fundamental to those goals was a sense of purpose, of meaning. I will return to the issue of meaning-making and purpose in Chapter 5.

81

I do not mean to imply that because of this one conversation, all was well with Dr. M from that time forth. AD is progressive and so, with the passage of time, her difficulties grew still more severe. Yet she was still in need of encouragement, patience, and acceptance, and of a non-anxious partner in conversation, all of which served to facilitate communication with her. That she reacted well to these forms of interaction was made clear when her husband commented that on the days when I was going to meet with her, she was more alert and energetic than she was on other days. She was able, then, to communicate a great deal about her thoughts and feelings, to evince wit and humor. In other words, the illocutionary force of her comments was clearly present despite her striking word-finding problems, and what she accomplished with her comments (the perlocutionary force) was to have made a contribution to our understanding of AD. We will return to the case of Dr. M in subsequent chapters.

The Case of Mrs. F: Extralinguistic Communication

The two words which form the title of this chapter, language and communication, are not synonymous, for communication involves more than words alone. Tones of voice, emphasis, facial expressions, gestures, and the like, all can have the effect of modifying what is transmitted via words alone. It is quite common for speech to be accompanied by and related to a variety of paralinguistic, gestural, and kinesic actions. A communicative act may be carried out through the use of spoken or written words, pictures, signs (as in American Sign Language), gestures (such as mime), or music. The case of Mrs. F (Sabat and Cagigas, 1997) underscores this point very well, for she had encountered severe word-finding problems and used extralinguistic forms of communication to convey her thoughts.

A snapshot

As previously reported,

> Mrs. F was 62 years old at the time of the presently reported observations. She had been diagnosed with probable AD by NINCDS-ADRDA criteria (McKhann et al., 1984) four and one-half years earlier, although she had experienced problems with spatial memory (getting

lost) and exhibited right-left confusion four years before the diagnosis was made. She had earned a Bachelor's degree in music while raising six children, the sixth being born during the period of time in which she was taking classes. Although she was a consummate homemaker and parent during the time her children were growing up, she was also very active, running her own business teaching children and adults to play a musical instrument, and joined her husband in teaching dance classes.

According to her spouse of more than thirty years, she had been the driving force behind many of the family projects, had been a teacher/counselor and in summer camps for children as well as a camp director, an actor, producer of plays at community theaters, a singer, and a musical accompanist on two different instruments. In ever so many avenues of her life, she had been an extremely assertive person, the one who could always get things done. In addition, Mrs. F had been an extremely expressive person via writing, and had been an especially effective teacher. She was very proud of her accomplishments as a teacher and as a musician and at the time of her association with us, she still exhibited an excellent singing voice. However, her speech was clearly affected by the disease as she exhibited severe word-finding and pronunciation problems. Thus, her spouse commented that she "converses with more animation than coherence". (pp. 342–3.)

She also evidenced problems dressing herself and in dancing, and although she was able to feed herself, she did have trouble coordinating simultaneous movements with a fork and knife. She was unable to sign her name, sight read music, or perform simple calculations, was no longer able to paint in the realistic mode that she used in the past, and was clearly embarrassed and frustrated by these losses. Although she wanted to help around the house, she often left tasks incomplete after having been distracted for a moment or two. Her spouse also reported that "she *purposefully* puts things away in random places." In many ways, her behavior matches with what would be predicted by her scores on various standard tests (Mini-Mental State, Boston Diagnostic Aphasia Examination, FAS, Buschke Selective Reminding Test), she could be considered moderately to severely afflicted (Folstein et al., 1975; Reisberg, 1982), and she was taking medication for anxiety.

Her compensatory skills

An example of her extralinguistic compensation for word-finding difficulties occurred when she was trying to describe someone with whom she did not get along at the adult day care center she attended. When she was asked to say something about how she felt about that person, she struggled for words and finally acted out her thoughts as evidenced in the following extract of conversation with Xavier E. Cagigas, my former student and co-author (Sabat and Cagigas, 1997):

> *Mrs. F:* But when she comes in anytime, she comes strutting . . . [*Her face changes expression, she rises from her seat in a very dignified manner, and proceeds to strut about with an obviously false smile, looks down at XEC and smirks. She walks right past XEC so that he must turn around to face her.*]
>
> *XEC:* [*laughter*].
>
> *Mrs. F:* then I say [*mimicking the person's voice perfectly*], 'Oh, don't you have anything better to do?' [*laughter*] And that was the very first time, of course, that I came when she came . . .
>
> *XEC:* The first time . . . um hum . . .
>
> *Mrs. F:* And I said, 'I have things to do, and I'm not gonna fuss about it" [*she laughs*]. Oh, it was terrible [*goes to sit down again*] . . . anyway, uh, I like to um . . . talk with her, you know, but . . .
>
> *XEC:* Um hmm . . .
>
> *Mrs. F:* but it's like pushing on you . . . pushing on me, I mean. [*Obviously feeling that she had not fully communicated her point completely, she stands up and over XEC frowning, with her hands extended toward him as if pushing him in an intimidating way. XEC feels as though she is invading his space and obviously feels uncomfortable, and responds by shifting his chair away from her. Mrs. F sees this response that she has evoked and thus feels that she has made the point she wanted to communicate*] See?

Again, referring to the same person whom she was discussing above,

> *Mrs. F:* . . . So I don't, I, I, really stay away from her after the way she . . . the way she comes . . . [*stands up and begins to mimic the woman's posture and tone again*]. She walks in 'Oh are you gonna have a, a session or somethin?' I said, 'Yes' [as in "Yes, and what's it to you?"]. I didn't tell her what [*laughter*] I mean it, she is twister . . . twists your arm and everything else. I [*chuckles*], but I like her, I really like her, uh, sometimes she's just [*winces*].

In this exchange, Mrs. F used a series of overt behaviors which were designed to imitate the attitude and comportment of the person about whom she was speaking and thereby communicate her perception of that individual. At the end of her last turn talking, Mrs. F winced to convey her reaction to the individual when she could not find the word she wanted to use. Herein, she seemed to use tone of voice and facial expression as a means of compensating for her loss of verbal fluency, and it is evident that her deficiencies in verbal communication were not matched by similar losses in nonverbal communication.

In another instance, Mrs. F indicated her feeling about a staff member with words, but then affected a bodily posture to indicate her perception of the staff member's attitude. It should be noted that the staff member in question has a very dry sense of humor and jokes in a caustic way with some participants: "She's great for smashing down people who want to, you know, you know [sits up straight, throws her shoulders back and forth like a strutting rooster]. Yeah, I thought . . . I can't speak to her, I don't know why."

With time, Mrs. F engaged more and more in her use of such forms of extralinguistic communication, which may have indicated her possession of intact implicit memory (Schacter, 1996) with regard to having had the experience of her interlocutor understanding what she wanted to convey. But in order for her interlocutor to understand her, he first had to take "the intentional stance" toward her. That is, he had to position her as someone who was indeed trying to communicate something intelligible, engage her with a readiness to understand, and provide her with feedback which indicated to her that he was actively involved in conversation. On the other hand, it is very often possible that, as a result of using such different means of communication because of their inability to communicate effectively via words alone, many AD sufferers can be innocently positioned or characterized in ways that emphasize their seemingly confused or irrational nature. Once positioned in such a way, AD sufferers can experience frustration and isolation as a result of the ensuing behavior on the part of caregivers. Such behavior can easily lead to negative reactions on the part of the afflicted, and such reactions might then be interpreted mistakenly as symptoms of AD. I will return to this issue in Chapter 3.

It was this use of her intact extralinguistic ability which led me to suggest to Mr. F that he encourage his wife to "show me what you mean" when he found himself having trouble understanding her attempts to convey something verbally. By approaching her in this way and thereby engaging her intact extralinguistic abilities, he might be able to understand her more readily.

From time to time, Dr. M also used gesture to convey that which she could not through the use of words alone. There were numerous times in our association when I tried to impress upon her that she was able to communicate effectively despite the fact that she couldn't find the precise word or words for which she was searching. In the following is an example:

> *Dr. M:* May I? He has a friend who is, uh, uh, she gives him uh, among other things she uh, gives, *ex*, . . . help me.
>
> *SRS:* Your husband has a friend who,
>
> *Dr. M:* Who uh, who uh, gives him air, uh, she does [*moves her arms about*] . . .
>
> *SRS:* Oh, exercise?
>
> *Dr. M:* Not exercise, but something like it. She's a, a person who . . . [*moves her arms and now her hands, with fingers spread out, in a kneading type of motion*].
>
> *SRS:* Is it massage?
>
> *Dr. M:* Yes, thank you.

And then, a few minutes later, in talking about one of her sons,

> *Dr. M:* And uh, he's uh, we are like both, we are like, he's very wor, word . . .
>
> *SRS:* He writes?
>
> *Dr. M:* Not uh, not write so much. He's very, uh . . . [*makes large "busy" movements with her arms*]
>
> *SRS:* Active?
>
> *Dr. M:* Exactly. Who needs words? [*laughs heartily*].
>
> *SRS:* [*laughter*] But you see, you see – this is something that I think you should be uh, pay, paying attention to. You see, you communicated, within the last five minutes, two different things. You communicated the word, "massage",
>
> *Dr. M:* Um hum.
>
> *SRS:* and "active", by gesturing.
>
> *Dr. M:* Um hum.

SRS: So you're absolutely right. Who needs words? You, you, made your point.

Dr. M: Um hum. I made *your* point!

Indeed, she had made my point as well as her own. When Dr. M uttered that last comment, I had not immediately seen the significance of what she said, but in another instant it was clear to me. Yet just as clear was what had to be true in order for her to have said what she said. That is, her short-term memory for the topic had to be intact, but also intact was her ability to appreciate the point of view of another person. Although this was not the first instance in which she manifested that ability, here there was, additionally, a sense of humor, an ability to reflect upon what had just transpired in that she had to be able to: (a) compare what I said about the use of gestures to what she did, (b) understand what I said, and (c) make use of the locution I used to turn it back on me with the knowledge that it was my point that she was making as well – that she could still communicate effectively without succumbing to the anger and frustration that often accompanied her word-finding problems. In that regard, there was a rather light-hearted, lilting character to her tone of voice when she said, "Who needs words?" that revealed a kind of relief, an experience of a kind of freedom to communicate, and a certain delight at being successful.

Part, if not all, of this interchange occurred because over the course of many conversations, I took the time to reflect on, and to call her attention to, her successful use of gestures following each such occurrence. My correct interpretations above seemed to be very rewarding to her. Underscoring those interpretations with an explanation of how they came about served to show her that she did, in fact, make her points and allowed the natural flow of conversation to be sustained. The process of natural conversation in turn allowed her to demonstrate a sophisticated ability to understand and use my comment to her that "you made your point," to indicate to me that her behavior also supported what I had told her all along – "I made *your* point."

I cannot overstate the importance of engaging in the process of natural conversation in addition to using standard measures of language function in which there is no real conversation at all. When we confine our approach and understanding to the results of the latter form of investigation, there is no room for the emergence of the ability to make correct inferences, to reveal humor, subtle thinking, caring, value, and reflectivity which are outcomes of natural conversation and examples of important aspects of cognitive function. To come to conclusions about the "language of Alzheimer's disease," or any disease for that matter, without examining natural conversation between people is to limit our understanding to a veritable pinhole relative to the entire visual field and spells the difference between studying a disease as opposed to interacting with a person who happens to be afflicted with a disease.

To Generalize or not to Generalize?

What are we to make of the foregoing?

It is true that two of the three AD sufferers whose words and experiences you have just encountered were highly educated, academic people. In that sense, they are hardly representative of the population of healthy people, and therefore hardly representative of those who have been diagnosed with AD. One could reasonably ask questions such as: How special are these people? Are they, perhaps, "high-functioning" AD sufferers? They are certainly special in terms of their academic accomplishments. Perhaps it is the case that, because of their life-long intellectual pursuits, they had built-up what some researchers call "synaptic reserve." That is, it is theorized that by using the brain in such pursuits over a period of decades, there is an increase in the extent of synaptic complexity – in the complexity of neural networks that are thereby established. As a result of such enhanced development of neural networks, it could be argued that Dr. B and Dr. M were able to withstand a degree of brain injury and still communicate a great deal about issues that other, less educated, AD sufferers could not, and that their experiences are unique to them and are not representative of those of most AD sufferers.

I would have little difficulty in considering the aptness of the hypothesis that the educational backgrounds of these people, and the possible "synaptic reserve" that may have existed, contributed mightily to their ability to communicate with me. It would be tempting to use this one feature of their lives, their academic background, as a means by which to argue that their experiences of the disease's effects were unique to them. However, one must remember that in many ways, these individuals' behavior showed marked dysfunction – enough to render them moderately to severely afflicted according to standard measures of cognitive function. In these latter ways, they were quite similar to other AD sufferers whose educational backgrounds are less highly developed.

Thus I offer the following:

1 It is clear that standard neuropsychological measures of language function do not give us a complete picture of what AD sufferers think or can think and feel, hope for or can hope for, or value – not even in the cases of Dr. B and Dr. M.

2 How could we know that less educated AD sufferers do not experience similar emotional reactions to their losses if those very people are not related to and engaged in conversation as were Dr. B and Dr. M? Would we have known about the ways in which Dr. M and Dr. B experienced and reacted to AD had they not been approached via the "intentional stance," positioned as being people who had something to say, and given the facilitative support that allowed them to express themselves?

3 Were Dr. M's depression, Dr. B's turmoil, and Mrs. F's taking medication for anxiety related to their ongoing experiences of the loss of cherished abilities and having their long-held hopes for the future dashed?

4 Might it be the case that Dr. B and Dr. M, in using possible "synaptic reserve," and responding positively to a supportive interlocutor, are actually speaking for many, if not most, AD sufferers in the moderate to severe stages of the disease? May theirs be the voices which allow us to understand what many, many AD sufferers endure as they experience emotional upheaval, social isolation, and a slow, inexorable end to long-held hopes and dreams and abilities?

I prefer to weigh a certainty against a doubt in these matters: If AD sufferers, regardless of their educational background, are not engaged in supportive ways and positioned as having something to say, to share, we will never know how they experience the disease, what they think, how they feel. Thus, I prefer to give the benefit of the doubt and engage people with AD with the same concern and interest they have been shown throughout the balance of their adult lives.

What can happen to people afflicted with AD when they are not treated in such a supportive manner and what constitutes a lack of supportive behavior? Are there identifiable behaviors on the part of the healthy which can have a profoundly negative impact on the afflicted? Let us explore some of these possibilities in Chapter 3.

Excess Disability:
The Potential Impact
of Others in the Afflicted
Person's Social World

Mrs. L, diagnosed as having dementia, was being interviewed by one of my students. Sitting in a wheelchair in the nursing home where she lived, Mrs. L was discussing meaningful aspects of her life when a staff member entered the otherwise empty room, told Mrs. L that it was time for lunch and proceeded immediately to wheel Mrs. L out of the room. The interview, never brought to a polite end, was interrupted, and as Mrs. L was being wheeled down the hall, she continued with her story, speaking in a louder and louder voice as she was being taken further and further away from the room in which the interview had been conducted. The staff member had an agenda: to take Mrs. L to lunch, and that agenda would be fulfilled without question. There was no attempt made to allow the two people to bring the interview to a smooth ending, no attempt to inquire as to how much time that process might take, no attempt to treat Mrs. L as a person who deserved the simple respect that one would accord to virtually any individual who was involved in a conversation with someone else.

What made Mrs. L worthy of such treatment? It would seem that at least one possibility deserves our attention: she was positioned by the staff member solely as being a dementia sufferer. What sort of powerfully influential narrative, or storyline, springs forth silently from this type of positioning? It would seem that because Mrs. L was viewed principally as a "demented" person living in a nursing home, she was judged as not being mentally competent enough to have a negative reaction to being treated in such an inconsiderate, peremptory way, and therefore not worthy of having her needs or desires taken into consideration at that moment. Thus, in the mind of the staff member, there was nothing wrong, inconsiderate, or impolite about subjecting Mrs. L to such treatment.

Interestingly, the following week, when the second interview occurred, Mrs. L appeared not in a wheelchair, but using her walker instead. Although there may have been a plethora of reasons for her using a walker on that occasion, one clear outcome of her having done so was that no staff member could summarily remove her from the interview without her permission and cooperation.

In addition to the afflicted person's experience of and reaction to the effects of brain damage, another avenue of investigation pursued via Romantic Science is the way in which others treat the person with AD and his or her reaction to that treatment. We saw, for example, in the previous chapter, that a supportive, interested interlocutor can facilitate conversation with Alzheimer's sufferers and that such facilitation can yield profoundly meaningful information as well as other positive effects for the healthy and the afflicted alike. It is not too great a leap, I think, to assume that if the person with AD can react positively to caring, considerate, thoughtful, facilitative treatment, he or she is also capable of reacting negatively to the opposite type of treatment. Suppose therefore, that the staff member's "narrative," in which Mrs. L was positioned as incapable of being negatively affected by impolite treatment, was itself incorrect. What effects might such treatment produce in her? One might hypothesize quite logically that the effects would be negative, perhaps calling forth anger, resentment, hostility, and depression as they would in any person subjected to such treatment.

But if caregivers assume the validity of the original incorrect narrative and positioning and treat the afflicted person in ways that have a negative impact on his or her behavior, that behavioral result will itself be interpreted according to the original narrative. That is, whatever resulting negative behavior is observed will be viewed as symptomatic of the disease rather than symptomatic of the treatment accorded to the afflicted person. Thus will the cycle of misinterpretation continue, much to the detriment of all concerned. One outcome of this sort of misinterpretation may very well be that the afflicted person's hostility, anxiety, or depression will be treated with medication given in order to "manage the patient."

In this process, healthy caregivers view the AD sufferer's anger or hostility toward them as "irrational" and this interpretation adds further to the original incorrect storyline or narrative that supports the positioning of the afflicted person as being defective due to the disease. Thus we have an ever enlarging list of "symptoms," a "syndrome" which is understood as being caused by the disease itself, having no connection to the social milieu in which the afflicted person dwells. What a powerful storyline it is! The person diagnosed with AD is viewed as being virtually unaffected, indeed, incapable of being affected, by the ways in which others treat him or her. Under such circumstances, it is surely possible to treat him or her as an object rather than as a person.

The Concept of Excess Disability

In the first chapter I noted that, as early as the work of Rothschild and Sharp (1941), there has been considerable reason to have at least some doubt that the myriad symptoms observed in AD sufferers are due to brain pathology alone. More than a quarter century ago, Brody (1971) coined the term "excess disability" to describe what he called "the discrepancy that exists when a person's functional incapacity is greater than that warranted by the actual impairment." But if there is such excess disability, there would seem to be only one possible realm in which that disability is rooted, and that would be the social world in which the person with AD dwells.

Unfortunately, for all too long, the focus of researchers' efforts has been through a lens which the late, esteemed, Tom Kitwood (1990) called the "standard paradigm," the medical model, which itself deals with the physical disease process and the behavioral and cognitive effects as measured by standard tests performed in the laboratory and the clinic. The standard paradigm requires that we measure abilities that can be easily quantified through such tests. Despite the rarely acknowledged fact that such tests allow us only a snapshot of the AD sufferer's cognitive and behavioral abilities, such a snapshot most often presents an extremely influential and mainly "defectological" picture – a laundry list of things he or she cannot do, along with

93

often unwarranted inferences about the incapacities of the afflicted. The defects are seen as being causally related to the disease, generalizations are made so as to create the stereotype of the "average" AD sufferer and add immeasurably to the predominantly negative storylines constructed by caregivers about the person afflicted with AD.

We may be in the midst of a tragic irony here: however objective and useful the standard approach may be in certain venues, it is relatively insensitive to the varied contexts of the social world in which all of us, including the afflicted, live our lives. Yet, on the basis of the results of research using the standard paradigm, we have painted a mosaic, created a narrative, about the afflicted person's abilities in the very social world which is not studied through that research. In other words, on the basis of the standard approach, incorrect negative assumptions can be made by those who interact with AD sufferers in the everyday social world. So, one must ask questions such as: What are some examples of incorrect negative assumptions? What bitter fruit might be borne of such assumptions, or storylines; that is, how might they affect the behavior of those afflicted with AD? What form do these incorrect assumptions take in the subsequent behavior of caregivers?

Briefly, some answers to the above questions may be found in the connection between excess disability and what Kitwood termed "malignant social psychology," a term that encompasses a host of dysfunctional forms of treatment faced by afflicted persons. The two would appear to be linked in that the former (excess disability) may be seen to follow from the latter (malignant social psychology). How these two phenomena interact will be seen in what follows, but first let us examine some hints as to the effects of positive, supportive interventions in the lives of institutionalized elderly people.

Preliminary Hints Regarding Environmental Effects

Some years ago, a study was conducted to elucidate the relationship between excess disability and social isolation (Dawson et al., 1986). AD sufferers were provided with a one-hour social group every day for two weeks, and then a weekly group for the next two months. The social interaction involved introductions among the participants, refreshments, and various forms of interpersonal activities. Before the program began, and then after two weeks and again after two months, the participants' performance on a mental status questionnaire and on the London Psychogeriatric Rating Scale (LPR) was recorded. After two weeks, nine of ten participants showed improvement on the mental status questionnaire and all ten improved on the LPR scale. After another two months, there were no measured declines, thus leading the authors to propose that planned socialization can help to reverse and prevent excess disability as defined by performance on the above tests. Although the study provided some hints about the positive effects of the social environment, the participants' behavior was not studied outside of their test results. Does such social enrichment have positive effects in the afflicted persons' behavior in day-to-day life as well?

A classic study in which this issue was examined was conducted years earlier by Langer and Rodin (1976), who focused their attention on how the ability to exercise a measure of personal control would affect elderly people living in an institutional setting. One group of elderly residents was given the choice as to how to arrange the furniture in their rooms; the group was told that it was their responsibility to make their complaints known to the staff, and to communicate what they would like changed; the residents were given the opportunity to choose plants for their rooms and, if they wanted one, to pick which one they wanted from a number of choices; if they wanted a plant they were told that it was their responsibility to care for the plant as they wished. Finally, this group was told that there would be movies shown on two nights in the following week and to decide which showing they'd like to attend if they wanted to attend at all.

The other (comparison) group members were not given the choice of arranging the furniture in their rooms, were given a plant (no choice involved as to having one at all or which one to take), and informed that the nurses would water the plants, that there would be a movie on two nights during the following week, and that the staff would let them know which showing they were scheduled to attend.

Thus, the first group was given the opportunity to make choices and exert a degree of control in their lives in a variety of ways, whereas the second group was told that most decisions would be made for them by others. The results were hardly surprising, yet powerfully instructive. The residents in the group given increased responsibility and choices reported that they felt happier and more active than did those in the comparison group; they were rated higher by staff nurses (who were uninformed as to the different treatment conditions) on measures of alertness, happiness, interacting with other residents, talking to staff members, and general improvement. In addition, this same group was rated as spending less time engaging in passive activities than were members of the comparison group. Interestingly, more residents in the group given increased choices and responsibility attended the movie than did members of the comparison group.

The enhanced psychological effects were mirrored on the medical level in that health ratings from physicians indicated an overall increase in health status for the group given increased choices as compared with a slight decline in health for members of the comparison group. Finally, during the 18 months following the study, 30 percent of the members of the comparison group died, compared to only 15 percent of those given increased choices. Such results may be linked to the fact that the feelings of increased control in normal everyday decision-making were actively fostered among the residents, thereby sustaining the positive results found during the study itself. It is almost poignant that the life-enhancing effects found in nursing home residents by Langer and Rodin would stem from the ability to make choices about what appear to be such fundamentally simple things.

More recently, Boschen (1996) found that among adults living with spinal cord injuries, satisfaction with living conditions could be predicted by their perception of the degree of choice they had regarding where they would live and the nature of their daily activities. Thus it would seem that the overall well-being of individuals, be they elderly nursing home residents, or those living with the effects of spinal cord injuries, is clearly related to the degree to which they can exercise some control over their lives through the fundamental ability to make choices for themselves and thereby feel somewhat responsible for their own well-being. It would seem only logical that this would be true, as these same adults had lived their lives for decades doing precisely those things. Rodin (1986) made it quite clear that the process of aging is smoother, happier, and healthier, as people retain, more and more, a sense of control over their own lives. In this context, the approach of Mrs. B toward her husband (Dr. B in Chapter 2) becomes even more meaningful. Recall that when Mrs. B picked up her husband at the day care center, he would often ask, "What are we going to do now?", and she would respond by saying, "What would you like to do?". She thus indicated to him that he had some choice in the matter and that his wishes were important to her.

Note that the very fact that Mrs. B asked such a question means that she had positioned her husband as one who was capable of making choices, as one who deserved at least to be given the opportunity to do so, as one who deserved to be heard. This form of behavior on her part was surely of the ilk found to be life-enhancing by Langer and Rodin. But what of the behavior of the staff member toward Mrs. L that I described at the outset of this chapter? Such behavior may be described as a form of malignant social psychology as delineated by Kitwood, and it is to this topic that we now turn.

Malignant Social Psychology and Excess Disability

Kitwood and Bredin (1992) and Kitwood (1998) outlined forms of behavior which are exemplary of what they called *malignant social psychology* – behavior which can be understood as being assaults on the afflicted person's feelings of self-worth and personhood, leading to his or her being depersonalized. Of course, no caregiver would intentionally inflict such potentially devastating treatment on a loved one or a client. Thus, we can understand such behavior more accurately as being rather "innocent" and not springing from ill-will, for the situations facing caregivers are often daunting and exhausting. The fact that healthy caregivers can and often do treat the afflicted in such ways, however, may be traced to (a) the ways in which people with AD are positioned in the first place and (b) that these people are often unable to refuse to be positioned thus. Let us first examine some forms of malignant social psychology and then delve into the ways in which such behavior can lead to excess disability. Note that the following is not an exhaustive list by any means, but is meant to highlight some common dysfunctional behavior patterns.

1 *Treachery* is understood as being one or another form of dishonest representation, trickery or deception used by others in order to achieve the compliance of the person who has AD. For example,

97

the afflicted person is told that they are going out for a ride and the ride leads to a nursing home or hospital where he or she is then admitted.

2   *Disempowerment* occurs when things are done for the afflicted person even though he or she can do them independently, even if not with the speed or agility of healthier days. For example, the caregiver cuts the afflicted person's food while they are eating in a restaurant, even though the afflicted person is able to do this, albeit with some effort.

3   *Infantalization* is a form of disempowerment and can be seen, for example, in the sing-song, patronizing ways in which others speak to the person diagnosed with AD, as if that person were a child.

4   *Intimidation* is seen in the impersonal treatment given to the afflicted person by professionals who exude power and competence in carrying out assessments which, themselves, are threatening because the tests often underscore the AD sufferer's failing abilities. As a result, he or she may become agitated, extremely emotional and possibly exhibit another "symptom," called "catastrophic reactions" by crying or becoming angry as a result of such failures.

5   *Labelling* occurs after a person has been given a diagnosis such as "probable AD" and, from that point on, is expected to deteriorate and is treated differently than before the diagnosis was made – the afflicted person may now be written off. Subsequent negative reactions to such treatment as well as any form of behavior which is not readily understood, or which is somehow deviant, are also labelled, or understood, as symptoms of the disease. For example, if the caregiver is confused about what the afflicted person is trying, but failing, to convey coherently, it is the afflicted person who is labelled "confused" and is then treated accordingly. Another example can be seen in the following: while being tested, the AD sufferer comments that the test questions are trivial. The comment is labelled as an attempt at "social masking – a strategy employed by the afflicted in order to conceal his or her defects." Interestingly, if a healthy person were to make the same comment, no such interpretation would be made.

6   *Stigmatization* involves the exclusion of the afflicted person in that he or she now becomes an outcast of sorts; friends and relatives slowly cease to visit the afflicted.

7   *Outpacing* is seen when others go about activities at a pace that exceeds that of the AD sufferer, thus having the effect of leaving the

afflicted person out of conversations, for example, because the latter cannot think and speak at the rate of healthy others.

8   *Invalidation* is the denial, ignoring, or overlooking of the afflicted person's subjectivity. For example, if he or she is anxious about something, the anxiety is viewed as symptomatic of AD and no attempt is made to interact with the afflicted person in a sensitive, supportive way, as the anxiety is not considered as being "real," but, rather, a symptom.

9   *Banishment* is seen in the instances in which others avoid the afflicted person, who is seen as being "confused" and thus removing him or her from the social world of others.

10   *Objectification* is seen when the AD sufferer is not treated as a person, but as some sort of matter which can be led around, and talked about in uncomplimentary ways by others even when he or she is present.

11   *Ignoring* is seen when healthy others carry on a conversation or engage in actions in the presence of the afflicted person as if he or she were not present.

12   *Imposition* is seen in the description, at the outset of this chapter, of way in which Mrs. L was treated by the staff member, as in forcing a person to do something without allowing choice on that person's part.

13   *Withholding* is the refusal to give attention when it is requested to meet a clear need.

14   *Accusation* is the blaming of the afflicted person for behavior of commission or of omission which proceeds from their inability or their having misunderstood the situation.

15   *Mockery* is seen in making jokes at the afflicted person's expense, making fun of his or her "strange" behavior or comments.

16   *Disparagement* is telling the afflicted person that he or she is incompetent, burdensome, and so on.

17   *Disruption* is the abrupt intrusion on the afflicted person's behavior, breaking what Kitwood refers to as the afflicted person's "frame of reference."

In addition to this list of malignant behavior patterns, we can also appreciate how they can interact when being brought to bear on the afflicted person. For example, suppose Mrs. L is consistently exposed to infantilization, disempowerment, and objectification, and as a result becomes depressed and apathetic. Such a reaction would be a result of what Seligman called "learned helplessness." Her depression and apathy, however, will instead be labelled as symptomatic of the disease, much as fever is symptomatic of malaria. As a result of this interpretation, the social behavior of others which has brought about her reactions in the first place will not receive any attention and will therefore continue unremittingly.

I have used the example of fever being symptomatic of malaria for a specific reason here: the person who has contracted malaria will have fever regardless of how he or she is treated socially by others. However, suppose a person with AD is exposed to one or another form of malignant social psychology in one setting but not in another. Will we see striking differences in his or her behavior in the two settings? If so, one might then propose that the difference in behavior is due to the impact of the two different social situations rather than to the neuropathology of the disease.

An important consideration which must be kept in mind is that there is great variability among AD sufferers in terms of their personal histories, the pathological process, and the quality of their social relationships, as well as their premorbid abilities and dispositions. How all these factors interact may be quite unique in each instance. Among those who have attempted to construct a rating scale to assess the severity of the disease is Berger (1980), who noted that "it is not uncommon, particularly before serious deterioration sets in, for the picture to vacillate each day." The author went on to say that such things as the AD sufferer's feeling of security in the environment can be followed by decreases in the measured level of severity according to the rating system. Feelings of security may be thought of as reactions to a supportive environment. There is some reason to presume, therefore, that an environment in which the afflicted is exposed to behavior which conforms to malignant social psychology would not provoke feelings of security and could therefore affect the severity of the illness as measured by such rating scales as Berger's. It is to these issues that we now turn.

The Case of Mrs. R

Mrs. R was 68 years old and had been diagnosed with probable AD according to NINCDS-ADRDA criteria (McKhann et al., 1984) four years earlier. According to her medical records, she had severe problems with short- and long-term memory, orientation, verbal communication (Mini-Mental State score of 5, Folstein et al., 1975), needed assistance with personal grooming, and was given to aimless wandering. At the time of our association, and for months before, she was given Amitriptyline 50 mg. as a treatment for depression. Her spouse indicated that she needed help with taking medication, that she no longer cooked or did housework or any other home repairs, no longer handled money, never wrote or used the telephone, and if left alone she watched television or did nothing. He also reported that she needed assistance when eating. Mr. R indicated that the areas which caused him the greatest stress were related to his wife's "keeping busy, socializing, and housekeeping," none of which she did any longer according to his reports. The couple had a history of a strong, loving marriage, and in much of their behavior toward one another that history was still very much manifested at the time of our association.

My association with Mrs. R spanned a period of more than two years, during which time she was a participant at an adult day care center three days each week. She was a very warm person who had a history, throughout her adult life prior to the onset of AD, of being extremely service-oriented in her community. Her husband's work involved them travelling to and living in a variety of countries around the world, and in each place Mrs. R took on volunteer work in hospitals, homes for abandoned children, and facilities for the frail elderly to name but a few. During the Viet Nam War, she campaigned actively against the further pursuit of that war. During the time of our association, she did not speak, save for some rare occasions. One such occasion occurred while we were looking through a magazine and the saw a picture of former President Nixon, which prompted her to say, "Ooh, I *hate* that man, I just *hate* that man!" She did not respond that way to photographs of other well-known politicians whose views were more resonant with her own, and so I concluded that she did indeed recognize him and recalled, perhaps, his policies in the pursuit of the war. For the most part, Mrs. R communicated through gestures and mime, and did so quite effectively. Whenever I arrived at the day care center, she greeted me with a warm, broad, smile and a wave of her hand.

As I mentioned earlier, one of the hallmarks of brain injury is variability in the behavior of the afflicted. Thus, an AD sufferer might

101

be able to perform a particular task at one moment, but not at another. Variability can be seen from day to day, even from hour to hour. However, if there are consistencies in behavior such that it is coherent in one environment and absent or incoherent in another, we might hypothesize that the crucial factor is the environment, and that the disability seen in one of the two environments is "excess." In other words, if the disability were due to neuropathology alone, one might expect to observe the disability as being randomly present in both environments.

The case of Mrs. R is quite instructive in this regard, for we can examine a variety of her "symptoms," the areas of her behavior which caused her spouse his greatest concern and stress, and see how they were affected by her social environment and aspects of malignant social psychology.

(1)   *Grooming*: Mr. R indicated that his wife was able to pick out which clothes she wanted to wear on a particular day. However, at the time of our association, he also indicated that he made the choices for her. On one particular occasion, he reported that she had become very hostile with him for "no reason." When we examine the situation surrounding this episode, it becomes clear that Mrs. R's hostility did not occur for "no reason." It seemed that two days prior to this incident, Mrs. R celebrated her birthday at the day care center, and that she wore a particular outfit for the occasion. Now, two days later, and the first time she was returning to the center since her birthday, she wanted to wear the same outfit again. Her husband refused to allow her to do so, and she became angry.

It is in the storyline, or narrative, constructed by Mr. R about his wife that we find the foundation not only of his refusal to allow her to wear the outfit she had chosen, but of her angry reaction as well. He commented that he did not allow her that choice because: (a) he assumed that she wanted to wear that outfit because she had forgotten that her birthday had already been celebrated, and (b) as a result, she thought her birthday was that very day and that she wanted to wear that outfit for her birthday party at the center. From his point of view, given that her birthday had already been celebrated, there was no reason for her to wear the clothes she had chosen. When I inquired as to whether there was any other reason why she shouldn't wear those same clothes, such as, perhaps, that they were soiled, or that they weren't appropriate for the weather that day, he answered "no."

What if his assumptions were incorrect, and that she wanted to wear those clothes simply because she liked them so much and felt like wearing them again? His refusal to allow her that choice could easily be seen as something that could call forth an angry reaction to what had been his *disempowerment* of her in this situation. Because he positioned her as he did, he interpreted her hostility as existing for "no reason" and therefore a symptom of the disease, and we thus have an example of *labelling* as well as *invalidation*. I should point out that even if he had been correct in assuming that his wife mistakenly thought her birthday party was going to be that day, there still would be no reason to engage in such behavior toward her.

Mr. R also reported that his wife was able to apply her own make-up, but that he did it for her because when she did it herself, she "used too much" in his opinion. It was clear that he thought his wife was beautiful and that she didn't need all that much make-up in the first place. However, further examination of this situation was quite informative. He indicated that his wife was preoccupied with her facial blemishes, that she touched them a great deal. As a result, they became irritated and very obvious, much to her consternation, for she was always quite fastidious about her appearance. Her facial irritations had become so apparent that she did not want to be seen socially, even refusing to go to the day care center, which she greatly enjoyed. On one occasion, he reported that when he picked her up at the center, her face looked "tan" due to her having applied more make-up while at the day care center. It seemed that she had surreptitiously placed some of her make-up in the purse which she carried with her. When I inquired as to whether her application of make-up was more successful at hiding her blemishes than was his, he allowed that she had done a better job than he had that morning.

Here we have another example of *disempowerment* in that Mrs. R was perfectly capable of applying her own make-up, but her husband insisted on doing it for her. In addition, however, we also find a form of *invalidation*, in that he wasn't taking seriously her powerful need to hide her troublesome facial blemishes when she was going to be seen in public. To ignore her subjective reactions, or not to take them seriously, means that Mrs. R was cut off from the kinds of reactions from her spouse that would allow her to feel accepted and understood. Such a lack can be viewed as a form of social isolation even when one is in the presence of others, for the afflicted person's point of view is being essentially discounted, rendering him or her alone in a very real sense.

In both of these situations, Mrs. R was being deprived of exercising choices which she was competent to make and to carry out because Mr. R positioned her in such a way as to view her desires as being somehow "dysfunctional," thereby not taking her subjective reality into account.

(2) *Eating*: Mr. R reported that he cut his wife's food for her, especially if they were eating in a restaurant. That she was capable of doing this herself was evident from her behavior at the day care center, where lunch meals are served daily. Her eye-hand coordination was clearly still intact enough that she was able to feed herself, cut the food when necessary, without outside help. Why did Mr. R insist on doing this for his wife? One reason seems to be related to the way he positioned her initially, creating a fear of being embarrassed by the possible fulfillment of his incorrect expectations of her. Thus, based on that incorrect positioning, he engaged in another form of *disempowerment*. One must wonder how Mrs. R might have felt while watching her husband cut her food for her when they ate in a restaurant, knowing that the process could be witnessed by others.

(3) *Following directions*: Mr. R reported that his wife was unable to follow directions when he asked her to do things at home. However, while at the day care center, she seemed quite capable of doing so when the directions were given in a combination of verbal and gestural forms. She was able, for example, to help arrange place settings at the lunch tables and did so whenever she was asked to help. Mr. R did not, up until that time, use gestures along with verbal directions. Based upon his assumption that his wife could not follow directions, he slowly and increasingly refrained from asking for her assistance with household tasks. As a result, she had nothing to do, save for watching television, and thus we have the basis for his report that she did nothing at home anymore, including housework. Again, we see *disempowerment* at work, based upon incorrect negative assumptions.

(4) *Keeping busy.* Another of the areas of his wife's behavior which was of great concern and caused great stress for Mr. R was that at home, she did not do anything to help with household-related work. At the day care center, just the opposite picture emerged. Mrs. R was consistently described by staff members as being exceptionally helpful. For example, she would aid in helping to set up chairs for particular activities, moving them from one location to another, arranging them in the requested manner, and came to the aid of other participants on many occasions such as helping some to find the restrooms, assisting those in wheelchairs who needed help moving through doorways, and providing warm, supportive consolation to those who were in pain physically or emotionally. Staff members commented that Mrs. R seemed to be "on the lookout" for those who might need extra help, and when she herself could not provide that help, she would signal to staff members, calling their attention to those requiring assistance. One participant, as a result of undergoing chemotherapy, began to lose hair, and Mrs. R sought her out each day, giving her smiles and warm hugs.

It would seem that at the day care center there existed for Mrs. R the opportunities to keep busy, to be of help to others, and that such opportunities did not exist at home. Thus, the fact that she didn't provide help at home cannot be traced to one or another disability caused by AD, but to the social situation confronting her. Part of that social situation, as I noted already, involved the way in which Mr. R positioned her and his resulting expectations of her. I explored this issue with him and, in that process, he commented that he thought that he was being "somewhat overprotective" in not asking for her help, because he did not want her to experience failure. His incorrect assumption that she would fail was the basis of his subsequent behavior toward her, and this led to her "doing nothing or just watching television" – a fact that caused him to experience great stress.

In a sense, Mr. R may have been being overprotective indeed – not of his wife as much as of himself, for he did not want to see his (incorrect) negative expectations of her fulfilled in fact. Although his desire to prevent his wife from experiencing failure was admirable and rooted in his great love for her, his extreme efforts in that pursuit seemed to have had adverse effects. That is, although he successfully removed her from those situations in which her behavior *might have* borne out his expectations, he *disempowered* her in the process and prevented her from doing all she was capable of doing. When I pointed out to him that by allowing her to do all she could do for herself, some of his own sense of burden would be lessened, he readily agreed. On the other hand, at the day care center, where the staff did not hold such incorrect negative expectations of Mrs. R, she was a vital member of the group who was counted upon by the staff to be of help.

(5) *Wandering*: Mr. R indicated that his wife "wandered aimlessly" at home, causing him distress. She did not do so at the day care center, for the most part. I say "for the most part" because most of the time at the center, Mrs. R was engaged either in the program of activities or in being of help to others. There were occasions on which she did walk about in the hallway by herself, and this behavior could be *labelled* as "aimless wandering" if engaged in by someone diagnosed with AD. However, these same occasions were marked by her choosing not to participate in the activity transpiring at the moment, coupled with her having nothing else to do. One might wonder, had she chosen to sit and look through a magazine instead, if that behavior would be described as "aimless sitting down and looking through magazines." Rather, having been an active person all her life, sitting in that manner was not part of her personality. At home, she enjoyed little or no opportunity to be of help. As a result, other than watching television, all she could do was walk about the house. In this situation, her walking about was hardly aimless, for it was, in fact, something to do.

It is unfortunate that many AD sufferers, when walking about as did Mrs. R, cannot give an account of the reasons for their doing so, perhaps because they have some linguistic problems, and healthy others do not facilitate what might be informative responses. That is, the AD sufferer, while walking about in the day care center hallway, cannot easily answer the questions, "Why are you walking about?" or "Where are you going?" by saying, "Well, I don't want to be part of the small group discussion, nor do I want to sit and thumb through a magazine, and there's nothing else to do, so I figured I'd stretch my legs and walk about for a while." Thus, because they cannot say why they are doing what they are doing, their behavior is *labelled* as "aimless," and because of the same linguistic problems, they cannot refuse to be positioned as "irrational, aimless, wanderers."

(6) *Socializing*: Mr. R was disturbed by the lack of socializing that occurred in his spouse's life. At the day care center, she was a consummately social person who enjoyed warm interactions with others, but at home the story was markedly different. The basis of the difference may be seen in *stigmatization* and *banishment*. Mrs. R had more than a half-dozen siblings and their families living in areas close to where she lived. Following the diagnosis and the progress of the disease, what used to be regular social gatherings among the families slowly but inexorably ceased, causing marked social isolation. Mrs. R became, in effect, an outcast among members of her own family and her husband was especially embittered as a result.

Malignant social psychology and the realm of losses

In addition to the losses that can be traced to the neuropathology of AD and the afflicted person's reactions to those losses, there are other clear and significant losses that the afflicted individual can experience, and such losses can be traced to the impact of the behavior of others. Mrs. R was essentially stigmatized and banished by her siblings, faced disempowerment, labelling, and invalidation, and was incorrectly positioned as being incapable in a variety of ways at home. She thus faced social situations, as Kitwood proposed, in which she experienced a decreased sense of agency – the sense of meaning that is bound up with the ability to have and to exercise choices, to have the opportunity to act in positive, life-enhancing ways with her remaining intact abilities. Therefore, it would seem not too great a leap to suggest that her depression was a result not only of her reaction to the effects of the disease, but also powerfully rooted in the effects of malignant social psychology. Her demeanor at the day care center was rarely worthy of being described as "depressed," and she had no previous history of depression.

Yet in places other than the day care center, she was experiencing significant losses in many parts of her life. Not to react negatively to such losses would itself be considered pathological! As Lipowski (1969, p. 1200) noted: "The response of the family caregiver and other meaningful people to the patient's illness or disability, to his communications of distress, and to his inability to perform the usual social roles may spell the difference between optimal recovery or psychological invalidism." In the case of Mrs. R, "optimal recovery" could be understood more precisely as the optimal use of her remaining intact abilities, for there is as yet no recovery from AD. It is clear that many of those abilities were manifest in the day care center environment but not at home, and the behaviors which were described by her spouse as being problematic at home were not present at the day care center. Her "excess disability" and lack thereof can be traced to the ways in which she was positioned and responded to by her spouse and the day care center staff respectively. Neither neuropathology nor random variability in the expression of symptoms can account for such consistent and obvious differences in Mrs. R's behavior. She was, however, innocently positioned in a negative way by her spouse and siblings primarily on the basis of some of her losses in recall memory, orientation, writing, and the like, that could be traced to AD. That incorrect, but potent form of negative positioning led, it would seem, to her being deprived of what Lipowski called, "personally significant needs and values" and would naturally evoke a response of grief, of depression.

An alternative approach: Focusing on indicators of relative well-being

It is devastating to witness a loved one being assaulted by Alzheimer's disease, all the while knowing that there is little that can be done to halt, in any permanent way, the downward spiral that is produced by progressive brain damage. Family caregivers, therefore, may also be affected by a form of learned helplessness, in that there is nothing they can do to reverse the course of the disease. The losses are all the more obvious and debilitating to those who have spent the preponderance of their lives bound up in close relationship with the afflicted and such losses rivet our attention. Yet, despite the plethora of losses in individual abilities such as spelling, writing, reading, verbal recall memory, grooming, calculation, finding the proper words with which to frame thoughts fluently, and the like, there may also exist a variety of intact abilities that represent the part of the glass that is half-full. By attending to and supporting those remaining intact abilities, caregivers can avoid positioning the afflicted incorrectly, decrease the likelihood of engaging in forms of malignant social psychology, and minimize excess disability. How can we characterize those remaining intact abilities such that they can be identified readily by caregivers? It is to the identification of such abilities that we now turn, for such abilities put the afflicted on common ground with healthy others.

There is another important reason to look into the matter of intact remaining abilities, and that has to do with the need of caregivers to see what might be called a "glimmer of light" still shining in their loved ones. Mr. R behaved as he did in part so as to avoid *his* having to experience what he expected to be his wife's failures in a number of situations. Therefore, if he had a way of being able to observe and identify the remaining "points of light" as seen in his wife's intact abilities and behavior, that would be likely to aid in reducing his experience of sadness, loss, helplessness, and stress.

Kitwood and Bredin (1992) referred to such characteristics as "indicators of relative well-being" and proposed 12 such indicators, while underscoring the idea that such a list is hardly exhaustive:

- the assertion of desire or will
- the ability to experience and express a range of emotions
- initiation of social contact
- affectional warmth
- social sensitivity
- self-respect
- acceptance of other dementia sufferers
- humor
- creativity and self-expression
- showing evident pleasure
- helpfulness
- relaxation.

A particular person diagnosed with AD may manifest some of these indicators, perhaps all of them. There is no "threshold" number of indicators which must be displayed in order to establish common ground between the afflicted and the healthy, no minimum "score" which means that the afflicted person is "still there." One common thread which seems to run through most of these indicators is that they become apparent only in social interaction between people. For example, one cannot display helpfulness if one is not given the opportunity to provide help; cannot display social sensitivity, humor, affectional warmth, and acceptance of others or initiate contact, if one is socially isolated.

The case of Mrs. R is illuminating even further when we note that she displayed a number of these indicators of relative well-being. For example, she initiated social contact and displayed social sensitivity and affectional warmth in her efforts to be supportive to a day care center participant who was suffering the effects of chemotherapy. She displayed helpfulness on a regular basis, coming to the aid of staff members and other participants wherever she possibly could do so, showed evident pleasure in performing well in certain programs and activities, and evidenced a wide range of emotions, from sadness to anger to humor to pride. In covering up her facial blemishes by applying more make-up than her spouse would provide, as well as in avoiding activities in which she knew she could not take part without being embarrassed, she showed a measure of self-respect and the assertion of desire or will. In addition, she took evident pride in her appearance. In all these instances, despite her clear and significant losses in a variety of individual cognitive functions, Mrs. R behaved in a way that would be considered quite normal, even admirable in some respects, for any healthy person. Such behavior would seem to demand that she be engaged by others in ways that took such behavior and ability into account – that is, engaged as someone who is not "defective" because of her diagnosis.

On one particular occasion, I walked into one of the rooms of the day care center holding a small towel over one of my eyes. I had an allergic reaction that made the eye itch and tear, and I needed to bathe it in some water and keep it closed. The room was crowded with participants involved in one of the daily activities. As I entered the room, Mrs. R noticed me and she immediately got up from her seat, approached me with a look of concern, and pointed to the towel I was holding over my eye as if to ask "What's wrong?". I told her why I had the towel over my eye and that I was okay and thanked her for her concern, at which point, she nodded and returned to where she was sitting when I entered. We can quickly see that her behavior here reflects a number of indicators of relative well-being, but we can also analyze the behavior in terms of still other cognitive functions that must have been intact in order for her to have behaved as she did. She had to have been able to focus her attention on one of many "stimuli" (me) in her environment, she had to have inferred from the towel I was holding over my eye that there might be something wrong and must have been able, without the use of words, to express her concern. Finally, she had to have understood what I told her such that she could show her concern to have been allayed, and she had to have had intact short-term spatial memory in order to have gone back and sat down where she had been sitting when I first entered the room.

One can describe Mrs. R's response to me on that occasion as an instance of *caring*. As renowned neuroscientist Karl Pribram observed in his influential book, *Languages of the Brain* (1971), caring is context-sensitive. That is, caring is not simply doing the right thing, but doing the right thing at the right time, in the right situation. In order to behave in a caring way, brain systems which involve connections between the frontal association areas of the cortex and the limbic system must be functional, for these systems are closely related to our ability to formulate and assess the context in which events occur. In this example, the context is social, and Mrs. R's ability to evidence caring would have been unobservable if those brain systems were not functional or if she were socially isolated.

It is seemingly evident then, that the ways in which the afflicted person is positioned by others will depend to an extent on the social environment in which the person is observed. That environment can either be rich enough to provide opportunities for the afflicted person to manifest indicators of relative well-being or impoverished so as to preclude those same opportunities because the AD sufferer is socially isolated. Realistic, accurate positioning would require healthy others to take into account the effects not only of the disease itself, and the afflicted person's reactions to the effects of the disease, but also the effects of the social environment on the afflicted person's behavior.

The presence of indicators of relative well-being carries another level of meaning which is of potential importance as regards how AD sufferers are positioned by caregivers. Kitwood and Bredin propose that underlying the indicators themselves, there are what they refer to as "global sentient states" which they identify as:

- the sense of personal worth
- a sense of agency
- social confidence
- a sense of hope.

The logic here is that without these states of mind, it would be difficult indeed for a person to display the indicators of relative

111

well-being. For example, one would not display helpfulness if one did not have the hope that such behavior might make a positive difference and if one did not have a sense of confidence or of personal worth. On the other hand, if the presence of indicators of relative well-being in the AD sufferer's behavior were not noticed, acknowledged, honored, by healthy others, one could argue that such behavior on the part of caregivers would undermine the "global sentient" mental states in the afflicted. This is another reason why such forms of behavior are called malignant social psychology, for how else, other than as malignant or dangerous, could we describe the effect of undermining a person's sense of confidence, hope, personal worth, and agency?

The Situation of Mrs. D at Home

Mrs. D, "the Life of the Party," whom you will meet more fully in the next chapter, lived at home with her devoted husband. Her behavior at home and at the day care center revealed marked differences and pointed out once again the importance of the social environmental as it bears upon the afflicted person's ability to behave meaningfully (Sabat, 1994b,c). At home, her mood was sullen for the most part and she would say very little as her husband would do most of the talking, including his speaking for her even though she could speak for herself (an example of *disempowerment*). On winter evenings at home, her complaints of feeling cold were interpreted by her husband as symptomatic of her disease, for he did not feel cold (an example of *invalidation* and *labelling*). That the maid would give Mrs. D an afghan under such circumstances was viewed as "over-indulging" behavior by Mr. D. At home, Mrs. D had no "work" to do other than trying as best she could to respond to her spouse's infrequent requests, for he took on many of the household chores. When she would fail to comply on those occasions, he reproached her and she would lower her head and eyes, staring at the floor in embarrassment. Mr. D treated his wife as though her behavior was primarily the result of AD, and thus would not speak to her about his own problems and feelings because, in his words, "she wouldn't understand." Ironically, as you will see in the following chapter, her remaining ability to show sensitivity to the plight of others and her willingness and ability to be of support to people at the day care center were not called into play at home, for there she was positioned principally as deficient. As a result, both partners experienced isolation and discouragement, and Mrs. D was unable to maintain her sense of self-worth as she so easily did at the day care center where the staff actively enlisted her help and allowed her to use her remaining intact abilities to the fullest extent. Thus, once again we can begin to understand the relationship between excess disability and malignant social psychology.

The undermining of the aforementioned global sentient states, through the various forms of malignant social psychology, can be seen as being assaults on what we commonly refer to nowadays as self-esteem. Given the losses that the person with AD experiences due to neuropathology and to impoverished social situations, how can he or she maintain feelings of self-worth, or self-esteem? Let us turn to the next chapter where we may delve into this very important issue.

Chapter 4

The Maintenance of
Self-Esteem

"They don't know *anything* anymore."
"Treating an Alzheimer's patient is like doing veterinary medicine."

The first comment, characterizing people with AD, was uttered by a caregiver while I was speaking to a group of caregivers about remaining intact abilities found among the afflicted. The second comment was made by a physician who was treating Dr. B, whom you met in Chapter 2. Both statements position the AD sufferer in extremely negative, defective ways, and exemplify the assumptions which underlie behavior characterized as malignant social psychology. In the face of such positioning, in addition to the losses in cherished abilities, how can the afflicted person maintain any sense of self-worth? Before we explore how self-esteem may be maintained by AD sufferers, it is important to examine specifically some of the ways in which those feelings of worth are assaulted, for such an examination may provide meaningful clues as to how caregivers may aid the person with AD in preserving important aspects of self-esteem.

Assaults on Self-Esteem

Soon after Dr. M received the news of her diagnosis, years before we met, she avoided telling friends and even her adult children about the results of her medical examinations. With regard to her reluctance to "come out of the closet" as it were, she wrote, with the help of her husband, "Why this reluctance to name my malady? Can it be that the term, 'Alzheimer's' has a connotation similar to the 'Scarlet Letter'

114

or the 'Black Plague'? Is it even more embarrassing than a sexual disease?" It would seem that Dr. M recognized something very significant here, for although the wearer of the "Scarlet Letter" or the person afflicted with a sexual disease may be looked down upon in terms of some dimension of morality, that same person's cognitive ability *per se* is never held in question. On the other hand, the diagnosis of AD surely puts the afflicted person at risk of being seen as somehow less than a person, something of which Dr. M seemed to be keenly aware. The idea that AD sufferers are those who "don't know anything anymore," or are no better at communicating with a physician than are animals (treating the afflicted is "like doing veterinary medicine"), certainly gives credence to Dr. M's reason for feeling embarrassment in the wake of the diagnosis.

Dr. M, a person of astoundingly powerful intellect, whose literary skills during most of her adult life were such that her prose and poetry could literally leave you breathless, now found that,

> Creating a single coherent sentence or paragraph is very difficult. Typewriting had been second-nature to me, with the process itself even pleasant since I was so facile at it. Now, it is so miserable a chore that I avoid it as much as possible. And all of these things take ridiculous amounts of time. Moreover, the expectation for the future is grim . . . As to how my symptoms affect me, do not think I am just being frivolous if I say, "they drive me crazy."

When she entered the hospital for further tests that would eventually confirm her diagnosis, her reaction to being asked "Orientation" questions such as "Do you know your name?", "Do you know where you are now?", was, "What a put-down! I feel the questions are disrespecting, disparaging, and dismaying . . ." These were her reactions years before our association began, years before there was further erosion of her highly developed and deeply cherished abilities to write, to read, to speak.

When a person is experiencing the loss of skills from the relatively simple and mundane, such as dressing him or herself or using eating utensils, to the more complex, such as those required for engaging in the pursuit of vocational and social interests, it is certainly easy to imagine reactions of annoyance, disgust, and the like. And, when formal testing of cognitive function indicates to caregivers what are

115

described to be serious decrements in memory, abstraction, concept formation, and word-finding, some may wonder not only how an AD sufferer can maintain feelings of self-worth, but even *if* such a person is able to understand the very concept of self-worth at all. This latter issue is hardly a flight of fantasy. We have already seen that malignant social psychology consists of behaviors on the part of the healthy which undermine the well-being of the afflicted person, and result in excess disability, and that such behavior is rather innocent as opposed to being malicious. Yet the very innocence of such behavior must itself rest on negative assumptions about the cognitive abilities of the afflicted person. That is, the basis for treating the AD sufferer in peremptory, patronizing ways must, to some degree or another, reflect the belief that the afflicted person is not, and cannot possibly be, cognizant of and reactive to such treatment.

We saw, however, in the previous chapter, that there can be striking differences in the behavior of persons with AD depending upon the ways in which they are treated and the opportunities that are made available to them to manifest remaining intact abilities. In this chapter, I should like to examine the proposition that, despite serious deficiencies in cognitive function as measured by standard tests, as well as deficiencies that are plain to see in everyday life, it is the case that AD sufferers in moderate to severe stages of the disease are still able to retain feelings of self-worth and, under the proper supportive circumstances, act in a variety of ways so as to maintain such feelings.

The Dialectics of Self-Worth, or Self-Esteem

In his *Principles of Psychology* (1890/1983), William James wrote,

> . . . we have an innate propensity to get ourselves noticed, and noticed favorably, by our kind. No more fiendish punishment could be devised, were such a thing physically possible, than that one should be turned loose in society and remain absolutely unnoticed by all the members thereof. If no one turned round when we entered, answered when we spoke, or minded what we did, but if every person we met "cut us dead", acted as if we were non-existent things, a kind of rage and impotent despair would ere long well up in us, from which the cruellest bodily tortures would be a relief; for these would make us feel that,

116

however bad might be our plight, we had not sunk to such a depth as to be unworthy of attention at all. (p. 281.)

In the case of the AD sufferer, the social situation is somewhat different from that described by James. It is not so much that the afflicted person is "cut dead," not noticed at all but, rather, what is noticed by the AD sufferer and others consists primarily of attributes that are negative. That is, the afflicted person is most often noticed for what he or she cannot do any longer, and is often reacted to in ways which produce in him or her, as James wrote, "an impotent despair."

Feelings of self-worth, or self-esteem, are not determined solely by being noticed favorably for, in this regard, one must be aware that one is noticed favorably in order to think well of him or herself. But what is it about a person that might be noticed favorably by others, and in what would one take pride? One way to begin an answer to this question would be to propose that it is one or another of a person's positive attributes which would be the focus of feelings of self-esteem, and such feelings would be included among one's beliefs about the quality of his or her attributes and skills. Therefore, as some of Dr. M's deeply cherished positive attributes were being eroded, so too were her related feelings of self-worth.

We can understand aspects of the AD sufferer's predicament here in terms of a *dialectical* type of reasoning as described in James Lamiell's research (1987, with P.K. Durbeck) on the formation of impressions. The afflicted person seems to be making negative judgments about him or herself on the basis of a type of reasoning that can be captured as "who I am not, but might otherwise be." That is, the person with AD has an awareness of his or her past valued attributes, a simultaneous awareness that those valued attributes have become eroded as a result of the disease, and how his or her life might have unfolded if those attributes were still intact. As a result, there is a tension between the afflicted person's knowledge of what used to be, what *could be* if not for AD, and an understanding of how the quality of life at present is lacking as a result of the disease. Here, the dialectical reasoning is intrapersonal, within and about the afflicted person. An excellent example of this type of thinking emerged from conversations with Dr. M. In one such instance, I was pointing out to her that, even though she couldn't find a particular word, she was still able to communicate her idea in another way. She then commented:

117

> *Dr. M:* But I can't do that now. I, I, it is as you say the, the way
> I have organized my li, self all the time . . . so I always have
> [had] that, but now I can't get it because . . .
>
> *SRS:* I'm not convinced that you never get it. Of course, you'll
> have some problems, but it's in those moments when you can't
> get it.
>
> *Dr. M:* But see, those are most of the moments in my life now
> and I don't want that.

The same type of dialectical reasoning may be appreciated as transpiring also in the minds of caregivers. For example, the spouse of the AD sufferer can often engage in "who my husband (or wife) is not, but might otherwise be," as well as "what our life together is not, but might otherwise be." Here, the dialectic is interpersonal, between people.

It is extremely important for our present purposes to understand clearly that the focal point in both the intrapersonal and the interpersonal dialectic is the effect of AD as it has manifested itself in the various deficits seen in the behavior of the afflicted person. Thus the assaults upon the self-esteem of the AD sufferer may be understood as having as their principal source the powerful focus of attention on what he or she can no longer do well, or, perhaps, at all. To see oneself and to be seen by others principally in terms of what one cannot do, cannot but weaken one's sense of self-worth, or self-esteem, and increase one's sense of being burdensome and deficient.

In addition, and in keeping with the concept of *social identity* as defined by Tajfel (1978), feelings of self-worth, or self-esteem, may spring forth also from "that part of an individual's self concept which derives from his [sic] knowledge of his membership in a social group (or groups) together with the value and emotional significance attached to that membership" (p. 63). In terms of what Tajfel is saying here, we can readily understand Dr. M's reluctance to reveal the nature of her illness, for being an AD sufferer was not only akin to wearing a "Scarlet Letter," but also to be seen as belonging principally to a group called "AD patients." The negative connotations and powerful emotional significance related to membership in such a group would, as well, be a damaging blow to her feelings of self-worth. Again, we can understand the intrapersonal dialectic as being something

118

akin to "whom I am not numbered among, but might otherwise be." Here, the "whom" in the dialectic refers to the healthy, "unburdensome," vital, independent people in the community who are not identified primarily as "patients."

Self 2 attributes and self 3 personae

Still another way to begin an examination of the matter of the maintenance of self-esteem among AD sufferers is to outline aspects of selfhood referred to as Self 2 and Self 3. As we saw in Chapter 1, the former consists of the person's attributes, both physical and psychological and can include characteristics which have long-standing histories, such as one's height, educational background, achievements, and the like, as well as attributes which have less longevity in terms of their existence, such as having been diagnosed with probable AD, or being retired. Self 2 also includes one's beliefs and one's beliefs about one's attributes. Although most of us have long-standing attributes which we may not particularly like, we generally have a larger host of attributes in which we take proper pride – such as having raised good children, having achieved this or that in our vocational lives, being valued friends and members of a social community. For the healthy among us, the valued attributes generally outweigh those which are less valued, and are noticed and respected by others.

However, this situation is often tragically different for the AD sufferer. As valued skills become eroded, and one's independence becomes curtailed, the attributes which are now focused upon principally by the afflicted person, as well as by healthy others, are the very attributes which are damaging to the AD sufferer's sense of self-worth, self-esteem. As Dr. M said regarding social situations, four years after the diagnosis, "I, uh, I can handle myself when I try to not let myself be presented as an Alcazheimer's, I'm very different." Her focus upon and reaction to her own losses of ability were patently clear in the following exchange:

SRS: When you walk around saying to yourself, "I can't stand the way these things are going, I can't do this, I can't do that, I have trouble with this and that . . ."
Dr. M: Ya, that's the issue. That's the issue. The issue is, what kind of life is that?

119

She spoke about about these issues again during a conversation we had after she had been given a battery of tests by a speech therapist, for her husband thought that speech therapy might have some beneficial effects. After the first visits which focused on assessments of her speech, she decided that she did not want to continue, and we discussed that very matter as she showed me the results of the assessments:

SRS: Well, I'm familiar with some of the tests that they gave you.

Dr. M: And uh, this was at the time, it was about three weeks ago and um, I was doing other things and it didn't, it didn't give me a feeling that there's something that I should have another thing.

SRS: It didn't give you the feeling that going back and doing some kind of speech therapy would be helpful to you? [Note the use here of indirect repair. In her next turn, she clarifies her comment in her previous turn.]

Dr. M: No, I didn't think about that and uh, I, d, it wasn't, it wasn't important and I, you know, at this time too, I found that I really don't like to be uh, talking about what, what's my trouble. It's gotten, I know what my trouble is. And I think that what I would like it uh, only if there's something that is, uh, a time, a uh, a time and with a person who there is a real [*gestures with hands, holding them upright, parallel to one another and moving them back and forth alternately toward one another*].

SRS: Back and forth – a relationship [another indirect repair].

Dr. M: Um hum. You know you could go out, out of this area and you could get so many people who would want to, to for one reason or another, to do uh, something uh, with me, and I don't want that. I don't want my life to be uh, not uh, I don't want to be part of what does this person can do, what that person do.

SRS: Let me back up for a second because I think I'm missing your point. You don't want your life to be . . . [I am using another indirect repair here.]

Dr. M: Going always to see people to see what's wrong with me.

SRS: Ah!

Dr. M: And how to, and how and how it could sometimes uh, what can we do about it? But otherwise, I've, I've, I've had it.

120

SRS: Ya . . . let me see if I understand. At least one of the things that you're saying is that it's, it's not something – you, you don't want to put yourself in situations where you're constantly being shown what you can't do. [I use another indirect repair here.]

Dr. M: That's one. That a real thing.

In this conversation, Dr. M makes clear her need to avoid being in situations in which she's "going always to see people to see what's wrong with me" for those situations focus her attention on those of her attributes which are in decline. Furthermore, she is aware that there are many people who would be interested in her as a result of her having been diagnosed with AD, but that she doesn't want to be involved in situations such as those: "I don't want my life to be uh, not uh, I don't want to be part of what does this person can do, what that person do."

She also makes quite clear that what she does want is a genuine social relationship with another person. Rather than having new relationships based upon her being the test-taker and the patient, and someone else being the test-giver, she wants to be able to enjoy social relationships which involve and acknowledge her social identity principally as a person and which do not limit her social identity, her Self 3 personae, to her being a "patient."

From the point of view of Social Constructionist thought, we have a multiplicity of Self 3 personae (such as loving spouse, devoted parent, demanding teacher) and in order for any or all of those personae to be manifested in appropriate behavioral forms, we need the cooperation of others in our social world. If others in the social world restrict their view of a person to "AD patient," it will be virtually impossible for the afflicted person to manifest any other social persona which may be a source of pride, or self-worth. Attempts by the afflicted to construct a more positive, valued, Self 3, such as "professor," or "teacher," or "academic person" may thus be ignored or even misinterpreted in ways such as, "Dr. B still thinks he's a professor." In other words, when the afflicted person is trying to say, "Look at me – I'm not just an AD patient – I'm a (lawyer, teacher, father, mother, etc.), his or her interlocutor, focusing solely on the Self 2 attribute of AD, may interpret the effort of the afflicted in terms of the disease process: the afflicted person is exhibiting delusional thinking, still believing that he or she is a professional. Thus the healthy interlocutor ignores what may very well be the afflicted person's cry for attention to and respect for, aspects of his or her of social identity which have been and are valued by one and all.

That the testing situations were detrimental to feelings of self-worth was also voiced by Dr. B. In the following extract of conversation, we pick up at the point at which Dr. B had begun talking about AD:

> *Dr. B:* I presume that I'm Alzheimer's. I must. I must start with that. So how do you test the best? How do you test the worst?
> *SRS:* That's a good question. Let's say, for the sake of discussion, that somebody was diagnosed as having AD six years ago. [*Dr. B interrupts here.*]
> *Dr. B:* Uh-let me break in right away so that it doesn't go in my head [I understood this as meaning "go out of my head"]. I had a testing of there was – my wife and I thought there was something right away in the hospital and I was there for quite a few times. I was in there, um, NIH. And I read and read and read for that for quite a long time and then I gave it up. I went in the NIH, so I went through the NIH batteries. We walked out of the NIH not because it was stupid, but what we began to think that we were doing um, sim, very simble projects or things like that. And, um, on the tests that have come through from NIH, nothing at all have we collected. Thought – this is *michigahss* [Yiddish for craziness].

In an interview, Mrs. B told me that when Dr. B went to the NIH for testing and the diagnosis turned out to be probable AD, Dr. B at first did a great deal of reading about the disease. They discussed the possibility of doing further testing but decided against it because there was no cure, and neither of them thought that it would be especially good for Dr. B to be subjected to any more test batteries, especially as they would cause him great consternation.

> *SRS:* When you took these tests, did you feel that the tests were annoying or simplistic?
> *Dr. B:* Um, very, very. It, um, I think nothing came out of it. NIH was, uh, sort of, sl, eerie. It took me a long time, it took me a long time for me to take my psyche and put it apart and

122

say, "Hey – this is nothing." My wife and I actually walked out of the hospital.

In this last comment, I understood Dr. B to be saying that it took him a long time to separate himself from the ordeal of the testing situation, from the assault he experienced by having his problems highlighted again and again. He had to take his mind, his psyche, and "put it apart" and downplay the experience of having many problems with the test questions by saying, "Hey – this is nothing" in order to salvage some sense of self-worth. In order to say, "this is nothing," Dr. B had to be aware of his other Self 2 attributes which were worthy, which were "something," in which he could take pride still.

Of course, one could easily interpret his commentary as being a species of denial – that he is being defensive about his defects – and thus label what he said ("This is nothing . . .") as a type of *anosagnosia*, a denial or unawareness of illness. Such an interpretation would be in keeping with viewing his behavior (his discourse in this case) principally in terms of his diagnosis, for very often one of the effects of brain damage is that the afflicted person seems to exhibit an unawareness or denial of illness and its effects. To jump to such a conclusion without further investigation would be consistent with Kitwood's notion of *labelling* which, as we saw in the previous chapter, is an example of malignant social psychology because such a defectological interpretation would patently ignore two important issues. One is the possibility that Dr. B did indeed have a host of worthy characteristics of which he was aware and for which he wanted to be acknowledged and respected. The second is that he actually did acknowledge, rather than deny, the effects of AD in a variety of ways, noting that he has to slow down, that he loses track of information, that AD gives him "fragments," that AD is constantly on his mind and makes him "mad as hell," to name but a few. Therefore, labelling his response as a species of *anosagnosia* would obscure the idea that he quite rightly wanted, as would any healthy person, to avoid being seen primarily in a negative light, that he knew that he possessed worthy qualities which were not undermined by the failures he evidenced on standardized tests, and that he did not, in fact, deny his illness or many of its effects on him.

To summarize, then, it would appear that the assaults on the AD sufferer's feelings of self-worth center upon:

1 The focusing of attention mainly upon the negative attributes of the afflicted person and the simultaneous lack of focus upon remaining intact abilities. Such a focus limits the Self 2 of the afflicted person, in the eyes of others, to those characteristics which are anathema and threatening to all concerned.

2 Forms of what I would call malignant positioning as seen in the quotations with which this chapter began. Such positioning involves a variety of incorrect, or at least questionable, assumptions and, if it is maintained, is reflected in caregivers' subsequent behavior (malignant social psychology) toward afflicted persons. The subsequent behavior further demeans the afflicted person and increases his or her sense of despair as being burdensome and possibly having nothing of value to contribute to others.

3 The restriction of the afflicted person's social personae to "the patient," who must be "managed." Because the construction of social personae, or forms of social identity, requires the cooperation of others, if the only social persona which will receive such cooperation and which can be constructed is that of AD patient, the afflicted person's ability to express him or herself in the social world is clearly restricted. This means that social personae in which the afflicted person may take pride are relegated to nonexistence, save for what might be occasional but vain attempts on his or her part to construct social identities other than that of "patient."

In all three forms of assault, the AD sufferer has become something of a prisoner of others' thoughts about him or her, and the bars of that prison filter out most of what is deemed worthy and allow through most of what is deemed threatening, defective, burdensome, and hopeless. Ironically enough, it is the AD sufferer who understands this situation best and who often feels the need to ameliorate it with great intensity of purpose.

So it would seem that the maintenance of self-worth, of self-esteem, among AD sufferers requires the cooperation of healthy others in the afflicted person's life. This is hardly different from the situation that confronts all of us except for the fact that the AD sufferer is far more vulnerable to the effects of the behavior of others. That is, the afflicted person's ability to act independently as he or she has in the past is severely compromised by the effects of the disease.

The avenues through which others might cooperate with the afflicted person include, but are not limited to:

1 That caregivers facilitate communication with the afflicted, as in the use of indirect repair in conversation. When communication is thus facilitated, the AD sufferer is spared some of the frustration accompanying word-finding and other linguistic problems and can thus find a measure of satisfaction (exemplified in Dr. M's comment, "Who needs words?!") in the process of communicating with others, along with the delight in being understood. Simultaneously, attention is diverted from some of the linguistic defects which accompany the disease – defects which do not, in and of themselves, render communication impossible.

2 The reduction of forms of malignant positioning and malignant social psychology. The former and the latter are intimately related and both serve to undermine self-esteem by emphasizing real and imagined defects. Persistence of this type of positioning and behavior by caregivers prevents the afflicted person from exercising his or her remaining intact abilities by removing or restricting severely the opportunities for the AD sufferer to engage and demonstrate those abilities.

3 Identifying, paying attention to and supporting the afflicted person's remaining intact, admirable characteristics, by aiding him or her in constructing social personae in which pride can be taken. Although such personae may be different in different people, the life history of the individual can provide important clues for the caregiver in the process of identifying those valued personae. For example, what has been abidingly important to the afflicted person in his or her relationship with others? How has the afflicted person behaved in the past in order to build his or her sense of self-worth? How can social situations be used now to help him or her to construct those valued social personae and thereby aid him or her in achieving some semblance of self-esteem?

With these suggestions in mind, let us now turn to some specific cases of AD sufferers and explore how cooperating with the afflicted person in constructing valued social personae can have a powerful effect on the person's feelings of self-worth and satisfaction and how

AD sufferers attempt to maintain and bolster those feelings. Some of these findings were reported by Sabat et al. (1999).

The Case of Mrs. D

A snapshot

At the time of our association, Mrs. D, a high-school graduate and homemaker, was 70 years old and had been diagnosed with probable AD five years earlier. According to standard tests, she was moderately to severely afflicted (Stage 4, Global Deterioration Scale, score of 7 on the Mini-Mental State test). She was unable to name (recall) the day of the week, the date, the month, the year, or the city and county she was in, and she displayed difficulty from time to time in finding her way to the restroom at the day care center. In addition, she evidenced a number of sensory-motor problems such as bumping into things occasionally, difficulty in picking up and using eating utensils, getting food to her mouth, imitating the movements of instructors in exercise classes, and distinguishing between left and right, and she underestimated her age by saying she was "60, 60-something." During the 18 months of our association, Mrs. D attended an adult day care center and lived at home with her husband. I met with her two to three hours per week at her home and at the day care center.

Her ability to use spoken language was not as compromised as were her recall and sensory-motor skills, but she still experienced frequent word-finding problems and often misprounounced words (displayed *paraphasias*) and these were, to her, the most frustrating of all her difficulties. An example of her word-finding problems can be seen in her response to the question, "Can you tell me about significant experiences in your life?" Mrs. D responded, "The only thing I can think of is when someone came and told me, 'come, there's a problem here.' It was all about Alfat, Alfased, no, it's not Alfased – Alzheimer's." (Note that in her attempts to find the word "Alzheimer's" both of her errors began with the correct initial sounds.) Although she expressed frustration in response to word-finding problems while speaking privately with me or with the social worker at the day care center, if such problems arose when she was among other participants, Mrs. D revealed a different response. If, after stumbling over a word and then making two or three attempts, she would substitute another word or stop and say, "It's that Alzheimer's." The social worker reported that the substituted word was often confabulated or had a different meaning than the word she presumably intended, and that she "can cover for herself and often start the crowd laughing by poking fun at herself."

How she maintained self-esteem

Social persona of "Life of the Party"

The AD sufferer's personality and pre-morbid proclivities can often provide us with clues as to the strengths or worthy characteristics the person exhibited in his or her life, and such strengths can be closely related to the ways in which the afflicted person will attempt to maintain his or her self-esteem during the course of the disease. This was certainly true in the case of Mrs. D, and we find an intimation of her approach to this issue in her means of "covering for herself" by getting participants laughing as she poked fun at herself.

Mrs. D was born into a family involved with show business. Her brother had been a stand-up comedian of note, having performed on television and in many well-known night clubs. She, likewise, exhibited a wonderful singing voice and a terrific sense of humor, often telling jokes to make people laugh. She noted, in this connection with true vaudeville *elan*, "I got a million of 'em." One example of her "delicate" sense of humor surfaced when she and I were chatting about poetry, which was something she had always enjoyed. At one point, she asked, "Why don't people read more poetry these days?" And, answering the question so as to provoke others to laugh, she said, "Because they're too busy making money, watching television, and thinking about sex." It was this aspect of her personality which turned out to be the foundation of her mode of maintaining her sense of self-worth. Yet, in the unfolding of this story, we also find an example of social misunderstanding on the part of her loving and deeply devoted husband who positioned her primarily on the basis of AD, and thereby created negative storylines about her and interpreted her behavior in dysfunctional terms that coincided with those storylines.

Her husband was overwhelmed by her inability to do the household chores and other tasks that had been her responsibility for many years. Some aspects of her behavior led to his creation of a storyline which painted her as deeply confused, even deluded. For instance, Mr. D reported that his wife had a delusion about having a job and that the delusion was due to Alzheimer's. He explained that, on mornings before taking her to the day care center, she would often ask him to hurry lest she be late for work. To him, this seemed odd at the very least and delusional at worst, for to his knowledge she did not have a job. After having heard this story from him, I approached Mrs. D at the day care center and asked her about this interaction with her husband.

My conversations with Mrs. D were always punctuated by jokes and kidding, for she was a very witty, warm and outgoing person. As she put it, "In our family [her nuclear family] we are clowns." Thus I said to her, "You've been holding out on me. Your husband tells me that you have a job. I didn't know that you were working." She seemed confused by this, so I explained further: "He said that on mornings before coming to the center, you sometimes hurry him because you are afraid to be late 'for work'." She then seemed to understand my question and explained that many of the people who attend the day care center are sad or depressed and that she cheers them up with jokes and songs. *"Some of them are in bad shape, you know, that they couldn't remember a thing. I would try to help them. That's what you have to do almost if you want to get along."* When asked, "Oh, so you have to help the others?", she replied, *"I think it's a nice thing to do. Instead of me sitting down with the little I have gone, a little bit, a little higher, and not trying my fellow person . . . as things went by I would work, you know, with somebody just to keep them happy."*

Bringing cheer to people at the day care center was her "work," her purpose, and she was so successful in her efforts that the social worker often asked Mrs. D to talk to new participants so as to help integrate them into the group, or to provide sympathy and understanding to those who were experiencing difficulties. Significantly, even when not specifically asked to do so, Mrs. D would strike up conversations with others who seemed to need some sort of diversion, and would provide humor and understanding. When she would begin to sing an old song, other participants would join in, and when she told jokes, she had everyone "laughing in the aisles." Mrs. D's social persona at the day care center was "the life of the party" and whenever a staff member referred to her in this way, she beamed with delight.

Here we have an excellent example of how the social worker, not-ing Mrs. D's good humor and caring nature, cooperated with Mrs. D in the construction of the valued social persona of "life of the party." As a result, Mrs. D was able to feel that she was a useful and worthy member of the day care community for, despite all of the symptoms resulting from AD, she was still able to be of help to others. Her strong sense of purpose was evident in her wanting to avoid "being late for work." Her "work" was not limited to helping other particip-ants, but also extended to some of her interactions with members of the staff. For example, the social worker reported that when she herself happened not to be in a good mood, Mrs. D would immedi-ately recognize the situation and would attempt to use humor to provoke a smile or laughter. Given all this, it was hardly surprising to learn from Mr. D that his wife "just loves going to the day care center," for it was there that she found the necessary cooperation from others (staff and participants alike) that resulted in numerous opportunities to use her remaining abilities so as to be a vital and valued member of the community.

Additionally, at the day care center, Mrs. D's difficulties, either with words or as exhibited in sensory-motor problems, were not the main focus of attention and she was never placed in a position in which her deficits were displayed over and over again to the exclusion of her intact abilities. Even when she did encounter problems, the social situation was such that she could rescue herself with humor by bringing some cheer to others. In that environment, "everyone makes mistakes," and Mrs. D found delight and safety in the combination of her admir-able social role and the simultaneous downplaying of her deficits.

Being a volunteer research subject

In addition to her being an important member of the day care center community, Mrs. D found still another way to shore up her feelings of self-worth by giving of her time as a research subject at the NIH. Although this may seem counterintuitive, especially given Dr. B's aversive reaction to being tested at NIH and Dr. M's negative reac-tion to her assessments by a speech therapist, one must bear in mind the psychological life of the particular individuals involved here and I will explore the differences in these individuals' reactions in the next chapter.

Mrs. D was quite aware of the serious problems caused by AD ("It's a hell of a disease") and was very open about its effects. For example, at times when she experienced word-finding problems or pronunciation problems in the course of conversation, she would say, "This is the Alzheimer's right now carrying on." She often expressed concern for other AD sufferers and also the hope that her participation in NIH studies would help researchers to find a cure. She told her husband that "when they make a breakthrough," he won't have to do the chores that she used to do but could do no longer. As Mrs. D said in a conversation with one of my graduate students (now Dr. Patricia Durbeck):

> *Mrs. D:* It took me a long time and they used me as what would you call it ? There's a word for that . . . anyway.
>
> *PD:* Subject? Is that the word you're looking for?
>
> *Mrs. D:* Yes, uh huh, they asked if I would take that. That was the nicety of it, cause I could have said "no", but believe me, if I can help me and my fe, [fellow] man, I would do it.
>
> *PD:* So you've been really helpful.
>
> *Mrs. D:* Yeah, yeah [*now begins to sing*]. "Like I give" . . . see if you can understand what I'm going to sing. I'm a singer. My father was a singer. We were all singers. [*Sings*] "I'll give to you and you'll give to me, true love, true love, and on and on it will always be, love forever true. For you and I have a guardian angel on high with nothing to do . . . but to give to me and to give to you, love forever true." Now, do you know who that person is?
>
> *PD:* Ah, let's see . . . is that Bing Crosby? Is it Bing Crosby?
>
> *Mrs. D:* No, it's Grace Kelly.
>
> *PD:* Oh, Grace Kelly. I was close – it was the right movie! And that's your philosophy, isn't it?
>
> *Mrs. D:* Why not? You know if we could all do this, we wouldn't have to have a lot of money!

Mrs. D's warm, generous, witty nature, along with her genuine concern for the well-being of others, found outlets at the day care center and at the NIH. Despite her serious cognitive deficits as highlighted on standard tests, she was able, with the help of healthy others, to bolster and maintain a strong sense of self-worth. She was, indeed, the life of the party, and she was doing what she could to aid in the search for a cure for AD. Everyone at the day care center recognized that about her and, most importantly, she was aware of that recognition.

In terms of Kitwood and Bredin's (1992) indicators of relative well-being which we expored in the previous chapter, we see that Mrs. D, in her personae of "Life of the Party" at the day care center and research subject at the NIH, revealed the assertion of will, helpfulness, the initiation of social contact, affectional warmth (greeting people and providing support to those in distress at the day care center), social sensitivity (accurately assessing and responding to the feelings of others), acceptance of other dementia sufferers, humor, creativity, and self-expression (initiating sing-alongs and telling jokes), and displays of pleasure ("that was the nicety of it"). It is possible, again using Kitwood and Bredin's ideas, to infer from her behavior a sense of agency in her ability to control situations through intentional action, her intention and willingness to help others, a sense of social confidence – she felt at ease with people and had something to offer them, and a sense of hope – she would attempt to affect others for the better so that their situations might be improved even for a short time.

Dr. B as "Scientific Collaborator" and Teacher

Dr. B, whom you met in Chapter 2, was an academic, a scientist, who attended the day care center two to three days per week. One of the striking things about his behavior at the day care center was his consistent refusal to participate in the program of activities led by the staff, in which virtually all participants were engaged. He eschewed games such as Bingo, Trivial Pursuit, bowling, and the various discussion groups which were held and, although he was always gracious and polite toward everyone at the center, he rarely engaged in anything more than superficial and brief conversation with other participants despite the encouragement given him by members of the staff.

Instead, he would often be found going into the office, seeking out one or another staff member for conversation and attention. If one were merely observing his behavior without knowing anything about him beyond his diagnosis, it would be rather easy to describe him as being aloof, antisocial, not a "team player." Knowledge of his diagnosis might even lead to other storylines about him, such as trying to hide his defects by avoiding a great deal of the activities which required attention, recall, and other key cognitive functions. Although this may be the case for many AD sufferers in specific circumstances, it was not altogether true for Dr. B. The motives behind his behavior were far more complex and also indicative of his own attempts to maintain some sense of self-esteem. Interestingly enough, although Mrs. D found avenues to achieve and maintain feelings of self-worth by being a vital participant at the day care center, Dr. B acted to achieve the same end by behaving in the diametrically opposite way.

It was readily apparent that Dr. B placed great pride in his achievements as an academic person, and, even though he was no longer actively engaged in scholarly pursuits, the same proclivities and tastes which led him to his vocational choices were still very much a part of his being. Yet, how was he to construct this aspect of his selfhood at a day care center in which the main activities consisted of things which never appealed to him in his entire adult life and which were also, in some cases, threatening to him? He was caught, as it were, in a situation in which the only social personae which he could find tacit cooperation to construct, were those of "day care center participant" and "AD patient," and these personae were anathema to him. Thus did he attempt to avoid the usual activities, and avoid being a member of the group, and thus did he attempt to restrict his social interactions to engaging healthy staff members in conversation. We will explore other aspects of these choices in Chapter 5. For now, his own words with regard to his situation at the day care center are telling:

Dr. B: And sometimes I have to fake, um, as to people that I deal with back and forth.

SRS: What do you have to fake?

Dr. B: Uh, I uh fake for uh, of course I feel I could have done more. Can I do better now? I don't know.

SRS: But when you say you have to fake, is that part of kowtowing to people?

Dr. B: Oh yeah. And, uh, it's a slick game.

SRS: When you say that you fake things does that mean that you have thoughts about what's going on and you don't say anything or try to be different?

Dr. B: Ya, or being different. The staff – I love them very dear, very, very much. I uh, don't necessarily need what's in the room [the room where games are played].

SRS: Where they play games? Trivial pursuit is one game.

Dr. B: Ah, that is impossible – like an asshole.

SRS: Do you think it's a foolish thing?

Dr. B: Ya, well, my wife and I are very strong academic people and uh, so, we start talking to each other, we talk to each other at a very high level right away. Uh, and uh, I mean, uh, most of these people here, most of them are good. But when I get closer, uh, I, uh, get information that's much, uh, that Trivial Pursuit. I wish I could find out how to make it break.

Here we find Dr. B expressing quite clearly both his warm feelings for the staff members and his disdain for the activities available to him at the day care center, indicating that Trivial Pursuit is "impossible," that he wishes he could "make it break." Of course, such a game requires the very recall memory that has been adversely affected due to AD, and that is one aspect of it which made it "impossible" for Dr. B. Then, too, the games were generally trivial and meaningless to him and he contrasted these with his interaction with his wife, characterizing the two of them as "very strong academic people" who talk at a "very high level." Just as revealing here is the way in which he contrasts the quality of his interaction with his wife with the nature of most of the people at the center – his manner was gracious and sincere when he commented that most of the people there are good, however he does indicate, in his behavior of avoiding them, that he does not consider the participants to be on the same level as that of himself and his wife. He was even more blunt about this issue in the following interchange:

Dr. B: Um, I, I, I'm groping as to how well can we do . . . I don't know if you get me right or wrong. I'm fishing for something.

SRS: Yes, I know.

Dr. B: I'm finishing [fishing] for something because the phenomenon of, of, if I'm working with you, I can – look, I can work in here for thirty times and all that but in *this* group, I'm nothing. ["This group" refers to the day care center participants.]

SRS: Maybe – that is, we could be working together a lot.

Dr. B: Yes.

SRS: But with the rest of the people in the day care center, you're nothing?

Dr. B: I'm nothing.

SRS: What do you want to be?

Dr. B: Well, I think in, in, very quickly, I think, I think it would be better, wait a minute. It takes on status . . . sometimes it's not a soft system between the two of us when I'm in the day tare [here he mispronounces "care"]. Maybe I'm crazy, but there's nothing that I can do about it.

SRS: Are you saying that you feel that you have no status with the rest of the day care people?

Dr. B: Oh, absolutely. Absolutely! There, there, should be some hier, hierarty.

SRS: So you feel that you're a pretty bright guy, but that you're not really treated differently than people who aren't as bright?

Dr. B: Ya, that's, that's forces me to do something like this. And I, I say that. Remember when you put the thing, when you gave me the letter [from the Dean]? It was a very strong statement that I am something above, or something like that.

SRS: You feel that you're not treated with as much deference as you think you deserve. Is that accurate?

Dr. B: Honestly, yes.

It was this lack of deference, the feeling that he was "nothing" among the group of participants, which led to his avoiding them and the activities at the center and to his being amenable to, indeed finding the necessity of, working with me. In our working relationship, I was ever mindful of his status as an academic person and treated him with the deference and respect which one would extend naturally to a senior colleague. I never addressed him by his first name, but rather as "Professor." The formality, however, did not in any way hinder the development of a strong, trusting, and warm bond between us. In this manner, I engaged him in a research project and in so doing, helped him to construct the social persona of "research collaborator," for in this project, he was indeed the subject, rather than an object, of study. Being the subject of study required nothing less than his collaboration and willing interest to participate, and furnished him with a means by which he could maintain his self-worth – by differentiating him from the rest of the group. In fact, he often asked me whether or not there were other day care participants with whom I was working, and the fact that he was the only participant with whom I was working at that time helped him to differentiate himself from the group even more. He took an additional step in differentiating himself from the other participants by asking the Director to place a sign with his name and mine as well as the times of our regularly scheduled meetings on the hallway bulletin board for all to see.

He recognized the significance of the project as I explained it to him, and commented: "Yeah, um and also like scientific stuff and uh, I uh, because I think as far as I'm concerned this is a real project, it's a monster." That he saw the project as "scientific stuff" further enhanced its value to him and, because he was a scientist himself, he found great value in his own role in the process.

As he became involved in what he would always refer to as "The Project," he also made himself available to some of my students who were doing an internship at the day care center. His interactions with the students provided him with additional opportunities to construct, with the students' cooperation, respect, and deference, the persona of "teacher" and he took pleasure in their presence:

> *Dr. B:* I don't mind the students . . . but I don't want three or four coming in.
>
> *SRS:* At one time?
>
> *Dr. B:* At one time, because you and I have pret, pretty good rapport.
>
> *SRS:* If one student wanted to walk with you?
>
> *Dr. B:* I have done that [indeed, he had] I've done that, because the students, oh heavens yes. So pull out good students.
>
> *SRS:* Thank you for doing that.
>
> *Dr. B:* Well, it helps me too.
>
> *SRS:* So nobody loses, huh?
>
> *Dr. B:* No, no one loses unless you have a schmuck.
>
> *SRS:* And you're not one of those and neither are my students.
>
> *Dr. B:* Oh, I know, they're sharp. Frequently the students are very sensitive.

It was clear from his comments above that he valued the opportunity to interact with the students, to be once again in a teacher-student relationship with young people. As it turned out, he was able to teach more than a deeper understanding of the experience of AD. An example of one such interaction involved a student who was taking a drawing course.

Because Dr. B had for many years been an artist, a painter, as a hobby, my student had shown him her work and asked for his opinion. Dr. B looked at the drawing and then indicated that she needed to add some things in order to make improvements. The drawing was of candlesticks and a few other mainly vertical objects in the center of the paper, and Dr. B told her that she needed something "like your eye" (something round or oval) in an area of the paper to which he pointed and made circular motions with his hand. It was to the left and toward the lower corner and then to the lower right corner that he motioned. The next day, she told me what Dr. B had said and also what her art professor said and I related all this to Dr. B:

> *SRS:* I had a conversation with Liz and she told me that you critiqued her drawing.
> *Dr. B:* I don't know that I did, you know, like that. In any event, what does this, uh, mean?
> *SRS:* Your comments were repeated exactly by her teacher – you and her teacher said exactly the same things.
> *Dr. B:* Yeah? And I'm a scientist, for Christ sake! [laughter].

He took great delight in this interchange, for his paintings were quite excellent, almost astounding in their surrealism, and here he was, in the throes of AD, giving critical feedback to a student and realizing that his own comments were virtually identical to those of the student's art professor. His last comment was uttered with a ringing pleasure, as if to say, "I'm a scientist by training, whose interest in painting and art is more of a hobby, and I was quite sharp in my artistic analysis of the student's work!" It was clear that he took a measure of great pride in the fact that his and an art professor's critical comments on the same work were identical. His final assertion that, "I'm a scientist . . ." further underscored how he viewed himself and how this episode gave him the opportunity to "show his stuff," as it were.

In these significant ways, Dr. B sustained and supported the healthy, positive Self 2 attributes he believed he still had. Likewise, he worked to construct valued Self 3 social personae by not associating himself with the day care participants who were "unhealthy" – instead, he associated with those, such as staff members, myself, my students, who were "healthy" and who were ready, willing, and able to recognize him as a person of accomplishment. In being recognized in this way, Dr. B was able to maintain some of his valued beliefs about his attributes and be treated with the deference and respect he had enjoyed throughout his adult life.

His need for and attainment of status

Although the construction of a Self 3 persona of "scientific collaborator" and "teacher of students" certainly helped Dr. B in the process of clearly differentiating himself from the other participants at the day care center, it became apparent that his need for status went beyond his own knowledge of what he was doing and the worthiness of his efforts. We may harken back to James' (1983) notion of being "noticed favorably" *by others* in this regard. The situation confronting the AD sufferer here is challenging to say the very least. Given his word-finding and other linguistic and recall problems, how could Dr. B explain to others exactly what admirable work he was doing? That is, how could he be noticed favorably in spite of the fact that he was at the day care center? He approached this issue and, at first, I failed to understand the profound meaning he was attempting to convey.

> *Dr. B:* I think I was very much wanting the project should go like faster and that I've lost something um which I may or may not really need. Again, the project is one that I feel very much uh, but from the professionals, they don't feel that is much status. Is there any name we could call for a project or would you rather not?
>
> *SRS:* You mean somebody to talk with about this?
>
> *Dr. B:* No, no, no, no – what is the name of this project? So what we can take a very decent project that, uh, something like a coordinous thing.
>
> *SRS:* Like a title?
>
> *Dr. B:* A title or a project or you – what's your name and what is it?
>
> *SRS:* I think we should work on a title.

I thought that I had understood what he was trying to convey to me, but that was true only to a limited degree. As I look back at it, I cannot imagine how I could have been so blind; it was Dr. B who would remove the blinders eventually. But at this early time, I thought that he wanted to work on a title and thus did not realize the significance of what would follow immediately in his words:

Dr. B: Let's think about it because it would bring a little more something.

SRS: Focus?

Dr. B: Focus. Now having said that, do you, we want that? Because I've had this, people talk to me and then I'm blum, blum, blum, what do I do? Well, blum, blum, blum. So it may I think, My G-d this is *real* stature to do! This is maybe picky, picky, picky, stuff.

SRS: I don't think so.

Dr. B: That's stature and what, who can be attached to somebody uh, in agreeable thing. Now if you don't like it . . .

SRS: Do you have any ideas for a title for this?

Dr. B: That's . . . I've been thinking about it for a long, long time. I thought about this before. I thought I had and now it's *tsuris.* [Yiddish for grief: he's saying that he thought about it but that now it's not retrievable.]

SRS: But it's in there somewhere.

Dr. B: Somewhere – where we can do status. If somebody calls me and says "what are you doing?" and then I write this thing, what is it? Now it could be a very long, long thing in the project from your university or something else. Do you think I'm silly?

SRS: No. No, not at all.

Dr. B: Some sort of status.

SRS: If you're going to write something it's a good idea to have a title.

Dr. B: Am I picky on this thing?

SRS: No, you're an active participant.

Dr. B: Oh sure, and I was thinking to myself, "Hey now wait a minute, I'm involved in this thing and it doesn't matter what it's called."

SRS: I was thinking about a title. It's got to be something that will grab the attention.

Dr. B: Okay, because I can be set or attached to some, some project, you know, a senior project or something like that so that I would have this sort of status.

At this time, I had been focused, not only with Dr. B but on my own, on the question of the title for the project and, as a result, I did not understand clearly the other aspect of what he was saying to me. He was saying, first of all, that when people ask him what he is doing and he wants to tell them about the project, what does he say? ("...what do I do? Well, blum, blum blum..."). He then comments that working on this project is "*real* stature to do," and then goes on later to say, "If somebody calls me and says 'what are you doing?' and then I write this thing, what is it? Now it could be a very long, long thing in the project from your university or something else."

Here we see the predicament he was facing:

1 Working on the project provides him with stature, with status, which is important to him.
2 Yet, given his linguistic and other problems due to AD, he cannot describe clearly to others exactly what he's doing, and thus cannot be looked upon favorably by others as one who has a certain admirable status despite AD. Recall that in his view, he was lacking status at the day care center.
3 He then hints at what he needs – something in writing from my university which would, essentially, "do the talking for him," by explaining to others exactly what he has done and is doing to have achieved the "status" that he desires and believes he deserves.

When I finally realized what it was he needed and wanted, I arranged with Rev. Robert B. Lawton, SJ, then Dean of Georgetown University's College of Arts and Sciences, to write a letter of commendation to Dr. B, acknowledging the wonderful contribution he was making not only to the Georgetown students, but also to furthering the understanding of the remaining intact abilities among people with AD. However, between the time that the letter was written, sent, and finally received, Dr. B had run out of patience waiting for the recognition he desired, and decided to remove himself from "The Project."

There was no mistaking the profound sadness in his voice and posture when he said:

Dr. B: We have got nothing now. Um, this is very difficult for me, I tell you. We have to leave the project.

SRS: You have to stop working with me?

Dr. B: Ya.

SRS: Is it something that I did?

Dr. B: No, no, no.

SRS: Or

Dr. B: Heavens no. Um, we . . . oh G-d, this is so difficult. I, we, feel that, uh, you have been just great, absolutely great. Yet, um, I am, I'm sort of, what do I, it's difficult for me to say. But the project, my wife and I want to do different things. We've been, I mean, we've spent fair amount of things. Because it's just too much for us. It came out very slowly. Uh, we feel, we feel that among other things we have not, our got what we think what we might have done. We're sort of tired on some of these things. But the big project, the big thing is we decided it's too much, it's too much.

SRS: It's a strain on you?

Dr. B: Well it is in a strain, yeah, the project from going through all kind of work, it's difficult. We had a long session as to what we're gonna do about this thing. It's very difficult right now. No real compensation in very ways. Um, I, I feel it's too tight. Bringing up more information, I feel sort of torn. I love the students. We have go, we have done a lot of work for the project and I'm sort of dry about the thing right now. I just can't do it for no compensation, for one thing. Um, for your friendship is wonderful. It pains me, it pains me.

SRS: What kind of compensation do you mean?

Dr. B: Well, the compensation is itself minor. I have sort of told over and over again. The students are wonderful. We've done a good service with things already done. I don't know what else to say. I think in the main if we did more, we could have had more. I'm torn in everything and the little squabbles that the university never really gave me, or something.

SRS: What sort of thing did you want from the university? Did you want some form of recognition?

140

Dr. B: I've been saying that for so long that I think it's over the hump.

I interpreted his last comment, "I think it's over the hump," to mean something akin to "it's too late now," but I then owned up to my own misunderstanding of what he was trying to convey to me:

SRS: I guess I was confused for a long time about what sort of recognition you wanted.

Dr. B: Yet I had or should or wanted – something should have been done. The university could have had *some* status.

SRS: So you feel offended?

Dr. B: I said that so long, or felt that so long. Right now I'm having difficult to work on it at all.

SRS: I'm sorry.

Dr. B: I feel so sorry too, but I never got some real status for me. What you started is fabulous as far as I can see. We could have done it before.

SRS: I can only thank you for the time we had. Was there something that I failed to do?

Dr. B: No. You were admirable. That's all I can say.

SRS: Well, I just want to assure you that anytime I'm here and you want to chat or go for a walk, that's fine with me.

Dr. B: I wished there were more things, more possible.

SRS: Why are you torn?

Dr. B: I wished the university had been – easily get something.

SRS: You wanted something more than a letter of commendation?

Dr. B: It would have been nice for the puniest . . .

SRS: If you had gotten a letter of commendation from the Dean, would that have made any difference to you?

Dr. B: It would have done.

SRS: Because I spoke with him and he said he would send one to you.

Dr. B: Who?

SRS: The Dean. I mentioned you to him and told him of the contribution you were making to me and to my students, and he said he would send you a letter. You haven't received it yet?

Dr. B: It's too late.

SRS: So you got angry?

141

Dr. B: No.

SRS: Disappointed?

Dr. B: Ya. I know that I was sending signals all the time . . . well, the signals were that I was wanting some sort of commend and some things.

SRS: I didn't understand immediately. I thought you meant something else.

Dr. B: I send out so many signals.

SRS: I know, but

Dr. B: I talked my ass off and I felt I was sending out so many signals.

SRS: I apologize. Your disappointment shouldn't be with the university, but with me because I was confused. You said something about a title and it was only last week that I realized what you actually meant. I never intended for you to feel slighted.

Dr. B: I never would think that.

SRS: Okay. Well, thank you for the time you've spent with me. I'll certainly never forget it.

Dr. B had made what he thought were several requests for some tangible recognition that he felt he needed and deserved, but which to date, he had not received. As a result he felt, with great and unmistakable sadness, that he could not go on with the project. I, on the other hand, had fallen prey to the trap I was determined to avoid: I assumed that when he spoke of status, of stature, of a title, that he meant a title for the project as opposed to some form of status for himself. When he said that when people ask him what he is doing he cannot say exactly what it is, that should have tipped me off, but I misunderstood and thought he needed clarification for himself regarding the nature of the project. I mistakenly did not pursue the matter initially. And now, having made what he thought was a reasonable request and having received nothing, his only remaining option was to act to preserve his dignity. Unfortunately, he had not as yet received the letter from the Dean.

This episode spoke multitudes to me and still speaks to me as I write. Here we have a man who had a number of serious problems in the cognitive realm and who, in addition, was experiencing great frustration about those problems and his own lack of ability to do anything about them. And yet, for all of those problems which are so clearly underscored by formal testing, he was clearly capable of acting in a way to preserve his feelings of self-worth. He was exercising control in the situation. His sensibilities had been assaulted and he was not about to accept that treatment for another day. It is a matter of great interest to me that, in formal assessments of cognitive ability, physicians and neuropsychologists ask people to do all sorts of tasks, from naming objects, to spelling, to reading, to following commands, to interpreting proverbs, and more. Yet, far more fundamental and, perhaps complex, than any of the test-based elements of cognitive function, is the cognitive function that is involved in the assertion of one's sense of dignity, of self-worth, and there are no objective tests to measure the extent to which a person owns such qualities of mind.

For a person who has, over the course of decades, worked hard and received recognition more or less commensurate with his effort, the absence of such recognition is anathema. This is to be expected. Yet here, in the case of a person who could be classified as suffering from a form of dementia – who could be called, in some circles, moderately to severely demented – is the preservation of all those cognitive and brain functions that involve the expression of pride and dignity. In addition, there is also the preservation of brain functions that are involved in the expression of disappointment, sorrow, the desire not to hurt someone who had been recognized as being "wonderful" and "admirable." It is unfortunate that in our formal assessments of cognitive function, we have not found it necessary to include fundamental aspects of human character and integrity. Feeling slighted or feeling as though one has been treated in an undignified way requires a highly complex combination of functions involving memory, attention, emotion, and abstract thought – such as the idea of fairness. And, even though Dr. B could not dress himself, he was still able to assert, and work to maintain, his sense of proper pride, and to understand and ask for reciprocity.

Dr. B did not truly want to remove himself from the project, but his sense of dignity and his need to preserve and maintain feelings of self-esteem, perhaps more important now than ever, required extreme measures. That some form of recognition was, indeed, the critical issue in this episode was made quite clear when I encountered him at the day care center in the aftermath of his having received the letter from Fr. Lawton.

This was the first time I had seen him since he quit the project and so I did not expect that Dr. B would be involved in anything with me beyond a few pleasantries. I did not know at that moment that he had received the letter, and so I just greeted him with the abiding warmth I felt toward him. I should point out again that one of Dr. B's problems involved finding the correct words to use, so that when he would say "weeks," he often meant "days" as in the extract of conversation which follows:

Dr. B: Everything's okay. First of all, how are you doing?

SRS: Well, thanks.

Dr. B: Everybody is telling me about this project.

SRS: Are they asking you if you're interested in doing it?

Dr. B: In a sense. Because two or three weeks ago, four weeks ago, I had, uh, just about given up on the project and the project, and said "oh the hell with it." But three or four people were telling me different things. I know this is crazy. Everybody was talking about it. I sort of wanted to give you what I'm been up to. And do we, do I, do you, do somebody else start working on this, or something like that? Um, in the meantime I was getting information for you and for me. At one time I was frustrated on who does the project.

SRS: You didn't know exactly what your part was?

Dr. B: Well, I did and I did not because people were assuming that I was off the thing. People were telling me that I was out of the project. You sent a nice letter to my wife.

SRS: [*thinking that he was referring to a letter I had sent to his wife many weeks earlier*] That was quite a while ago.

Dr. B: It just got to me. I still feel, of course, I have still feel that I would just, you know, continue for the two of us.

SRS: Did you get a letter from the Dean?

Dr. B: Oh yeah, I've got it right in my pocket.

SRS: Terrific. I'm glad.

Dr. B: Have you seen it?

SRS: No.

Dr. B: Oh, you haven't?

SRS: What do I know? Who am I? [*joking*].

Dr. B: You're just a peo, just a peon [*chuckling*].

144

He then showed me a copy of the letter and I read it immediately.

SRS: That's lovely. The Dean . . .
Dr. B: Ya, is he a nice guy?
SRS: He's very nice.
Dr. B: Oh, good . . . I still absorb things, but I lose things – a sweater here, a sweater there.

During this conversation, I chose not to remind him that he had taken himself out of the project the previous week. It was clear that the letter from the Dean had made a huge difference in his outlook. He was so delighted, in fact, that he asked his wife to make copies so that he could carry a copy with him and save the original at home. When he arrived at the day care center for the first time after having received the letter, he showed the letter to the staff members. The director of the center read the letter aloud to the rest of the participants who responded with resounding applause. Dr. B acknowledged the response with his head slightly bowed and a shy, modest, smile as if to say, "please don't, but thank you just the same."

The letter gave Dr. B what he so desperately needed and wanted: a form of acknowledgement so that he might be looked upon favorably by others, a way to enhance and maintain his feelings of self-worth. For a person who had always been involved in some significant work, and who had earned great admiration for his efforts, the thought of having nothing tangible to show for his present efforts – which he himself could not accurately convey – was deeply distressing. Simultaneously distressing was the thought that he would be viewed simply as an AD sufferer who attended an adult day care center while his wife worked. His distress made a great deal of sense to me. After all, he chose not to participate in the usual activities in which just about everyone else was involved, and was directly involved with a number of students, that he might teach them his experience of the disease. So why should his selfhood be defined solely in terms of AD and its various symptoms?

That he did, in fact, teach students a great deal was evident not only in their comments during the course, but also in a letter which I received from one student who had since graduated, Heather Markey, after she heard of Dr. B's death:

Dr. Sabat,

I spoke with Beth yesterday and she informed me of Dr. B's death. I cannot find words to express my feelings as I heard Beth's words. He was a wonderful man who taught us all so much. I can still hear his voice as he ran his fingers through his fiery grey hair: "the project," "it comes in blobs," "everyone loves Christina," recognizing me as "you're with the man," the pipes out front that he wanted to paint, pointing out the different directions we could walk in the park out back. The images of him are endless. He struggled so much. It is nice to know that he is now at peace though he will surely be missed by many. No other person and no book could ever have taught me as much as Dr. B did. It is truly a shame that your future classes will not have the opportunity to meet this wonderful man. But I can already hear you as you tell them the many stories you have of the times with him and our class. I don't doubt that he will play a large role in many of your lectures. Fortunately, there are many other wonderful people at the center who will touch the lives of all who know them. Please give my best to everyone at the center. I miss them all. Dr. B's greatest quality was his ability to affect all of us who knew him. He will continue living in all of us and in all that he showed us.

Henry Adams said, "A teacher affects eternity; he never knows where his influence ends." Dr. B wanted acknowledgment for his work as a teacher and collaborator. Having received that acknowledgment from the Dean, he continued to teach my students and to collaborate with me on "The Project." The man who had problems putting on his pants and keeping track of his sweaters was able, nonetheless, to fulfill his mission to teach young people and to affect their lives in a lasting, positive way. Here we have qualities of dignity, motivation, persistence, and caring, all of which were clearly present in Dr. B, but none of which is assessed or revealed through formal standardized testing. His test scores did not predict that he had, in abundance, the qualities that would earn him the highest accolade that a teacher can receive. The test of his performance in the arena of everyday life, however, told a completely different tale, as he worked diligently to add to the lives of others and simultaneously to preserve and maintain his own self-esteem. All that was necessary for him to achieve both goals was the opportunity which could be given only by healthy others in his world.

146

Dr. M as Social Worker, Teacher, and Guide

Dr. M, whom you met in Chapter 2, had also been an academic for decades and was deeply embarrassed, angered, and depressed by her inability to find words and speak with the grace and incisiveness as she had for most of her life. There was, however, some variability in the fluency of her speech, such that she was more fluent on some days than on others. On one such occasion in spring, she and I took a walk in the woods near her home; she walked with bare feet and I wore dress shoes. She navigated the woods rather well and I spent an embarrassing amount of time slipping and sliding. The next time we met, we talked about that walk:

SRS: Well ya, and you know what? I'll tell you something. While we were taking that walk, you didn't seem to have a great deal of trouble making yourself understood at all.

Dr. M: No, I had no trouble. *You* had the trouble!

SRS: [*laughter*] It's true. That was a very humbling experience.

Dr. M: What?

SRS: Well, I mean here you were walking barefoot through this whole place and there I was uh, being a little uncertain about myself, and, and you noticed, you pointed out everything to me, you showed me what was where and you knew exactly where we were going and uh, uh, but when you spoke with me, when you asked me something or when you said something, you were very clear.

Dr. M: Well, I guess my role was a different one.

SRS: I think that makes a lot of sense. I wonder if, when you're taking a walk, you have fewer problems finding words.

Dr. M: Yes, probably. But, well you see, I, I'm the teacher, not the, the thing, and uh, uh, being a teacher uh, wasn't, isn't something very – I can see the flower. It's not, I'm not, that I understand all the flowers and all the other things, it's just I guess what it is, and I have the role of a person who, and maybe I'm losing some of that too. I guess so. I guess you're right. I had, wouldn't, didn't think of it.

SRS: So when we were taking a walk you had a different role in the sense that you were leading,

147

Dr. M: Um hum.

SRS: guiding, showing,

Dr. M: And I, and I've, don't have very much of that now.

SRS: Ya.

Dr. M: Um hum, so thank you!

SRS: Thank *you*!

Dr. M: All right! Come on, we have some uh, time. Let me be the teacher for about 15 minutes. I hope you appreciate what I'm going to show you.

In what was, and still is to me, a moment of powerful insight, Dr. M articulated something fundamental about the relationship between the social situation confronting the AD sufferer and the effect of that situation on his or her behavior. Here she was the leader, the teacher, the guide (for when we were walking in the woods I had no idea of where we were or how we got there). Her role, as she put it in the sociological argot which was hers by training, was different from the role she found herself in so very often since her diagnosis. In social constructionist terms, I cooperated with her in the construction of the valued social persona of teacher, of guide, and in that position, her fluency of speech improved. That this situation brought her satisfaction was clear not only in her thanking me for giving her the opportunity to construct the persona of teacher or guide, but also in her final comment in the extract, in which she seeks to return to that position, that role which she "doesn't have very much of" anymore, in order to show me something that she hopes I'll appreciate. Here she is in the position of giving something of value to another person and she clearly relishes the opportunity.

Her reaction to being diminished

This situation may be contrasted with another social situation which occurred when she first went to a support group for people with AD. Her deeply devoted and loving husband attended a support group for caregivers every other week, and at the same location there was a support group for AD sufferers which met at the same time as did the caregivers' group. In this way, caregivers were spared the problem of having to find someone to stay with their afflicted family member during the caregivers' meeting. As a result, Mr. M prevailed upon his wife to attend the AD sufferers' group, believing that the groups could benefit them both. However, Dr. M's great reluctance to continue to attend her group meetings was a source of consternation to her husband, for he wanted her to understand that her going to her group helped him to attend his without having to worry about her well-being at the same time. Her reasons for not wanting to attend, however, were significantly connected to the issue of maintaining her own self-esteem. One such reason emerged in the following extract about her initial experience of going to the support group:

> *Dr. M:* When I came in to the program there uh, the person thought I was a uh, a person – not a group person.
> *SRS:* Um hum.
> *Dr. M:* And then when she found out that I had *that*, I, I uh, I was feeling very bad about it and uh, because she said, "I'll, I'll talk to your hu, your husband." And I got out and I said I, I don't want to be in it at first. I have to think about it and do this. What's in it for me? That's awful.

Here, one of the support group leaders approached and began to talk with Dr. M, initially thinking that Dr. M was "a person" and not an AD sufferer, or a "group person." The moment Dr. M's diagnosis became known ("And then when she found out that I had *that* . . ."), the leader abruptly ceased speaking with Dr. M and announced that she would speak with Mr. M, who was "a person." The conjunction of the two events produced in Dr. M a feeling of great distress, for the group leader, now aware of the diagnosis, placed Dr. M in a junior position even though she is an intelligent adult. If Dr. M had not been identified as having the disease, her interlocutor would not have acted as she had.

In such a situation, the person with whom Dr. M was speaking might have explained briefly *why* she needed to speak with Mr. M, thereby granting Dr. M the social status of an equal instead of abruptly placing her in some sort of implied junior, in other words less competent, position. I do not for a moment believe that it was the intention of the group leader to act in a derrogatory or demeaning way so as to cause Dr. M anguish. However, in the immediacy of the moment, Dr. M was not granted the status she deserved and *which she was indeed being granted* until she was identified as being an

Alzheimer's sufferer. Here we have another example of malignant social psychology and we see the profound assault that it has on the afflicted person's sense of self-worth.

It is quite a journey from being a "Doctor," a "Professor," to being a "Patient." After decades of living as the former with all that that entails, it is difficult to be viewed by so many, so much of the time, as the latter with all that that entails. Having a diagnosis of Alzheimer's disease, however, does not entail the loss of one's advanced degrees or of the education that the degrees represent. It need not entail the loss of the respect and deference usually given to a person of that stature or any person for that matter, regardless of educational background. Nonetheless, this experience was deeply troubling to Dr. M and was one of her reasons for not wanting to attend the support group.

Finding a strategy for maintaining her self-esteem

Another reason, also connected to the issue of self-esteem, emerged in another conversation. Keeping in mind Dr. M's reaction to her word-finding problems, it should come as no surprise that, once she began to attend the support group meetings, she would be emotionally reactive to the situations she confronted there. We begin to understand her wish to avoid the meetings in the following, which began with my comment that she still had the opportunity to teach others about the abilities which remain intact despite AD, and Dr. M begins to discuss a situation which arose in the support group meeting she attended:

SRS: Maybe if the fates had it differently we wouldn't even have met because there wouldn't be any Alzheimer's disease and you'd be doing social work. But, what I want you to know is that you have a chance even now to be teaching.

Dr. M: Uh, that, that makes me think of what happened yesterday, one of the things that happened yesterday. Uh, we go to group. Did I tell you about that? I'm in a group that has about five people and uh they're all Alzheimer's. Then there is a teacher – not a teacher, a uh, probably a sociologist or a psychologist. The people in the group are not very uh, out of the four or five there's one or two who, that interest me and uh, and then last

150

night, uh yesterday the, the people, the caretaker in the group uh, uh was good that day . . . I felt, she, she told the people who uh had uh ability to come and talk uh and I had a very neat thing, a statement and I had to, I, I couldn't handle it. Um anyhow, they were talking about how they could make it organized. I couldn't put that in them. I knew exactly what they should do and uh, and I, I at least – I don't mean that I was perfect – I mean there's a way of bringing in and uh, and so I say I watched them and I saw what was going on and I was not a hero. I couldn't, I, I, I said nothing. And at the end, the caretaker said, "You haven't said anything, what do you think? We haven't heard from you." Now the fact was that I knew that it was something that had been done and would have and should have been done and that was good. And it was good with a good person who could pick it up. I know what to do with it . . . But it was not appropriate at all to, to, to say this. I wanted to say that I felt very bad about it when they said "why aren't you saying anything?" And then the good caretaker [group leader] said, "what do you think?" And I said, "I think I'll tell you the next time [*chuckles*] what it is." And it was, it made me, I, I felt that I wasn't myself, and I couldn't in my role, I couldn't do, I couldn't have done the thing and the good caretaker said, "Remember, you said you'd talk." And then when Mr. M and I got in the car, I felt so awful. It was, it was here's the opportunity in place I didn't like very, I wasn't appreciating, uh what should be, could be. And now I have the, the, the problem of saying "why didn't you say?" or "You said you promised to be there" and I don't know quite how to handle that. See, we don't know each others' backgrounds at all, and our experiences are different, and uh, I, I don't know how to – I think the good caretaker is there we may do a good thing. I haven't seen very much of it. Nobody says uh, what – that's a problem. What do you do, doctor? You told me I could call you "doctor" [*chuckles*].

SRS: Let me see if I understand you here. You see an opportunity to give some constructive criticism.

Dr. M: Well ya. People are not all there at the same time.

SRS: And you have some thoughts about how to organize it.

Dr. M: Ya, *but* it's not my role.

SRS: Well, you know what? There's a word in Yiddish.

Dr. M: What it it?

SRS: *Chutzpah.* And it means nerve.

Dr. M: Uh huh.

SRS: I think a little *chutzpah* on your part wouldn't hurt.

Dr. M: But it would if I could talk.

SRS: Oh, you mean, you'd be

Dr. M: That's the rest of the story! [*laughs heartily*].

SRS: You mean you'd be very barbed in your criticism?

Dr. M: No, I would not. I would be if – I know I would not be barbed. I wanted to, to, to say things but not in a nice way but, but I

SRS: You held back?

Dr. M: Ya, but I don't know how to hold back.

SRS: Then don't!

Dr. M: [*laughs*] But if that group is not uh, ...guess I don't want to go.

SRS: Are you fearful that you might offend somebody?

Dr. M: No, I, I don't think I'd . . . I would be careful not to.

SRS: Well then, why make a big deal out of it? You can offer an opinion, why not? It might teach something . . . if you have some suggestions to make about how to improve things,

Dr. M: But I can't talk!

SRS: Well you just explained the whole thing to me!

Dr. M: No, but you understand very well, uh, both parts of the problem. I don't want to go.

SRS: It's a challenge, though.

Dr. M: But I – okay, it's

SRS: A challenge. If you want to say something to the group,

Dr. M: Um hum.

SRS: you have an idea about what you want to say.

Dr. M: Um hum.

SRS: And you said to me, "But I can't talk." You're talking to me and you say, "well, you understand." Now what you have to say to the group is, "Bear with me."

Dr. M: Um hum. I have a problem, and . . .

SRS: and I need some time to talk about this because I can't find the words that easily. But if you give me time I'll be able to – I'll try.

Dr. M: That's a neat thing! [*chuckling*].

SRS: You think?

Dr. M: Ya [*chuckling*].

SRS: But you see what it is? It's taking a certain amount of control. *Taking* the control for yourself. If someone else has not *given* you the opportunity or doesn't seem to understand that you need time to develop, to find, the words that you want to use, then *you* have to say, "Wait a minute, bear with me, please don't interrupt, I'll get to it, you have to be patient."

Dr. M: "That's what I'm here for."

SRS: Right! I think you can do it and I think you can do it very nicely.

Dr. M: Thank you. Want to come over?

SRS: I think I might very well want to do that.

Dr. M: All right! Now let's, let's think of in terms of uh, getting some cl, cloat, closure for this day,

SRS: Um hum.

Dr. M: and what's going to happen for the next day.

SRS: Okay. See, now, there you go! You see what you just did? You said "let's do this, and let's do that" very nicely, but direct.

In this conversation it is possible to see clearly how a word-finding problem can have far-reaching effects. Here Dr. M who, for a lifetime, exulted in her ability to use language beautifully now finds herself behaving in ways that go against her nature – she held back, but in her words, "I don't know how to hold back." That is, it was never her nature to be silent about an issue which she could address intelligently. Now, in the support group meeting she doesn't offer an opinion even though she has the knowledge and background to provide insights. She is reluctant to attend the support group and to offer constructive suggestions about how it should be conducted for two reasons. One is that she is convinced "can't talk" and be "herself" and is embarrassed as a result. The other reason is that it wasn't her "role" to organize the group, in her opinion. She did, however, explain to me the aspects of the situation that gave her discomfort despite her word-finding problems. Thus she was able to communicate effectively. But why was she able to talk to me and at the same time believe that she could not do so in the group setting?

Her reason, as she presented it to me, was that I "understood" her. My ability to understand her, however, derived in part from my willingness to give her all the time she needed to formulate and to express her thoughts, for I understood that her word-finding problems required such time and imposed no pressure on her. Thus, I gave her the control and the time that she needed. In the group, she didn't feel that she was given the control she required in order to express herself. My point to her was that she, herself, could do something to establish control over the situation by stating her needs and asking the group to cooperate. Her response to that suggestion was one of somewhat bridled glee, saying, "That's a neat thing" with a warm, almost giddy, chuckle in her voice.

At the end of this conversation, she took control of the topic by saying, "All right! Now let's, let's think of in terms of uh, getting some cl, cloat, closure for this day . . . and what's going to happen for the next day." Such a suggestion is reflective of the way in which a clinical social worker/therapist would speak, and it was precisely with the intention of doing clinical work that Dr. M earned her M.S.W. degree after she retired from teaching. Thus, with my cooperation, Dr. M was able to construct a social persona in which she took great pride and satisfaction. In so doing, she was also taking a very active part in bringing our meeting to an end and planning ahead for our next meeting. Taking a very active and instrumental part in interpersonal interaction was one of the abiding and, to Dr. M, defining attributes from which she derived great satisfaction and in which she took great pride.

The Dialectics of Self-Esteem and Taking Control

It is plainly apparent that there is a loss of control over various aspects of life as a result of AD. Some functions, such as word-finding, are clearly and directly compromised. In the present situation, the loss of control needed to speak one's mind is not due to the disease alone. Rather, such loss of control and the related ramifications also result from the person's *reaction to* the effect(s) of the disease, as well as the subsequent behavior of others. It is in these latter areas that modifications are possible, because it is possible to alter the person's reactions to the effects of the disease and to alter the behavior of others. In other words, although Dr. M had word-finding problems, they alone did not prevent her from speaking her mind and communicating, for

154

she did so with me. And if I was able to provide optimum conditions for her to communicate, others could do so as well. She could help others toward this end by telling them exactly what it is that she requires of them. In altering their behavior, she would gain control over the situation and could now behave in a way more consistent with what she views as being positive aspects or attributes of her nature.

When we examine the fruits of the above conversation, we find Dr. M reflecting on her own behavior possibly in the following way:

- I can't speak well. This is not me, for I have been able to speak well since I was a child.
- I have always spoken my mind directly. I don't do that now. This is not me.
- I have always made constructive suggestions when I was asked to provide them, but I don't do that now. This is not me.

Thus, the Self 2 attributes which she manifests at present are diminishing and constitute for her a source of lowered feelings of self-worth. Such thinking is similar to that of the dialectic of "what I am not, but might otherwise be" that we encountered toward the beginning of this chapter.

Of the three features described above, the second and the third are outcomes of the loss of control over situations in which others are present, and can be the sources of great anxiety, sadness, and embarrassment. Her embarrassment was so great that she did not want to attend the group anymore. Such reactions also may contribute to what some might call "personality changes." In these instances, the "personality changes" follow directly from the problems stemming from the reactions to the loss of control and of feelings of self-worth. Dr. M, however, took seriously what I said to her and, at our next meeting, informed me of what she planned to say at the next support group meeting in an attempt to regain some control over the situation and thus to allay her feelings of embarrassment:

Dr. M: I think I told you that uh, I find it hard to talk, uh so uh I and so I didn't talk [at the group meeting]. Did I tell you that?
SRS: Um hum.
Dr. M: And uh, I said I'll do it next time. So we had all these people getting together and so here's what I'm going to say for

155

this thing. Something like this: What I'd like to say, uh, for my, me as a member of the group, uh where, uh, uh, I, I wanted to tell you about myself and this is very, very little talking. Uh, and but, I, but it's at this I look at where I'm c – oh – people coming from everywhere, so this mixes the people and me personally and anything,

SRS: Um hum.

Dr. M: That is relevant. Uh I think that uh, I, I was a person who has spent all my life as a professor, all about talking. But in the last two and three years I've have much decreased ability. My big plo, problems is words . . . [*Now as an aside to me*] I don't have these people knowing.

SRS: Oh I see, they don't realize what your problem is.

Dr. M: They don't – no and that's, *that's crazy* . . . So I, I had prepared, I just thought that what I need, uh, what the group needs, to introduce themselves to each other.

SRS: I understand. It's kind of like going out on a blind date every week.

Dr. M: [*laughs heartily*] It is! [*Again as if to say to the group*] My big problems is words: finding, speaking, remembering. So I need to have some time. [*Now to me*] Each one has to say what they want, okay? I need to have some for, some time for, to tell . . .

So here Dr. M has put together some thoughts to share with the others in her group so as to alert them to what her main problems are and what she needs from them in order to speak to them. In this way, it is possible for her to create, with the cooperation of others, the optimum circumstances for her own participation. At previous meetings, she told me, she didn't talk very much:

SRS: Wow. That's pretty amazing to me that you don't talk very much there, because you have so much to say.

Dr. M: [*laughs*] Ya, uh huh, okay. [*Again, as if to the group*] So we should take a little bit of time to help each other relating problems.

SRS: That's very important because if someone else doesn't know that you need a little more time to find the words you want, then you don't get the time you need.

156

Dr. M: Um hum.

SRS: And then you can't participate, and somebody else might have a different problem,

Dr. M: Ya, and that's good and I wanted it for the that other people should be aware that they could do it.

SRS: What you've put together here is wonderful for a couple of different reasons I think – I'm not perfect, so I don't know all of the reasons, but

Dr. M: You're not? [*laughs*].

SRS: Amazing isn't it? It's taken me all these years to figure it out.

Dr. M: When you're older, you know.

SRS: [*laughs*] You see, what you're doing here is you're asserting yourself.

Dr. M: I'm what?

SRS: You're asserting yourself by making suggestions about what you need and you're also thinking in terms of the group and how to make it better.

Dr. M was hereby creating the groundwork for enlisting the cooperation of the other members of the group – the very cooperation required for her to express valued Self 3 social personae and manifest her own valued Self 2 attributes. She was also manifesting an aspect of Self 3 with me in the very same process: her training as a sociologist and a social worker involved the study of group dynamics and now, in order to deal effectively with the issues surrounding her participation in the support group, she was calling upon skills and concepts that were part of her life as a member of the academic community. As she went through the various points and suggestions she was planning to make to the group, the intonation and rhythm of her voice reflected thoughtful, poised, bearing. Here was the teacher, the guide, the concerned member of the group – all present in the style she manifested, all deeply valued by her as she prepared to reclaim feelings of self-worth in the support group setting. She related her success in that effort when we met again after she attended the support group meeting:

Dr. M: It's important to say that for in the time I got into the place I uh, told them as I had not done in other times that I had uh, I, I told them what I felt – why I did not – remember they asked me why I didn't talk and I sa, I explained them and I said uh I uh, I don't know exactly but it was, the point was that I did a lot of talking and it was part of my job and uh, but I can't do it now because I, I can't speak in the way that was necessary, or something like that.

SRS: Uh huh.

Dr. M: So that was all right and we had it.

SRS: That was wonderful that you were so direct about it.

Dr. M: Well, this was after the talking we had.

SRS: Ah – well, I'm very glad.

Dr. M: Oh yes – you should be!

Dr. M's intial reluctance to attend the support group meetings was not based upon a lowered sense of group self-esteem – that is, the belief that being part of such a group would diminish her in her own eyes. Rather, her reluctance was based upon her estimation of her own diminished linguisitic abilities and her wish to avoid being embarrassed as a result. That this was the case was evident in her positive reaction to attending the group once she had developed a way to make her thoughts and feelings known to the group. In the process, her beliefs about her positive attributes were supported as were her feelings of self-worth and pride in being able to have a positive effect on the group dynamics and thereby make worthy contributions to others. There is a great deal more to the story of Dr. M and her support group which I will take up in Chapter 5.

Summary

Mrs. D, Dr. B, and Dr. M did not base their estimations of their self-worth on a simple assessment of their understanding of others' assessments of them. Instead, their sense of their own self-worth reflected a far more complex set of interactions between their attributes and beliefs about their attributes, along with the social opportunities available to manifest their valued attributes while minimizing potential sources of embarrassment and humiliation. These persons faced the problem of dealing with the dysfunctional attributes they now had due to AD while at the same time trying to manifest the worthy, valued attributes they enjoyed for the preponderance of their healthy, adult lives. The problem could be compounded in the social world, when healthy others viewed them principally in terms of their diagnoses and thus attended mainly to their current disabilities. As a result, each person desperately needed healthy others with whom they could construct social personae (Self 3) which reflected the cherished attributes they once so easily displayed. In order for such personae to become manifest, healthy others had to refrain from (a) focusing attention mainly on the dysfunctional attributes resulting from AD, and (b) creating the associated storylines which represent behavior in terms of dysfunction alone. Instead, healthy others had to look into the totality of each person with AD in the context of his or her own interests, needs, proclivities, values, and dispositions, as developed and maintained over the course of decades of healthy adult life, in order to gain clues about the social personae in which the afflicted found value.

On the basis of the foregoing, perhaps the following points can frame in words what the afflicted person apprehends to one degree or another:

1 There are within me even now, attributes I have from my past in which I have taken and still take great pride.
2 There are, within me, still other attributes which are a result of AD, and these attributes constitute a source of tremendous embarrassment and torment me; they indicate my decline, and prevent me from being seen in a variety of positive, worthy, and valued ways. I am aware of the difference between my former abilities and my present ones, and this negatively affects my sense of self-worth tremendously. If I do something which healthy others do not at first understand, they interpret my behavior as dysfunctional and symptomatic of my disease, and treat me accordingly. They often do not look further and help me to communicate my solid reasons for doing what I did or feeling as I felt. Most of what I hold to be worthy about me is being obscured, most of what I find humiliating is being emphasized, and this is driving me crazy and depresses me. I am becoming, more and more, a bundle of burdensome symptoms in the eyes of others, and when I voice my objection, I am often called "obstreperous" and other demeaning things.

3 I have a variety of remaining intact abilities which I can use to some extent, and when others ignore them in favor of my AD-related problems, salt is being rubbed into my wounds.

4 I would prefer to be able to interact with others in such a way that they pay at least equal, if not more, attention to (1) and (3), instead of (2) alone – as if (1) and (3) no longer exist. I am still willing and able to some degree to work toward calling attention to (1) and (3) and avoiding situations which emphasize (2).

5 My clear and ever-present vulnerability in social settings nowadays lies in the fact that, in order to accomplish (4), I need the determined, caring, and sensitive cooperation of healthy others around me. When I receive such cooperation, I am able to present myself in ways that give me the delight of being seen in positive and valued ways, I can still use my remaining abilities and valued attributes to achieve some good ends, and my feelings of self-worth grow tremendously.

6 Although I don't want to be viewed as a mere moral consequentialist, it is the case that when my feelings of self-worth are strengthened, my caregivers feel better too.

In order for persons to be able to react negatively to, and attempt to avoid, situations which cause them embarrassment and humiliation, to react positively to and attempt to increase the frequency of situations which provide them with enhanced feelings of self-esteem, they must have the ability to make, and to derive, meaning from the situations which confront them. In other words, they must be what some cultural psychologists call *semiotic subjects*. We will explore, in the next chapter, some specific ways in which the AD sufferer behaves as a semiotic subject despite striking losses on standard tests of cognitive function.

Chapter 5

The Alzheimer's Disease Sufferer as a Semiotic Subject

"I just love going through things like that."
"Doc, you gotta find a way to give us purpose again."

The first sentence quoted above, spoken by Dr. M with a clearly zestful joy, followed a long conversation we had about a situation which occurred at one of her support group meetings. She obviously derived a great deal of pleasure from the conversation, for it concerned issues which were very much a part of her own abiding interests. One could say that the subject of the conversation and the conversation itself were very meaningful to her in a variety of ways and I will explore some of them in this chapter. The second of the above quotes was uttered by a person with AD to whom I was about to administer a battery of neuropsychological tests in a hospital outpatient clinic. He was living at the time with his two sons and daughter-in-law, his wife having died some years earlier.

In this chapter, I should like to explore and provide support for the idea that it is still possible for AD sufferers in the moderate to severe stages of the disease to display behavior which is driven by the meaning that situations hold for them. It is especially curious that this should be the case, for the information that emerges from traditional studies of people with AD paints a very different picture of their cognitive abilities.

For example, what I refer to as "traditional" studies often involve giving neuropsychological tests to afflicted persons in order to come to an objective, quantifiable, understanding of their cognitive abilities

161

and skills. Such studies can be subsumed under the category of "Classical Science" as discussed in Chapter 1. Neuropsychological tests are administered in the hospital clinic, laboratory, or nursing home, and other assessment measures such as Activities of Daily Living Questionnaires are given to caregivers for their assessments of certain of the afflicted person's abilities (handling money, grooming, using the telephone, shopping, doing laundry, etc.) in day-to-day life at home. From the results of such tests we learn that AD sufferers are often described as being confused, emotionally labile, guilty of engaging in inappropriate emotional and social behavior, wandering aimlessly, suffering from deficiencies in problem-solving, word-finding, conveying information, and concept formation, and the like (Allender and Kaszniak, 1989; Bayles, 1982). Some authors (Neville and Folstein, 1979) have indicated that dementia sufferers are unable to perceive, attend, and recall.

The clear implication of such descriptions is that people with AD in the moderate to severe stages of the disease do not have the cognitive abilities required to behave in ways that would reflect deliberate action which is guided by the meaning of the situations which they confront. Specifically, if a person were confused, emotionally labile, unable to perceive, attend, and recall, unable to convey information and understand concepts, he or she would be rendered bereft of the tools necessary to behave in ways that require an understanding of the situations before them. One must be able at least to perceive and attend to one's environment in order to derive meaning from environmental situations and then act accordingly in appropriate ways.

But why should I propose that persons with AD can act in meaning-driven ways when the results of their cognitive assessments via standard tests would not predict such behavior on their part? Are the assessments completely incorrect? Am I engaging in wishful thinking? I should like to address these questions by examining some aspects of how we come to know what we know about people with AD. That is, we must explore some of the *epistemological* issues and assumptions behind the traditional, Classical approach as well as the Romantic approach which, as I have adopted it herein, focuses upon the discourse of the AD sufferer. In examining such discourse, I focus not on the fine details of linguistic performance, but rather upon what the speakers accomplish through their speech acts – such as the display of feelings, making complaints, and the expression of desires and beliefs, all of which can be communicated frequently despite the AD sufferer's linguistic problems in word-finding, pronunciation, syntax, and so on.

Epistemological Issues Revisited

Rather than arguing that the results of standard tests are inaccurate, and rather than accusing myself of engaging in wishful thinking about the ability of AD sufferers to act on the basis of the meaning they can derive from situations they confront, it seems more prudent to explore the subtleties involved in the methods of investigation which yield these strikingly different conclusions. By doing so, we can put these disparate claims in some perspective and, I think, arrive at a more complete way of understanding the abilities and behavior of those who have AD.

Therefore, I will propose herein that the results of standard testing are not inaccurate in the technical sense and that, in a variety of cases, their results sometimes mirror some of the problems which caregivers and the afflicted confront in everyday life. However, for a number of important reasons, they often simultaneously prevent us from understanding certain aspects of the cognitive life of AD sufferers, and that these same aspects of cognitive life are, indeed, rendered observable and understandable through the approach of Romantic Science by examining the discourse of individual afflicted persons. Let us begin by examining some of the issues involved in traditional studies which are exemplary of Classical Science.

Do averages and medians really denote "typical"?

The conclusion that dementia sufferers cannot attend and perceive, for example, is said to be accurate in that they, *on average,* or on the basis of *median* scores, performed significantly worse in the statistical sense than did their normal counterparts on tests which were said, by the investigators, to measure attention and perception. However, there are two important issues which must be addressed here:

(1) Can we say that such results describe all dementia sufferers? The answer is "no," because only group medians (50th percentiles) were

163

used and the related statistical data (the ranges of scores) show that there is considerable overlap between the scores of dementia sufferers and normal subjects. Therefore, at least *some* dementia sufferers performed as well as did some normal, healthy subjects and, in these cases, we would not be able to identify the dementia sufferers and the normal subjects simply by looking at their scores on the tests given to them. As a result, it would be a mistake to assume that the median score of the group of AD sufferers applies to every individual in that group.

(2) Can we say that the tests used to measure perception and attention were, themselves, valid measures? The measure of attention used by the authors was a letter cancellation task. The subject is given a matrix of random letters and is asked to draw a line though as many "target letters" as he or she can, such as the letter "e," for example, in one minute's time. The median score (50th percentile) of dementia sufferers was significantly worse than that of their normal counterparts. However, the answer here is also, "no," because if it were indeed the case that dementia sufferers could not perceive and attend, they would not have been able even to engage the tasks at all, because they could not have attended to, and thereby understood completely, the instructions given to them. That they did follow the instructions indicates that they must have been able to pay attention to and recall the instructions to some extent. If, instead, the issue at hand was, "Can some dementia sufferers sustain, for extended periods of time, vigilant attention and process information with speed and accuracy as well as they did before they became ill?", the answer would clearly be, "no," but that is hardly the same thing as saying that each and every dementia sufferer cannot pay attention at all!

The test of perception consisted of exposing a picture for short periods of time, via a tachistoscopic device. The subject had to name the picture, and the total exposure time needed to do so was the measure of perception. The median score (50th percentile) for the group of dementia sufferers differed significantly from that of the normal group, although again, there was considerable overlap in the scores of the two groups. Many dementia sufferers have problems recalling the names of objects even though they can recognize the correct name when given a group of names from which to choose.

Thus, in this case, perception could have been confounded with the way in which the subject had to show he or she knew what the object was. There are other forms of perception, such as depth perception, figure-ground perception, perception of movement, person perception, which were not measured by this particular task. Thus, to say, on the basis of this one task, that dementia sufferers cannot perceive would be overstating the results tremendously, for the task used is hardly representative of perception in general.

So, if one were to assume that (a) average scores (or median scores, as the case may be) represent the performance of the group members "in general" (which is quite debateable in this study and many, many others for reasons which I will address further in a later chapter); and (b) that the tests given were valid measures of the ability in question (which they were only in a very narrow sense), then the tests and their results are not inaccurate in the technical sense of the word.

However, the implications drawn from the tests (that dementia sufferers cannot perceive and attend, for example) are not borne out on the level of each and every individual dementia sufferer in both the clinic and everyday life situations. This latter issue is one of great import as it bears heavily on the way in which people with AD are positioned and treated. To wit, if I assume in advance that a person with AD, by virtue of having been diagnosed as such, cannot perceive and attend, my behavior toward that person will be quite different from what it would be if I were to assume the opposite.

Creating "psychometric persons"

One of the results of using batteries of tests (psychometric instruments) and group statistics is the creation of what cultural psychologists Shweder and Sullivan (1989) call *psychometric persons.* These authors call attention to the idea that when we confine our understanding of the cognitive life of persons to their performance on psychometric tests, persons become defined in terms of "a statistical aggregate, an average across occasions . . . expressed in probabilistic terms." In other words, instead of understanding individual persons in detail, persons are grouped in some arbitrary way according to one or another characteristic (such as being diagnosed with probable AD), their test results are averaged and what is born, following the calculations, is a mythic "average normal person or average AD sufferer" who is defined in terms of a profile of averaged scores on a battery of tests.

This mythic average psychometric person is then taken as being "typical" of all the people who form the group from which the average is drawn and, by extension, all people who have the characteristic in question, such as AD. It is the case that in most studies, the major findings have cast light on the ways in which AD sufferers' performance on average, or via median scores, is inferior to that of normal control subjects. Thus is a stereotype created and, on the basis of this stereotype, AD sufferers are positioned in defectological terms – they are viewed primarily in terms of their deficits and those deficits are assumed to have been caused principally by the disease process. And, to the extent that conceptions of this mythic average AD sufferer inform the actions, attitudes, and interpretations of clinicians and caregivers, particular AD sufferers' actual intact abilities will necessarily be rendered more or less invisible, because afflicted people will be reacted to principally in terms of their deficits. Social interactions which have defects as their focus necessarily limit the range and quality of those interactions and often result in malignant social psychology. This outcome is bolstered further for reasons which form the second methodological issue that we must confront.

The use of standard tests and the testing situation

Another aspect of the Classical Science approach to studying the cognitive abilities of AD sufferers is the type of test materials which are used and the testing situation itself. The use of psychometric tests involves the breaking down of cognitive function into discrete elements, such as attention, language, memory, perception, learning, and the like (mirroring the chapter headings of introductory psychology textbooks), such that there is a separate test for each of these functions. Some functions are broken down even further on the tests, so that language tests, for example, involve separate subtests for naming objects on command, repeating what one hears, auditory comprehension (as in following specific commands, pointing to particular body parts on command), spelling, and so on. The results of the tests are expressed in quantitative terms and are thus thought to be object-ive measures.

One underlying assumption in this approach is that it is valid to decompose and test cognitive ability in a way which does not mirror the situation that exists in everyday life. In other words, in everyday life, attention, perception, language, memory, and so on do not occur in isolation from one another. Rather, they are most often engaged simultaneously in inextricable combinations which take on a character of their own, unlike that of any of the elements individually (much as the atoms of hydrogen and oxygen, when combined, form water). In a sense, this simultaneous activation of many cognitive functions occurs to some extent even in the testing situation, for the subject must attend to, perceive, remember, and understand the spoken instruc-tions in order to begin to answer the test items. However, unlike the situation which exists for us normally, each of the separate functions is then tested by using particular types of questions, or particular tasks, which are removed from the contextual ebb and flow of normal social life. It is highly uncommon, for instance, for someone to be asked, out of nowhere as it were, to point to his or her left elbow, or repeat individual words or phrases.

In fairness however, it is clear that, despite the uncommon situ-ation I have just described, normal healthy adults can respond correctly to such commands and many AD sufferers cannot. But the fact that many AD sufferers have more difficulty in such situations does not mean, *ipso facto*, that they have similar difficulties in normal social life, for brain-injured people often depend more heavily than do normal persons on information from the social context (Sacks, 1985) in order to behave coherently. A small example in the case of Mrs. D serves to illustrate the point. One type of test for movement problems (praxis problems) involves asking the person to make certain movements on command – such as "blow a kiss" or "wave goodbye." Mrs. D was unable to make the appropriate movements on command. However, using her show business background, she then began singing the old song, "Toot, Toot, Tootsie, Goodbye" and waved goodbye. She also sang the beginning of "Give Me a Little Kiss, Will Ya, Huh?" and blew a kiss. By singing these songs, she provided herself with a type of context and was able to make the appropriate movements.

There can be a world of difference between how a person with AD performs on such tests and how the same person engages the entire

167

host of cognitive functions in everyday life (Sabat et al., 1984). Specifically, the test results may mirror certain aspects of performance in everyday life in some respects but not in others. For example, AD sufferers who show striking word-finding problems on tests, also show word-finding problems in natural conversation. On the other hand, however, the findings gleaned from standard tests of conversational ability, which are said to indicate that AD sufferers cannot use language to convey information (Hier et al., 1985) are not at all borne out when the afflicted are engaged in true conversation in natural social settings and within the confines of more natural social relationships (see Chapter 2).

Now, if a researcher is particularly interested in one or another cognitive function and how it might be affected by a drug, it might be very helpful to use the Classical Science approach to try as best one can to isolate that one function from the others and examine the effect of a drug on that particular function. However, the ultimate test of the drug's efficacy would be how it affects the person's performance in meeting the demands of situations in everyday life. That is to say, there would be limited utility of a drug which produced positive effects on standard clinical tests of a narrowly defined cognitive function but which did not do so in natural social situations. There is yet another important assumption involved in the use of such tests, and that has to do with the testing situation itself.

Just as researchers attempt to isolate and test one cognitive function apart from others, the testing situation in the hospital clinic or laboratory is used so as to avoid the contamination, or confounding, of the results by "situational factors" such that existing deficits might be "masked." That is, an afflicted person may have problems with one or another function, but in normal everyday situations the person may be able to use a variety of social cues from other people to make up for, or minimize, a particular difficulty to one degree or another. From the standpoint of Classical Science, it is important to test cognitive functions in a "pure," or controlled, way, so that they aren't affected in such ways by social cues.

Ironically and paradoxically, this attempt to isolate individual functions from social situations cannot possibly succeed for a very fundamental and important reason: the test situation is itself a type of social situation and it provokes psychological reactions in those being tested.

Such psychological reactions could, themselves, confound or contaminate the performance of the afflicted person.

Imagine for a moment, how you would feel if some authority figure, such as a scientist or professor, suddenly told you that you were about to be given a test of one or another of your mental functions. Most normal, intelligent adults, react to such a situation with a significant degree of trepidation and often "freeze up" to some extent. (I recall, with some amusement, the hostile reactions I received from my classmates when I requested that our teacher give exams in our adult education course.) Famed neurologist MacDonald Critchley (1953) noted that the test situation and the attitude of the examiner have a great bearing on the performance of brain-injured people. To assume that being in a test situation cannot, itself, have an effect on a person, brain-injured or not, is to assume that the situation has little or no meaning for the person being tested. Such an assumption, from Critchley's point of view, is patently false. Thus, the test situation cannot be thought of as being "pure" in such a way as to minimize or eliminate social influences which can have an effect on a person's behavior. Recall Dr. M's reaction to being put in the testing situation:

> *SRS:* Let me back up for a second because I think I'm missing your point. You don't want your life to be . . .
> *Dr. M:* Going always to see people to see what's wrong with me. [And, on another occasion]
> *SRS:* Ya . . . let me see if I understand. At least one of the things that you're saying is that it's, it's not something – you, you don't want to put yourself in situations where you're constantly being shown what you can't do.
> *Dr. M:* That's one. That a real thing.

I do not propose that all people with AD react exactly as did Dr. M (Mrs. D, for example, did not react this way). Rather, I am suggesting that it cannot be assumed that the afflicted person is not in any way reactive to the testing situation, nor can it be assumed that when such reactivity occurs, it does not affect the person's performance on tests.

Critchley also pointed out that there are many aspects of behavior which cannot be reduced to, and understood in terms of, numbers.

This is yet another issue that affects the extent to which we can understand the AD sufferer's cognitive ability via standard tests, for there is an entire realm of human behavior and thought which is not tested at all for this reason. For example, psychological characteristics or functions such as proper pride, the desire to avoid humiliation, the desire to be of help to others, the need for genuine human relationship, expressions of generosity toward and concern and love for others, the need and expressed desire to have purpose in one's life, and the like, are extremely important and highly valued aspects of human psychological life even though there are no objective, quantitative tests to measure these characteristics. At present, there is no way to contrive truly valid "standard" situations to evoke such behavior in laboratory or clinical settings such that these functions might be tested in an objective, quantifiable way and replicated by scientists in different laboratories and clinics. As a result, traditional psychometric measures, while not to be abandoned, are clearly limited in that they tap only a restricted sample of the sufferer's cognitive and social abilities, and do not take account of the afflicted person's experience from his or her own point of view.

Therefore, if we were to ignore the existence of these characteristics in our attempt to understand the cognitive abilities of AD sufferers, simply because these abilities or functions cannot be studied via the methods of Classical Science, we would eliminate from the picture of their psychological lives some very compelling and valuable features. The outcome of such a strategy would render our understanding of the AD sufferer's cognitive abilities incomplete to say the very least and such an incomplete understanding can have far-reaching effects on the lives of the afflicted and their caregivers alike especially in terms of the ways in which the afflicted are positioned by others.

Where Classical Science ends and Romantic Science begins

In order to gain an appreciation of the meaning-making abilities of AD sufferers, one must bring to bear methods of study other than those of Classical Science. In this regard, the approaches employed by Romantic Science, especially that of examining the discourse of the AD sufferer, are ideally suited and can serve as a valuable complement to Classical Science techniques. Herein, we examine in great detail, the behavior of individual AD sufferers as they confront everyday life situations. Although, in this manner, no attempt is made to arrive at large generalizations about groups of people, what we learn from fine-grained analysis of individuals may be seen to apply, in possibly a variety of ways, to many others as research continues.

There is not a great deal that could be called "standard" in the Romantic Scientist's toolkit. Instead, there is the careful, relentless observation of and interaction with the afflicted person as he or she attempts to navigate the social world. In the process, the psychological reality of the individual is kept in sharp focus. Controlled replicable situations and methods are sacrificed to a large extent in order to obtain information which can be gathered only by observing life as it is lived and unfolds in the everyday world. Let us, then, begin to examine the lives of some AD sufferers, the situations from which they derive meaning, and how that meaning is expressed – that is, let us explore the proposition that the person with AD can be a semiotic subject.

What is a Semiotic or "Meaning-Driven" Subject?

To say that one's behavior is driven by meaning requires that we come to some provisional understanding of what "meaning" means! For present purposes, meaning will be understood in three different ways (Sabat and Harré, 1994):

1   acting out of intention – reflection and intention are built upon systems of meaning, as outlined by Geertz (1973) and Shweder (1983);
2   the interpretation of events and situations; and
3   the evaluation of events, situations, or actions.

Semiotic subjects are those individuals who can act intentionally given their interpretations of the circumstances in which they find themselves; they are people who can evaluate their own behavior and the behavior of others in accordance with socially agreed-upon standards of propriety and reason. The meaning of a situation takes into account all of the possible interpretations or inferences which a person can make in light of what Shweder and Sullivan (1989) call a "conceptual scheme," in which specific situations, or texts, are understood in light of some overarching interpretive way of thinking. For example, the view of dogs in Hindu culture is quite different from that in North American culture. In the former, dogs are considered to be polluted animals who are cursed to mate in public, while in the latter, they are loved and showered with great economic resources and care. Thus, the same physical situation may be understood to have entirely different meanings depending upon the conceptual schemes of the observers.

The test situation is a case in point. Although the test-giver views the situation as an opportunity to gain information about the afflicted person, and does not find the circumstance threatening to him or herself, the situation can have quite a different meaning to the test-taker, as we saw in Dr. M's comments earlier. In the formal report of the results of her neuropsychological tests, it was noted that "at times she became annoyed with the tests and stated that there was a 'trick' to them." She also stated that she saw no purpose in the tests, for they were not going to help her to help herself in any way. She was entirely correct in her inference. Therefore, in her conceptual scheme, if the tests would be of value to her, she would not object to them. If, however, the tests would not serve such a purpose, and served only to humiliate her, she would conclude, quite rationally, that there was no purpose in her taking them.

The application of Shweder and Sullivan's approach to understanding meaning-driven behavior has opened up the possibility that, even though the person who studies another culture may not, at first, understand the meaning behind the behavior of those in that other culture – because the latter have systems of meaning (conceptual schemes) which are different from those of the investigator and so appear to the investigator to be odd or strange – those in exotic cultures still do, in fact, have lives animated by meaning. There is, then, the possibility that human beings who are categorized as being ill share a type of predicament similar to those in an exotic tribe, in that a cursory examination of their behavior might result in defectological interpretations which are not accurate once a closer examination is undertaken.

For example, her neuropsychologist noted that Dr. M had "an unsteady gait" and that this was evidence of praxis (movement) problems which result from brain damage. Completely ignored in this interpretation was the fact that she was extremely nervous and uncomfortable in that situation. More than a year following her being tested, I walked extensively with her and never noticed any such unsteadiness in her gait. Presumably, given the fact that AD is a progressive disease, her gait when walking with me should have been worse, not better – if her "unsteady gait" was, in fact, due to the disease alone and not to her trepidation.

The approach taken here is that the behavior of the afflicted person is assumed in advance to be driven by meaning rather than viewed as being defective, incoherent, inappropriate, or aimless simply because the behavior in question might be "nonstandard" in one or another way. Such an assumption is akin to what philosopher Daniel Dennett (1990) refers to as "taking the intentional stance" toward another person. Let us, then, begin our examination of the AD sufferer as a semiotic subject with the case of Mr. R.

Mr. R – "The Top Guy"

Mr. R was 68 years old, had been diagnosed with probable AD in the moderate to severe stages according to standard tests, and was a participant at an adult day care center, where our association of approximately one year unfolded. My initial encounter with him was his first day at the center and I stopped to greet him as I entered. A retired executive, he was well dressed and looked as if he were about to play a round of golf. He spoke rapidly, with great emotional agitation, his face full of frowns, shaking his head. Although I could understand virtually every word he spoke, I could not understand the totality of what he was saying. After some ten minutes of listening to him and having observed that he seemed to be extremely upset, I noticed that he paused for a moment, and I asked him, "Do you feel like crying?" With his eyes almost darting out of his head in response, he immediately shot back, with crystal clarity, his first completely coherent sentence: "You're damn right I do!"

His interpretation of events and situations

The program director of the center had spent quite some time with Mr. R that morning and had concluded, by piecing together many of Mr. R's disparate comments, that Mr R feared that Mrs. R was having

173

an affair. Given that fear, it would have been entirely appropriate for the man to be in turmoil and to "feel like crying." Let us examine two possible conceptual schemes with which we can analyze his behavior.

One interpretation could focus on the fact that the man has AD in the moderate to severe stages, his speech is largely incoherent, and we conclude that he has developed a delusion about his wife, because *we* know that his wife is consummately faithful. In this case, his disease and its connotations form the conceptual scheme, the driving force, behind the interpretation. However, closer examination of his situation, attempting to take into account his point of view and the larger context of his situation, can reveal a very different interpretation.

Mr. R had spent every day of the previous three years with his wife. The disease had advanced to the point at which she needed some respite from caregiving as well as time to take care of the sundry details of everyday life which she could no longer do efficiently when he accompanied her. As a result, she placed him in the adult day care center for a couple of days each week. He knew that he had the disease and that he was now unable to do the things that he once did easily, that he was not able to give to his wife and be with her as he had for the previous decades of their marriage. His recall memory was affected and thus he could not recall exactly what she had told him about his being in the day care program. Given all this, and the knowledge that his wife was a healthy, vibrant, intelligent, and attractive woman, might it be reasonable for him to fear that she might want the company of a man with whom she could share her thoughts and her life more completely than she could with him, and that she was leaving him at the day care center so that she could have something of a life of her own?

Taking the second interpretation as a starting point, I thought of his fear as being real, for it was real to him, and worked to assure him that what he feared was not, in fact, actually happening. In order to do so, I could not simply dismiss his fear as a delusion, as symptomatic of his disease. Rather, I had to recognize that there was an inherent logic in the way he was thinking, that the faulty premise from which he began resided in a certain insecurity he felt about himself at present – an insecurity which was not without due cause. He had felt burdensome to her in recent years, but he needed to understand that she still loved him as much as ever – which she, herself, confirmed strongly in a later interview and showed unstintingly in her behavior toward him. Further, in order to reassure him, I had to be willing to "be" with him, to earn his trust, to enter into a human relationship with him. That is precisely what happened, and with time his fear subsided but the relationship between us grew to be strong.

It was clear that he could not recall what day of the week it was, the name of the month, the season, where he was, and so on, he had great difficulty expressing himself verbally much of the time, and his word-finding problems were severe. Yet he was quite responsive to those individuals who tried to make contact with, and who expressed interest in, him.

At first, when I entered into conversation with him, I tried to focus his thoughts on specific topics that had mostly to do with himself. I wanted to come to know more about him. Given his age, it seemed to me that it was possible that he was in the military service during World War II, and so I asked him if that was the case and it was indeed.

SRS: Were you in the Navy?
Mr. R: No.
SRS: The Army?
Mr. R: Yes.
SRS: The Air Force? [I asked this question just to see if he'd say "yes" to something that seemed, from his previous response, not to be the case.]
Mr. R: Yes.

At this point, one might have concluded that Mr. R was evidencing a symptom of confusion. He was not at all confused, however, because at the time of World War II, the US Army and Air Force were a combined service that was, in fact, called "the Army Air Force." One would have to know that in order to see the accuracy, the sense, of his answer and not attribute his seemingly contradictory responses to confusion caused by AD.

SRS: What did you do in the service?
Mr. R: I was the top guy, the top guy.
SRS: Were you a General?
Mr. R: No.

175

Then what, exactly, did "top guy" mean? I learned, from speaking with his wife, that he was the pilot of a large aircraft on which a number of other servicemen formed the crew. He could not find the word "pilot" but, in fact, on his plane he was indeed the "top guy" – the pilot.

As a result of many such conversations, in which I clearly expressed a strong interest in trying to understand him, to get to know him, to reassure him, and help him find some moments of calm, he came to refer to me as "good friend." "You're a good friend, G-d bless you," he would say to me every time we met. He had been able, despite the disease, to understand my intentions toward him (that I was interested in him as a person and willing to work with and help him) to interpret and to evaluate my efforts to engage him, and to respond to me in kind. There was always a handshake and a warm greeting from him when we would meet. That he interpreted and evaluated my intentions and behavior accurately was made clear in the following interchange between Mr. R and a Georgetown nursing student, Ms. T.

A staff person had asked the group of day care participants a question:

Ms. T: Do you know the answer to that question?
Mr. R: No, I don't. That man is still trying to get in [*pointing to me, making motions with his hand on his face indicating a beard – I have a beard*]. He wants in but I can't tell many others. He's trying, though, G-d bless him!
Ms. T: What does he want? Do you know him?
Mr. R: Yes, yes, dear. He wants in like all of your friends [*points to other nursing students*]. He wants in. [*Mr. R becomes teary-eyed and holds his head in frustration.*]

He was quite correct. I did "want in" – into his mind, his thoughts, his experiences. And I wanted him to know that I wanted in, for then, during at least some hours when he was away from his wife, he would not feel completely alone and adrift. His response of frustration at the end of this extract also indicates semiotic behavior in that:

1 Mr. R has interpreted and evaluated my behavior toward him as indicating that I wanted to understand him, that I was trying to "get in" to his mind.

176

2   He wanted to be understood, and was able to evaluate his ability to communicate as being such that he could not do so as clearly and as well as he would prefer.
3   He reacted with perfectly appropriate and understandable sadness and frustration.

His status as a semiotic subject was again clear in another episode, extending over a period of two days at the day care center. On the first day, he was sitting alone at a long table when I sat down across from him, to keep him company. Soon we were joined by another man who had Alzheimer's and a woman who had suffered a right hemisphere stroke which resulted in paralysis on the left side of her body, but which had not affected her speech. At one point, Mr. R became upset about something, stood up to his full and considerable height, and began the rapid-fire speech reminiscent of my first encounter with him. He went on and on and his sentences were, again, difficult to decipher.

The woman said, "He's confused."

The other man with Alzheimer's said, "He's upset."

I said, to the man, in a voice loud enough for Mr. R to hear, "You're right. He is upset, and he knows what he is upset about, and he's trying to tell us. But we're having trouble understanding exactly what it is that he means, what he is trying to say. Therefore *we* are confused."

I looked at Mr. R, found a moment in which to speak, and said, "I know that you're upset, but I'm having a lot of trouble understanding exactly what you're saying." With time, he did seem to calm down and whatever it was that troubled him had apparently passed. How ironic it was that the other Alzheimer's sufferer had assessed Mr. R's emotional-cognitive state accurately, and that the woman who was not suffering from any form of dementia had not.

The next day I arrived at the center and walked into the room where the participants were eating lunch. From the far side of the room, Mr. R stopped eating, arose from his seat at the table and walked over to me (indicating that he was able to focus his attention on me). In a very circumlocutory way, he apologized for his "ranting" (his word) the day before, and thanked me for being so understanding and good to him: "G-d bless you, good friend." Thus, the meaning of what I had done and said the previous day had clearly been encoded in his long-term memory, and it was possible for him to retrieve it from memory a day later. As a semiotic subject, he had interpreted and evaluated the significance of, and intentionally responded appropriately to, how he was treated. He knew that his dignity was not being erased, that he was being treated with understanding, and it made a difference to him.

His intention in acting

Yet another episode at the day care center shed further light on Mr. R's semiotic behavior and also helped to make clearer the distinction between the interpretation of behavior as an AD-related symptom as opposed to a successful adaptation. He went to the closet where the participants' coats were hung and began examining the contents of the pockets of each coat, one by one, starting from the left side of the closet and moving to the right. In each case, he reached into the pockets, pulled out and examined the contents, and then put them back. Now this is hardly appropriate social behavior.

One conceptual scheme would lead to the following interpretation: Perhaps Alzheimer's has resulted in a loosening of his social inhibitions so that now he is acting, with no hesitation or remorse, in ways that in healthier times would have been understood as being taboo. Such a defectological interpretation is clearly possible and often dominates the way in which AD sufferers are positioned in poor clinical practice and by caregivers. In this instance, however, there was more to his behavior than a socially inappropriate AD-produced symptom, and only careful observation would reveal the "something more."

As he moved from one coat to another, he reached into the pocket of a particular coat and looked at the contents. As with the other coats, he put the contents back, but then he took this particular coat off the hanger and put it on, for *it was his coat.* In this situation, he could not recognize his coat from among the others by sight alone. He wanted to find his coat, however, and so he engaged in an adaptation that would allow him to take advantage of an intact ability – he could recognize his own property in the pocket, and when he saw his "stuff," he knew that it was his coat.

I am not suggesting that this sort of behavior is completely asymptomatic, because clearly that is not the case. However, if he were stopped in the midst of this process because he was engaging in what might be interpreted as being purely symptomatic, confused, impolite behavior, the logic of this form of successful adaptation would have been missed completely, the stereotype about the Alzheimer's sufferer would have been "confirmed" once again, and would have affected the ways in which the staff treated him on subsequent occasions. It was clear, however, that his purpose was not to invade the privacy of others, but to find his own coat. It was also clear that he was not about to steal anything, for each item that he recognized as not belonging to him, was returned to its proper place. That he could not identify his coat by sight alone was a symptom. That he found an alternate way of achieving his goal without really hurting anyone else signals a form of adaptation in that he used one of his remaining intact abilities (recognizing the contents of his own coat pocket) with success. Thus, he acted out of intention to achieve a goal and thereby exhibited meaning-driven, or semiotic, behavior.

His intention in and his evaluation of two situations

During the period of my association with Mr. R, a number of nursing students from Georgetown University were spending time at the day care center as part of their training and I involved them with Mr. R, giving them a mini-course about everything I knew about him along with how to interact, what to do, what seemed to work well. They were wonderfully caring and warm with him and he responded in kind. The students and I met and discussed their experiences and one of them persented part of an exchange she had had with Mr. R:

> *Mr. R:* I'd like to talk to you dear, but you see . . . well . . . you know.
> *Ms. T:* I understand.
> *Mr. R:* Yes, you see. I'm glad. G-d bless you. You know my head.
> *Ms. T:* Does your head hurt?
> *Mr. R:* It's this darn thing, you know. Sometimes it hurts, it pounds, too many noises.

Here, it seemed as though Mr. R was doing two things. He was indicating his desire to speak with the student, but explaining that he

179

could not do so because of "this darn thing" with his head. He was also complaining of something like a sensory overload, that he couldn't filter out all of the extraneous noises in the room filled with people who were involved in a game being led by one of the activities coordinators. This comment resembles that made by Dr. B ("too many stimuli") under similar circumstances. Both comments indicate an evaluation of his situation and the events surrounding him, which is a dimension of being a meaning-driven subject.

A final example of Mr. R's meaning-making ability can be seen in the following episode. In the presence of one of the nursing students, Mr. R insisted upon going out to the front of the day care center to "see if those guys were coming yet." Once outside, he didn't see the people for whom he was looking and the student assured him that there wasn't anyone around. He was then quite cooperative about going back inside.

On the way, he said to the student, "You thought I was going to try to leave. I don't want to leave. I just wanted to check." He was correct about what the student thought about his possibly wanting to leave, for the students had been alerted by the staff to be mindful of such situations with participants. Here again we see that his inability to speak with fluent coherence or to show signs of intact "orientation" did not mean that he could not understand the possible implications of his behavior in the eyes of others (interpretation and evaluation), and still function as a semiotic subject.

He struggled mightily, and he taught me the virtue of patience. It was meaningful to him that I was "there for him" even when I didn't immediately understand the point he was trying to convey, and even when I couldn't "fix" the problems that AD created for him. It was especially meaningful to him that I recognized and validated his emotional state, which is itself a cornerstone of validation therapy (Feil, 1982). He taught me that his problems painting his experiences and feelings through the use of words did not mean that his nascent thoughts themselves were disordered or diseased. Mr. R taught me to be honest in letting him know when I didn't understand what he was trying to tell me. He showed me that the confusion was mine rather than his and that if I was a good enough detective, I would be able to find the coherent ideas that he often wanted to but could not express, and he showed me that, despite all his AD-related deficits, his meaning-making abilities were still alive.

After almost a year of being a participant at the day care center, he was placed in a nursing home. Now as I think and write about him years after his death, he is still the "top guy" to me and I am honored and touched that he called me "good friend," for I, too, am a semiotic subject.

The Case of Dr. M

At the outset of this chapter, we heard Dr. M comment, "I just love going through things like that." She was referring to a conversation we were having which included some discussion about a situation that transpired at one of her support group meetings. There were other issues which arose as well, and they, too, reveal her meaning-making ability.

Interpreting and evaluating interpersonal dynamics

The first topic of conversation on this particular occasion was initiated by Dr. M. It is important to note this fact along with the fact that Dr. M had initiated other topics of conversation in past meetings. One of the signs of damage to the anterior cortical areas of the brain (prefrontal lobes) is the lack of initiative shown by the afflicted person. Another symptom of damage to the prefrontal areas of the cortex is what is termed *perseveration*, which is seen in the person's repeating the response to a previous question on a test, for example, even though a new question has been asked. In our interactions, Dr. M never showed signs of passivity or a lack of initiative apart from instances related to her feelings of anger toward herself as a result of word-finding problems and her resulting reluctance to speak in group situations. Nor did she engage in perseverative behavior. Interestingly enough, this stands in sharp contrast to the interpretation given by a neuropsychologist about the results of the battery of standardized tests which she took approximately two years before our association began: "There is some suggestion of greater involvement of the anterior cortex than the posterior. This was evident from the perseverative quality of many of her responses as well as her ability to verbalize solutions but not follow through with the corresponding behavior."

181

When I arrived at her house on what was a lovely spring day, Dr. M began:

> *Dr. M:* If someone asked why you came here, what uh, would you say?
>
> *SRS:* Well, I'd say I was coming here to talk to, well I wouldn't even mention your name, but
>
> *Dr. M:* [*laughing*] Of course!
>
> *SRS:* but just because you know who you are, I would
>
> *Dr. M:* [*laughing*] *I'm glad you know and I know.*
>
> *SRS:* I'd say I'm coming here to talk with Dr. M uh,
>
> *Dr. M:* Since when? You are not talking to me as Dr. – that.
>
> *SRS:* That too,
>
> *Dr. M:* Really?
>
> *SRS:* That too, I never forget that. And that, that's important for me not to forget, actually.
>
> *Dr. M:* Okay. *It's very, I, I find it hard to use that name rather than doing it.* I, I really don't. Anybody whom I've talked to as, so long as I have talked to you in such a, a point of understanding, that, that's not what it's, it's, has it's own way of speaking. That's why I could say could we be on the here [that's why she can say, "where would you like to sit – inside or outside?]
>
> *SRS:* Uh huh, so "Dr. M" has a more formal connotation – you would use that in a more formal kind of setting?
>
> *Dr. M:* Um hum.

Here, Dr. M initiated the topic of why I'm coming to visit her and when I used her title, she questioned me intently by wondering why I would use her formal title when she and I had reached "such a point of understanding." In so doing, she reveals her ability to evaluate and interpret the meaning, the nature, of our relationship and the seeming contradiction in my referring to her in such a formal way. She also reveals her sense of humor in the first italicized portion, and her sense of difficulty in using her title when she's not doing things that are coeval with that title (second italicized portion). Earlier in this extract, she clearly recognized the meaning of confidentiality in my comment that "I wouldn't even mention your name" when she responded "Of course" while laughing – she understood this aspect of my response from her own training. The conversation continued with my validating her sense of the contradiction in my using her formal title, given our level of relationship and understanding, while at the same time I tried to convey why it was important for me to think of her as having achieved all that she has achieved in her life. At first, she challenged me again, by saying that I myself don't insist on being viewed in such terms, but then she seems to make an about-face in the italicized comment below:

SRS: Well yeah, I understand that, but at the same time I think that it's very important that, at least for purposes of understanding um, aspects of the way you think and feel, that it's very difficult from your point of view,

Dr. M: Yes,

SRS: it's kind of hard not to be Dr. M who studied those things, who taught and wrote,

Dr. M: Um hum.

SRS: and did all of those things, that's very much tied up with you.

Dr. M: Ya,

SRS: So I remember that.

Dr. M: But *you* don't say "I'm a person who uh, who also has uh, a life of his own" and the other things. So I can't and I don't real, I guess I, I don't like so much when people talk to me – that I really care to talk to – *uh, I see – No, it's, it's better to have all the other things come in.* Now for instance, uh two things that I, I didn't ever uh, know uh that I like very much – not about you, but about the whole thing here – I mean incl, incue, including you, a tree I never saw – the white one.

Intention in the subtle use of words

In what was a flashbulb-like instant, Dr. M concluded that it was better for me to think of her in terms of some of her admirable accomplishments as summarized in her professional title, again revealing her ability to evaluate and interpret the meaning of a situation in light of new information (my reasons as stated). She then called my attention to a lovely tree behind her house:

SRS: The dogwood tree?

Dr. M: Not that one. That one I was saving for this, but the white uh tree.

SRS: Uh huh,

Dr. M: And I have never seen that tree.

SRS: There it is!

Dr. M: Um hum!

SRS: All of a sudden. A present!

Dr. M: Yes, and present in two senses is the word.

SRS: Uh huh.

Dr. M: Gotcha!

SRS: You did, that's right! Present as in "a gift" and present as in "here".

Dr. M: Yes, um hum!

SRS: [*laughs*].

Dr. M: [*also laughing*] And all the while I'm asking what do you want to do today?

Note that Dr. M has spontaneously initiated the play on the double meaning of "present." She actually called my attention to it, for I had used the word in the sense of a gift without seeing the other meaning. She thereby revealed her still very much intact gift for playing with the interpretation of words and their meanings.

Interpreting and evaluating group dynamics

We moved on to a discussion of her support group and some of the interactions that occurred at the previous meeting. It was clear that she had come to some conclusions about the dynamics of the group as well as revealing her reactions about an interchange involving herself and another group member. I was at that meeting, the first of many I was to attend, and how that came about is another example of Dr. M's semiotic behavior which I will describe in Chapter 6. First, let us turn to the discussion about the group in general:

SRS: You were saying that there were things about it that you didn't like and,

Dr. M: That was not a, a uh, word system right now, but it wasn't like all other things. It was a, a, *completely* different in many ways.

SRS: You mean that what you didn't like was different from – I'm not sure that I understand. Help me. [Dr. M often said "help me" to me when she was stuck for a word, so I used this locution when I was having difficulty understanding her point.]

Dr. M: The feeling of the group,

SRS: Yes.

Dr. M: uh, no one asked uh, right now it doesn't come to mind. Uh, the feeling in the group was more uh, connecting with people to people.

SRS: Um hum.

Dr. M: And that was good and it, it was largely because of you.

SRS: Oh, so when I was there, there was more of a feeling of connection between people.

Dr. M: Um hum.

SRS: Well, I'm delighted to hear that.

Dr. M: I know you would! [*chuckling*].

In this extract, Dr. M is comparing the "feeling" in the group on those occasions on which I was not present to this occasion on which I was present. In her evaluation, she notes that on this particular occasion there was more of a connection between the group members, and she attributes that positive outcome "largely" to my presence. She has clearly engaged in semiotic behavior of evaluation and interpretation of situations and events here, and she did so again as the conversation continued.

Interpreting and evaluating the behavior of herself and another person

SRS: [*laughs*] It felt good for me, it seemed very natural, you know, the, the people seemed very nice.

Dr. M: There was, the group, the group was uh, also. I had something I had uh, uh, one thing I was sad about. It wasn't about you. It was about me. Um, when uh, you asked uh, we had, woman sel uh, starts uh, shows us, uh say something about Dr., not Dr., but uh, I don't know wha, what they used. Uh, uh, ten, tense, what's his name?

SRS: Was it Dennis?

Dr. M: Yes, Dennis. And he had this thing.

185

SRS: Oh the speech he gave? The tape? [a tape of a speech Dennis gave, played by the group leader].

Dr. M: Uh huh. And I was very glad because I like him and also I wanted to, to, and I want to, I want to talk to him more in that. And uh, he's the uh, most one of how did you get. And how come you're here? This, would have been my thing. [Dr. M is saying that he was, in her opinion, the brightest and most well-spoken member of the group and that she wanted to ask him why he was a member of the group, given his ability. Although this interpretation is not easily found in her words, I knew about her reaction to him from previous conversations in which she had discussed this man.]

SRS: Um hum.

Dr. M: And since that we, we were more connected with each other as you could, you couldn't fully know, because you weren't there [at previous meetings]. I thought it was very good that he should be the person who was talking about himself.

SRS: Um hum.

Dr. M: And, and um then, but we talked about something that I can't remember but after uh, and you might maybe, maybe you didn't even knew it was something that [was] happening. Uh, people gave him uh, an impre, impression of having a good thing done and someone, somewhere in the talk, after he had made his whatever words, uh people clapped – a little heh, hesitant, but that was just because we never, we don't do these things like that.

SRS: Um hum.

Dr. M: And then uh, someone said something about uh, how good it was or something that uh, brought it up more. And, and something made him uh, and he was very pleased with the first things, and then everything was ever, uh very nice except since it was everything was so nice, I was playing with the idea and uh, and uh, I was, I, I thought it made him less feeling, feeling less. Did you sss, see that?

SRS: You mean after we listened to his talk,

Dr. M: And then we talked about his talk.

SRS: Um hum.

Dr. M: And while we were talking that something, *something* came in, in, and I think because I tend to be playful when I'm

186

happy, I said something that made him feel un, uh, not in, it didn't make him happy at all. Did you see that?

SRS: Oh! I saw something like that but it was at a different moment. Um, that I remember. I mean, that could have happened exactly as you put it, but I didn't see *that*, but I did see something else.

Dr. M: What?

SRS: It was later on when I was, I was talking about, um, I can't remember now! *Oy!* [Yiddish for something like "egad"] I was talking about, I think I was talking about how it's important to let other people know that you need time to come up with words and ideas and that that's a good thing, a good strategy to use when you're talking to people. And he was, he was looking intently at me,

Dr. M: Uh huh.

SRS: and *you*, at one point you, you said something to him. You, you were, you were telling him that while I was talking, you said to him – to Dennis – "you were so" and you were making this movement with your hands as if to say, as if his attention was riveted and he was so focused. You were trying to say something to him along the lines of, "You were so focused on what he was saying" – you were saying, "You, Dennis, were so focused on what Dr. Sabat was saying" and he did not quite understand what you were getting at when you said that at first.

Dr. M: Um hum.

SRS: And he was looking at you and he didn't understand what your point was. And, and he, then he said, "I, I really don't know what you're getting at."

Dr. M: Ya and he had that luh [look] and it was almost as if I did a, a wrong thing.

SRS: Oh no! I'll tell you what I felt.

Dr. M: All right!

SRS: What I felt in that moment was that he was feeling, I thought that he was feeling a little bit self-conscious.

Dr. M: Yes, that, that was there.

SRS: And, and, and I thought the reason he felt self-conscious was that he didn't understand what you were getting at and he might have felt, in that moment, that there may be something wrong with him because he didn't understand what you were saying, or it was difficult for him to say, "I don't understand what you're trying to tell me."

Dr. M: So you found him a little confused.

SRS: Yes, I, I think he didn't understand quite what you were getting at and I think he

Dr. M: And he was far away from me.

SRS: Um hum, and I think he was a bit reluctant at first to say, "I don't understand what you're getting at." And so at that point, he might have felt lost. See sometimes, here look – if you know that sometimes you have trouble uh, understanding some things, and if someone says something to you and you don't understand what the person says,

Dr. M: Um hum.

SRS: you might be attributing to *yourself*,

Dr. M: Um hum, *exactly* I suppose.

SRS: the problem. That is, you might be saying to yourself, "I don't understand what that person is saying to me because oh, it's, I just can't focus", instead of saying "I'm sorry, I didn't get what you just said."

Dr. M: That ended. He said that *finally*.

SRS: Finally. And I think he was trying at first to understand and then he really wasn't able to,

Dr. M: And he didn't know and what did I, what did I did?

SRS: Well, you tried to repeat yourself and he, you know, then he was caught in trying to think about what you had just said a moment ago, and then what you were saying now, and he was sort of caught. And at that point I jumped in and I, I, I said, I said, "What Dr. M, I think," and I asked you – "I think that Dr. M is trying to say that while I was talking, you were so focused and so attentive to what I was saying," and you confirmed that that was what you were saying. And then he understood.

Dr. M: Um hum.

SRS: But at first I think he was feeling very uncomfortable because he didn't understand and maybe he was blaming himself for not understanding.

Dr. M: It seems to me uh, that that's int, interesting and I just *love* going through things like that and what it seems like and when and it uh, it's very, I like to do it. And I like to do it with you.

SRS: Oh, well thank you! It's mutual.

In this segment of our conversation, Dr. M did not recall exactly what led to the look of consternation on the face of the man in the group (Dennis), but she recalled correctly that it had to do with something she had said and further interpreted incorrectly that what she had said was, itself, a bad thing. It was wonderful that she chose to discuss this issue because had she not mentioned the incident, I would not have been able to analyze the situation with her and thereby help to ease the burden or sadness she felt given her initial interpretation.

It is clear from the foregoing that Dr. M was able to interpret correctly the meaning of the facial expression of another person. Although after a week, she was able to recall only some aspects of the incident, she was still clearly reactive emotionally to its construed meaning. It is important that caregivers recognize that even though it may be difficult for an Alzheimer's sufferer to *describe* his or her feelings and recall accurately the incidents which gave rise to them via words, the same person may be very accurate in recognizing, interpreting correctly, and reacting to the outward signs of emotion on the face of another person – that is, acute in his or her meaning-making ability.

Also clear from the foregoing is that Dr. M truly enjoyed analyzing the interpersonal dynamics of the situation. She was completely involved in what was, for her, a very meaningful and interesting discussion. Throughout our conversations, I kept in mind that, years earlier, she had studied interpersonal dynamics at a very high level, and I thus recognized her as someone whose understanding and whose personality were clearly geared to such discussions. This is an example of what I meant when I told her, in the first extract, that I do not forget that I am speaking with the Dr. M who has a history of intellectual interest and achievement. As a result, I was not positioning her as a "patient" whose identity was determined primarily by her having been diagnosed with AD. If, however, I had positioned her principally as a "patient," she and I probably never would have had this conversation, and she would have remained burdened by the sadness she felt about seeming to have caused another person to be distressed.

Meaning-making as intention in acting: Using gesture to communicate

In the same conversation Dr. M began to use gestures to communicate when she was having problems finding words. This was the first

189

occasion on which she did so a number of times in succession. It is important to note this, for on several previous occasions I had spoken with her about another person with AD who had used gestures with regularity and who had been able to communicate quite effectively through their use. In this segment of the conversation it was Dr. M who, once again, initiated the subject, speaking about her husband at the outset:

> *Dr. M:*   May I? He has a friend who is uh, uh, a, she gives him uh, among other things she uh, gives ex, help me. [Here I had to assume that she meant her husband – in another conversation Dr. M had mentioned that her husband has a friend and so I drew on that as a possibility and, as it turned out, I was correct.]
> *SRS:*   Your husband has a friend who,
> *Dr. M:*   Who uh, who uh, gives him air uh, he, she does [*she now makes movements with her arms, hands, and fingers*]
> *SRS:*   Oh, exercise?
> *Dr. M:*   Not exercise, but something like it. She's a, a person who, who's year, who's um,
> *SRS:*   Is it massage?
> *Dr. M:*   Yes. Thank you.
> *SRS:*   Do you know how I got "massage?"
> *Dr. M:*   No.
> *SRS:*   Well, you said your husband has a friend who gives him, and you started moving your body, moving your arms and so the first thing I thought was exercise. But then I thought well, moving arms, you move your arms like that with your hands spread, fingers spread out, when you're massaging someone.
> *Dr. M:*   Um hum.

Her wish to communicate was accomplished here by her intentional use of gesture, and she succeeded admirably. Her success was achieved in part by the fact that I was not attending primarily to her loss for words, but to the totality of her communicative actions.

Her further intention in the subtle use of words and her evaluation of a situation

The conversation about her husband getting a massage continued:

190

Dr. M: So he's getting it and she's a, she's a very good person and a good friend and he eats lunch with her

SRS: Oh my!

Dr. M: if they get the time to do so.

SRS: That's terrific! Have you ever gotten a massage?

Dr. M: Sure.

SRS: Do you still?

Dr. M: No, not – I don't like 'em.

SRS: Why don't you?

Dr. M: They're too, they're too passive for me.

SRS: Oh, too passive.

Dr. M: Um hum.

SRS: And you really want to, you're a swimmer.

Dr. M: I guess so.

SRS: Well, you're a very active person.

Dr. M: So I don't have to uh, uh, do it.

SRS: So you don't have to get a massage?

Dr. M: Yes, really. I mean I have, have uh, our uh, youngest son does that and uh, he, he's a very active person if that's the thing we're talking about now. And uh, he's uh, we are like both, we are like, I'm trying to think why. He's very wor, word-working.

SRS: He writes?

Dr. M: Not uh, not write so much. He writes some and he likes to, he's very uh [*gestures with arms*]

SRS: Active?

Dr. M: Exactly. Who needs words? [*laughs heartily*].

SRS: [*laughter*] But you see how, you see – this is something that I think you should be uh, pay, paying attention to. You see, you communicated, within the last five minutes, two different things. You communicated the word "massage,"

Dr. M: Um hum.

SRS: and "active" by gesturing.

Dr. M: Um hum.

SRS: So you're absolutely right. "Who needs words?" You, you made your point [*chuckles*].

Dr. M: Um hum. I made *your* point [*laughs*].

Indeed, she had made my point as well as her own. When Dr. M uttered that last comment, I had not immediately seen the significance of what she said but in another instant, it was clear to me. As well, just as clear was what had to be true in order for her to have said what she said. That is, she had to be able to (a) attend to and understand what I said, (b) compare what I said about the use of gestures to what she did, and (c) make use of the locution I used to turn it back on me with the knowledge that it was my point that she was making as well – my abiding point to her being that she could communicate effectively without succumbing to the anger and frustration that often accompanied her word-finding problems. There was a rather light-hearted, lilting character to her tone of voice when she said "Who needs words?" that revealed a kind of relief, an experience of a kind of freedom to communicate, a kind of delight at having been successful. Such delight about having communicated clearly and such insight into her having "made my point" both represent an interpretation and an evaluation of events, which spell meaning-driven, or semiotic, behavior.

Part, if not all, of this interchange occurred because I took the time to reflect on, and to call her attention to, her successful use of gestures following each such occurrence. My correct interpretation seemed to be very rewarding to her. Underscoring those interpretations with the explanation of how they came about served to show her that she did, in fact, make her points and, in turn, allowed for the continuation of the natural flow of conversation.

Evaluation of subtle differences in the impact of words and expressed intent in action

Another example of Dr. M's ability to evaluate the communicative quality of a subtle difference in locution can be seen in the following interchange. Also, notice that she is still focusing upon her inability (in her estimation) to talk. In response to her statement, I maintain that there is a difference between her own abiding standard of graceful speech and her ability to communicate her thoughts. In regard to her ability to evaluate important differences in the verbal approaches one can employ to make suggestions to others, I should point out that it is possible that her training could have had a bearing upon this, but it is possible that a person without such training could have made similar observations:

SRS: Well, it might be an idea to talk about one or two things that you would like to have happen in the group.

Dr. M: Well, I'll tell ya, I'll do it only if you're there.

SRS: I'll be there.

Dr. M: That's what you said. Some people – you need someone who knows that how you can run a clu [club, perhaps], and uh, I'm not the one in my group who does it particularly since I can't talk. [Here, she wants me to be present at the support group meeting because in her estimation, I have the ability to run a group and that she herself could not do so given that she "can't talk."]

SRS: Could have fooled me [*chuckling*].

Dr. M: You didn't notice? [*laughter*].

SRS: Well, to say you can't talk is a bit of an extreme interpretation. I think you can, I think you can speak and make your points. I think if you're upset or nervous, then that stands in your way.

Dr. M: I fear, yes. Ah! That's present uh, one in the three things you told me to do.

SRS: That's interesting because when you're relaxed you're much more fluent and much more

Dr. M: Um hum.

SRS: able to communicate what you're thinking. So if you go into the group and you're nervous, then that just stands in your way.

Dr. M: Um hum, I know. But you know if you do this [*she then breathes deeply and slowly to stay calm*] it will be better. But better is some, not something you could get right away.

SRS: Oh, that's right – you have to practice.

Dr. M: [*laughs*]

SRS: Does that make sense?

Dr. M: Yes.

SRS: So . . .

Dr. M: It's practicing for anything you're doing, of course.

SRS: That's true.

Dr. M: Did you just make that up? [*laughs*]

SRS: [*at first wryly, clearly with humor*] Well, I don't know, some angel just whispered it in my ear and I just repeated it. But I think, you know, talking, saying something to the group about how you feel, what you think should happen, I think that's very important.

Dr. M: I have a some, something.

SRS: Okay.

Dr. M: Different people have different ways, and so if you, who are not uh, a per, what kind of [group] what we are, come up and say uh, here's how I'd like to talk about it or something – I lost it.

SRS: No, you've got it. Let me see if I understand you. If I were to say I would like to see certain things happen here,

Dr. M: Um hum.

SRS: that is, *I could make a suggestion about how the group ought to go, or something the group ought to think about or do,*

Dr. M: Ya. *"Think about" is a better word I would say, wouldn't you?*

SRS: Ya.

Dr. M: [*laughs knowingly, as if I got the point that she just gently taught me.*]

SRS: Gives people a little more freedom.

Dr. M: Yes, sure! [*laughs*].

In the first italicized portion of her comments, she is quite clear in expressing her intention to explore what she'd like to see happen in the group only if I were present. In essence, she is setting up something of a contingency for future action – she will speak up only if I am there, because she thinks that I have the ability to lead such a group. In the second italicized portion of her comments, Dr. M discriminated between my first locution, "how the group ought to go" and my second, "something the group ought to think about or do." She clearly evaluated the second approach as better than the first, and she encouraged me ("wouldn't you?") to see the difference and recognize that the advantage of using the latter form was that it offered more freedom to the group and carried less of a dictatorial message. I was literally being instructed gently, in a Socratic way, and when I came to the right conclusion and verbalized why (it gives people more freedom), she chuckled as if I had realized finally what was so obvious to her in the first place, and what she had led me to understand with clear purpose. There was a palpable delight in her

194

facial expression, for she was teaching me something here and I was a willing and quick student.

Her intention in planning and her self-reflection

She then went on to suggest a topic for discussion:

> *Dr. M:* In my head I had the idea that uh, people could each tell the other what they can't do.
>
> *SRS:* That's a good idea, what you just did here and some of your work would fit into this.
>
> *Dr. M:* [*laughs*] Of course! You think I don't listen?
>
> *SRS:* Oh I know you listen. It's just that I don't think clearly sometimes. And they could talk also about what they can do well. It would be very interesting and I think very helpful because that way, people start to learn about each other.
>
> *Dr. M:* Um hum.
>
> *SRS:* You really do know how to run a group!
>
> *Dr. M:* [*chuckles*] But not in this point.
>
> *SRS:* But you know how. You have, you have the sense of, um, of the dynamics.
>
> *Dr. M:* Kid, I want you to know that I learned it when I was uh, at my father's knee.

Again, we have an example of the ability of a person with moderate to severe Alzheimer's disease to think clearly about an issue of great import to her and to bring to bear abilities that were "learned at her father's knee" and elaborated upon and developed over decades of study. She obviously evaluated her own abilities when I commented to her that she really knows how to run a group, and she responded by saying, "But not in this point" (not at this time). Here I am pointing out to her the distinction between her clear and admirable knowledge of how a group should be run and her comment that, at present, she could not actually do so. Thus, it is entirely possible for the Alzheimer's sufferer to be able to evaluate situations even though there may be no opportunity to exhibit the evaluation and act upon it through overt behavior. In the case of Dr. M, the combination of her own reluctance to speak in the group setting and the flow of the group process led to her silence on some important matters. It should be clear from the foregoing that it would be a great mistake to assume, on the basis of the lack of the overt behavior, that the evaluative ability is not present. To make such an erroneous assumption, based on the positioning of the AD sufferer as a "patient' could result in a variety of social misunderstandings and render the meaning-making ability of the afflicted invisible to one degree or another.

Evaluation and application to herself of the meaning of a story

This next extract occurred toward the end of about two hours of conversation. Dr. M was aware that we had only a short time left to converse, because we were going to have some lunch and then go to the support group meeting, and she wanted to communicate that to me:

> *Dr. M:* We want to get to the, we can have a little more time because we, it is necessary only to get uh, food and uh, we can have a little uh. One of the things, one of the more things that uh, I can't quickly say uh, "Look if we uh, we have to be there, here." It's so hard for me.
>
> *SRS:* Ya, I see that. I could almost feel just in these last few moments,
>
> *Dr. M:* Um hum,
>
> *SRS:* when you looked at your watch,
>
> *Dr. M:* Um hum,
>
> *SRS:* it was almost as if you wanted to say, "Well the only thing we have left to do really, is to have some food before we go to the support group meeting and it takes a half an hour or so to get to the support group meeting and we have to be finished eating by one, we have some time now,
>
> *Dr. M:* Ya, but that's not, it's not like we, I used to do.
>
> *SRS:* Oh ya, ya, I know. But I want you to develop a habit not to flash on how it used to be and keep on track, because thinking of how it used to be just blocks your thinking now. Let me tell you a story.

I went on to tell Dr. M about two men, each of whom had had a stroke. One was middle-aged and very angry about the stroke's effects and about other things as well. His speech was not affected by the stroke and he could engage in conversation to whatever extent he wished. The other man was in his seventies and the stroke initially affected him in that he was not able to speak, for Broca's area in the left hemisphere of his brain had been damaged, and Broca's area is quite heavily involved with the motor aspects of speech production. Now, five years after the stroke, he was able to say some words and could make himself understood but not without a struggle. The older man said to the younger man, "You know I'm really happy with my life now compared to the way it was when I first had the stroke, because now I can say some things." The younger man said, "But you're not as good as you were before the stroke." And the older man said, "Well, that's irrelevant basically. When I first had the stroke, I couldn't say anything. Now I can say some things." And so the younger man said, "Well, I can't stop thinking about how it used to be for me before my stroke."

Upon hearing this story, Dr. M responded:

Dr. M: Oh, that's not a good thing to do.

SRS: That's what the older man said,

[*Dr. M chuckles*]

SRS: so in a way, it applies to you too.

Dr. M: Ya, I know.

SRS: So you could say to yourself, "All right, so it's not the way it was when I could utter 5700 words a second, but I'll get to it." It's shifting goals.

Dr. M: All right, I'll do that.

SRS: Good.

Dr. M: I'll try to.

SRS: And I'll, I'll do everything I can to help you.

Dr. M: Okay! Um, the, maybe what you had talked about will be helpful um, mostly now I see things um, maybe this isn't what we need to say. I, I said it once or twice that things are, are not getting better at all. And uh, the man that who's having some happy moments, I suppose that's, I think that's probably about like the guy, for me when we go walking, or something like that, without saying "We're going out to . . . uh, put uh, do something that is yoush, uh yoush, youshable [useful]."

SRS: So, maybe what the older man said applies to you too?

Dr. M: Yup. All right, if I can't get anything better, I'll take that.

In this exchange, Dr. M immediately recognized that it wasn't a good thing for the younger man in the story to dwell on how things used to be before his stroke, and she immediately acknowledged that she understood that the maxim of the story applied to her as well. She was in the process of shifting her expectations of herself based on her standards of the past and shifting her related emotional reactions toward accepting her present condition as seen in her final comment. This process entails evaluation and interpretation, for she was applying the reactions of the men in the story to herself, and deriving meaning in the process.

Her evaluation of a support group situation and her action to effect change

Dr. M was deeply sensitive to the dynamics of the group, particularly to the idea that at certain times there were "in" people and "out" people. In other words, at certain times, the conversation would be dominated by a few people, leaving the others silent. Dr. M preferred to see everyone in the group included in one way or another and was instrumental in bringing one woman, who was particularly silent, into the discussion. As a result of her effort, the conversation took on a new life with topics that I never anticipated arising in such a group. It is, perhaps, an example of my own failings that my expectations did not allow for the possibility of what actually occurred. I have since changed my expectations! What follows is some of the dialogue in which Dr. M indicates her acute perception of the group process (which occurred a week earlier) and I will then provide some dialogue from the group meeting itself.

> *Dr. M:* I, I felt . . . see, all the things that were going until they got to the last part,
> *SRS:* Um hum,
> *Dr. M:* that uh, I think was not, not – there were in people and out people.
> *SRS:* Um hum,
> *Dr. M:* I was one of the out people some of the time.
> *SRS:* Um hum.

We then went on to discuss the situation of another woman in the group, one of the "out" people for some of the time:

198

Dr. M: There was a lot of people with people. You know, two people getting with two people and that made a good connection.

SRS: Ya,

Dr. M: So that people were ahead. It had another problem and that was the person, the other woman who was made more away because she wasn't, because there was so much uh, dealing with this lady who talked a lot . . . because uh, when the woman who was alone uh, wasn't, she wasn't there.

It was important to Dr. M to include the woman who was one of the people who was silent throughout. This same woman had been present at other meetings and had been silent most of the time. Dr. M succeeded in bringing this particular woman into the discussion when the group began to discuss the subject of cursing when frustration is experienced. One of the women who was an "in" person most of the time commented, "I find 'shit' is a wonderful word. I don't know why, I don't understand why it's such a great word, those four letters together. It's very relieving." Dr. M, during this comment, turned to the otherwise silent woman and asked her if she liked what was being discussed and the woman responded by saying "No."

I then turned to one of the men in the group and asked him if he liked poetry because I thought I remembered him saying so during an earlier meeting. He responded by saying "absolutely," and then another person responded in kind. While this was going on, I noticed that Dr. M was leaning toward the usually silent woman and saying something to her. Suddenly, Dr. M said (about the woman whom she wanted to include in the group and to whom I will refer as Mrs. N) "She said it in a very nice voice. 'Yes', she said."

SRS: Really?

Mrs. N: I was a literature major. English literature. I had a double major.

SRS: What was the other one?

Mrs. N: It must have been art history.

SRS: Would you like to come to my office sometime and tell my students that they should be majoring in those kinds of subjects?

Mrs. N: Yes!

SRS: Is there a poet that you really love?

Mrs. N: I think in American literature it was Walt Whitman. I also did a paper on Henry Adams, the education of Henry Adams. He had a very wonderful career.

Mrs. B: He knew Washington, DC when there, when you went out into the street and fell into three inches of mud.

SRS: He said something that I have never been able to get out of my mind. He said that a teacher affects eternity because he (or she) never knows where his (or her) influence ends.

Mrs. L: That's true of anybody, not just a teacher.

Mrs. N: Or any teacher or any person.

SRS: Or here, right now. You're teaching me things all the time. So Whitman was one of your favorites?

Mrs. N: Yes, that's right. He had several versions of his poems, probably five of them, and uh, so you never know which one you're reading probably. Because there were many additions and corrections, because he apparently continued to correct the uh, drafts. He was writing in the period of the Civil War. And he was a male nurse in the Civil War and he was just appalled at the carnage of the Civil War.

SRS: So he re-wrote poems?

Mrs. N: Yes, that's right. Because he was never satisfied with the revision that was in process at that point. And so he would write another.

SRS: I didn't know that.

Mrs. L: I didn't know it either.

This discussion continued, but it never would have taken place had it not been for Dr. M's desire and successful effort to bring Mrs. N into the group conversation. Dr. M's sense of group dynamics, her sensitivity to the situation of a person "just sitting there," as it were, her making the effort to bring the group's attention to Mrs. N's otherwise unheard response to the question about poetry, not only allowed Mrs. N to participate but also opened up a discussion that was enlivening and informative. Thus, Dr. M not only evaluated a situation as being one that she wanted to change, but found a lovely, graceful way to precipitate that change.

When Mrs. N spoke, she seemed somewhat nervous at first, perhaps shy, but she was so obviously interested in the subject that her enthusiasm was not to be denied. It was as if she had suddenly come to life. She was full of energy and dignity, her tone was graceful and erudite. Interestingly, Mrs. N was in the early stages of the disease, and could obviously express herself well, yet until Dr. M intervened, Mrs. N, perhaps due to the social situation of the group, had been an "out person." But once she became involved, others in the group were drawn into the conversation and there was a flow of ideas that commanded the attention of everyone in the room. Afterward, I could not help thinking about the personalities that came to life in that room, the knowledge that was shared, the mutual give and take of conversation that occurred, all because of the insight, meaning-making ability and effort of the woman who, in her words, "can't talk" and who literally could no longer sign her name. A host of cognitive and brain functions must be brought to bear in order to achieve what Dr. M achieved in those moments.

Among the cognitive operations involved are planning, attention (in that Dr. M had to be attending to the conversations and to what Mrs. N said), context-sensitive operations which would allow her to pick the right moment during the speech of others to interject what Mrs. N had said, memory of what she wanted to accomplish in terms of the group and in terms of Mrs. N's involvement, to name but a few. Among the personal qualities that were involved was a sense of concern about the group as a whole and about Mrs. N in particular, the desire to make a tangible positive contribution to both, and the determination to seek and find the moment.

How ironic and beautiful it was that Dr. M, the woman of letters who now suffered severe word-finding problems, would be the person to find exactly the right words and the right moment to allow Mrs. N to become involved in the group's discussion for the first time, to make a wonderful contribution, and to manifest a thoughtful and charming personality. Interestingly enough, Dr. M did not say a word after she brought Mrs. N into the discussion. The conversation flowed with a life of its own. In a way, Dr. M did exactly what a good group leader would hope to do: say very little, but create the circumstances through which everyone, including the reticent members of the group, becomes involved.

I never expected that Walt Whitman and Henry Adams would be topics of discussion at an Alzheimer's sufferers' support group meeting. My own surprise served to signal the subtle bias I had brought with me. Once again, Alzheimer's sufferers brought home to me the idea there are semiotic abilities which remain intact, but which require the necessary social context in order to be realized.

Her evaluation of me and her ability to shift her view of another person

As I became more of a "regular" at the support group meetings, Dr. M and I discussed those meetings more often, with her giving me feedback about her experience and about my performance as a facilitator and as a source of information. In what follows below we began talking about the previous week's meeting, at which two of her poems, written decades earlier, were read by the group leader. The group seemed to enjoy the poems immensely, and the group leader thought at first that the poems were authored by me (Dr. M was not identified as the author until quite some time after they had been read and discussed).

> *Dr. M:* The uh, the way uh, you handled the last group, I think it was very good.
>
> *SRS:* Oh really? Well, I was hoping you were going to want to talk about that.
>
> *Dr. M:* Ya, of course, my goodness!
>
> *SRS:* I think it was wonderful that you brought the poetry.
>
> *Dr. M:* Oh! Everybody believes in poetry!
>
> *SRS:* Isn't that something?
>
> *Dr. M:* I, I was really surprised. Not, not everybody.
>
> *SRS:* Yes well, Len was sort of lukewarm about it,
>
> *Dr. M:* Ya, he's, ya but he uh, he's not a man who could look at ideas of feeling, feeling things. He tries to put it away, but you don't let him or we don't let him.
>
> *SRS:* Ya, well he is an emotional guy.
>
> *Dr. M:* You get that because . . .
>
> *SRS:* Because after, I think it was a couple of meetings ago, the end – I think it was the time Rita was saying how she loves the word, "shit",
>
> *Dr. M:* Ya, uh huh,
>
> *SRS:* at the end of that meeting he came over to me and his eyes were very teary, and he just said to me, "I want you to know that I appreciate what you're doing here."

Dr. M: Oh! I, I feel right, right for you and good for him.

SRS: I was touched, I was so touched. So I think he's a sweet, emotional guy, I think that men in that generation didn't necessarily take as many opportunities as they could to express their feelings.

Dr. M: All right, I understand.

Indeed, Dr. M did understand. I found her comment about "feeling right for you and good for him" to be particularly interesting. In this statement we see evidence of her ability to put herself in the position of someone else (myself) and her ability to be happy for another person and to change her view of that person based upon new information. Her desire to evaluate Len's behavior began with my saying that I thought that he was an emotional guy, and her immediately probing me with, "You get that because . . ." (you think so based on . . . what?). She wanted to know how I came to my conclusion and when I told her, she indicated flexibility of abstract thought and the ability to shift perspectives, to change her evaluation of him. Dr. M's life before AD was one permeated by and with meaning. And, although AD robbed her of many of her cherished abilities and thus caused her great anguish, even in the middle to severe stages of the disease, she was still very much a semiotic subject and our time together was nothing but meaningful to both of us.

The Case of Dr. B

In previous chapters, we have seen a great many examples of meaning-driven behavior in Dr. B's discourse. I will revisit a few of those examples here and also provide additional evidence that he was able to interpret and evaluate situations and events as well as to reveal intention in his actions.

His evaluation of his abilities as affected by Alzheimer's disease

Dr. B: What the things are? Uh, I have, uh, delumision [diminution] of what, what I could read, uh, and that's very important to me, and, and my wife is an absolute doll and uh, so it doesn't,

203

uh, so like I have times when I can't, I can't get up in terms of, um, that I sort of gone fooey sometimes. And then I don't think I, uh, I know that I am slowing down. I don't know how to put an end, and a quarter or a thirty of something. But, but I do works I, I can't work for that I used to do, that I used to do. And then, on the other hand, I get a spurt.

SRS: Um hum.

Dr. B: I get a spurt and it, uh, I have, I have, uh, a good time but, uh, it doesn't, doesn't hold.

SRS: It doesn't last very long?

Dr. B: No. And I, you know, love, I love my wife very much and she works her tooshie off because she, I have, I have to give her, you know, and uh

SRS: How do you feel about that?

Dr. B: No thing you can do. Wife and, uh, I pray for Alzheimer's things, you know. What do I do? What do I do? [*laughs*] I don't have any more.

SRS: Do you feel sometimes that you're almost a fraction of the person . . . [*Dr. B interrupts*]

Dr. B: Oh, I do that almost every day! What, what does it mean? It doesn't mean anything, though. I've, I've hard, hard work and I have to *schlep* [carry, haul, in Yiddish] stuff sometimes now for, for my wife, and sometimes it works okay and sometimes it doesn't. Now I don't have it constantly . . . Well, I get wisps of people, of thoughts, that show me that Alzheimer's is right on top of me. And, uh, that there's nothing I can do about it . . . Well uh, I'm, and I'm, something has knocked me down, something's knocked me down and I can't do anything about it.

In this extract, Dr. B indicates that he is slowing down, that there is a diminution in his ability to read, that sometimes he gets a "spurt", he experiences moments when he feels more able to have a good time, feels more coherent, but that it doesn't last ("it doesn't hold"). Each statement involves an implicit evaluation of his present abilities as compared to those same abilities in his past, healthier days. Knowing the difference is, itself, revelatory of the ability to evaluate and to compare. In the last sentence in this extract, he indicates his understanding of the nature of the disease, that there is no cure or means of reversing its effects, and his own impotence in the face of its effects.

His desire to preserve privacy and his cooperative action with his wife

When Dr. B first agreed to work with me, I was explaining to him some of the things I wanted to explore in the process of working with him:

Dr. B: Where do we go from here?

SRS: I'd like to know about meaningful events in your life, what really mattered to you.

Dr. B: Well, there's, you know, gonna be a lot of probing there and um, we'll see what's what . . . I wanna think about what this is about and secondly, have Mrs. B, if she thinks it's, uh, doesn't dest, des, destroy the family. So look – bear with me, bear with me. Mrs. B is the uh, and I will have to talk about that. Okay, uh, I'd like to, I like to see what Mrs. B does. That's the linch, the linchpin, the linchpin. I don't want to give out, to give out personal family and we are, you know, I think the next step is for, um to talk with Mrs. B I will definitely have a long talk first with Mrs. B – how to handle it . . . Right now I have to chew out a lot of things, um, and uh, let's see how the lay of the land is, because we have a very strong family any which one of them could knock your socks off.

SRS: You have really strong personalities in your family?

Dr. B: Well we have, we have, um, we *are*, we all um, is pretty strong. I may be that this is as far as I could go.

A year after this conversation occurred, Mrs. B told me that I knew more about their family than anyone who wasn't in their family. It was obvious that this was an incredibly strong, loving family and that their sense of privacy and propriety was well developed. Dr. B, in the throes of AD in the moderate to severe stages, was not at all hesitant about setting early limits on what would be revealed to me about him and the rest of his family. The meaning of family privacy and his own diminished abilities were clear to him and so, before he would agree to discuss such important aspects of his life, he intended to discuss the issue with his wife, who was his partner in every way throughout their marriage.

This clear, meaning-driven behavior may serve to inform some of the studies of language ability among AD sufferers. Kempler (1984), for example, studied the semantic abilities of the afflicted by asking them to respond to questions about their families. It is unclear as to what extent the issue of privacy as expressed by Dr. B had an effect on the results of Kempler's study. However, it is apparent that researchers must take account of the fact that some AD sufferers' responses to such questions may be affected by issues that have little to do with their language functions, and that some AD sufferers may not be as forthright or informative about their concerns regarding privacy as was Dr. B. So to assume that AD sufferers would not be reluctant to speak about private family matters would be to assume incorrectly, perhaps, that maintaining privacy has no meaning for them – that is, that they are not semiotic subjects.

The issue of his independence

For many years before the onset of AD, Dr. B enjoyed taking walks as a form of exercise. This proclivity, coupled with the fact that he did not enjoy participating in the daily program of activities at the day care center, conspired to bring about another source of frustration, as he was not allowed to go outside for walks by himself. From the point of view of the day care center staff, this prohibition was quite understandable, but from Dr. B's point of view it was something quite different:

> *Dr. B:* Um, I want so very much, this is another block, I want my very much to have, um, being independent. Right now I can't go out without anybody else.
>
> *SRS:* Um hum.
>
> *Dr. B:* And, um, it irritates me.
>
> *SRS:* Maybe something can be worked out where you can be a bit more independent, but recognize the limits that you need to stick to. Would you like to go out on your own?
>
> *Dr. B:* Well, yes! And, uh, I find that I want to get away from this lock-step, or something like that.
>
> *SRS:* You feel like you're closed in?
>
> *Dr. B:* Oh yes, very much.

As a result of this conversation and others with his wife and the day care staff, Dr. B was given the opportunity to go for a walk with one

206

of the staff members so as to find out whether or not he could walk a short distance and then find his way back to the center without any trouble. It turned out that he could do so, and he even chose a landmark to help him locate his position relative to the center. The landmark was a mailbox to which he referred as "the infamous box" or, at times, "the lodestone." As a result, he was allowed to take short walks outside and he described this new development to me:

> *Dr. B:* I think I have one resolution that I, uh, think I got now – taking walk. And [director's name] and others are letting me be. When I assure them they were not to worry because I'll go there and come right back. It's just the tightness that I get because I used to, I'm certainly used to walk a lot and for someone to encapsulate people, that got me and maybe you know about it now or something like that.
>
> *SRS:* I know now that you just told me. And yes, to fence people in is not . . . [*Dr. B interrupts*]
>
> *Dr. B:* Fence me in. I look for people to take a walk, everybody else is turning their own thing. But I, for Christ's sake, you know I can't. I love to walk and if I don't, I'm, I'm, I am really upset.

His use of the words, "lock-step" and "encapsulate" in the above extracts indicated to me, in the context of the conversation, his feeling of a lack of flexibility, of independence, in the case of the former word, and a feeling of being hemmed in, enclosed, or fenced in, in the case of the latter word. Again, through the use of indirect repair, we can see that that was precisely how he was feeling. In his last comment above, he indicates his frustration at not being able to find someone with whom to take a walk, as "everyone else is turning their own thing" – is otherwise engaged, as it were, usually in activities in which he had no interest or could not take part.

All of the foregoing reflects his ability to interpret and evaluate the meaning of the situations which he confronted, for these situations were powerfully connected to his sense of loss, of decline. Specifically, to remain unable to go outside for short walks and return, even though he could do so without any problems, would mean that he would have to admit that he was being correctly positioned as incompetent and that AD had robbed him further of an important aspect of his personal identity which he regarded as being central to his sense

207

of self. On the other hand, to have reached the resolution of being able to go out for short walks, was consonant with his past history and this enabled him to see himself as being differentiated in still another way from the rest of the participants at the day care center.

Retaining the ability to educate

Because I had seen and had been tremendously impressed by photographs of some of his paintings, I mentioned my reaction to him and I thought that perhaps he might like to do some sketching. I arranged some objects on a desk and gave him a pad and pencil and he began to sketch the still life but did not seem to enjoy it, going through it quickly rather than deliberately, although he did do a fairly decent job.

Dr. B: I do the work [painting] and I do rather slowly.

SRS: Oh, I see.

Dr. B: Now, some people do like that [*making quick motions with the pencil*], but I don't. I do my painting in my place and uh, it takes me quite a while to shape. I'm a shaper if you want to call it, a shaper . . . I'll work and I'll work and I'll be constantly working on it if it's, if it's worthy. But other people just go like that: bang, bang, bang. I don't do that. I mold and I mold and I mold.

SRS: So with you things take shape very slowly.

Dr. B: Ya.

SRS: And you work with different colors and tones.

Dr. B: Ya.

SRS: That's why you don't like to sketch. Because sketching is quick.

Dr. B: Well, ya. With me, I'll work here, and then I'll work here, and then I'll go another piece here [*all the while pointing to the paper he used to make the sketch*] and then I may even turn it around.

SRS: Oh, I see.

Dr. B: That's the way I work, I have worked for, with paintings. Does that put a lynch in there somewhere? [I interpreted this as, "Is that a problem?", although he may have meant, "Is this meaningful somehow?"]

208

SRS: Not at all, not at all.

Dr. B: What do you mean?

SRS: Well, it just tells me that – you see you're educating me –

Dr. B: Oh?

SRS: because, see, I made an assumption that I shouldn't have made.

Dr. B: What?

SRS: Well, I've seen your paintings and I've admired them, and I said, "Well, this fellow paints – why don't I ask him to sketch something?" not thinking that painting and sketching are very different kinds of things.

Dr. B: Ya, ya.

SRS: And you've just explained that to me.

Dr. B: We're, we're educating each other.

He was absolutely correct about this situation and virtually every other encounter we shared. Slowly, but surely, he explained to me the difference between his view of sketching and painting and why sketching was less meaningful to him than was painting. In addition, he would ask quite often during our association, "Does this mean anything?", or "Does this have any value?", or "Does that put a lynch in there somewhere?", and I took these questions as reflecting his constant desire to provide useful information for the Project. He was being utterly faithful to and conscientious regarding his position in this project as would any scientist who was engaged devotedly in the search for understanding.

His work on and position in "The Project"

Dr. B had spent the preponderance of his vocational life as an academic scientist, a professor, and an author, and as an administrator. As a result of his background, the idea of working with me to help elucidate the experience of AD sufferers had an intrinsic appeal, for it was, in his estimation, "a sort of scientific thing," and as such carried significant meaning for him.

It was in the third week of "The Project", as he called it, that an issue arose which I must say came as something of a surprise. Dr. B had already learned to recognize me by sight, although he did have trouble recalling my name. He could recognize my name, however, once again pointing out that remembering is more than simply being able to recall. Already he was looking forward to our meetings, for the director of the adult day care center often would tell me that, before I arrived, Dr. B would be asking about my expected time of arrival. He was involved in research again and this excited him, as that part of his life had been shortened by Alzheimer's. And now, despite the problems posed by AD, he was once again engaged in a pursuit that had always been compelling to him. And, as I was to find out, he was very protective of his position in The Project.

Dr. B: Somebody said that Bob (the director of the adult day care program) was the project and doing all the work. So let's clarify on this. You and I are the projects. You may not like it, or something like that.

SRS: That's fine.

Dr. B: We can embellish in whatever we want. My G-d! I'm doing nothing? I'm not saying this is absolutely right and something like that . . . I put quite a mount in myself. This may be a little piss in the pot, really, or something like that . . . But I hear people telling me that this is your project. Yeah, I buy that, but when people start telling me over and over again that Bob . . . so I'm beginning to say, you know, that something in me has got to be, you know, in this. And so I'm not being picky, picky, picky, picky, picky picky, picky, picky. I'm perfectly apple [happy? able?] to identify a project as a project that and certainly doing whatever you want to do. There are areas, not areas, what I'm trying to say, for example, Bob – he's putting himself into the project. That's about all that I can say. I feel, uh, my sons and daughters they will – what's cookin'? – this kind of thing. It's probably a piss in a pot. Because you, you, I know you started the project. You did, I know you did. So I sort of had 3, 4, 5, days thinking "what's going on?" I'm probably rambling.

It happened that the previous morning I was at the day care center and had been discussing a number of things with the staff. Some of my students were beginning to come to the center as interns and I wanted to discuss related issues as was our custom at the beginning of a term. Dr. B already knew that I was not usually there in the early morning, and he saw me through a glass window as I was talking with staff members in the office. Following that discussion, I spent some time talking with Dr. B, and he expressed some concern that I was bringing people on the staff into the project. I immediately assured him that that was not the case, and told him exactly what I was talking to the staff about. He was quite aroused about the issue and I sought to allay his fears.

However, under conditions of heightened emotional arousal, even among completely healthy people, the ability to process and retain information is often compromised. For the Alzheimer's sufferer, the situation is even worse. And so we spent about 20 minutes beyond the dialogue above sorting out exactly who was in the project and who wasn't. I treated his concern with great seriousness and without any hint of comments such as "Don't you remember that we had this conversation just yesterday?" (After all, didn't *I* remember?) That comment would have been irrelevant on the one hand because if he could recall the conversation of a day ago, he would not be saying all this now. On the other hand, if I made such a comment, it probably would have increased his arousal even further, thus perpetuating the problem. He himself had told me that he absorbed "in globs." It turned out that the "glob" he absorbed concerned my talking with the staff, and the "glob" he didn't absorb was my explanation regarding the subject of my discussion with the staff members. Thus, I treated his concern as quite real, for it was nothing but real to him, and he deserved to be reassured and have his calm restored.

There was still another issue involved in Dr. B's urgency about who was part of the project and who was not. If I were to involve others in the project without telling him, or without asking him, he could easily experience a sense of loss of control regarding his position in the project. The idea of loss of control could be a very powerful issue for someone who (a) had generally, for decades, been in control regarding important issues and (b) was suffering from a disease that, by its very nature, compromises one's control over some of the most mundane aspects of life, not to mention the control one is accustomed to having over one's thoughts and use of words and ability to retrieve information from memory.

Finally, what I came to confront with him was still another issue regarding the meaning of his position in the project:

Dr. B: It's your project, in a sense, really. I know that.

SRS: But there isn't any project without you.

Dr. B: Ya, ya.

SRS: I can't do this by myself.

Dr. B: I know, well I know that. Maybe get status – you being number one and I'll be number two.

SRS: We'll work on a par.

Dr. B: Okay, alright, enough of that. We have concluded that it's ours, really, it's ours because one of these times if I spect and hope for both of us that, uh, we can get glory, you know, something like this.

SRS: I agree.

In this dialogue, so early into the project, the academic-researcher in Dr. B is being manifested and recognized. I knew that Dr. B was a distinguished man and I wanted to avoid having him feel like something of a guinea pig, or object to be studied. (Actually, I have interacted this way with all AD sufferers with whom I have been associated, without regard to their academic achievements.) He as much as asked me early on if he was going to be a "guinea pig." On the contrary, I wanted to see him be himself, act naturally, and so I wanted to interact with him in a human context as one person to another. In other words, I wanted to avoid positioning him (and having him feel positioned) as someone being tested, and I wanted to avoid positioning myself as the tester-experimenter. Thus, we were doing this project together. As it turned out, he grew to be very excited about the project and related his excitement to his wife. He knew that his cognitive abilities had declined considerably. To be working on a project, doing research, with the possibility of "getting glory" gave him a sense of meaning and pride in the reconstruction of the academic person that he had been for so many years of his life.

Additionally in the dialogue, he established our relative positions in the project as "number one and number two," recognizing me as what would be termed in professional parlance, "the principal investigator," but reserving for himself the position of "number two," which is far more meaningful than is a mere subject in a typical study. One can see also in this form of positioning that he was creating a means by which he could establish and maintain feelings of self-worth.

212

In his last comments in this extract, we see yet another example of the project's meaning for him. Not only is the project now firmly established as "ours," but perhaps we "can get glory, you know, something like this." The prospect of doing significant work once again, especially in the confines of an adult day care center, where he assiduously avoided being part of the community of participants, made the project and his role in it all the more meaningful to him. Where the other participants were engaged in doing what he called, "filler" (which he defined as "something that doesn't mean anything") and in which he would not participate for a moment, he now was engaged in doing "a scientific sort of thing" that might bring us "glory."

His participation in the project with me, to the exclusion of everyone else at the day care center, differentiated him further from the rest of the participants in a way that bolstered his pride and simultaneously reconnected him with an aspect of his lifelong vocational pursuits. Recall that he commented that, among the day care participants, he was "nothing," and that, in his view, given his accomplishments and abilities, there should be some hierarchy – which, presumably would locate him as being "special" in ways that were not shared by any other of the participants. Note also, that he was very upset about the prospect of other staff members being involved in the project, and that when he came to understand that the project involved just the two of us, he was calm and content. Although the project was going on at the day care center, none of the other participants and none of the staff was involved, thereby insulating us as a unit from the larger social context in which we happened to be working. It was precisely the larger social context with which he wanted nothing to do, for his being associated with that environment was, to him, emblematic of his decline. In fact, he evinced a great deal of urgency about moving the project along, because he knew, from having read extensively about the disease immediately after he was diagnosed, that he was fighting against time and the progression of the disease.

His urgency about the pace of the project

Dr. B was very keen for his wife to be involved in the project and he told me as much. I had spoken with his wife and then with him and explained that, before I met with her, I wanted to spend a good deal of time with him so that I could form my own judgments about him without being biased in one way or another by the observations or attitudes his wife might offer. At this point, I had no idea that Mrs. B would turn out to be one of the most remarkable human beings I had ever met. Nonetheless, I explained my plan to each of them.

At the same time, however, Dr. B was becoming increasingly restless about when his wife would become involved, for he wanted the project to move along swiftly. Toward that end, he believed that his wife could provide important information and was urging her to meet with me. I had no idea of what was transpiring between them until the following conversation. It began with Dr. B clearly distressed about something that transpired between himself and his wife and he was trying to explain the problem to me. However, because of the combination of his own sense of urgency and his word-finding problems, that proved a formidable task.

SRS: It's kind of hard to reconstruct?

Dr. B: It's hard to reconstruct . . . the *will* is there.

SRS: That I know.

Dr. B: Ya, of course, of course. We're in tandem. Uh, when the thing is, when he comes into the project – this is my wife talking – I will be able to talk to him.

SRS: Was she saying that she'll talk to me when the time is right?

Dr. B: Well, approximately that, she said when you come to me then I will something or something like that.

SRS: I think she's perfectly willing to be involved.

Dr. B: If we started from scratch right now, what should we be doing – in order for her –

SRS: If we were starting from scratch, I wouldn't talk with her until I got to know you for quite a while, just man to man.

Dr. B: Yeah, here's what she says: "When you get there, when you get to that point of being able to do this project, then I will be able to talk to you," or something like that.

SRS: That's fine. I don't feel any need to be upset. I think she understands.

Dr. B: Along with that, what's the time that you look, that you first, last, um, because I keep telling her, and I keep telling her, and telling her and I have the feeling that she's getting more and more upset.

SRS: When you say you keep telling her, what is it that you keep telling her? Let me back up. You said, "I keep telling her and telling her."

Dr. B: That . . .

SRS: Yes, what are you telling her?

Dr. B: What do I telling her – I want her, I want you to this prah, to work with this project.

SRS: Good, okay, so you're saying to her over and over, "I want you to be involved with this project," right?

Dr. B: Yeah, so that uh, can I think preferably that she sees him, or something like that. [Here he is having problems with the use of pronouns, so what he means is, he said to his wife "I think it preferable that you see him" and he is saying this to me, so he is referring to his wife as "she" in the statement "I think preferably that she sees him" while not using "you" to refer to me.]

SRS: Yeah, and so now I think I'm beginning to understand.

Dr. B: Yeah, I wish you would.

Here, he indicates that it is valuable to him that I understand the situation that occurred between him and his wife, with the understanding that if I did understand it, I could then explain to him what had happened and what might be done next.

SRS: Here it is: You're saying to her over and over again, "I really want you to be in this project, I really want you to be in this project, I want you to talk to him, I really want you to be in this project. [I did this emphatically and in this manner in order to communicate the sense of urgency that I sensed he felt.]

Dr. B: Yeah, yeah.

SRS: And she's saying "Enough! When he calls me I will talk to him!"

Dr. B: Yeah. I want to review this thing because maybe I'm getting uh, is there a loop that I have not gone through?

SRS: I think so, I think so.

Dr. B: Well, for G-d's sakes tell me!

SRS: I think that you are very eager to have her involved,

Dr. B: Yeah,

SRS: and for us to get together,

Dr. B: Um hum, yeah, "when he talks to me." [His wife's words to him.]

SRS: and what she's saying is, "he said he will call me

Dr. B: Um hum

SRS: and when he does, I'll be involved. And what I'm trying to make clear to you is that – look – when people are married for a long time and they love one another the way you and your wife love each other, the way you behave with her is different from the way you behave with any other human being

Dr. B: Yeah, but I'm afraid that, ah, it's something is eroshing [eroding] in our life.

SRS: Is it because of this – what you're telling me now?

Dr. B: Well, of course!

SRS: Is that the main issue?

Dr. B: Well it's enough to get us in this the heebie jeebies.

SRS: I will talk to her. But I think the loop you're missing is that she's perfectly willing to be involved, and she just wants to wait until I call her because that's what I said I'd do.

Dr. B: Fine. Because that's what I'm looking for.

SRS: Well, now is the time for me to get in touch with her.

Dr. B: So that's the lodestone.

SRS: So what she's saying to you is, "Look, sweetheart, when he comes to me, I'll be involved. Calm down." That's what I think she's saying to you.

Dr. B: And you will have to carry the ball.

SRS: Hey, I'm a New Yorker!

Dr. B: All right. Having said that, I want to do it as fast as we can because she's prepared to give this information or and "when he comes" that's the key, critical thing.

SRS: She's waiting for me to call her which is precisely correct.

Dr. B: All right. If it will be, that was pushing too much.

SRS: Yes, I think that's what it was.

Dr. B: Yeah.

SRS: I think that's what it was. I think that's a wonderful insight.

As it turned out from my meeting with Mrs. B, what I understood from the above conversation was exactly what had happened. The first thing that had to happen in order for me to understand the situation was that I had to conduct something of a friendly, caring, interrogation (if there is such a thing). I had to get him thinking *with me* instead of reacting still to what had transpired between him and his wife. In the process, he expressed the fear that his marriage was eroding as a result of his wife's being upset with him for his having harped on how she needed to meet with me. Only after his visceral reactions were somewhat calmed, could he recognize what had happened and then arrive, on his own, at the notion that he had been pushing too much – which is, itself, an interpretation of his own behavior toward his wife, along with an evaluation of his own behavior ("too much").

This insight, in my opinion, was profound. For all of his problems in finding and producing words, keeping tenses of verbs uniform, pronouncing words correctly, keeping track of dialogue accurately, he was able to see, in the end, that his wife's exasperation was due to the fact that he had been pushing his case too much and not really hearing what she was telling him. Such an insight is not found as frequently as would be desirable in relationships among people who have no brain injuries, and is certainly not examined through the use of standard neuropsychological tests of cognitive function. It is, however, one of the most important abilities that one must have if one is to make a marriage, or any meaningful relationship, work. And the uncovering of the ability to have such an insight can occur only in the natural flow of human, social interaction. This conversation was not only helpful to Dr. B, but it allowed his meaning-making ability, even with Alzheimer's disease, to be revealed yet again.

This conversation required that I not become exasperated with him, that I stay with him, and that I search for the meaning that I knew – or at least assumed – he was trying to convey. All too often, our attention can become hooked by the linguistic errors committed in the speech acts of AD sufferers. However, if we look past them and search for the deeper, underlying meaning, which often is expressed through extra-linguistic communication such as tone of voice, facial expression, gesture, and the like, we can eventually enjoy at least some success. Exemplary of this notion is an interaction I had with the daughter of an AD sufferer who told me that her mother would often wear on her face a very troubled, clenched expression. However, when the daughter asked repeatedly, "what's the matter?", her mother was unresponsive. I suggested that the daughter ask instead, "Are you upset?", and when she did so, her mother responded immediately and quite fully.

Clear to me as a result of this and other conversations with Dr. B, was that I should not judge Dr. B's ability to understand what I was saying to him on the basis of the way he himself *produced* speech. Production is often far more difficult than is reception, or under-standing – just think about how, when learning a new language, we are able to understand what is said to us far more quickly than we can say the same thing spontaneously. Production requires recall of vocabulary, the complex process of articulation, and tremendous coordination of over three hundred different muscles. Reception requires none of the above. I therefore gave him *a priori* credit for being able to understand me; it was my task simply to find the right ways to get the point across to him. If I had judged his ability to understand on the basis of his speech production, this and other con-versations may not have occurred in the first place, and that would have been terribly sad for personal, as well as human, reasons.

The conversation helped restore his calm and strengthened his understanding of where we stood. We then discussed the next step:

SRS: I'll call her and see if she and I can meet.

Dr. B: And, uh, without me?

SRS: Yes, without you this time.

Dr. B: Without me.

SRS: Is that okay with you?

Dr. B: Of course, of course!

SRS: And then we can arrange another time when the three of us can get together because that's important as well.

Dr. B: Fine.

SRS: Because that's important too. It's like chemistry.

Dr. B: It is chemistry. I talked to her for quite a long time early and I was talking, and I was talking, and I was talking, and *maybe* um, I wasn't talking the little things coming through, or something like that. I mean, [I'm] an honest person . . . you know, maybe I screwed this up. Who knows? And she make think very offendive [take offense about] on some of the things I'm trying to show. So what do we, what are we saying now?

SRS: We're saying that I'm going to call her and set up a time when she and I can meet alone.

Dr. B: Alone, fine.

SRS: She and I can talk.

Dr. B: Yeah.

SRS: And then we can go from there.

Dr. B: Okay. So right now I sit tight.

SRS: Right.

Dr. B: I just sit tight.

Thus did Dr. B express his sense of urgency about the pace of the project, his fear that due to his insistence, his wife had taken offense and that his marriage was being hurt, and thus did he come to some resolution as to what would transpire next. In all of this, he had to be able to evaluate and interpret the meaning of the circumstances which he confronted and come to define what his role would be as the project moved on.

His concern about my continuing the project with him

Not only did he express urgency about the need to move along with the project, but he also expressed his concerns about my continuing to work with him.

Dr. B: So – are you gonna throw me out of the shed?

SRS: Not me. Not for a minute. Are you kidding? [I took his question to mean "Are you going to stop working with me?" or "Are you going to end my work on the project?"]

Dr. B: What keeps you going about me?

SRS: What keeps me going about you? Now there's a question. You mean why do I keep coming and talking with you and doing this?

Dr. B: Um hum.

SRS: I think that you have a lot to teach about the effects of Alzheimer's, especially in terms of the things you can still do. The person who has this disease is not, in my opinion, well understood. I want to change that with your help. It's a matter of human dignity.

Dr. B: Well, I got a lot of dignity.

SRS: You certainly do. I want also to show that the person with Alzheimer's can learn new things, can remember new things, over a long period of time.

Dr. B: Um hum. What I want I think I've got. I've got that you have stayed with me. I have a lot of feeling for my family and, uh, so I'm hoping you can stay with me.

Here he begins by expressing his concern that I might "throw him out of the shed," or cease working with him and his curiosity about what keeps me "going about him," what keeps me working with him. He evaluates himself as having "a lot of dignity." Present here as well, is his ability to evaluate his needs ("what I want") and compare them to what he has, in fact. Finally, we see that he is able to conclude that he has what he wants. The conversation continued:

SRS: I'm here and I will be.
Dr. B: You're here, cause that gives me what I need for Alzheimer's but it also gives me, you know, other things.
SRS: I will be here and I will work with you.
Dr. B: I will never say I'm going to give up.
SRS: You'll never say you're going to give up?
Dr. B: I'm never going to give up.
SRS: That's wonderful.
Dr. B: Why?
SRS: That's what I'm hoping you'll feel.
Dr. B: Um, I don't think so. I don't think I'll quit or anything like that. I know that if I wanted to I could make a stance, uh, that will maybe do a couple of things. And I'm glad that you are staying with me. You stay with me, I stay with you and we're gonna help each other.

He recognized that my working with him fulfilled his needs "for Alzheimer's" and that it gives him "other things" as well; he expresses his intention to stay with the project, and not to give up, and evaluates the outcome of the arrangement as being "we're gonna help each other," indicating his understanding of our work on the Project as involving mutual cooperation and mutual benefit.

SRS: Well I'm glad too. You are a terrific person, you really are.
Dr. B: Well good. So I will be working right with you.
SRS: Thank you.
Dr. B: Because you need it and I need it, right?

SRS: Ya, and because a lot of people out there need it too.

Dr. B: Okay, so we can work together. So we will stay on this procedure. You know I don't, I don't, you know, oh I've had enough of my *tsouris*. What else do we have?

SRS: Well, would you like to take a short walk?

Dr. B: I'd love it.

After the walk, I was stunned by what had transpired, for it seemed that Dr. B had found a deep well of resolve in the face of the insidious disease that was killing his brain's ability to function, that the time we spent working together had cemented a bond between us, that some deeper level of communication had been reached, that he still had much to live for and so much of a contribution yet to make. And although we were fighting the inexorable ticking of the clock, and the accompanying progress of the disease, Dr. B's resolve to work on a meaningful project remained heroically intact.

Of course, there were many other examples of his semiotic behavior throughout our association, some of which I discussed in previous chapters: His "quitting" the project because he hadn't received the recognition he desired, and his returning to work on the project once he received the letter of commendation from the Dean; his refusal to take part in the games and other activities at the day care center because he saw them as having little meaning for him (they were "filler"); his purposeful estrangement from the other participants with whom he felt he had little in common. In all cases, he was guided by a conceptual scheme comprised of his own tastes and dispositions, and used that scheme to compare what he was being offered at the day care center with his abiding way of life. In making such a comparison, he found the activities at the center lacking in quality and substance. His reactions in these instances would have been essentially the same decades earlier, for they were deeply woven, fundamental aspects of his being.

Some Words of Summary and a Word of Caution

G.H. Mead (1934) observed that, "Mind arises in the social process only when that process as a whole enters into, or is present in, the experience of any one of the given individuals involved in the process" (p. 134). Thus one can conceive of mind as something of a process involving discourse, akin to an internal conversation. From such a vantage point, the AD sufferers you have met here have minds that are far better preserved than would be assumed on the basis of their performance on standardized tests of cognitive function drawn from the domain of Classical Science. Using the tools of Romantic Science to investigate their discourse in the ebb and flow of everyday life, however, we can find:

1 ample evidence of meaning-driven, or semiotic, behavior among AD sufferers in the moderate to severe stages of the disease;
2 that taking the "intentional stance," and thereby not positioning the afflicted person primarily in terms of the defects associated with being "the patient," can allow for clearer communication with and better treatment of, the afflicted; because by doing so,
3 we are able to enter more deeply into, and thereby understand and appreciate more clearly, the AD sufferers' coherent hopes, fears, insecurities, needs, frustrations, intentions, and reasons, which animate their lives; and
4 we can see how such needs, reasons, hopes and the like can form the bases upon which they act intentionally in attempting to navigate the terrain of a social world that is partially veiled for them due to the effects of the disease.

However, we must be vigilant about another extremely important issue: In many cases, caregivers often do attribute intention to the afflicted person in that caregivers may believe that he or she is acting deliberately to annoy them, when in fact the annoying behavior is due to cognitive impairment. If the afflicted person's recall memory is severely affected, he or she may ask the same question repeatedly. This is hardly due to an intention to annoy anyone. It is of utmost import that caregivers identify the circumstances in which intention is present and healthy and not meant to annoy. An example can be found in the case of Dr. M's initial reluctance to attend her support group meetings. At first, Mr. M concluded that she was deliberately disregarding his needs (their support groups met simultaneously, thus relieving him of the task of finding someone to stay with his wife while he attended his group's meeting). When we delved further into the issue, we found that Dr. M's reluctance was based not on any desire on her part to annoy him or to inconvenience him, but upon the fact that she was not "getting anything from the group" and that she was embarrassed to be put on the spot by the group leader given her word-finding problems.

Many examples of meaning-driven behavior seen in AD sufferers can be found to be rooted in abiding aspects of their character, aspects which seem to survive the ravages of the disease after the ability to sign one's name, recall the date, speak fluently, or dress oneself have long since become extinct. Thus, the goals, intentions, and dispositions of the AD sufferer are related and a closer examination of this relationship is the subject of Chapter 6.

Goals, Intentions, and the Alzheimer's Sufferer's Predicament in Light of Critical Personalism

Although the bathroom was literally steps away from the bedroom on the main level of the house, Mrs. D, "the Life of the Party" whom you met in Chapter 4, would often use the bathroom in the basement when she awoke in the middle of the night. Mr. D confided that he thought that his wife was being irrational, and was fearful that her condition was deteriorating further. Before offering Mr. D a reaction or advice, I asked Mrs. D why she used the basement bathroom in the middle of the night instead of the one that adjoins the bedroom. "Mr. D is a very light sleeper," she told me. I asked her if she thought that her use of the bathroom next to the bedroom would awaken her husband, and she said, "oh, *sure!*" (I could imagine her thinking me a fool to have asked that question given what she had just said – in that I "failed" to draw the correct inference.)

In addition to the problem that can exist with regard to a caregiver's misunderstanding of an afflicted person's behavior, we can learn a great deal about an AD sufferer from this situation:

1 Mrs. D showed that she was able to retrieve accurately a long-term memory regarding her husband being a light sleeper. This may not be terribly surprising, but it is true nonetheless.
2 She showed that she was capable of engaging in "if...then" thinking: "*If* I use the bathroom near the bedroom, *then* I might

awaken my husband and I don't want to do that. Therefore, I will use the basement bathroom so as to avoid disturbing his sleep." She accurately understood the potential consequences of her choices regarding which bathroom to use, and chose an appropriate course of action based on that understanding.

3 She showed that she knew where the basement bathroom was and how to turn on the necessary lights to illuminate her path, although she often did not flush the toilet and turn the lights off afterward (which is how Mr. D knew that his wife had used the basement bathroom during the night).

4 That by assuming incompetence or dysfunction in the first place and by creating storylines that conform to the positioning of the AD sufferer primarily in defectological terms, caregivers frequently may be oblivious to actions that reveal clear intentionality and complex, healthy, goal-oriented planning and behavior on the part of the person with AD.

5 Mrs. D revealed her intact intention to act with consideration toward her husband – a consideration which was emblematic of her behavior during decades of marriage in which she enjoyed good health.

In this chapter, I should like to illuminate more fully not only the existence of intact goals, intentions and long-standing dispositions as revealed in the behavior and discourse of afflicted persons, but also attempt to clarify further their experiences and predicaments. To do so, it will be helpful to use another tool taken from the realm of Romantic Science: the perspective of a "lost star" of psychology, William Stern (1871–1938). Stern's most personally cherished work, upon which I will draw herein, had gone largely unnoticed in the pantheon of modern psychology until the last years of the twentieth century when my colleague and friend, James Lamiell, undertook to translate Stern's works from the original German.

Stern was best known, much to his own chagrin in retrospect, for the creation of the concept of the intelligence quotient, or IQ, and a variety of statistical approaches to the study of individuals and their differences (known as Differential Psychology). His subsequent, and personally more valued, approach to the study of persons and their social interrelationships, known as Critical Personalism, is a valuable heuristic device, or conceptual scheme, by which we may understand more completely the situations confronting, and the experiences and cognitive life of, the Alzheimer's sufferer. So as to provide a framework for the balance of this chapter, let us explore some of Stern's thinking on the subject of persons and how best to study certain aspects of their psychological lives.

The Whys and Wherefores of Critical Personalism

Although Stern's quantitative approach was used in significant research efforts aimed at identifying highly gifted and talented children, he believed that there were sundry aspects of a person's psychological life which could not be elucidated by using those same quantitative (psychometric) tools (Lamiell, 1996). He was quite blunt about his beliefs on this issue. And, although he was not referring specifically or even allusively to our methods of understanding people afflicted with AD, his comments that follow apply to them as well:

> In the first place, tests provide only a momentary snapshot of the performance capabilities of the examinee. To be sure, we seek to use the most diagnostic tests available. But even then, it will never be possible to eliminate completely factors which can exert a momentary influence on performance (bodily indisposition, temporary lapse in attentiveness, test anxiety). Consequently, the results of the tests do not provide a sure indicator of enduring psychological characteristics of the examinee . . . by their very nature, tests require the examinee to react, and for this reason can tap only reactive behaviors. Such spontaneity as might be manifested by the examinee's interests and inclinations, or in play or artistic activities, or through aesthetic or ethical or religious modes of experience, escapes tests entirely and can be captured only, if at all, through the observations of sensitive persons who have spent some extended period of time with the person whose psychological profile is being constructed . . . Tests yield a number on the basis of which that examinee can be located somewhere along a quantitative scale, but which obscures things qualitatively peculiar to that individual. For all of these reasons, the methods of direct observation of an examinee must always be used to supplement the test methods, and the former must be developed and refined with the same care as the latter. (Stern, 1921, pp. 3–4.)

226

As if to anticipate, by approximately sixty years, Shweder and Sullivan's concept of the "psychometric person," Stern made clear that, "The person is a unified whole, and has depth . . . A human being is not a mosaic and therefore cannot be described as a mosaic. All attempts to represent a person simply in terms of a sequence of tests scores are fundamentally false" (Stern, 1929, pp. 63–4). In Stern's view, a person is more accurately represented fundamentally and irreducibly as a goal-striving, intentional being.

So as a supplement to the psychometric, quantitative approach, Stern proposed Critical Personalism as a method of understanding more completely the unified whole, the depth, of a person's cognitive or psychological life. Critical Personalism includes a number of ideas about the nature of persons, their interactions with the world at large, and the psychological dimensions which will have a strong influence on the quality of the person's social interactions. The basis of this approach is the systematic and detailed study of individual cases, which serves to allow researchers to formulate questions which may then be pursued in order to uncover knowledge that can be generalized (Lamiell and Deutsch, 1999). Let us take a brief tour of Critical Personalism and we can then begin to see how its lenses help to bring into sharper focus the experiences of AD sufferers and the predicaments they face.

Mental-physical and Person-World relations

In his book, *General Psychology from the Personalistic Standpoint* (1938), Stern explored these two aspects of psychological life. His statement that "[t]he person makes use of his body as an implement in the service of his experience" seems to indicate rather clearly that there is a profoundly intimate connection between the person as agent or actor, one who has intentions and goals, and the vehicle of the body as a means by which those intentions and goals may be carried out and achieved – that is, through the body the person acts upon the world. Additionally, the body serves as the vehicle through which the person's psychological-mental experience of the external world becomes intelligible. In other words, through the body, and perhaps through the brain most importantly, the external world is made manifest in the psychological-mental experience of the person. If this is the case, and there seems to be no reason to doubt that it is, it would then follow that if the brain were damaged, the afflicted person's ability to employ the body as a vehicle to serve his or her experience would be compromised to one or another degree. Presumably, the degree to which the person would be affected in this way would depend upon the location and extent of brain injury. But how would such an effect be manifested?

Renowned nineteenth-century neurologist, John Hughlings-Jackson, delineated two general types of effects stemming from brain injury, calling them "Negative" and "Positive" symptoms. The former encompasses losses in ability – things one can no longer do; not being able to find the word one wants to use is an example. Positive symptoms are alterations in surviving patterns of behavior. The person who cannot find the word "physician" may use a circumlocution ("the person who takes care of me when I'm not well physically") to convey his or her meaning. When we examine the existence of surviving goal-directed behavior among AD sufferers, we will be examining instances of Positive symptoms in some cases, for afflicted persons may work to achieve their goals in ways far different from those which they employed in healthier days.

One example may be seen in Dr. B's discourse concerning his experience of the effect of AD: He commented that "Alzheimer's gives me fragments," and "I absorb in globs." Here, his ability to use his body as a means by which his experience of the world may be made intelligible is affected in a specific way. That is, by saying that he "absorbs in globs" and that AD gives him "fragments," he is saying that his ability to maintain vigilant, focused, consistent attention to his surroundings has been adversely affected. Now, because of AD, he is able to experience clearly only pieces, or chunks, of what used to be a steady, coherent stream of external events. This was especially true for him in situations in which there were many events occurring simultaneously and he found great difficulty in "filtering out" what was not salient in order to become more clearly aware of what was of consequence to him. Two examples of Positive symptoms, one from his discourse and one from his non-verbal overt behavior, serve to illustrate the point further.

In the first case, he and I were sitting in the day care center office trying to have a conversation. It was a busy office, with people coming in and out, others talking to one another, others speaking on the phone, still other phones ringing. Dr. B shook his head in frustration, and asked if we could go out of the office, because "There are too many stimuli in here." Many months later the disease had progressed further and in the identical situation, he said nothing, but instead shut his eyes, put his hands over his ears, and began to cry – for he could not cope with the surrounding "stimuli" by using his brain so as to filter out, to intentionally diminish the experiential intensity of, what most of us regard as "background noise." In these examples relating to the willful ability to focus attention, then, we see how AD affected Dr. B's ability to "use his body as an implement in the service of his experience" and how he attempted nonetheless to reduce the effect of "background noise." Even his weeping is mute testimony to his realization of the vast gap that separated his earlier capacities from his current and irremediable predicament.

There is an important, yet subtle, aspect in this conceptual scheme: to wit, Dr. B *wanted* to filter out the extraneous stimuli, but could not achieve that goal easily due to the fact that the "instrument" (in this case, the relevant brain mechanisms) which used to serve him in achieving similar goals so well in healthier days, was now damaged. Thus, his intention was coherent and intact, he was able to formulate clear plans for goal-directed behavior, but was not able to execute, to carry out, that intention as he did routinely throughout the decades of his life before becoming afflicted with AD. Using such a conceptual scheme, then, one can observe in the example of Dr. B:

1 intact intentions and goals along with attempts at realizing them;
2 that the ability to behave in "normal" ways so as to carry out those intentions appropriately is compromised as seen in his positive symptoms;
3 that despite (2), Dr. B did respond appropriately in both cases, given his intentions.

That is, in the first example, he recommended going elsewhere, and in the second example, he reacted to his inability to filter out the "background noise" with understandable, obvious frustration and used alternate means (shutting his eyes and covering his ears) as a meaningful sign that he was being "flooded" by the cacophony of stimuli surrounding him. The same analysis would apply rather well to Mr. R's successful attempt to find his coat in the day care center wardrobe which was related in the previous chapter.

With the help of Stern's concept of Person-World Relations, we can understand aspects of the phenomenon of the defect-based positioning of the AD sufferer in another way. The body has what Stern called "radial significance," in that ". . . bodily states and movements portray the nature of the person." In a sense, then, bodily states and movements may be understood metaphorically as the "cover" of a book. Thus,

1   if the observable movements of the AD sufferer are the principal means which portray his or her nature for others; and
2   if those movements are in one way or another abnormal or difficult to comprehend (be they related to poor articulation, syntax, or other speech problems, or to how one finds one's coat, how one reacts to surrounding background noise, etc.); then
3   the normal observer will "read" those abnormalities as being a true and complete portrayal of the afflicted person, and will henceforth position that *person* as being defective in one way or another; and
4   create storylines about the afflicted person's subsequent behavior which emphasize defects and obscure intact, "normal" abilities still inherent in the person and his or her cognitive life.

We know, however cliché-sounding it may be, that "one should not judge a book by its cover." Aspects of Stern's Critical Personalism may serve as methods by which we can look beneath the "cover," or surface structure, of the AD sufferer's behavior and see the clarity of intention, the intact goal-directed behavior, and the healthy dispositions of the afflicted person which otherwise might be obscured.

Another of the analytical tools which Stern provides within the realm of "Person-World Relations" is his concept of "convergence." Persons meet with the world at large. One's life can thus be understood in part as a set of interactions with the world. But here again, as one attempts to realize personal goals when engaging the world, one may be constrained to some extent not only by one's own limitations as seen in the aforementioned examples, but also by the limitations of the world in understanding and responding appropriately to the person's attempts. Stern noted that,

> The milieu of the person is not that portion of the objective environment that happens to be nearby and consequently influential; the environment

is rather the portion of the world that the person *brings* near to himself because he possesses receptivity or sensitivity for it, and to which he also *seeks to give* that form which is appropriate to his essential nature. (Stern, 1938, p. 89.)

Rather than seeing a person as responding to the environment in some mechanical, reflexive way, Stern sees a person as an active agent, "bringing receptivity and sensitivity" to the world on the one hand, and on the other "seeking to give" to the world in a way that is in accordance with his or her own nature. This may be seen as being akin to what I described in the previous chapter as a "meaning-driven" or "semiotic" subject. One dimension of meaning which Stern calls to our attention has to do with the person's needs: "The person seeks in the world that which he *lacks*, and reacts against the world with the force of *counteraction*, whenever his own being must be asserted in opposition to the process of assimilation" (1938, p. 91).

In Chapter 4, we saw some examples of AD sufferers seeking in the world what they lacked when they acted so as to maintain feelings of self-worth in the face of the assaults of AD. Stern uses the term "assimilation" to refer to the process of a person being made into a homogeneous member of the human order (as in being made into a "number" among other numbers and thereby losing concrete individuality, for example). We will see that this same process may apply to the ways in which healthy others in the afflicted person's world may position him or her primarily as a member of a group such as "the demented," or "Alzheimer's patient" and thereby overlook, or pay less heed to, other qualities in which that person may take pride. Once such an attribution is made, it is very difficult for all concerned to see the individual *person* anymore, for the fate of the categorized individual may be to be lost in the stereotype.

Personal dimensions

In addition to relations between the person and the world at large, Stern also discussed "personal dimensions" of psychological life, which can be employed as well to understand the predicament of the AD sufferer. Two of these personal dimensions are what Stern called the *inward-outward* dimension, and that which he referred to as the *personal present.*

In the case of the inward-outward dimension, Stern asserted that the world of any individual person has what he called, "a natural center from which and toward which everything pertaining to it extends; this is the person himself, about whom it is oriented" (p. 92). This natural center may be understood as corresponding to what Harré refers to as the Self 1 of the person – the sense of one's continuous experience as an individual in the world; the location, in relation to the place of embodiment, of the individual's psycho-social space of beliefs, attitudes, responsibilities. So, to Stern, one's thoughts, feelings, and reactions, are "inside," and things and other persons in the world are "outside." I will explore, in the following chapter, discursive evidence to support the continuity of this "natural center" in AD sufferers even into the moderate to severe stages of the disease. For present purposes, however, it is abundantly clear from their behavior as meaning-driven, or semiotic subjects, that the AD sufferers you have met herein, do indeed display such a natural center. Additionally, springing forth from this natural center, AD sufferers display a variety of social personae along with the ability to evaluate and interpret the significance of social situations in such a way as to reveal their intact sense of pride as well as the desire to avoid humiliation and embarrassment (Sabat and Harré, 1992; 1994a).

The second personal dimension which Stern enumerated was that which he called the "personal present." For me, this is an extremely informative way of understanding aspects of a person's psychological life and behavior. Although it may seem obvious to one and all, the recognition and appreciation of its meaning and consequences is, I believe, of great import to our understanding of the AD sufferer's predicament. In complex language, Stern notes that what we usually call the present time is, "spatio-temporally neutral; it is the unseparated here-now," and that what is here and now is always determined "according to the personal perspective" (p. 93). What does this mean in everyday terms?

It means that I can bring into the "present moment" any aspect of my life, even though that particular aspect may have been lived by me in what we might call the "distant past" in terms of linear time. So a person may be, at the present moment, an AD sufferer, but that same person's "personal present" may include being an attorney, author, homemaker, son, daughter, mother, father, and the like, even though the person is not actually living out those aspects of his or her life course at the present moment. Thus, the various and sundry attitudes, dispositions, and inclinations that go along with those aspects of one's life can be alive at any "present" moment, if one "brings" them to that moment. Presently, I may be a day care center participant, but my personal present also may include aspects of my life which flourished in healthier days, so that my psychological characteristics, attributes, from the "past" can live easily within me in my personal present – at *this* moment in time. Hence, Mr. K, a day care center participant, when being introduced to a third person by Mr. G, the day care center director, commented:

Mr. G [to the third party]: This is Mr. K. Mr. K was a lawyer.
Mr. K [interrupting]: I *am* a lawyer!

Although it was true that Mr. K was no longer a practicing attorney, an important aspect of his personal present, even at that moment, was the fact that the dispositions, education, and attitudes which were coeval with being an attorney, were very much alive within him even though he was suffering from AD and going to a day care center three days each week. And, as we see in his comment, these characteristics were important enough *to him* that he demanded that they be recognized as being part of him even then. He was, in his comment in the above situation, showing the force of "counteraction" to the process of being "assimilated" into a category of "once was, but no longer is an attorney, but now is a day care participant and an AD sufferer." Something within him led him to the study and practice of law, and that something was not merely "in the past," nor dormant, nor erased by the passage of time or by Alzheimer's, but was very much with him in the present. So here he "seeks in the world, that which he lacks" in this situation, namely the recognition by others of who he "is" in a much larger sense of the word.

What holds for the dispositions and attitudes of time past, holds also for time future. Each time we engage in behavior which is geared to achieving some future goal, we bring into our personal present one or another vision of the future. And to the extent that we engage in such thinking, planning, and behavior, a repertory of possible futures is made very much alive for us in the present moment. Whether it be planning for the arrival of a new baby, or for retirement, or for a summer holiday, or for the possibility of having to place a loved one in a nursing home, we are incorporating into the present moments of our lives a time that is yet to come; so even though that time is in the future in one sense, it is also very much a part of the present for us as well. Thus, to Stern, cognitive life in the present moment can include times distant both in the past and the future by the mere shifting of one's "personal perspective," thereby making the present moment "unseparated" from moments at other points in linear time. Thus is psychological time quite different from linear time.

Goals

The idea that time future can be a very potent part of our present moment is clear in the fact that we often define goals in our lives, and goals themselves can be understood as taking different forms. What might be examples of such different forms, or types, of goals? One set of goals defined by Stern is called *autotelic* and these are, as implied by the prefix, "auto," related to the maintenance of the self (preserving what exists for the person and his or her relationship to the world) and to the development of one's self, for example, as a conglomerate of skills and dispositions such that one can achieve individual growth in ways yet to have been realized. Other goals, which Stern saw as being part of what he called "productive self-development," and described as *heterotelic* are those which extend beyond the individual, reaching into the areas of family, humanity, deity, and the realization of abstract ideals such as truth and morality. It is the pursuit of these "higher" (heterotelic) goals which extend beyond one's own narrow, individual, interests that gives the person "living coherence" with the world according to Stern (Lamiell, 1996).

From Stern's point of view, goals such as these "determine the factual life of the personality," and the psychological experience of a person is not understandable without our being able to relate that experience to goals and their realization. So from Stern's point of view, we could not understand the psychological experience of the AD sufferer without exploring the goals and intentions of the afflicted person, what fills his or her personal present, the ways in which he or she engages the world and behaves with counteraction, and how he or she attempts to satisfy needs.

In one of the quotations which began Chapter 5, an AD sufferer said, "Doc, you gotta find a way to give us purpose again." From his

234

comment, it was not clear whether by "purpose" he meant autotelic or heterotelic goals or both. However, it is surely clear that the absence of goals, of purposes was, to him, a profound lack in his life even though his cognitive ability as seen in his performance on neuropsychological tests was strikingly poor. Because quantitative measures of cognitive function cannot reach into that part of a person's psyche wherein the need for, and character of, purpose lives, we need to employ other means by which we can comprehend this and other related aspects of the AD sufferer's psychological reality. Critical Personalism may aid in our efforts as a supplement to the quantitative approaches employed, and we will turn now to specific persons with AD and explore their psychological lives from Stern's point of view.

Dr. M From a Personalistic Point of View

NB Among the extracts in this section are some which were used earlier in other contexts.

Autotelic and heterotelic goals

I

In my first encounter with Dr. M, she began by asking me about the sort of work that I do, with whom, and how often. I told her about my work with people at the day care center, and soon she began to spell out what was fundamentally important to her with regard to me:

Dr. M: Well, you're given me several kinds of peoples that, uh, have come there and how, how do you, uh – show me how he uses that, that person, uh, with the, with what you have noted.

SRS: Ah, now I'm not sure I understand what you're getting at here.

Dr. M: Yeah, I'm not s-s-s-s too. Uh, I want, t, to know is, how do you do, s-s-s, could do something that would be useful for me.

SRS: Ah!

Dr. M: Because it's, how do we put those two together? [my work and her needs].

What was uppermost in her mind was to try to find a means by which her word-finding problems could be alleviated to some degree. As you will recall, Dr. M had been an exceptionally literate, well-spoken person ever since she was a young girl, and her word-finding and other speech related problems were terribly distressing, even tormenting to her. In expressing her desire to alleviate these problems, she expresses an autotelic goal of self-development.

II

Another example of the goal of self-development was contained in her reasons for not wanting to attend support group meetings (Sabat, 1991a):

> *Dr. M:* Ya! And I don't want to do that. I, I guess I don't want to go – that I don't get enough.
>
> *SRS:* Oh – you don't get enough out of the group?
>
> *Dr. M:* I think I don't get the group and it's not that I don't want to be in a group like that, it's that I – That's what makes me feel bad, I think. It doesn't give me anything. I don't want to go with people who . . .
>
> *SRS:* So you're going to sit around for an hour saying, "Gee, I don't know what we're going to do, where we should go . . ." [this said in a tone implying the quandary she described as characterizing the group sessions].
>
> *Dr. M:* Yep, exactly. That is it. At least it's a part of it.
>
> *SRS:* You're impatient.
>
> *Dr. M:* I don't get enough. Whew! That, that uh, clarifies a lot!

Here, she has expressed some impatience with the seeming lack of direction of the group and also that she was not "getting enough" out of the meetings to justify her continued attendance. We may assume, without stretching credibility too far, that not "getting enough" refers to enough help, information, enlivening experience, and the like, that would add to her life. In the face of so many and varied distressing losses, Dr. M sought avenues which would provide additional joys and meaning to her life and she reacted with "counteraction" to attempts to assimilate her into a homogeneous group which emphasized for her that which she herself lacked, much to her distress.

III

From the beginning, and at many times throughout our association, Dr. M evinced obvious concern about our relationship being reciprocal in nature. Although she expressed her appreciation for my visits and help, she did not want our relationship to be a one-way street, as it were, with her gaining the lion's share of benefit. Her position on this issue was quite clear in the following interchange (Sabat and Harré, 1994):

> *Dr. M:* Now – then, I want to tell you something uh, that has some – I hope you're getting something out of this.
> *SRS:* Oh yes! Oh yes! No question about it.
> *Dr. M:* Because I, I feel, I don't want to, to use your time.
> *SRS:* I appreciate your concern very much, but I want to assure you that this time is so important to me and you teach me so much.

Her wanting me to be "getting something out of this" and not wanting to "use" my time, reveals her position that there had to be mutual benefit in our association, for if it were otherwise, she could not continue in good conscience. Not only is she evaluating the situation in accordance with public standards of fairness and propriety here, but she is also expressing a heterotelic goal – that our meetings should be of help to me as well as to herself.

IV

After she had retired from her university faculty position, Dr. M pursued her M.S.W. degree, as she wanted to become a Licensed Clinical Social Worker who could provide psychotherapy and thereby make a positive contribution to the lives of others (heterotelic goal). Although she did complete her M.S.W. degree, the onset of AD symptoms prevented its realization in her becoming a psychotherapist. Now, beset with AD, she was still able to see what her support group lacked in coherence, and she encouraged me to attend a meeting, thinking that my presence might make a positive difference. I told her that I had spoken to the relevant people at the Alzheimer's Disease Association which sponsored the group:

SRS: So it's all arranged.

Dr. M: Ya.

SRS: This is great. I'm a little nervous, I have to tell you.

Dr. M: Why?

SRS: Well, "opening night jitters", you know.

Dr. M: Oh no! I don't feel that. I find that if I were in your pray, place, I think it would be wonderful.

SRS: Well, I think it's great, but before I start, I get nervous; but once I'm involved I don't think about it anymore. I just get involved.

Dr. M: Well that's how you should do and will do!

SRS: This is a very different kind of thing for me.

Dr. M: I don't know this kind of you.

SRS: You don't know this part of me?

Dr. M: Um hum.

SRS: It's okay, I don't mind it, it's good to have a little tension sometimes.

Dr. M: You, you, there's nothing to, to do there for you unless you are different to them as you are to me.

SRS: So I have nothing to worry about?

Dr. M: Ya.

Given her goal of becoming a psychotherapist, and knowing a great deal about how to lead a group, Dr. M indicated clearly her enthusiasm for working with people in such a situation when she commented, "... if I were in your pray, place, I think it would be wonderful" in response to my confession of feeling some trepidation before going to my first meeting with the group. Her sense that it would be wonderful if she were in my position reveals that she still put great value on her heterotelic goal of helping others. She then went on to give me a great deal of encouragement by expressing her confidence that I have nothing to worry about, as it were, unless I am "different to them as you are to me" – unless there's a big difference in the way I behave with the group *vis à vis* the way I interacted with her. In this manner, she sought to allay my trepidation and be of help to me in my "hour of need" as it were. She thereby sought out in the world that which she lacked; that is, she was able to serve as a nurturing, encouraging force in my life and such a role was now less and less available to her even though it was historically very much a part of her character to behave in such a way.

V

On a number of occasions, I had explained to Dr. M that I was interested in learning about her experience of AD and what abilities remained intact during the course of the disease. Her encouragement in getting me involved with her support group seemed geared toward the realization of two main goals which can be understood as being autotelic (helping herself) as well as heterotelic (helping others): (a) making the group better for everyone (heterotelic), including herself (autotelic); and (b) helping me in my own quest for the production of knowledge which could be shared with the wider community (heterotelic). Both are seen in the following interchange, which began with her thanking me for encouraging her to speak at the group meeting which I attended:

Dr. M: When I was put on the – what do you get put on?
SRS: The spot?
Dr. M: Yup! Thank you.
SRS: You're welcome!
Dr. M: When he uh, when you asked me very in, in very nice uh, knowing, knowingly, knewingly you were a knewingly, I, I think that uh, it was I – I didn't know anything in the whole wide world to do. That and then uh, somehow it worked itself out uh, and uh, and to have seen me talk to a group and a group whom I, I don't really know as friends or, I just wanted you to know that.
SRS: Oh, so that was good?
Dr. M: Oh, it was *real* good.
SRS: I'm *so* glad. I think that everybody has something, everybody has something to offer.
Dr. M: Oh, that's very good, kid!
SRS: To me the angels speak sometimes. You know how it is when you have that feeling that somebody's tapping you on the shoulder and saying, "Hey – would you just wake up and look at this for a minute, will ya!"

Dr. M [hearty laughter]:

SRS: That's how I felt when the group leader asked me if I would come back. Inside my head I was saying, "Would I? Are you kidding? I would love to!"

Dr. M: I knew that! *I knew that, I knew that it gives you just what you're looking for. So uh, and I think it gives, gives the group some.* You repeated, I mean I repeated what you had said in a sense.

SRS: Yes indeed! I think we learn more about what people *can* do (when we observe them) in very rich social settings.

Dr. M: Um hum, *and you can have it for the next uh . . . paper.*

SRS: That's right!

In her final comment in this extract, very much a kindred academic spirit, she is well aware that her bringing me into the group was going to give me "what you're looking for" and would also help the group as well as a professional audience through my writing a journal article, my "next . . . paper." My cause had become part of her own cause. She saw how the group dynamic could provide me with information that would be valuable to me, and how my presence would also help the group and herself.

VI

Another example of her making my cause her own can be seen in the following extract, in which we were talking about one of the men in her support group and an interaction between him and me in which I was able to facilitate his speaking in the group setting:

Dr. M: You can tell me – I must tell this to your, for you. Uh, the guy who doesn't . . .

SRS: The man who doesn't talk?

Dr. M: Yes. He was so um, ooh! I asked Mr. M about the lady who was in the room, our room and uh we were talking about . . . I can't do it.

SRS: Now let's see if we can find it. See, I know that you know what you want to say.

Dr. M: Yes, I do.

SRS: You were talking about your group and the man who doesn't speak very much,

Dr. M: *And then you made him be uh, so, you were so wonderful about that because uh nobody would else would ask him.*

SRS: Oh, you mean I tried to, I said some things to him that he could answer "yes" or "no."

Dr. M: *Yes, yes! Nobody has said that to him. I, I thought you were great about that.*

SRS: Thank you! That's, that's part of what I think is so important – that we all recognize that he has thoughts, you have thoughts. You have difficulty sometimes in saying what you want to say, he has much more difficulty, but

Dr. M: But when you brought out that uh, that, nobody has asked him for ages what he did,

SRS: Um hum, and then I did.

Dr. M: and I told you that earlier on he could say just a little. Now he has lost, but now he's got it back and that was so good.

SRS: If other people can learn how to help the person use the words he or she has available, if other people can learn how to listen and how to translate, then you don't have to be that quiet.

Dr. M: Um. That's nice! That's nice of you!

SRS: My goodness! We're people aren't we? Everybody, we all have our problems don't we? And we, we need each other. Nobody can do it all by him or herself.

Dr. M: *I would think that you would hold this part of the work that we're doing now*

SRS: Um hum.

Dr. M: *uh, for if you were writing the thing.*

SRS: *You want me to include what I just said*

Dr. M: *Yes, um hum.*

SRS: *in what I'm writing.*

Dr. M: *Um hum.*

SRS: Yes, I shall. I think it's very important. We have to work together.

Not only is her discourse here revealing of meaning-making, semiotic behavior, but also appears to be aptly described by Stern when he wrote:

> . . . perhaps the last and highest secret of the human personality, [is] that it takes up the heterotelic into the autotelic. The outer goal indeed

remains, after as before, directed to the not-I, but is appropriated with and formed according to one's own self. Only in this way does it become possible that the surrender to the suprapersonal and nonpersonal goals nevertheless does not signify any depersonalization, or any degradation of the personality into a mere thing and mere tool . . ." (Stern, 1917, p. 47.)

Put another way (Stern, 1923, p. 63), "People must, therefore, incorporate the ends of others into their self ends." This type of behavior may be understood to be the highest form of "higher goals." Dr. M's ability to act in such a manner was still clearly intact in the moderate to severe stages of AD, but this fact was neither identified nor predicted on the basis of her performance on neuropsychological tests, for the tests provided no social context in which this aspect of Dr. M could be observed.

Her personal present

I

We can see quite clearly how the concept of the "personal present" can have a powerful impact on one's life when we examine Dr. M's reaction to her word-finding problems and how they affected her ability to engage in conversation. The results of the neuropsychological tests she took two years before our association began indicated that her

> reading comprehension is within normal limits compared to the average person her age . . . her writing was slow and laborious, was adequate in content, spelling and sentence construction. This appears to contrast with Dr. M's perception of declines in reading, spelling, and writing. However, the tests are not sensitive to the changes in functioning from Ph.D. level verbal skills to the average range.

Even if the tests were sensitive to such changes in functioning – if there were data about the mythical "average person" with a Ph.D. – we would still know nothing about the *meaning* of such changes in functioning to any individual person. In the following extract of conversation (Sabat, 1991b) we can hear quite plainly her reaction to being described as being "within normal limits":

SRS: You have to tell me what it is that you want to be able to do.

Dr. M: I don't know how you go through the various steps, but I want to have a, a feel that when I talk, that when I caw, talk, I, I can talk.

SRS: Um hum.

Dr. M: I can't always do that.

SRS: Um hum, well, you're doing it pretty well right now.

Dr. M: No, but when I haven't, we're just talking uh,

SRS: Light

Dr. M: Light, light stuff, and even light sa stuff are problems because I miss and word and I can't find it.

SRS: Um hum.

Dr. M: *And I'm probably able to do it as other people can, but uh, not it that good, it's not good enough for me.*

In her final comment she has done two things: first, she has concluded that she might be "able to do it as other people can" – evaluating herself vis à vis other people; and second, she has evaluated her present ability in light of the abilities she demonstrated and enjoyed over the course of her healthy adult life – "it's not good enough for me." In this case, "good enough" is being defined in terms of what she was able to do in the past, rather than in terms of what "other people," whomever they might be, can do at present.

II

Thus, not only is her ability as affected by AD part of her "personal present," but so too is the cherished level of ability which was hers in decades of healthy days. In addition, her perception of the blatant difference between the two levels of ability is also a powerful part of her personal present. The dialectic of "what I am not, but might otherwise be" may therefore be seen as having one possible basis here in the clash, in her personal present, of her abilities in two different times of her life, thereby causing her feelings of great despair. She revisited that same theme in another conversation:

Dr. M: *Well. I just show you, as I showed you the last week how many things I are, I am, and how many of them come from far,*

> *far back – and then making it include the present – that kind of*
> *thing, that's a . . .*
> SRS: *That's a tough one to swallow?*
> Dr. M: *Ya, um hum, that's a lot.*
> SRS: It's hard to accept. Am I right?
> Dr. M: Ya, I guess it is.
> SRS: The present is so different from the past?
> Dr. M: The working is different. Uh I go into the off [office],
> into my room, and I uh, say this time I'm going to get the, all
> the papers I want to have used for what was. Um, that's a lot.
> And uh, I it's not like if I were, I have someone who sets a de,
> a program. And what I get from the days, the years, everything
> that are still left . . .

In one sense, the present was indeed very different from the past, but
we can hear quite clearly that her personal present included both
times quite prominently. She had revealed "how many things I are, I
am, and how many of them come from far, far back." And now, in
her personal present she was confronted not only with "those many
things," but also with the immense and insurmountable problem of
trying to be those things in the present time – "making it include the
present." She was so utterly tortured by this, that it was, indeed, "a
tough one to swallow" in that she could not bring to the present
moments in linear time, so much of what she is, as she lived it in the
past, and is thus tormented by the prospective waste of "the days, the
years, everything that is still left."

III

This same "tough one to swallow" – this bringing into the present
her memory of her past ability and her present predicament of enduring the effects of AD – was also evident in our discussion of her
behavior in her support group. The conversation began with our
talking about one of the group members:

> SRS: I made some contact with him at the end last time.
> Dr. M: You did, uh huh.
> SRS: We have some mutual acquaintances as colleagues and I
> told him about that.

Dr. M: Oh, that was a great thing to do! [Dr. M always appreciated the initiation and building of connections between people.]

SRS: I just wanted to make a little contact with him.

Dr. M: Oh, that was good.

SRS: So I'll talk with him if I can. I think he has trouble speaking, he [*she interrupts*]

Dr. M: The words, well then maybe that, he's like me.

SRS: I don't think you're like that by any means. [Here I referred to the severity of his problems.]

Dr. M: Well uh no, I, way in a, I have my own

SRS: Um hum,

Dr. M: incomplete way of getting with uh, people.

SRS: Um hum. There's a certain irony in that.

Dr. M: Why?

SRS: Because you explained it completely and you were saying that you have your own incomplete way of being with people. But that was a complete idea.

Dr. M: You know, I, I think you over, well anyhow.

SRS: You think I'm overstating things?

Dr. M: Yes, I do. I do. Or maybe I've learned to fit in the each person I'm talking to in a way, so.

SRS: Maybe. I'm not overlooking, I'm not overlooking that fact that you will have trouble finding words sometimes.

Dr. M: Sometimes? Tell me, tell me because I don't know what it is. What if you don't, what if you, if we weren't talking here, what would you say that this person was like? [She is asking me "If you never encountered me here in my home and only in the group, what would you say I was like?"]

SRS: You?

Dr. M: Ya.

SRS: I'll tell you something, if the only contact I ever had with you was at the group meetings,

Dr. M: Was it?

SRS: I'm saying *if, if . . .*

Dr. M: Ya.

SRS: If the only time I ever met you was at the group meeting, I would have a very different impression of you than I do as a result of meeting you this way.

Dr. M: Oh, oh please tell me what it seems like.

SRS: My goodness! Here in, in this context you are much more verbal, you, you,

Dr. M: Who? What?

SRS: Just you and me – like this.

Dr. M: Um hum.

SRS: You're much more verbal, much more assertive about what you say, you, your humor comes out much more. Over there, I think you're much quieter, I think maybe, you can tell me if I'm wrong, maybe there you feel more pressure to speak quickly. I'm not sure.

Dr. M: You might be right that way too, too, because I spend time before I tell people because I have so much problem with what I really want to see [say]. And so I take all that time and that's why, in part, I'm asking you now about it because I don't feel myself. You know, all my life it seems to me that I said, I did the the things I wanted to say and what it means and all that stuff. Uh and I don't, I don't go think this is the right thing, that's the bad thing, uh I ought to think about it, I, I play, I played with it.

SRS: Um hum.

Dr. M: And I never had it that way and this way.

When Dr. M commented that I "overstate" her ability, there was a clear difference in what she thought of herself and what she interpreted my reactions to be. She had a view of herself based upon her behavior as affected by AD in a variety of situations and was comparing that behavior to what she would have or could have done in the past, and she therefore had her own "incomplete" way of dealing with people. However, if she were allowed to believe that she could not communicate, *qua* communicate, she would become more and more silent, more and more isolated. Thus, from my point of view, it was imperative that she understand and believe that although she is not as able as she once was, she is still able to communicate and should not underestimate the value of her present ability. In a sense, I was encouraging her to live more in the linear present and less in her "personal present" in Stern's terms.

All her life she expressed herself artfully and effortlessly, never having had the experience of being any other way until being struck by AD. Her verbal ability was an extremely important aspect of her sense of self going back to the days of her youth. As a result of the profoundly negative impact of AD on her ability to use words, it comes as no surprise that she says, "I don't feel myself." Her personal present was dominated just as much by the memory of her lifelong gift of literary and verbal expression and of what she therefore "should" be able to do, as it was by her clear awareness of and torment about how it was affected by Alzheimer's. This fact of her personal present prevented her from accepting her situation, if it truly can be accepted at all.

It would seem important that caregivers recognize, and sympathize deeply with, the pathos of such situations that confront the afflicted person, and try to understand the powerful, often tormenting effects of living in the personal present. As a caregiver, no matter how much one might wish to, one cannot "fix" what is amiss but if, in such situations, one can show a clear and sympathetic understanding and honor the reality of the afflicted person, his or her torment can be eased to some degree simply by the fact of feeling understood. I hasten to point out that this is also true for the healthy among us. In addition, as seen in the cases of AD sufferers you have encountered herein, there may be great value in what he or she has to say, however, "incomplete" it may be. This approach adds to that of "validation therapy" (Feil, 1982). One of the tenets of validation therapy is that the behavior of the afflicted should not be judged as being appropriate or inappropriate outside of the context of the person's psychological and social needs and physical strengths. What I am proposing herein may be viewed as being helpful in identifying those needs within the context of the afflicted person's life and that to validate is to encourage and to encourage is actually to amplify the intact cognitive skills of the sufferer.

Planning, intentions, her personal present and goals in combination

I

As our conversation continued regarding the difference in her behavior in the support group as opposed to her behavior in one-on-one conversations with me, we explored more thoroughly these two very different social situations and how they affected Dr. M's behavior:

SRS: That's tremendously difficult but you see, one-on-one here, you're much, you come out and speak much more than you ever do at the group. And I'm not sure exactly why. You speak much more clearly and much more

Dr. M: Than when?

SRS: Than when you're at the group meeting. When it's just the two of us speaking, you're much more verbal

Dr. M: Ya, sure.

SRS: than you are . . . at the group.

Dr. M: At the group. I, I didn't get that, okay.

SRS: So a lot of your personality that I see here isn't as evident in the group.

Dr. M: Um hum. Of course it's a one-one-and one. [Here, she clearly understands the difference in the social dynamics of the two different situations.]

SRS: Ya, and that makes a difference.

Dr. M: Um hum.

SRS: But I'll tell you what. You might want to think about, next time, next time you have something to say at the group, pretend whomever you're talking to is me

Dr. M: Uh huh,

SRS: and that we're sitting here,

Dr. M: Uh huh.

SRS: And speak.

Dr. M: Okay if I would do that, maybe try it, I'd say, "I'm trying something out" and then it would.

SRS: Ya, because you're much more animated here.

Dr. M: There's such a difference between a two-some as a group-some.

SRS: I agree, I agree.

Dr. M: Maybe I'll try and see if how it works.

In this discussion, Dr. M is not exhibiting what was indicated by her neuropsychological assessment two years earlier. In that assessment, she "had extreme difficulty with a test of the ability to apply principles in the solution of problems . . . perseverated the incorrect responses and failed to benefit from feedback. She also had a tendency to overcomplicate the problem and focus on irrelevant details."

In the above extract, she clearly understands that there is a difference in her behavior in, as well as in the social dynamics of, the two situations. When I suggested a possible strategy ("pretend that you're talking to me") she immediately saw that as being potentially useful and began to rehearse a way of presenting herself when using the approach I suggested (". . . I'd say, 'I'm trying something out' . . ."). Her appreciation of the two situations was right on target and she never overcomplicated the problem. Indeed, in all our conversations, she never once overcomplicated any issue that was of concern to her.

In other respects, such as word-finding problems and using circumlocutions, the neuropsychological tests did reflect her behavior quite accurately. Thus, it would seem that we do, in fact, need to use means other than the psychometric alone to gain a more complete appreciation of the AD sufferer's psychological life and abilities by tapping into the person's spontaneous behavior in social situations that are important to him or her.

II

Dr. M initiated the next subject of discussion. Again, she incorporated the ideas that we had discussed and then pressed on in an attempt to find the general principle that was involved and also to ascertain the practical benefits of the points we discussed. There was an underlying logic to her thinking. First she explored an idea with me. Through the veils that the disease creates, she asked questions and sought answers and offered her own views. Underlying her efforts was an analytic mind that was still analyzing, and a deep desire to improve herself (autotelic goal) as well as the group (heterotelic goal). In both cases, it seems that these characteristics are not new to her but, rather, are enduring aspects of her personality as it had developed over the course of decades. Thus she began:

Dr. M: Okay, I think when I think of what we've said uh, on this, I wonder what, what is it's usefulness? We probably spent how long? What do we have to bring out to another time? [Here, unbeknownst to me at this moment, she is talking about what can be brought to the group.]

SRS: Ah! What, what lesson do we get out of this to go forward with?

Dr. M: Um hum.

SRS: Well, gee, that's a good question. What, what do you think?

Dr. M: I think that it wasn't, there are several ideas that people were talking about. I think they went away with different ideas, like uh, the lady next to me was different and not leaving out uh, with people who don't speak, or who do say the same things all the time, or something like that. That there are different things for different people who gets the thing. That was the point. You know, my friend, if you uh, you, you, your being in the place makes difference from other people being in there and uh, if uh, when that lady [a former co-leader of the group who left to care for a new baby] uh, she wanted to have uh, children – very young children it was more comfortable – if that's the case, it's a different thing and everyone is different and I don't, for me I should, I don't know how to say it yet, we're all different, how do we make the consistent with the group?

SRS: Um hum.

Dr. M: *That's, that's why it's useful for your being not only for uh, what I'm supposed to get for me but how the, how the whole thing gets together.* Don't you think that's true?

SRS: Well, I don't know what it was like before I came.

Dr. M: *I think it was better with you, I, I know that is. And so it seems to me that there needs to be . . .*

SRS: *Some kind of cohesiveness? A plan?*

Dr. M: *Yes, yes, yes!*

SRS: Well, one thing that can happen is that, as with Rita, a person can bring up a problem and by talking about it, it can be solved. Now she can go to a restaurant without being fearful about calculating the tip.

Dr. M: *Okay, then it seems to me that, that there are some things that are uh, uh useful immediately.*

SRS: Ya, that's a practical solution to a problem. Now there may be other things, like reading poetry [one of Dr. M's poems from decades back was read to the group], that was just a nice experience and people can enjoy that. That, see now, that serves a purpose in that it's not a solution to an immediate problem in a sense,

Dr. M: Um hum,

SRS: it's just a lovely experience, just fun. Everybody got to hear something that was very, very well said and an interesting observation and everybody got a laugh and got to know you a bit. So a different use was that you were speaking – your sense of humor was coming out, your creativity was made evident. It was certainly made evident to the group leader.

Dr. M: It did?

SRS: It had to – she thought I wrote those poems!

Dr. M [laughing]: Oh, that's right!

SRS: It's very interesting, isn't it? She didn't guess that anyone in the group had written that. Think about it. In order for her to think that I wrote that she had to assume that it wasn't written close to sixty years ago, and she had to assume that it wasn't written by anyone in the group who she has experienced as having problems with words, right? Otherwise, she would have guessed someone else. So I think that that was a good lesson. It also sparked other discussion so it was very useful. So the plan might be that you should all be yourselves and what you bring to the group through yourself enhances everybody else in the group.

That the group leader assumed that I had written the poems in question was a powerful indication of how she viewed, or positioned, the members of the group. I wanted very much to emphasize for Dr. M that that issue had an important effect on the group dynamic and may have been one of the reasons Dr. M felt that she wasn't getting anything from the group. Yet, despite her initial dissatisfaction and despite her AD-related problems, Dr. M was still extremely interested in finding ways to improve the group and her own situation within the group. She clearly assessed the group dynamic as having improved due to my presence, which she herself had orchestrated in the first place. Thus did she demonstrate the ability to identify a problem and express the desire to work toward its solution for the good of herself as well as others, both of which are prominent goals from a personalistic point of view and neither of which is part of a standard neuropsychological assessment. When Dr. M said to me, "*Ya, but there aren't very many yous, and many people that (I) would, ah, free myself to put, uh, the way we were talking,*" it was, I think, poignantly clear that Dr. M was acting in a way that was, in Stern's words, ". . . according to her inner disposition, simultaneously goal-striving and in need of supplementation . . ." (1917, p. 51).

251

Dr. B From a Personalistic Point of View

As in other sections of this chapter, some of the dialogue extracts use material from earlier in the book.

Autotelic and heterotelic goals

I

As a person who spent his vocational life as a scientist in the academic world, Dr. B's interests and inclinations were vastly different from what was offered in the activities and daily events of the adult day care center. As a result, he assiduously avoided the activities as well as interaction with other participants, never becoming part of the center's community. His comments that, "I don't necessarily need what's in the room," referring to the room in which others were engaged in a group activity; his referring to the activities in general as "filler," when combined with his eschewing interactions with other participants and his comment that he was not treated with the deference he thought he deserved ("There, there should be some hier, hierarty") all point to his attempt to maintain himself (autotelic goal). That is, for him to become part of the day care community would be a powerful signal of his decline, and this was anathema to him. And so, he reacted with "counteraction" to any attempt to assimilate him into that community. Simultaneously, he associated almost exclusively with staff members and with myself in an attempt to "seek from the world that which he lacked:" the deference and respect that would place him at a higher point in the community's hierarchy. In light of Critical Personalism, these forms of behavior can be understood as attempts to realize an autotelic goal of self-maintenance. In the absence of such an analysis, Dr. B might easily be described as "a loner," "reclusive," "uncooperative."

II

An attempt to realize another autotelic goal involved his request to go to a large bookstore, where he and his wife bought two books (one of which was about Jimmy Carter). He had always been an avid reader but had experienced declines in reading ability with the progress of AD. Nonetheless, books were central to his academic life, and he pursued reading still. Some time after he told me about his purchases, I asked him if he had read any more of the book about President Carter:

Dr. B: Well, the book that I bought?

SRS: Yes.

Dr. B: I've got – this is a problem. This is it, sort (of) silly [*chuckles*]. We bought the book, we bought two books, and um, *for a week or so I was being able to, to do the very much, you know. I can write and stuff like that. So it was, it was grandeur, but um, it uh, it didn't [last] – I was tensed, you know, as to is it mine? Is it still mine?*

SRS: With the book that you were reading,

Dr. B: Well, you know, the two books I told you about. And um, it's, it's, I listened to about two or three daw, uh, pages, and uh, it, it was difficulty. I had some difficulty. I think the difficulty is that I really was not on a rhythm, there was not, there was not a rhythm of that kind of thing. And I get all over the place. So, that's it – I bought the two books, I have the two books, and I thought, you know, it was, it was pretty good. *Uh, and I think I was getting some good, um, also the Alzheimer's is uh, tears me apart on it. I comes to the point of how to read, for me. I try keeping notes, but frequently it's not.*

SRS: It doesn't work?

Dr. B: *It doesn't work for me and um, I fell [feel, felt] a lot of antagonize to myself.*

SRS: You get annoyed with yourself?

Dr. B: Yeah, pissed off.

We see in this episode his attempt to maintain an important aspect of his sense of self through the purchase of books and attempts to read them. Also, in his reaction to having achieved some success ("So, it was grandeur"), we hear his joy at momentarily recapturing a valued aspect of his personhood in the sense of the capacities that make up the valued parts of his Self 2. And, as if to express delight while also recognizing the effects of his illness, he asked himself, with some degree of anxiety, ". . . I was tensed, you know, as to is it mine? Is it still mine?" In other words, he is saying, "Given that I was able

253

to do some reading in spite of AD, do I still have this ability that I enjoyed so much throughout my life? Is this ability still part of me?" In this last comment, we also hear how he has brought the awareness of his level of functioning in the past into his personal present when he uses the word "still" – he would not use such a term if he were referring to an ability which he did not own in the past. In expressing himself in this manner, he seems to be expressing some hope but, in his later comments, we see that his hope was dashed: ". . . it had some difficulty . . . and I get all over the place . . . the Alzheimer's is, uh, tears me apart on it . . . it doesn't work for me and um, I fell (feel or felt) a lot of antagonize to myself."

Thus, in his personal present, we see how his clear understanding of his past level of functioning clashes with his present level, causing him to be angry with himself even though he knows that it is AD which is causing his difficulties. It is not difficult to understand how these stark comparative differences of ability in his personal present contribute to his utter despair and deep feeling that he is not himself anymore. Furthermore, we must understand that such feelings of despair may be present in him a great deal of the time even though he does not specifically speak about them constantly. Recall that he did allow that Alzheimer's was ". . . constantly on my mind."

III

His attempt to realize still another autotelic goal is seen in his carving out of a special niche for himself as the only day care participant who was working with me on a "scientific sort of thing," what he called "The Project:"

> SRS: So you feel that you are a pretty bright guy, but that you're not really treated differently than people who aren't as bright [at the day care center]?
>
> Dr. B: *Ya, that's, that's forces me to do something like this [work with me on the Project] . . . remember when you gave me the letter [from the Dean of Georgetown College] . . . it was a very strong statement that I am something above or something like that.*"

We can see, then, that his interest in working with me signalled at least two major autotelic goals: first, to be involved in something that

254

was "scientific," something intellectually formidable, which was emblematic of his own vocational life in the past; and second, to set him apart from the rest of the day care participants; to create for himself a special position relative to the others ("something above" them) so as to avoid being assimilated into the group.

IV

But in addition to these self-related goals, he was engaged in the Project for heterotelic goals as well – for higher goals that went beyond his own immediate personal interests. It had become clear to me early on in the project that he was functioning as a colleague, a co-worker, as opposed to being an "object of study." As such he was making my cause his own, and on many occasions he would punctuate his comments to me with questions such as "Is this of any value?" or "Is this useful?" In these ways, he indicated his strong interest in providing me with information that would be of help to me, and indirectly to the wider professional audience with whom I would share my findings. Even at a time that was very close to his entering a nursing home, his sense of fairness was very much alive:

Dr. B: Maybe we can go and walk and do some work. It's not fair for you, it really isn't.
SRS: Why do you say that?
Dr. B: Well, it's not fair for you to work on this.
SRS: But all of this is information. All of this is valuable. No matter what, it's not unfair for me. You're saying that it's not fair for me because you think you're not doing enough, giving enough information?
Dr. B: Ya.

A striking example of his desire to add to the Project was his creative attempt to bring me into contact with someone whom he considered as being able to provide important information. In a series of conversations that extended over a period of weeks, he desperately tried to tell me about this person, and I had to work with the single-pointedness of a bloodhound to try to identify who she was, given that Dr. B "absorbs in globs." He had described her as "attractive," "a real chirper." He could not piece together all "the fragments" that AD gave him, as he put it, and I was left with many such fragments, but also with the desire to work with him to find the connections, for he clearly felt urgency about finding this person, and I wanted to honor that feeling. Finally, one day while we were talking about another issue, he picked up a pamphlet published by the Alzheimer's Disease Association, and the identity of the mystery woman was about to be revealed. Also becoming clear in this conversation, was that the reason for his urgency was that Dr. B saw possibilities for improving, strengthening the Project:

> *Dr. B:*   Here – this is, I think this will (holding the pamphlet) pull together three, four, five things right away. This is, this is what I think is, you know, we should get it. *Now there is a woman, there wis [was and is] a woman two weeks, uh, two weeks ago, or two weeks and she will, she can give me information, she will give me information.*
>
> *SRS:*   Is this woman very attractive?
>
> *Dr. B:*   Yes.
>
> *SRS:*   You told me about her.
>
> *Dr. B:*   Ya . . . It's a woman, who is very sophisticated, no flim flam.
>
> *SRS:*   Is she a physician?
>
> *Dr. B:*   No. She is very, very sophistic, sophisticated.
>
> *SRS:*   Is she a researcher?
>
> *Dr. B:*   Um, yes she has, in fact she does, because *she is working on the same project say pojedic, project, and, uh, ironically enough, it, uh, this is what it is.*
>
> *SRS:*   It has to do with dementia?
>
> *Dr. B:*   Yes it demention. *I think, I think that, that we could meld, we can meld two things.*
>
> *SRS:*   *Something that she's doing,*
>
> *Dr. B:*   *Yes.*
>
> *SRS:*   *with something that we're doing.*
>
> *Dr. B:*   *That's right.* I know that you see what *you* see and it could be a real slambam.
>
> *SRS:*   It could be really good. Now the thing that I need to do,
>
> *Dr. B:*   Ya,
>
> *SRS:*   is to figure out who this woman is,

Dr. B: Yes.

SRS: and where to find her.

Dr. B: I know where she is!

SRS: You know where she is?

Dr. B: Yes.

SRS: Is she at NIH?

Dr. B: No, not NIH. Is she right, right, high, it's difficult. But uh, she brings material, paper, paper.

SRS: Can you tell me where you met her?

Dr. B: *Yeah – this!* [*waving the pamphlet from the Alzheimer's Disease Association*].

SRS: The Alzheimer's Disease Association? Does this woman work at the Alzheimer's Association?

Dr. B: Yes!

SRS: She does?

Dr. B: Yes!

SRS: Did you go to the Alzheimer's Association?

Dr. B: Yes!

SRS: And that's how you met her?

Dr. B: Yes! And she is a somebody is a fighting a fighter, a fighter center f, fighter. If you can get, get that. [As it happened, the office of the Alzheimer's Disease Association was near a fire department station – where there are fire fighters. Thus, his comments are not of the word-salad variety, but are related to the topic at hand. He understands, has insight into the fact, that what he has said may be difficult for me to comprehend, for he says, "If you can get . . . that." Although his words here would be difficult to understand if the information about the fire station were not available to the listener, what he was saying constituted an attempt to communicate relevant information.]

SRS: Bear with me now.

Dr. B: You bear with me because I got just a screw loose! *But we can match . . . we can meld this, this, this, this. We can, we can get material like this (snaps his fingers) just like this.*

SRS: *Oh, so she can help us get information.*

Dr. B: Yes! Here it is [*waving pamphlet from the Alzheimer's Association*].

SRS: She can help us get information about dementia and that kind of stuff.

257

Dr. B: There it is . . . *If we could get things together we would have a very sophisticated thing . . . It's, it's worth it that you and I go look, look at it.*

SRS: Was she a nice person?

Dr. B: Awfully nice. We could work with her with, like that [*snaps fingers*].

SRS: So if there's some information that we might be able to use or need, she could help get it.

Dr. B: Right. And it's only five cents a piece.

SRS: Oh, so she can make copies?

Dr. B: Sure! And she has a copy machine . . . *we could meld together, to meld Alzheimer's. I think, I think we, we can have sort of a tri-ite [triad] thing.*

SRS: We can try it out and see.

Dr. B: *I'm not, I'm not pushing you for push, push, push, you know that.*

SRS: Oh ya, I know. *We're working together to find out some information about this.*

Dr. B: *That's right.*

In this conversation, I tried as much as possible to use his recognition memory rather than recall and this strategy bore fruit even at this very advanced stage in the progression of the disease. For two weeks, the identity of this woman was something of a mystery to me and now, finally, the mystery was solved. Dr. B's description of her as "no flim-flam, sophisticated, attractive, a chirper" was all directly on target. She was a very straightforward, outspoken, extroverted, animated, kind, loving, and extremely dedicated person named Harriet Fridkin, who was, at the time, the information specialist at the local Alzheimer's Disease Association chapter. Dr. B had all this information in long-term memory. His problem was retrieving it through recall and then finding the words to communicate it clearly.

For all his linguistic and attention-related problems, his need to carry a flashlight in the evening, his inability to dress himself, and the like, Dr. B urgently pursued the realization of a heterotelic goal – to improve the Project through the added information that Ms. Fridkin would provide and which we could then "meld" with our own work. He was acting as a member of a research team, trying to provide all he could, to do his part, for the good of the research itself. Dr. B had come upon a situation which he was able to see as having great potential for the advancement of the Project. He had made what was initially my goal, his goal as well ("... *It's, it's worth it that you and I go look, look at it*"), and that goal remained alive and burning within him.

In his last comment in this extract, "I'm not, I'm not pushing you for push, push, push, you know that", he was assuring me that it was not his intention to be dictating to me, as it were. In so doing, he was employing a sophisticated display of politeness – something which characterized his interactions with others before and after becoming afflicted with AD, and something which has been observed to exist in other AD sufferers in the moderate to severe stages (Temple et al., 1999).

When I met with him the following week, his level of energy was extremely low; he looked and acted as if he were exhausted. His sleep was becoming more irregular and interrupted and his anxiety had been increasing markedly. Yet, when we discussed AD and the Project, he would become energized and focused for minutes at a time. In addition, his concern for me was still clear, for when I arrived at the day care center and realized that I had forgotten the clip-on microphone that I used to record our conversations, I was extremely annoyed with myself for having made such a blunder. I knew that the quality of the recording would suffer if I used the tape recorder's built-in microphone. Dr. B read my annoyance immediately, and asked what was wrong. When I explained the situation he said, "Don't blame yourself," in an attempt to ease my annoyance. It was still important to him to be involved with the project, but he wondered as to his ability to continue to provide information as seen in his first two comments, and his sense of humor was also still alive as evidenced in his third turn in the following conversation.

Dr. B: Oh, I think I'm a baby.

SRS: Why do you say that?

Dr. B: Because it takes ... I don't know ... maybe I can, maybe I can do some work. I don't know. Maybe yes, maybe no.

SRS: We'll see, before lunch.

Dr. B: Gee you get a lot of meals for nothin' don't you? [*chuckles*].

SRS [laughing]: It's an occupational hazard. What's on your mind today?

Dr. B: I don't know. Maybe nothing, maybe yessing. I'm not in the best shape, that's for sure.

SRS: Is there something on your mind that you're thinking about?

Dr. B: I don't know, normal – whatever normal means – this thing. The other thing is I could walk over there and I would just drop slowly like this and I would not, it would, it would poop, really poop me. What are you doing?

SRS: I'm running around like a chicken without a head.

Dr. B: You mean both of us are running?

SRS: I think so.

Dr. B: So how's your daughter?

SRS: She's well, having a good time in school.

Dr. B: Good.

SRS: And she sends her love to you.

Dr. B: Thank you, thank you, thank you. *I'm not going to get very much out, but whatever I do, I'll do as . . .*

SRS: You really seem exhausted.

He then brought up the topic of the Alzheimer's Disease Association:

Dr. B: There's an Alzheimer group, you know, it's right over here near a *frice*, where the people are, where the people, the people, the people, the people.

SRS: Near the fire station? [I took "frice" to be something of a juxtaposed synthesis of some of the sounds that make up "fire station".]

Dr. B: Ya, the fire station.

SRS: You went over there?

Dr. B: Ya and foolishly I didn't bring it out.

SRS: The brochure from there?

Dr. B: Ya, and I don't know where it is. I think my wife has it.

SRS: That's where that woman you met was?

Dr. B: That's right. We did it. *We should have that, that article that thing right away. It's, it's about, it's about ten pages of material of Alzheimer's.*

SRS: Do you have any concerns that you want to talk about?

Dr. B: I think no. Now this, wait, now this, this, this woman – I uh, very, I feel very, very nice. I feel, I feel very, very, very nice. And uh, Alzheimer's. Um, I fix you up with the same, the same gal.

SRS: That's very nice of you.

Alzheimer's disease and Critical Personalism

Dr. B: I was very, very impressed with this woman and they have an enormous amount of material. Now the fext [next] question is what are we, what, what are we talking, what are we talking about now? What, what, what are we – Alzheimer's?

SRS: Ya. You went over to the Alzheimer's association and you met that woman, and that was what we were talking about. And she was very attractive and you want to fix me up with her.

Dr. B: Fix you up. Why not? It can't hurt. Did, did you, did you think of doing what, what I was I was doing so that I can, the man, no the woman talked gave us this thing. I think it's a tremendous book. Did you see it?

SRS: Yes.

Dr. B: *Because the first time I saw, I saw it I, I took it and I yanked if off because it was on the ball and I, I said, "holy shit, this is what we have got to need, what we need."*

SRS: You probably got pretty excited about that.

Dr. B: Oh ya! She was a nice gal, a woman. See, I'm fixing you up also too.

SRS: Well, I can't thank you enough.

Dr. B [laughs]: Oh boy, I think I'm flipped my lid.

SRS: Do you?

Dr. B: All right. What do we want to do right now?

SRS: I want you to tell me how you've been feeling.

Dr. B: Well I'm feeling just like that. Just uh, hard, hard but I, so I have well I'm really in this. I'm not making much sense.

SRS: You think so?

Dr. B: Ya, I think I'm making mess.

SRS: What words describe how you feel?

Dr. B: Well, I don't know because . . . um, I, I feel drained and I, I really, I really don't have any, any, any uh, any juice as it would be [as it were] and so I'm that [*whispers "oh boy, oh boy"*].

SRS: What happened just now?

Dr. B: Well no, by, by, by looking at somebody and say "holy crap what are we got in or something like this." *Okay – now let me ask you this: what, what, what do you, what do you want? Do you have, do you have anything? Is there anything here that, that you want to put on, on a high level so that you and I will be in consort [concert] and, and think about and, and get, get some meal or something.*

SRS: What's the Alzheimer's business?

261

> *Dr. B:* Well Alzheimer's just takes its piece.
> *SRS:* Does it?
> *Dr. B:* Ya it, it, it does.
> *SRS:* What does it do that's the most disconcerting?
> *Dr. B:* Well, things get sort of wacky out of town, if you want to use that thing. And uh, it's so prevalent because you, uh you know, with, with you I would be able to do, to go like that. But the next one, it would be a lot of problems. Sometimes I need sand, sometimes I do other things.

Working on the Project still held great meaning for him, as reflected in his comment, ". . . Is there anything here that, that you want to put on, on a high level so that you and I will be in consort [concert] and, and think about. . . ." Here, putting something on a "high level" means that he and I would be "in concert" with one another, for the Project, being a scientific sort of thing, was itself on a "high level." Here again, the definition of what is on a "high level" is based for Dr. B upon how he defined the idea in the past, and he is bringing that definition into his personal present in order to evaluate the worthiness of his present work with me.

More and more frequently, however, I experienced increased difficulty in understanding what he was trying to say. By this I mean I was having more difficulty in joining the threads of some of his thoughts given the words he used. Yet in other moments,

> *SRS:* It's very frustrating, I suspect.
> *Dr. B:* Ya.
> *SRS:* Did you ever feel like banging your fist against the wall?
> *Dr. B:* Oh, I've done it, I've done it.
> *SRS:* Have you ever been so frustrated in your life?
> *Dr. B:* Well, some people will go ahead and, and just uh, kill themselves.
> *SRS:* Um hum. But you're not that type.
> *Dr. B:* No, I don't think so. *The thing, the worst thing is that I'm just wrung out and wrung out and uh, well let's do some work if we can.*

Here, the thought of "doing some work" was still very much in his mind and he was still highly motivated to continue. In this respect, he was able to remain connected with what was for him decades of vocational life and the attitudes and motivations that go along with that way of life. Following up on his suggestion to "do some work," he said:

> *Dr. B:* We have materials. *So, because you and I are gonna talk an awful lot and uh this woman is, is a very attractive, wonderful gal.*
> *SRS:* The woman at the Alzheimer's disease association.
> *Dr. B:* Ya, the Alzheimer's. And uh, so she uh, she's very, she's very, very, very good. And she also is a very beautiful gal. She's a staff member. So you have it? You know her?
> *SRS:* I don't know her, but I know of her and where she works.
> *Dr. B:* You do? *You might want to get a booklet and work as we work together as, as to what, what do we can do. What can we not do, stuff like that.*
> *SRS:* I think I will contact her.
> *Dr. B:* It's a police woman.
> *SRS:* Well, it's near a police station or a fire station?
> *Dr. B:* Right, right, right, right ya, you you picked it up very quickly.
> *SRS:* Thank you!
> *Dr. B:* So that's what I have.

Again, he suggests that I contact this woman because she might be of help to us as we continue on with the Project, for in his words "you and I are gonna talk an awful lot." He thought that whatever information the woman would be able to provide might be of great help to us as we continued with our work, and continued to discuss this matter. Even when I tried to change the subject, he came back to it time and again. Some might refer to this as "perseveration," but to use such a negative descriptor would be to ignore the fact that no other subject was nearly as important to Dr. B as was the idea of making contact with the woman at the Alzheimer's Disease Association, for he saw this as a way to enhance the Project.

As our conversation continued, he became increasingly fatigued, and his voice grew weaker. Yet, the idea of working more kept him going nonetheless, for in this he had a higher (heterotelic) goal. During his many months of work on the Project, Dr. B had been able to delineate and realize autotelic as well as heterotelic goals with tremendous intensity and devotion. In barely six weeks after this last extract of conversation, he would be in a nursing home.

V

Another aspect of this is his concern about his position in the family. Soon after Dr. B's only daughter had arrived in town, he asked me, with a chuckle, "How do I work with these strong, dominant women?" Quickly, it became clear that he was not enjoying the same undivided attention from his wife as he had received before his daughter had arrived.

> *SRS:* Is it easier to talk with your wife when the two of you are at home and none of the children is around?
>
> *Dr. B:* When just the two of us, it's much easier for me to talk to my wife, but when our daughter is in, there's controlled chaos . . . one of the things that bothers me – my wife, she's a tough gal, but I think I get pushed away.

I found this to be curious, because by this time I knew that Mrs. B was an extraordinary person, whose love, care, and respect for her husband were great and deep, who encouraged him to make decisions, and who did not usurp him in ways that Kitwood characterized as "malignant social psychology." So, perhaps, his reaction was delusional? The answer came when I met with his daughter for the first time and she was kind enough to speak with me for more than two hours, talking about her parents. A physician herself, she was especially observant regarding the changes that had occurred in her father over the past eight years, and I will be forever grateful for the open, honest, manner in which she spoke with me.

As a result of my interview with Dr. B (the daughter), and given the present context of the family, I was able to understand her father's statement about feeling pushed away. The clues were to be found in his earlier comments about how to deal with "two strong dominant women." His daughter was in town for business reasons and was visiting at the same time. During the days, both she and her mother went about their respective jobs and in the evening, Dr. B, his wife, and daughter would be at home. Naturally, mother and daughter had a great deal to say to one another and wanted to spend time together especially because the daughter lived many hundreds of miles away and her visits were not frequent.

In the interview, Dr. B's daughter, without referring to the above context at all, but rather discussing her father's style over the course of years, indicated that he was always "very possessive" of the family. She described him as being "independent within the family, but dependent on us." The family was always the anchor in his life. So naturally, under the present circumstances, Dr. B would feel "pushed away." This was not something that derived directly from the effect of Alzheimer's, but perhaps indirectly in that Dr. B was no longer able to be as independent within the family as he was before. In addition, he was by now accustomed to having the undivided attention and company of his wife virtually every evening – something that clearly changed with the arrival of any of the adult children.

When we take all this into account, we can see that Dr. B was reacting ("with counteraction") to a situation which worked against his ability to maintain his present situation at home in terms of the amount of attention he received from his wife. He wanted this situation to change and was, in this respect, formulating an autotelic goal.

VI

Dr. B's devotion to and love for his family was truly abiding. Often, he spoke about his adult children, revealing his great pride in and love for each. At times, as our relationship grew closer, he discussed some of his concerns, such as that contained in the following extract in which he spoke of his concern for one of his sons:

Dr. B: My son is handicapped [he refers to something physical here], um, but he gets who – in the Who's Who.
SRS: Well, he's obviously not handicapped . . .
Dr. B [interrupting]: at all
SRS: so badly that . . .
Dr. B [interrupting again]: So how come he hasn't got all the girls?
SRS: Well, obviously, a girl with good taste has just not crossed his path.
Dr. B: Yeah,
SRS: There are some out there. It's not easy to find someone so special.

Dr. B: *I know, I know. So what do I do? I'm thinking what do I do? You know, with my son?*

SRS: Pray. That's always a good thing to do. I think it's probably the best thing to do. [Dr. B was a very spiritual man and his family was religiously observant.]

Dr. B: Ya.

SRS: *You can't make it happen for him, you can't pull strings over his life.*

Dr. B: *Ya, that's right.*

SRS: You know, something could happen when you least expect it. Who knows? Out of nowhere you could get a phone call from him and he'll say "Guess what? I'm getting married!"

Dr. B: Um hum.

Here, he expresses not only his concern for his son but his own sense of helplessness in doing something to find a suitable partner for his son. He understands quite clearly that, in my words, he "can't make it happen." Yet, he obviously wants his son to find the sort of happiness and fulfillment that marriage brought to him and Mrs. B. In this situation, he expresses another heterotelic goal – in that he is wondering what he can do to help his son. Many months later, at a time that would turn out to be just a few months before he died, he and his wife received a long-distance phone call from their son, who informed them that he had become engaged. Soon thereafter, the couple came to visit and share their happiness with Dr. and Mrs. B. Within a year of Dr. B's death, the couple had a son, who was named after Dr. B.

VII

Stern's observation that ". . . the environment is rather the portion of the world that the person *brings* near to himself because he possesses receptivity or sensitivity for it, and to which he also *seeks to give* that form which is appropriate to his essential nature" may be seen to apply quite well to features of Dr. B's behavior beyond the intellectual and academic sides of his life, as in the incident of the gift of flowers.

From what his daughter revealed about Dr. B, it seemed that a great many of his personality characteristics from decades past were still very much in evidence in him despite his losses due to the disease. He was always, and continued to be, a person who was demanding

266

and a go-getter, albeit in a gentle manner. When he wanted to talk to a staff member he was direct; when there was urgency he made it very clear. His manner had not changed in this respect. He was always and continued to be a very sweet, kind, and caring person. These characteristics were manifested not only with my daughter, Deborah, but also with the day care center staff. One instance occurred when one of the staff members whom Dr. B liked very much became ill and was unable to come to work for some days. It had been five or six days since Dr. B had seen her, but he brought a bunch of beautiful rhododendrons from his garden for her even though he did not know she had already returned to work. He was thereby "seeking to give that form which is appropriate to [his] essential nature."

At one point during our association, it was spring, flowers were in bloom, and their scent in the air sparked within me memories of my childhood. We had taken a walk, and on our way back to the adult day care center, as we passed the entrance to a park, and moved toward the "infamous (mail) box" that was his landmark, Dr. B told me that we had to go into the park, for there was something that I "had to see." We walked along a dirt path and suddenly before me was a row of shrubbery in full bloom. "Look at that," he said, "isn't it beautiful?" I agreed wholeheartedly. We stood for a few moments in silence, the sight of the flowers filling our eyes, the sound of birds' songs filling our ears. Here, I thought, was the biologist enjoying the beauty of nature in a way that I could not. But then, breaking the lovely silence, he said, "You should take some of these to your daughter, she'll love them." He knew that when I left him I would go immediately to pick up my then ten-year-old daughter at her school.

I proceeded to pick some of the flowers and we took them back to the day care center where I wrapped them in a water-soaked towel. When Deborah entered the car at her school, I handed her the small bunch of flowers and explained that Dr. B thought she would love them. And so she did. Her face lit up in a smile as she held the flowers in her hand. This scene was repeated a number of times in the coming weeks and its significance grew to a crescendo at Dr. B's funeral.

Listening to his daughter's eulogy on that occasion, I gasped and then smiled. She spoke about how, when she was a child, she and her father used to take walks together and on those occasions she would receive mini-lectures concerning the different facets of nature that surrounded them. Generally, before they returned home, Dr. B would search for and find some kind of flower – wildflowers, heather, whatever was available – to bring home to his wife. Indeed, in a weekly expression of love renewed, on his way home from work, Dr. B had always brought flowers home for his wife. I flashed to those moments in spring when he and I took walks in the park, and he suggested that I pick some flowers for my daughter. Despite his increasing problems finding words, absorbing only in "globs," switching subjects of conversation in stream of consciousness ways that required my careful attention to decipher, having trouble taking care of details that once were automatic, and despite the frustration of having the disease tell him to "slow down, slow down," there were abiding features of his personality still immune to the effects of Alzheimer's. One such feature, part of his personal present, was the inclination, the intention, to give flowers to a loved one, and thereby to express that love. In so doing, he realized an autotelic goal in maintaining an aspect of his own being, as well as a heterotelic goal in pleasing someone else.

These aspects of his being, of his cognitive life, do not "count," as it were, on standard tests of cognitive function, because there is nothing in such examinations which addresses them. That fact does not, however, mean that such aspects do not count *per se*. Here was expression of a heterotelic goal that was woven so deeply into Dr. B that the disease that robbed him of many significant abilities did not yet rob him of the ability to express love or affection – even for people he had come to know only recently. He was still, as Stern would say, "seeking to give to the world" in a form that was reflective of his nature – a nature that was still evident in these moments of every day life.

The natural, spontaneous, flow of interaction between people in rich social contexts allows room for the demonstration of abilities that are not assessed or measured in the context of formal testing and research. It was in the rich fabric of natural social life that Dr. B was able to express, with great coherence, an abiding feature of his personality and bring a smile to the face and warmth to the heart of the little girl of ten years of age that was my daughter. After meeting and speaking with Dr. B for the first time, Deborah asked me if he had "that disease" that I had mentioned to her, as if to ask the name of the disease. When I told her that he did have Alzheimer's disease, she responded by saying, "He seemed okay to me." I wondered, in that moment, how to respond. Here was a bright and sensitive child, having heard two men engaged in conversation, and having herself exchanged and shared thoughts, feelings, and humor with Dr. B, now, making an assessment based upon what a child can see and feel. In some ways, perhaps, a child can see further into the fabric of a person than an adult can.

Do I tell her that the afflicted person can "mask" the effects of the disease in social situations? Do I tell her that although some aspects of his memory, information-processing, and language skills have been negatively affected, there are other aspects of his being that remain intact despite the effects of the disease? I chose the latter, for it seemed to be the most honest way to respond. One cannot deny the effects of the disease, but likewise one cannot deny the truth and importance of remaining abilities by calling them a "mask." Dr. B did reveal much of himself to Deborah, and what he revealed was as significant as it was abiding in him. He responded to her as if she were his grandchild, seeking to give her reassurance when she made a mistake in a game she was playing, seeking to communicate warmth and affection to her. I can still hear him say, as he looked at her with overflowing warmth in his eyes, "She's a doll, she's a doll."

Displays of love, affection, friendship, and humor are far more complex than are many of the functions which are examined on neuropsychological tests, and are not expressed in the same ways by all people and to all people. Dr. B expressed affection to Deborah in a different way than he did to me or to the social worker or to the director of the adult day care center. These sorts of displays, or types of behavior, are highly valued in those who are healthy. It would seem only fair that the ability to feel and express love, friendship, humor, affection, should be valued as highly when assessing the cognitive abilities and lives of those who are afflicted with AD. From Dr. B's perspective as a scientist, surely it would be the honest thing to do.

Brain Function and Aspects of Critical Personalism

Intentions, setting goals and working to attain them, planning for the future, engaging in "If . . . then" thinking whereby one calculates in advance the potential consequences of various different courses of action, behaving in ways that are deemed appropriate by the larger social community of which one is a part, thinking in abstract terms, are all subsumed by neuropsychologists under the general heading of "Executive Function." It is not uncommon to hear researchers comment that such function is a cornerstone of what makes us human. The fruits of research and observation dating back more than a century have pointed to the operation of the frontal association areas (prefrontal lobes) of the brain as being of tremendous importance in our ability to behave in such ways (Fuster, 1995; Milner, 1995). Milner was quite specific about the importance of the left frontal lobe in the programming of voluntary actions, specifically the ability to plan ahead and achieve goals. Finally, among the most widely accepted changes that follow in the wake of frontal lobe damage are: tactless behavior, puerile joking, sexually disinhibited humor, lack of concern for others, blunted feelings, a vacancy of facial expression, and indifference (Stuss and Benson, 1984).

For decades, renowned neuroscientist Karl Pribram investigated the operation and significance of the prefrontal lobes and, in his *Languages of the Brain* (1971), offered an instructive example of how this area of the brain is crucial to what are called "context-sensitive" types of behavior. One form of "context-sensitive" behavior is what we frequently call "caring." The ability to behave in a caring way goes well beyond simply doing the right thing. What may be the proper way to show caring in one situation with one particular person, may not be proper with another person in another situation or even in the same type of situation. Caring involves doing the right thing at the right time. Thus, it is "context-sensitive" and requires that one calls into play "If . . . then" thinking along with aspects of other complex functions such as memory, emotion, motivation, and knowledge of the social rules of the local community. Pribram proposes that complex connections between the prefrontal areas of the cortex and subcortical structures in the limbic system are required in order to manifest such abilities, for in the absence of such connections, one does not observe the sort of flexible thinking and behavior that is required to achieve context-sensitive goals. One does not observe such deficits following damage to other areas of the brain.

Behaving politely is a form of context-sensitive behavior, for it requires us to plan and modify our behavior on a moment-by-moment basis in order to meet the demands of particular situations as they arise. For example, when Dr. B evinced urgent interest in making a connection with Ms. Fridkin at the Alzheimer's Disease Association,

270

he seemed extremely interested in communicating that he wasn't "dictating" to me. In so doing, he had to be:

1 monitoring his own behavior on a moment-by-moment basis;
2 evaluating its meaning and potential meaning insofar as how his behavior *might* appear to me (dictatorial); while
3 calling into play his knowledge of the standards of proper behavior established by the social community of which we both were a part; and then
4 acting in a way so as to assure me that his behavior was not to be interpreted as being outside those standards, and willing and able to communicate that any appearance that he might be acting in an impolite way was hardly his intention.

Although the exact pattern of cortical and subcortical damage caused by AD is not the same for every afflicted person, one can arrive at an understanding of the areas most often damaged by looking at a large number of cases. The cortical areas most often damaged include the association areas of the occipital, temporal, and parietal lobes' lateral surfaces, and the medial and inferior surfaces of the temporal lobes. As well, there is subcortical damage to parts of the limbic system, including the hippocampal complex and entorhinal cortex, and also to various neurotransmitter systems. Areas which are relatively spared include the primary projection areas of the occipital, temporal, and parietal lobes, and the classical motor strip (meaning that the seeing, hearing, sensing touch, and movement respectively are not damaged *per se*). Perhaps most important to our discussion here, the prefrontal areas of the cortex are relatively spared in AD sufferers (Brun, 1983), thus providing people with AD with an important set of brain mechanisms through which they can behave in socially sensitive ways toward others, formulate the context of a situation, plan ahead, and set and work to achieve goals of the autotelic and heterotelic types.

The Gap Between Intentions, Realizing Goals, and Being Understood

Ironically, although AD sufferers in the moderate to severe stages of the illness may be able to plan ahead and set goals, it is often possible

271

that, because of the damage to other areas of their brains, it may be difficult for them to explain clearly the nature and purpose of those goals and their subsequent behavior without the benefit of help from others. Because of linguistic problems for example, the afflicted person might not be able to explain clearly his or her intentions and behavior without help, such as indirect repair, from healthy others. As a result, intact goal-directed behavior and coherent intentions often may be misinterpreted or misunderstood, as in the case of Mrs. D with which this chapter began, the case of Mr. R in his attempt to find his coat from among others in the day care center wardrobe, and the case of Dr. M, whose spouse did not initially understand correctly the reason for her reluctance to attend support group meetings.

Such misunderstanding may easily proceed to characterizations of the afflicted person as "irrational" or "confused" and thus these descriptors are added to the list of symptoms of the disease. To the extent that these terms refer to that which is not understandable or sensible, they may apply more accurately to healthy others in that it is the healthy others who often do not understand the basis for and meaning of the afflicted person's behavior. That is, it is not the AD sufferer, but the healthy observer who is confused.

Another case in point may help to clarify this situation: Mrs. L was the primary caregiver for her afflicted mother, who was now living with Mrs. L and her husband. Mrs. L, distressed by the fact that her mother was inconsolable and spent a great deal of time crying without any obvious provocation, attributed her mother's "irrational" crying behavior to AD. When I asked Mrs. L if she had any siblings in the area, she commented that her brother lived nearby and that when her mother was with the brother, her mother did not cry, and "behaved herself." I then asked Mrs. L to think back through the years and to tell me if her mother had a history of being more open emotionally with her rather than with her brother. It seemed that that was indeed the case, and when I then commented that it seemed to me that her mother was still being more open with her, Mrs. L began to understand her mother's behavior in a different light. Rather than expending a great deal of effort trying to stop her mother from crying, Mrs. L now saw her role as being the one person with whom her mother felt comfortable enough to cry, and that her mother had many valid, understandable, reasons to cry under the present circumstances.

272

To illustrate the point further, recall the following interchange in which Dr. M was trying to communicate something to me, but was having great difficulty in doing so:

> *SRS:* Now let's see if we can find it. See, I know that you know what you want to say.
> *Dr. M:* Yes, I do.

How profoundly tormenting it must be to know on some level what one desires and feels, that those desires and feelings are perfectly reasonable, and then not to be able to use one's body in the service of achieving or explaining the desired goal, or thought, to healthy others in a way that is immediately understandable. Without the help of others, the afflicted person is extremely vulnerable to being characterized as "irrational," "confused," or by some other similarly defective terms, and then treated accordingly. Any subsequent attempt on the part of the afflicted to resist such treatment, to refuse to be assimilated into such a defect-based category, can itself then be easily misunderstood as being symptomatic of the disease, and the cycle of misunderstanding and counteraction continues inexorably. Under such circumstances, high levels of cognitive function as delineated by Stern in his Critical Personalism, can easily be rendered invisible.

Conversely, if our methods of assessing cognitive function include the realm of goals, intentions, person-world relations, the personal present and the like, as expressed in the flow of natural social interaction in which healthy others facilitate communication with the afflicted, it is possible that our understanding and treatment of afflicted people would improve dramatically as remaining abilities would thereby be recognized, honored, supported, and even enhanced. Such improved understanding and treatment of afflicted persons would itself enrich interactions with caregivers, reducing the stress that exists in dysfunctional relationships which are characterized by malignant social psychology.

Another important aspect of the totality of a person is the person's sense of self. We have seen how, by using Stern's concept of the personal present, AD sufferers can feel as though they are not "themselves" as a result of the brain damage caused by the disease. Does this mean that AD causes a loss of self? Let us explore this issue in Chapter 7.

Selfhood and the Alzheimer's Disease Sufferer

When Dr. M commented, "I don't feel myself" she was expressing the sense of loss that she felt with regard to verbal abilities she had enjoyed and valued highly over a period of many decades. It might appear that her comment lends support to the title of Cohen and Eisdorfer's (1986) book about Alzheimer's disease, *The Loss of Self.* Indeed, as the disease progresses into the moderate to severe stages as defined by standard tests, descriptors such as confusion, emotional lability, disorientation, neuroticism, hostility (Chatterjee et al., 1992), agitation, diminished ability to think (DSM-IV; American Psychiatric Association, 1994), loss of interest in usual activities, paranoia, phobias, hallucinations, delusions, anxiety (Reisberg et al., 1987), uncooperativeness and apathy (Bozzola et al., 1992) and personality alterations (Hamel et al., 1990) have been applied to the person with AD.

Given descriptors such as these, when combined with deficits in memory functions such as recall, especially of more recent events, it is not surprising that it would be surmised that the afflicted person also experiences a loss of self as a result of the disease. It has been said that persons without the symptoms enumerated above, but who had suffered a severe memory loss of the anterograde amnesia type due to Korsakoff's syndrome, had nonetheless experienced a loss of *self* ("The Lost Mariner," and "A Matter of Identity," in Sacks, 1985). Anterograde amnesia manifests itself generally in a striking inability to recall and sometimes to recognize information to which the person has been exposed after the onset of the brain damage. Other than the fact that AD results in a disorder of similar memory functions, there is little further commonality between AD and Korsakoff's syndrome with regard to symptoms and the areas and types of brain damage involved.

Philosophers have discussed the topic of the self from the writings of Lao Tse in the sixth century BC onwards. Socrates asserted that to "know thyself" is important, to say the very least. Surely, it would follow that if knowing one's self is a good thing, then losing one's self would be horrific. And, if one were to assume that a person afflicted with AD had, at some point, indeed lost his or her self, one would undoubtedly react to and treat that person quite differently from the way one would treat that person otherwise. But what, exactly, could it mean to lose one's self? If there is, in fact, a loss of self due to AD, what exactly is lost? Is such a loss an inevitable part of the disease process or could it be prevented and if so, how? What would it mean to the AD sufferer and to caregivers if such a loss could be prevented?

In this chapter, I should like to explore these issues in light of recent Social Constructionist theories of selfhood and the role of discourse as it relates to the process of expressing and experiencing selfhood. Rather than presenting Social Constructionist approaches as the definitive answer to the abiding question of the nature of selfhood, I will attempt herein to use this approach as a heuristic device such that we may appreciate still further the AD sufferer's vulnerability as well as his or her remaining abilities in the domain of selfhood. Toward that end, I will explore three main ideas:

1 That in one sense, selfhood, experienced as the sense of personal singularity, remains intact despite the many and varied deficits in cognitive function produced by the disease;

2 That there are attributes of the person which can be assaulted by the disease at the present (linear) time, but which can remain alive nonetheless in the afflicted person's "personal present;" that there are also new attributes which result from the disease process itself, and still other abiding attributes which survive the ravages of the disease. These features pick up the sense of selfhood as the totality of attributes a person has;

3 That there are aspects of the self, those which are presented socially and publicly, some of which can be lost, but that such losses are indirect rather than direct results of the disease. In this domain

of selfhood, the losses that may be experienced by the afflicted are directly related to the ways in which healthy others position and treat the AD sufferer.

The Constructionist View

The Social Constructionist view developed from recent advances in psycholinguistics, inspired in part by the writings of the philosopher Wittgenstein (1953), who asserted the central importance of language in the creation of social reality, and in part by rediscovering the work of Vygotsky (1965) who discussed the contribution of the acquisition of linguistic skills as they bear on the organization of thought and experience. The Social Constructionist point of view, then, as described by Coulter (1981) and Harré (1983, 1991), is based upon the idea that selfhood is manifested publicly in many types of discourse which include, but are not limited to, the telling of autobiographical stories, assuming responsibility for one's actions, expressions of doubt as well as interest in social situations, cries of unfairness, and the like. The ideas of William Stern also mesh with the constructionist view in that Stern viewed a person as a *unitas multiplex*, a diversity in unity (Stern, 1938), the implication being that there can be many and varied forms and expressions of selfhood all bound up in the individual person.

The self of personal identity: Self 1

In the case of personal identity, we must first distinguish between two issues: how the identity of a person appears to others, and how that person experiences and expresses his or her own identity.

In the first case, others make their initial judgments about the identity of a person in terms of the material, or bodily, attributes of that person. Thus, if such bodily attributes are judged to be the same from time to time and from place to place, we will say that this is the same person, for we take for granted that each person is embodied in the same physical form throughout his or her life. Likewise, we assume that a person's life runs along a continuous temporal course, such as can be captured in autobiography or biography.

From a Constructionist point of view, a person's experience of his or her personal identity is expressed most often in linguistic terms – in his or her discourse – specifically through the use of first-person pronouns such as "I," "Me," "My," and adjectives such as "Myself," "Mine." Through the use of such pronouns, we express our own sense of self as a singular person, a particular individual who has a continuous and single point of view in the world of space and time and objects. That one point of view, indeed the only point of view from which an individual experiences the world, is located at each moment in a particular point in space, necessarily grounded in the body. In Stern's (1938) words, it is the "natural center from which and toward which everything pertaining to it extends; this is the person himself, about whom it is oriented" (p. 92) and this is what constructionists refer to as Self 1. Multiple-personality disorders would thus be understood as pathological forms of the normal singularity of Self 1. The normal, singular point of view is located through the use of first-person pronouns. Therefore, such pronouns are said to have an "indexical function" in that they allow us to locate the source of beliefs, opinions, responsibilities, and the like in relation to the place of the individual's embodiment in space and in the social-psychological world. So, when a person says, "I am sorry," he or she is locating for others the source and ownership of the feeling of regret with the speaker. In addition, the use of first-person pronouns also indexes with the speaker the moral force of an utterance. That is, saying, "I will get this information for you," commits the speaker to what has been promised.

In principle, a person could suffer from a severe form of amnesia which prevents the recall of his or her name, age, personal history, what city or town he or she happens to be in at the moment and the like, and still have an intact Self 1. The moment the individual uses one or another personal pronoun, or even uses gestures, in such a way as to indicate "I" or "me," or "mine" or "my," that person is experiencing and expressing his or her personal identity and indexing for others the location of his or her singular point of view in the world. Of course, one might argue that the use of first-person pronouns might be merely a verbal habit that persists as something of a vestigial reflex, thus producing the illusion of the survival of personal identity, but such an illusion would likely be shattered by studying the person's discourse in further detail (Sabat and Harré, 1992).

If we adopt this way of understanding the expression and experience of personal identity, it follows that if a person with AD employs first-person indexical pronouns in a coherent manner in his or her discourse, he or she has experienced and displayed an intact Self 1. An examination of the discourse of the AD sufferers you've met in this book reveals that each of them, despite being in the moderate to severe stages of the disease, had an intact self of personal identity (Self 1). I will concentrate in this section on a detailed examination of the Self 1 presentations in Dr. B's discourse.

The case of Dr. B

Throughout our association, Dr. B used a variety of first-person pronouns to index as his own a plethora of autobiographical statements about his experience of the effects of the disease, his feelings about his situation at the day care center, his beliefs about his relationship with his wife, and his pride in, concern about, and love for his adult children. Throughout our association, he was in firm command of his sense of personal identity. For example, listen to one of his descriptions of how Alzheimer's affects him: "Well, I get wisps of people, of thoughts, that show me that Alzheimer's is right on top of me. And, uh, that there's nothing I can do about it . . . Well uh, I'm, and I'm, something has knocked me down, something's knocked me down and I can't do anything about it." Here he is not only indicating his insight into the fact that AD is affecting him, but also his ability to index, as his own, the experience of that insight as well as the location of the autobiographical report of his belief that he is powerless to do anything about the effects of AD.

Perhaps most telling for our present purposes is that toward the end of our association, in the last months of his life, he was still using first-person pronouns to index his experiences as his own. In the following extract, I engaged him in conversation about the fact that he was feeling more and more anxious with each passing day:

SRS: And you're upset most of the time?
Dr. B: Yeah, most of the time, all the time.
SRS: Is this new for you? Were you that way all your life?
Dr. B: I, I jump all, all over the place, but you do too I know.

SRS: Years and years ago when your children were young, were you upset all the time?

Dr. B: No.

SRS: No?

Dr. B: No, because that's ridiculous.

SRS: So being upset all the time is a relatively recent thing?

Dr. B: That's right, that's right.

SRS: Would you say that it has to do with Alzheimer's?

Dr. B: Yes! Yes. I think so. I don't know what the linking is, but I think it, it's there.

Not only is he is quite clear still about the difference in the degree to which he felt anxiety when his children were young as opposed to the present time in which he was experiencing the onslaught of AD, but he is clearly indexing, through his use of first-person pronouns, his thoughts and feelings as well as his uncertainty about the exact connection between Alzheimer's and his increased levels of anxiety as belonging to him.

This next extract occurred some hours after he experienced incontinence for the first time at the day care center:

Dr. B: I was, is, ill.

SRS: Were you ill this morning?

Dr. B: Ya.

SRS: Was that a real pain in the neck?

Dr. B: Oh, ya.

SRS: Did you get through it?

Dr. B: I got through it, but it hurt me.

SRS: Physically?

Dr. B: Physically.

SRS: Did it hurt you psychologically?

Dr. B: Ya.

SRS: That too?

Dr. B: Ya. What I want to do, I want to go home, I think, and just talk about it.

SRS: I bet you do, I bet you do. The problem is that I can't take you home and your wife can't take you home, so we'll just have to stay here and make the best of it.

Dr. B: I'll call my wife, because, as a matter of fact, I called her this morning.

SRS: You did?

Dr. B: Yes.

SRS: And what happened?

Dr. B: It was [the director] I think, I think he got like this [*shaking his hands nervously*].

SRS: Panicky?

Dr. B: Panicky and then and then, lo and behold, he was, he was pretty good.

SRS: He was?

Dr. B: He was pretty good. He wants, wants, he says we, we need newer things. [The director was referring to a change of clothes.]

SRS: What kinds of things?

Dr. B: Well, uh right now I have not quite to think.

SRS: Would you rather not talk about it?

Dr. B: No I don't want to [garbled]. You know and I know some of the things. Here, let me just sit up. I'm drunk, I'm drunk in water.

SRS: You seem pretty exhausted.

Dr. B: I am. My wife came here today.

SRS: She did?

Dr. B: Ya. Let's go, let's go, I want to tal, talk to you. Let's think about it, let's think about it, let's think about it, and then hopefully something pull, pulls out. But I'm tired; I am exhausted. My wife came here in the middle of the afternoon.

SRS: In the middle of the morning she was here? [I knew that she was there in the morning, after the episode of incontinence occurred.]

Dr. B: Ya.

SRS: What happened? Why did she come?

Dr. B: Yes. The thing fell down. There was some, some sort of, yeah. Someone was very upset and I couldn't, I couldn't take it.

SRS: Somebody at the center was upset and you couldn't take it?

Dr. B: Ya.

SRS: So why did your wife have to come because . . .

Dr. B: Well, the water, the waw, the water of all kinds, of all things, got down.

280

SRS: I'm not sure about what you mean. Would you rather not talk about it?

Dr. B: Ya, I don't like, as a matter of fact, I may go home.

SRS: We can talk about other things if you like, or we can go for a walk.

We went for a walk and, because the subject of this conversation provoked great anxiety and embarrassment in him, he avoided further discussion of the issue. He was hardly oblivious to what had happened and, although word-finding problems interfered with his recounting of the incident exactly, he successfully indexed a variety of feelings and desires as his own through the use of first-person pronouns. Notice, however, that his comment, "Well, the water, the waw, the water of all kinds, of all things, got down," seems closely related to the meaning of incontinence. If one were unaware of what had actually transpired, however, this sentence might not hold a great deal of meaning. This example may be informative to professional as well as family caregivers in that often utterances made by the afflicted person may appear, at first blush, to be meaningless or confusing, but such appearances may be just those – appearances – because, given the context of events which actually occurred, the utterances are related to those events and do contain meaning.

In discussions with his wife, I learned that Dr. B increasingly wanted to be with her all the time rather than going to the day care center. Unfortunately, this was impossible and at times he expressed annoyance about that fact. I brought this up in conversation with him:

SRS: It seemed to me that your wife thinks that you would like her to be around you and paying attention to you all the time.

Dr. B: Well I have had a couple, I have had some, some stuff things.

SRS: Have you been annoyed with her?

Dr. B: Oh good grief no! She's the light of my life. No.

SRS: So you're not annoyed that she goes to work? Resent the fact that she goes to work?

Dr. B: Oh no, no. She is the biggest love in my life.

SRS: If Mrs. B is the biggest love in your life, what is Alzheimer's to you?

Dr. B: I don't think they're incompatible, I really don't. I see, I see the two people are, can uh, easily carry.

SRS: So you think two people can still have a good relationship even though one of them has Alzheimer's?

Dr. B: Uh, yes, definitely. Nevertheless I feel why not, why not?

SRS: Would you say that Alzheimer's has caused you difficulties?

Dr. B: Oh sure, of course, of course. Oh ya, definitely, definitely.

SRS: What makes you happy?

Dr. B: Well, number one is the light of my life [his wife]. So that's one thing. Um, and then uh, the rest of my life is the uh, my children about three or four [actually, four].

SRS: So your children and your wife are sources of happiness for you?

Dr. B: Sure, sure. Oh ya! So the world, the world to me still lives.

If we take him at his word here, it could be said that he was not actually annoyed with his wife, *per se*, but with the fact that he had to be at the day care center twice a week while she was at work. His ability to index, as his own, his autobiographical reports regarding his experience of difficulties due to AD, as well as his ability to do likewise for the sources of his feelings of happiness is clearly established in his use of first-person pronouns. Here, in the midst of great inner turmoil and sadness, we see that his family, as it had always been, was still central to his joy and the cornerstone of meaning in his life. It was the abiding love of and for his family that inspired him to index as his own his feeling that, "So the world, the world to me still lives."

As this conversation continued, he asked me:

Dr. B: Why, why are you asking that? You know you and I, both of ours [us] go ahead and we, we talk and we both talk as it comes.

SRS: I was curious about how you see the world and your life even though you have this Alzheimer's business.

Dr. B: Um, I have been finding that the Alzheimer's is um, in, in, it all coils up. I think I can do it.

SRS: You think you can deal with it?

Dr. B: I think I can. I have, I have, I have. Now when I say that, when your people say, "hey this is what we have to do," and somebody comes up and says, "yeah we got something, we got something, something hot, hot, hot, hot, hot, hot." Um, but we do it. I'm not, I'm not incom, incompatible to Alzheimer's. I'm not, I'm not. I feel I can do it.

In his last comment, he again indexes as his own, and so stresses and highlights his belief that he can continue working on the Project in spite of the effects of AD, in that the disease won't prevent him from continuing in his efforts with me. Thus he continues to experience and display in his discourse his "self of personal identity."

On the last day I was to see Dr. B at the day care center, his exhaustion was extremely pronounced, and his periods of inconsolable anxiety and sadness had grown longer and more frequent. Staff members who had grown to love and respect him found themselves less and less able to help him find islands of peace even though his "spirit was willing." Throughout the course of our association, whenever I arrived, he greeted me with a warm smile and seemed happily relieved to see me. The day on which the following conversation took place was different, however, for he was clearly angry and said as much. When we tried to go for a walk, he lost his balance in the hallway and I literally caught him before he fell down and held him against a wall until a staff member could aid me in getting him to a chair (Dr. B was quite tall and solidly built).

SRS: You said you were angry.

Dr. B: Yes.

SRS: What were you angry about?

Dr. B: Look – could you get water, please?

SRS: There's the water.

Dr. B: [*He drinks a good deal.*] I'm so pissed off.

SRS: What are you pissed off about?

Dr. B: The son of a bitch.

SRS: Who's a son of a bitch? [I was shocked at this. He had never spoken this way before – either in words or tone.]

Dr. B: I'll tell you soon. Let's, let's take [the social worker]. Could you and I, just the two of us get, get on, on someplace to the idea of what you and I do? [I took this to mean, "Can we do some work on the Project?"]

SRS: Well, that's why we're here.

Dr. B: So now I want to establish, this is ugly.

SRS: How so?

Dr. B: How so? [The social worker.]

SRS: What happened with her?

Dr. B: She says, "I don't think you shou, shou, you should be working anymore." And then, "I don't think you should be doing this work." So, in a sense it's good. It's good.

SRS: Why?

Dr. B: Because um, they dividit it.

SRS: So she said that she didn't think that you should do any work today.

Dr. B: Ya. That's, that's one of the, the things.

SRS: She didn't mean forever, she meant today because you were exhausted.

Dr. B: Ya. Let's go out. Let's walk, okay?

SRS: You see, the thing is, that I'm concerned about that because you were trying to walk before and you were losing your balance.

Dr. B: Yeah?

SRS: Yeah and I don't want you to fall.

Dr. B: Oh.

SRS: And I don't think *you* want to fall.

Dr. B: What?

SRS: You don't want to fall down, do you?

Dr. B: Okay. Well tell me, let's, let's, let's fix it up.

SRS: I think just to rest is a good idea. Have you been sleeping well?

Dr. B: Ya.

SRS: You have?

Dr. B: Ya, ya. I may be, I may be over. Let's go outside and walk.

SRS: Well, I'm really concerned about that because we were just trying to walk and you almost fell.

Dr. B: Did you see it?

SRS: I caught you.

Dr. B: Oh. Okay. All right, let's, let's, let's, let's put this away for a time.

SRS: Put the tape recorder away?

Dr. B: Ya.

SRS: Okay.

In this extract, one can observe the same discursive abilities to use first-person pronouns as indexicals as he demonstrated at the outset of our association. His comment, "I'm so pissed off" indicates an intact ability to use the first person so as to index the force of and commitment to his utterance. Additionally, he shows what we may refer to as a "reflexive grasp" (Sabat and Harré, 1992) of the conditions for maintaining a social persona ("Could you and I, just the two of us get, get on, on someplace to the idea of what you and I do?"). Here, we see that, despite his turmoil, his working cooperatively with me on "The Project" is still of utmost importance to him. In his comments about the social worker and what she said ("She says, 'I don't think you . . . should be working anymore.' And then, 'I don't think you should be doing this work.'"), he displays the highest order of indexical skill in using what Urban (1989) calls, "the story telling voice." In technical terms, he uses "she" as an anaphoric pronoun which stands for "social worker" as a way to introduce an "embedded indexical." That is, in his telling the story of what the social worker said to him, he uses the indexical "I" to communicate what she said to him about her feeling that he shouldn't be working on the project given his state of turmoil and exhaustion. Thus he used the pronoun "I" in this story to index the responsibility of social worker's comment as being hers, and shows that it is this comment which led to his being legitimately "pissed off." In addition, his comment toward the end of this extract, referring to the tape recorder, ". . . let's put this away for a time," that is, "let us, you and I, put this away for a time" indexes as his own the desire to talk for a time without the conversation being recorded.

After a few minutes, with his consent, we began again:

SRS: A few minutes ago, we were walking up the ramp here and you lost your balance and almost fell and I caught you.

Dr. B: I know.

SRS: So I don't want to risk . . .

Dr. B: Ya. Okay, let's walk outside.

SRS: Now wait a second, wait a second. Listen to what I'm saying to you, okay?

Dr. B: Okay.

SRS: It's very important. You've got to focus everything you have on what I'm about to say, okay?

Dr. B: Yeah.

SRS: I don't want to walk outside because just a few moments ago when you were walking, you almost fell. You lost your balance and I had to catch you.

Dr. B: Okay.

SRS: So that's why I don't want to walk outside.

Dr. B: Well, let's not, let us not do nothing now and let's thought about it, assuming that this is whatever it is. Okay?

SRS: We don't have to do anything. All I want to do is to relax, actually.

Dr. B: Let me go for a while outside.

SRS: Well, you see if you go outside, it means that you're walking.

Dr. B: Which means what?

SRS: Which means you might fall. Your blood pressure is really up.

Dr. B: So what's the wise, best thing to do?

SRS: The best thing to do is to sit down and calm down. Do some deep breathing.

Dr. B: I want my wife. I wanna, I haven't talked to my wife. Think about.

At this point he became more and more insistent about talking to his wife and so we went to the office where a staff member made the phone call to her. He became teary-eyed, then cried convulsively. This pattern was repeated a number of times in the days following, and within the next two weeks he was hospitalized. I have presented this extract of conversation and the one that follows not only to show that he was still using the first-person pronouns, "I," and "me," to index his desires and understanding as his own, but also to allow the reader to understand the depth of his turmoil. The next time I saw him he was in the hospital.

As I stood in the doorway of his hospital room, my eyes recoiled at the sight of the distinguished, gentle, warm man I had come to know, care for, and respect, alone and strapped in a chair, head bowed down, seemingly staring blankly at the tray that crossed the armrests. The room was stark. Except for the radio and the pictures of his family brought by his wife, there was little of the human touch to be found. I was struck by the irony of it all, for here in the psychiatric unit one would imagine that the importance of a warm, human touch would be most clearly appreciated and celebrated. Sadly, that was not the case. Nonetheless, it was time to meet with Dr. B.

SRS: Hi, Dr. B, it's Dr. Sabat.

Dr. B [in a crying tone of voice]: I don't know where, where to go. I don't know where, where I'm going, I'm not going.

SRS: You're really upset aren't you? Are you afraid?

Dr. B: Afraid, afraid, afraid, where are you going, where, where are going, going, going [*trails off in a mumble*]?

SRS: Maybe if you look at my face, you'll recognize the beard.

Dr. B: Some schools, some schools.

SRS: I have a daughter. You met Deborah a number of times.

Dr. B: I have it cover for [not clear].

SRS: Is it difficult for you to speak?

Dr. B: I don't know, know, know, know . . . 95, 96, 97, 97, 98, here, here, here, here.

SRS: I'm with you.

Dr. B: Good, good, good, good.

SRS: Can you tell me how you feel?

Dr. B: Oh G-d. [*mumbles*] Telephone. *I wanna, want to spend telephone,* phone and see how, how they fear, how they fear, how they fear, how they fear, how they fear, how they fear, how they fear. No, no, no, no, no, no more, no [says oldest son's name six times].

SRS: Are you thinking about [oldest son's name]?

Dr. B: Ya, ya.

SRS: He's a real blockbuster, isn't he?

Dr. B: I don't know. [*louder*] I don't know what it is.

SRS: You don't know what's bothering you?

Dr. B [angrily]: I don't know what to do.

SRS: You know what?

Dr. B: I don't know, I don't know what to do, what to do, to, to, to, to [*mumbling*] say hello, hello [*mumbling agitatedly*].

SRS: Try to relax for a minute. I'm here. It's okay.

Dr. B [crying]: When can channa, channa, channa, my favorite [says youngest son's name three times], what, what can I come? *What can I want?* Come what I come, come what I come, come what I come. She was, was in, in there. She was in one too.

SRS: Who was she? I talked to your wife this morning.

Dr. B: Yeah?

SRS: Do you feel like you're out of control?

Dr. B: Not out of, out of croll, it's just that, it's just that, in for, in for, in for, in for.

SRS: You don't feel like you're out of control?

Dr. B: That what?

SRS: Do you feel like you're out of control?

Dr. B: In this, in this place, yes.

SRS: In this place?

Dr. B: *I'd kill them anyway.*

SRS: You just don't want to be in the hospital?

Dr. B: Tell me what do you know I know, know, know, know [*fades*]. No, no, no, no, no, n-n-no, n-n-no [*cries*] Who knows? Who knows?, Who knows? who, nobody knows. *I don't know, I don't know (louder).* They never were very, very, very, very, very, in the same thing, the same thing, the same [*crying*].

SRS: So what do you think?

Dr. B: Okay, all right, that's, this is the best them all things. *I wanna do this, I wanna do this.*

SRS: We're doing it.

Dr. B: We're doing it. I want a hundred. Now take off the day care, the day care, the day care, the day care.

SRS: That's right, we worked at the day care.

Dr. B [crying]: *I know, I know, I know.*

SRS: I know you know. I know you know. Does everything seem like a fog to you?

Dr. B: No [*cries*].

SRS: What's got you so sad?

Dr. B: It's sad.

SRS: What's sad?

Dr. B: *Yeah, because it's sad, it's so sad because, because I sit in that corner and I come, I come over, I don't even know, even know where I am, I don't even know where I am [louder], (screaming, crying) I don't even know where I am, AM, AM, AM.*

SRS: I'll tell you where you are. You're right here and this is [name of] Hospital.

Dr. B: And that's, that's what they, you calling.

SRS: That's what they call it [name of] Hospital. I guess this is not one of your favorite places, huh?

Dr. B: No, no.

SRS: Well I can understand that. It wouldn't be one of my favorite places either. Is today a pretty rough day?

Dr. B: Ya. 1,2,3, 1,2,3, positive. Okay, *I'll give it to you if you want it.*

SRS: I want it.

Dr. B: Okay. Everyone has a good stack, everyone has a good stack . . . yes, yes, yes, yes. Make it easy, make it easy. [His waist was bound too tightly by the seat belt and I loosened it somewhat.]

SRS: Okay?

Dr. B: Okay.

SRS: Ya?

Dr. B: Okay.

SRS: How's that?

Dr. B: All right.

SRS: Is that better?

Dr. B: Right.

SRS: Good. That's what we want to do – make it easy.

Dr. B: How?

SRS: I'm not sure.

Dr. B: Everything is terrible, terrible, terrible, terrible, terrible. All right, now the first thing is, he is not supposed to try to do [*mumbles*]. Yeah. Oh.

SRS: You have pain?

Dr. B: Yes.

SRS: Abdominal pain? [He had a history of feeling such pain when he was under stress.]

Dr. B: Yes.

SRS: Can you show me where?

Dr. B: Right over here . . . everything's got to work, but it doesn't work to work, to work . . . It's *too much, too much anxiety, too many anxiet, anxiet.* What, what are you, what are you going to do to me?

SRS: I'm not going to do anything to you. You feel anxiety?

Dr. B: Yes. *I hurt, I hurt, I hurt, I hurt, I hurt.* It gets worse.

SRS: In your abdomen?

Dr. B: Yes. Please can somebody do something else?

He began to cry once again, his head bowed. There was great rigidity in his face – much like a "Parkinsonian mask" – the rigidity was a side effect of one of his medications, and affected his speech as well. Rigidity was also revealed in his gait when he was helped to the bathroom. He shuffled rather than walked. Yet, he persisted in the use of autobiographical indexing of reports of his experiences of anxiety, torment, and pain as his own, thus demonstrating an intact Self 1, the self of personal identity as a uniquely embodied being.

It is of note that at this same time in the progress of the disease there was, in his behavior, evidence of new learning. During his stay in the hospital, he used the bathroom in his room. There was, however, a small step at the entrance to the bathroom. At first Dr. B, because of his shuffling gait, would catch his foot on the step, but eventually learned to lift his foot at precisely the right time when entering the bathroom and thereby avoided tripping over the step. Even in the nursing home, weeks later, he persisted in lifting his foot when entering the bathroom (even though there was no step to avoid). This behavior is an instance of what cognitive psychologists call implicit memory – wherein there is evidence of a change in a person's behavior as a result of prior experience even though the person may not be able to tell you, in words, what he or she has learned or even *that* he or she has learned. This occurred at a time approximately eight years after the first appearance of difficulties with his memory.

The self of mental and physical attributes: Self 2

Each of us possesses a unique set of mental and physical attributes which differ at least in some ways from those of any other person. Some attributes may have had great longevity, whereas others may be short-lived in comparison. Thus, a person's physical features, level of education, vocational pursuits, sense of humor, having a "good memory," are attributes which may have a long-standing history, whereas being retired or diagnosed with AD would be still other attributes which are relatively recent aspects of one's Self 2. In some respects, then, what a person is in the sense of Self 2, changes with the passage of time. The person whose eyesight was excellent for decades may now need glasses, for example.

290

In addition to mental attributes such as perhaps, having a good memory, a well-developed sense of humor, and having a facility with language, there are also one's beliefs, which include beliefs about his or her attributes. So, a person may have had a life-long set of spiritual or religious beliefs, a particular political orientation, a commitment to serving others, to which he or she has adhered, and one may have a set of beliefs about these attributes such that they may be sources of pride or strength, for example. Likewise, one may have beliefs about attributes such as one's height and weight, level of education, tendency to procrastinate, vocational pursuits, such that one prides oneself on some, but not on others. Furthermore, because some attributes change with the passage of our days, so too is there a multiplicity of our beliefs, for we have beliefs about what we were, what we are, and what we may someday become.

In keeping with this line of thinking, one may have beliefs about the attribute of being afflicted with AD. A person might believe that having been so diagnosed and now suffering from AD is a source of embarrassment, sadness, shame, and that the life one had anticipated living in later years is now a possibility no longer. Dr. M, you may remember, commented that soon after having been diagnosed, she was very reluctant to tell friends and relatives the exact name of her problem. "Why this reluctance to name my malady?", she asked. "Can it be that the term, 'Alzheimer's' has a connotation similar to the 'Scarlet Letter' or the 'Black Plague'? Is it even more embarrassing than a sexual disease?"

Some Self 2 attributes such as one's height, weight, previous achievements, religious orientation, family oriented style, nurturing disposition, sense of humor, and the like may not be easily affected or affected at all by AD in the moderate to severe stages, and therefore may still persist as aspects of Self 2, as we can see in one way or another in the all of the individuals whom you have encountered in previous chapters. Likewise, these same afflicted persons still held strongly positive beliefs about many of these attributes. Other attributes, such as having had a good memory, a facility with language, being able to dress oneself, to drive, to pay constant, vigilant attention to salient events occurring in one's immediate environment, to calculate easily the amount to leave as a tip in a restaurant, may be severely affected by the disease and are, therefore, replaced in the linear present by new, dysfunctional attributes. And, to the extent that the afflicted person is aware of his or her difficulties, that person's beliefs about these new, dysfunctional attributes will be negative. For example, listen to the following interchange with Dr. M:

SRS: You're not just any ordinary person who has some problems finding words. You're a person for whom words, words to you are kind of like a musical instrument.

Dr. M: Um hum, um hum. That's exactly right.

SRS: And so the kind of frustration you feel would be greater than for a person whose focus in life was not so literary. That could give you cause for a lot of grief.

Dr. M: I think the issue is, that is, for me maybe especially this day for some reason or other, but for last, maybe four years, that I am not satisfied with myself because what I want isn't here. I've, uh, thinking of it and it makes me angry as well as, that is part of the . . . and I guess that is what is happening now. Don't you think?

Finally, to the extent that the person with AD can no longer engage in formerly enjoyable activities due to the inability to speak or to move in as fluent a manner as in healthier days, he or she might be observed to avoid those activities for fear of embarrassment, all of which constitute still another set of new attributes brought about directly or indirectly by AD.

As we saw in the previous chapter, there can be a clash in one's "personal present" between valued attributes which a person has enjoyed for decades and the weakened forms of these attributes, as a result of the disease, which appear less admirable at the present time. As a result, another Self 2 attribute of the afflicted person may be sadness, anger, even depression. The degree of depression may be related to the extent to which others in the afflicted person's social world define him or her in terms of the very attributes about which the AD sufferer has negative feelings and beliefs.

The overarching point here is that, even in the moderate to severe stages of the disease, the afflicted person's Self 2 is hardly bereft of attributes of the mental and physical variety. Interestingly, although the afflicted person may be embarrassed, even tormented, by new dysfunctional attributes which follow in the wake of AD, the extent to which the person will speak about such attributes and his or her beliefs about those attributes may well be intimately connected with the social context. For example, Dr. B and Dr. M were obviously embarrassed and angered by the loss of certain cherished attributes they enjoyed in the past, and were unwilling to place themselves in social situations in which the potential for embarrassment was great. When I first met her, Dr. M would refrain from speaking at her support group meetings primarily because of her word-finding problems and her beliefs about them. Indeed, this was one of the reasons for her reluctance to attend meetings at all. Yet, there were other social situations in which these same people were perfectly willing to share their thoughts, feelings, and beliefs about those very attributes which caused them anguish, despite the fact that they would encounter tormenting word-finding problems, for example, in the process. Dr. M showed no hesitation whatsoever in speaking with me about her concerns and frustrations. Why would there be such a striking difference in behavior in these two different social contexts?

One way to analyze the effect of the social context, is to recognize that different social contexts offer either great opportunity or the lack thereof for the afflicted person to construct other valued aspects of selfhood, namely, the social personae or public presentation of self, the Self 3. Thus, when Dr. M was in her support group, she was viewed by the original group leader primarily as "a patient," and that was something that caused her to feel great disquietude. On the other hand, when meeting with me, she was able to construct the honorable, valued, persona of academic person-social worker and, in that context, she addressed a plethora of problems and her beliefs about the dysfunctional attributes stemming from AD which caused her anguish. In this context she could explore her disabilities and her beliefs about them in the thoughtful, careful, analytic style which was a source of pride for her in her healthier days. The same was true for Dr. B, who was able to discuss his experience of AD in the context of his persona of "Scientist-Research Collaborator," for this persona was one in which he had always taken pride and was fundamentally related to his sense of honor. And finally, we see the same phenomenon occurring with Mrs. D, who, as "Life of the Party" was able to joke about her AD-related problems ("It's a helluva disease"). By being seen in a positive way at the outset through the construction of a valued social persona, each person could, from that position, feel comfortable enough to discuss the very Self 2 attributes which were anathema to them. One might say that the social conditions which allowed the afflicted person to preserve some dignity and pride, by being recognized in a positive light, also allowed them to be open about their problems and their beliefs about those problems without feeling humiliated.

Thus, when Dr. M said, "I don't feel myself," she was referring in part to her awareness of the negative alterations in many of her valued and long-standing attributes as caused by AD. I say "in part" here because there were other ways in which Dr. M did not feel "herself," but these other ways had to do with aspects of this other dimension of selfhood, the public persona, what constructionists refer to as the socially presented self, Self 3.

The socially presented selves, or personae: Self 3

On the social constructionist account, there is a multiplicity of Selves 3, for these are the variety of different social personae and patterned and coordinated forms of behavior, the display of any of which depends upon the social context within which one finds oneself at any one moment. Thus, among the many Selves 3 of a particular individual person, there may be the respectful child who speaks with deference to an elderly parent, the authoritative teacher who has the right to determine a student's grade, the parent who acts from a senior position when helping his or her child with school-work, the patient who acts from a junior position when visiting a physician or dentist, the devoted friend who acts as an equal in conversation with his or her neighbor. In each of these interactions, the quality of the persona, the entailed beliefs, the codes of conduct and associated behavior will be different as befits the specific social context.

It would follow, then, that one person can be seen as having many different sides or personae when viewed in a variety of situations. Hence, if we were to experience a person in only one social context, we may find ourselves surprised at the behavior of that person when we first observe that person's "different" Self 3 in another social context. Seeing the serious, senior research scientist behave in a jok-ing, warm, almost silly way when playing with his or her young child might "shock" a junior colleague. Such "shock" or surprise would spring forth from two things:

1 The fact that the junior colleague has experienced the senior scientist only in professional situations in which the latter has, with the cooperation of others, manifested a Self 3 of "senior scientist" along with the attendant cluster of behavior patterns, and

2 The fact that, on the basis of such limited experience, the junior colleague has constructed in his or her mind, a "storyline" or "narrative" with regard to the senior person and has positioned the senior person on the basis of that storyline. The particular story-line accompanying the behavior of the "senior scientist" does not allow for behavior patterns which one would display with one's child, and so such behavior observed in the senior person would be unexpected and seen as surprising and, perhaps, even improper by the junior colleague.

In this regard I recall vividly how, as an undergraduate student, I was stunned to discover that my esteemed, eloquent and distinguished professor was a devoted sports fan. I had positioned, and had created story lines about, professors in such a way so as to exclude them from having such "trifling" interests, entailing a wholly distinct form of public presentation of "who he is."

Self 3 is unlike Self 1 and Self 2 in yet another way. In order to experience and display Self 1 and 2, it is not necessary for an individual to receive the cooperation of any other person. Self 3, however, does require the cooperation of at least one other person in order for that persona to be manifested, for it is in the dynamic interplay of mutual recognition of one's own and another person's position in the social situation that the particular Self 3 is constructed. Put another way, it would be impossible for the individual to manifest the persona of teacher without the recognition and cooperative behavior of his or her students, impossible to manifest the persona of helpful parent without the recognition and cooperative behavior of one's child. We may appreciate the fact, then, that any particular Self 3 is continuously created in the course of the interaction between two or more people.

In like manner, for the AD sufferer to construct, and to manifest, a particular Self 3, he or she would require the cooperation of healthy others. The afflicted person is thus strikingly vulnerable in social situations. For, to the extent that healthy others focus upon the Self 2 attributes of AD and its negative effects upon other Self 2 attributes to the relative exclusion of attributes which the afflicted person values, that person will have difficulty in gaining the needed cooperation required in order to construct Self 3 personae which reflect attributes in which the sufferer can take pride. In other words, if healthy others position someone as defective, confused, and helpless and act out story lines about the afflicted person that emphasize his or her defects, it will be difficult if not impossible for the afflicted person to gain the sort of cooperation needed to construct a Self 3 other than that of "The Burdensome, Dysfunctional Patient." Shortly, others will come to believe that that is all the afflicted person *can* be.

Therefore, if there is a loss of Self 3 personae in an AD sufferer, such losses may be seen in many cases not to have been caused by the disease itself. This loss has come about more directly by the lack of the necessary cooperation he or she receives from others. It is, unfortunately, all too common for people with AD to be defined and positioned by others primarily as "patients." For example, one intelligent and otherwise sensitive caregiver introduced me to her husband by saying, "This is my husband, he's the patient." If the afflicted person does, however, receive cooperation from others, we will see that valued, healthy, Self 3 personae can be constructed even in the moderate to severe stages of the disease.

The case of Dr. B

Dr. B refused to be a part of the day care center community. We hear in his own words how he viewed himself in terms of Self 2 attributes and Self 3 personae:

- First of all, "I don't necessarily need what is in that room," referring to the day care activities, calling them "filler." For him to be assimilated into such a group of people and involve himself in the usual activities would mean undermining his beliefs about who he was (Self 2) and would prevent him from constructing the public persona which was of profound importance to him.
- That he saw himself as a distinguished, respected, intellectual academician (Self 3) is seen in his comment that, "Yes, well my wife and I are very strong academic people and, uh, so we start talking to each other, we talk at a very high level right away." If he

allowed himself to be assimilated as a member of the day care center, the community of participants was such that he would never find another person who would be able to cooperate with him in the construction of this valued Self 3 of academic, intellectual, scientist. Indeed, despite the negative attributes caused by AD and his related beliefs about those attributes, the fact that he still saw himself as a scientist as seen in the following interchange:

SRS: Your comments were repeated exactly by her teacher – you and her teacher said exactly the same things.

Dr. B: Yeah? And I'm a scientist, for Christ sake! [*laughter*].

As a result, he had a negative reaction to being treated in a way that did not take into account his "standing" in the social order of the day care center:

SRS: Are you saying that you have no status with the rest of the day care people?

Dr. B: Oh, absolutely. Absolutely. There, there should be some hier, hierarty.

SRS: So you feel that you're a pretty bright guy, but that you're not really treated differently than people who aren't as bright?

Dr. B: Ya, that's, that's forces me to do something like this [working with me on the Project]. And I, I say that. Remember when you put the thing, when you gave me the letter? [The letter of commendation from the Dean of Georgetown College.] It was a very strong statement that I am something above, or something like that.

SRS: You feel that you're not treated with as much deference as you think you deserve? Is that accurate?

Dr. B: Honestly, yes.

That Dr. B found his working on the Project to be satisfying, so as to speak of himself in a way that reflected his commitment to being a fellow researcher, was evident in many conversations. In the following extract, from Chapter 6, he was trying to put me in contact with Ms. Fridkin at the Alzheimer's Disease Association in order to add to "our work" in a positive way, for she would be a valuable source of information for us:

Dr. B: Um, yes she has, in fact she does, because *she is working on the same project say pojedic, project, and, uh, ironically enough, it, uh, this is what it is.*

SRS: It has to do with dementia?

Dr. B: Yes it demention. *I think, I think that, that we could meld, we can meld two things.*

SRS: *Something that she's doing,*

Dr. B: *Yes.*

SRS: *with something that we're doing.*

Dr. B: *That's right.* I know that you see what *you* see and it could be a real slambam.

His use of the first person plural in the locution, ". . . we can meld two things . . ." indicates the successful construction of Self 3 as scientist-researcher-collaborator, for he and I have become "we" in the workings of the Project. He has now become an active contributor to what he saw as a "sort of scientific thing," and is functioning as a collaborator rather than as an AD sufferer. Working with me on the Project meant a number of things:

1 He was singled out from the rest of the day care participants, thus being someone "special" in the "hierarchy" of participants.
2 He was working on a research project which he viewed as a ". . . real good, big project . . . a sort of scientific thing . . . others go with stature and what I feel, I think, my G-d, this is real stature to do!"
3 He was thus positioned primarily as one who had a contribution to make to science rather than as a helpless, confused, burdensome AD sufferer, or "patient".

All of these resulted from my providing him with the necessary co-operation with which he was able to construct the Self 3 of "academic person-research scientist-collaborator", which, in turn, signalled that he was doing something important with his time and effort. Goffman (1969) has pointed out many times that honor and reputation are fundamental to moral lives and are precious in the eyes of most people. A person's standing in the local moral scheme of social life, that is, a person's "position," is intimately related to the presentation of Self 3 personae, for it is through such personae that we can maintain our valued standing among others. Dr. B understood this very well and continued to maintain his position and career as a scientist despite being at the day care center. But note that this would not have been possible without the cooperation of others such as myself and members of the staff. His avoidance of the routine activities could easily have been interpreted as meaning that he was "a loner," reclusive," and "uncooperative", when in fact his behavior was a statement of his willful desire to construct a Self 3 other than "AD patient at a day care center" along with all the dysfunction that such a Self 3 would connote. Thus, had Dr. B experienced a loss of this Self 3 persona of "academic person-scientist," such a loss would not have been due to AD itself, but rather to the constraints of the social circumstances surrounding him.

The case of Mrs. D

Mrs. D constructed the Self 3 persona of "Life of the Party" at the day care center, and here we see similar phenomena at work, although the social dynamics between her and the community of participants were entirely different from those in the case of Dr. B. Mrs. D, a high school graduate, did not pride herself on Self 2 attributes of distinguished academic achievement, scholarly abilities and the like. Rather, it was her Self 2 attributes of humor, her extroverted, warm personality, her nurturing and caring disposition along with her positive beliefs about these attributes which were central to her. As a result, she did not mind being part of the community of participants, but instead carved out the Self 3 persona of "Life of the Party." She had a fountain of knowledge of old songs which were familiar to many of the participants and also knew scores of jokes ("I got a million of 'em"). She clearly explained that many of the participants were sad or depressed and that she cheered them up with her songs and jokes, for she initiated sing-alongs and her jokes were greeted with raucous laughter. In this dynamic, she was able to obtain the participants' cooperation in manifesting her Self 3 persona of "Life of the Party." She commented, "I would work, you know, with somebody just to keep them happy" and "Some of them are in bad shape . . . I would try to help them. That's what you have to do almost, if you want to get along." In so doing, she became an important member of the day care community – someone who was valued by the staff as well as by other participants.

Mrs. D was able to construct this and other Self 3 personae because in addition to that given her by participants, she also received the cooperation of the day care center staff members who asked her to help integrate new people into the group (Self 3 of "liaison between staff and participants") or to provide sympathy and understanding to those experiencing particular difficulties (Self 3 of "nurturing group member"). Mrs. D would often initiate conversations with others even though she was not asked directly to do so. In addition to her role at the day care center, Mrs. D often volunteered herself as a subject in research efforts at NIH, even though she was confronted with failure on the numerous test batteries to which she was exposed in the process. The pride she took in constructing a Self 3 of "volunteer in the service of others" was far more important to her than whatever mistakes she made on the tests. As she commented, "That was the nicety of it, 'cause I could have said, 'no,' but believe me if I can help me and my fe (fellow) man, I would do it." Note that this last comment of hers reflects the existence of autotelic and heterotelic goals as defined by Stern (1938) and discussed in the previous chapter.

The fundamental importance of the cooperation of others in the process of constructing Self 3 personae was powerfully evident in Mrs. D's case, for her situation at home, as we saw in Chapter 3, was quite different. Her husband, though he loved her dearly, had positioned her mainly as an AD sufferer who was incompetent and therefore treated her as if she were not an agentive adult with intact powers and capabilities to act in meaningful ways. As a result, at home she was sullen, quiet, and experienced failure far more often than not when trying to respond to her husband's infrequent requests to do menial tasks such as moving small trash cans from one location in the house to another. The only Self 3 persona which could be constructed at home was that of "AD sufferer-burden."

Ironically, Mr. D reported that he would not speak with his wife about his own problems and feelings because he believed that, "she wouldn't understand." The very sympathetic and understanding nature and ability which she demonstrated with day care participants, her ability to experience and express a range of emotions, her sensitivity to the moods of others, her ability to express herself creatively, could not be called into being to aid her husband at home not because she was incapable of such, but because he did not give her the opportunity to behave in such a way. And, the lack of opportunity given to her by her husband was, itself, founded on his positioning of her as incompetent in the first place. Thus, at home, Mrs. D's loss of the same Self 3 personae constructed and displayed at the day care center was due to the social situations she confronted there rather than to the neuropathology of AD. Her husband's positioning of Mrs. D as "incompetent AD sufferer" resulted in the creation of an environment in which, sadly, both partners experienced isolation. Yet, ironically again, this resulted in something of an "honored" Self 3 presentation for Mr. D as the burdened and devoted caregiver.

The case of Mrs. R

You first met Mrs. R in Chapter 3. Here we find again the powerful effect of the cooperation of healthy others in AD sufferer's ability to manifest a valued and respected Self 3. Recall that Mrs. R had spent a great deal of her adult life as a volunteer in the service of others. In the many different countries in which she and her husband lived, she engaged herself working with the infirm in hospitals or with abandoned children. Years after becoming afflicted with AD and while she was a participant at an adult day care center, she was described by staff members as being extremely helpful in spite of her linguistic problems. Staff members commented that, in some ways, she functioned as did other healthy volunteers in that she helped setting tables for lunch, helped to set up for various activities, pointed out to staff members those participants who needed help that she could not provide, aided those in wheelchairs as they tried to navigate doorways. She had, with the cooperation of the staff members, created a Self 3 of "helper" and "nurturer" as she also provided those in distress with warm hugs and her smiling, evidently caring, presence. Staff members encouraged her with their thanks and praise, often engaged her to help with specific tasks, and she appeared to revel in the pleasure of being of service to others.

At home, the situation was quite different, for her devoted and caring husband had taken it upon himself to fulfill the responsibilities of the household, rarely asking her to help. Because of her linguistic problems, he assumed that she was unable to follow directions, and even went so far as to apply her make-up for her in the mornings, pick out her clothes for her each day, and cut her food at meals. Interestingly, she was able to do all of these tasks herself when she was given the opportunity, but before that time, her spouse complained that she did nothing to "keep busy" at home, did no housework, and either watched television or did nothing. Although it was an abiding aspect of her character to be helpful to others, she was unable to construct the Self 3 of "helper" and "nurturer" at home due to the way in which she was positioned by her husband – which itself prevented her from receiving his cooperation in constructing a valued and valuable Self 3 persona. What was the basis for his positioning her in such a way?

Mrs. R was positioned by her spouse as being incapable of doing at home many of the things which she routinely did at the day care center. His grounds for positioning her in this way were based upon her linguistic problems along with behaviors such as her putting soiled clothes into the bathroom trash can instead of the hamper, and refusing at times to change into sleepwear before going to sleep. Thus did he develop a storyline about her that portrayed her as being a "confused", "helpless" AD sufferer. At the day care center, she was still positioned somewhat as an AD sufferer by the staff, but positioned also as being someone upon whom they could count to be of service in a plethora of ways. And it was this latter, and crucial, type of positioning which spelled the difference between Mrs. R's ability to construct a worthy Self 3 at the day care center and her inability to do so at home.

Ironically, she was able to be somewhat nurturing at home in a way that played into the story line which her spouse had created. That is, although she could and did apply her own make-up at the day care center, she allowed her husband to do it for her at home, even though his doing so did not cover her facial blemishes and irritations to her own satisfaction. This was made clear by her applying more make-up at the day care center. Her spouse allowed that she did a better job than he did, but still thought she was using "too much" make-up. He also allowed that, perhaps, he was taking on too many tasks out of a need to "protect her" from failure. Mrs. R for her part was nurturing her husband's need to be needed by allowing him to do things for her which she, in fact, could do herself. Thus did she nurture him by allowing him to position her as being incapable of being helpful. Behavior patterns such as these have been described as "psychological symbiosis" (Shotter and Newson, 1974) and as a species of "undifferentiation" by Bowen (1990) such that two individuals function in some ways as one, each supplying an essential piece so as to create a whole coherent picture.

At the day care center, Mrs. R was also found engaged in actions which were aimed at protecting her honor and dignity. She would be observed, from time to time, walking along the length of the corridor, seemingly without any particular destination. If one were to ask her where she was going, she would not be able to furnish an answer. The storyline which is often woven about such behavior emphasizes "aimless or irrational wandering," which itself derives in part from the previous positioning of the AD sufferer as "confused." By investigating her behavior, however, a far different story line could be constructed.

On the majority of occasions on which Mrs. R walked about in the corridor, the only activity in which she could be engaged otherwise was a small group discussion in which each member of the group is asked to talk about the particular issue at hand. Mrs. R had extreme difficulty speaking coherently and, as a result, could not engage in the very behavior which was fundamental to the activity itself. Under these circumstances, if there was nothing else for her to do, if there was no staff member whom she could assist in some way, she went for a walk in the corridor instead of risking the humiliation of losing her standing in the community of participants as the Self 3 shown in her cooperative and nurturing behavior in other situations.

Therefore, instead of the "irrational wanderer" which is typical of the "confused" AD sufferer, we have something very different in the second storyline. Namely, we have behavior which reflects Mrs. R's grasp of the social situation, the rational decision to avoid embarrassment, and the desire to take a walk instead. This interpretation fits rather well with another of Mrs. R's Self 2 attributes. Recall how she displayed fastidiousness about her appearance in wanting to hide facial blemishes, which her spouse's application of make-up failed to do, by applying more make-up on her own after Mr. R dropped her off at the day care center. She was clearly concerned with how she appeared in the eyes of others. The first storyline, that of the "confused patient" ignores the very possibility that Mrs. R was capable of being humiliated, of feeling embarrassed, and so paints her behavior of walking about in the corridor as anything but a successful adaptation to a potentially embarrassing situation. As well as this, the first storyline serves only to support and perpetuate the original defect-based positioning of her. Had Mrs. R chosen to thumb through a magazine instead of walking through the corridor, one can only wonder if such behavior would be interpreted as "irrational, aimless thumbing through a magazine." I say this not to be droll, but simply to point out the power of how an AD sufferer can be positioned in defectological terms so as to label as "symptomatic of disease" the very same behavior which could be seen quite easily as being just as reasonable, healthy, and worthy of respect as it would be in anyone not afflicted with AD.

The case of Dr. M

Dr. M commented, "I don't feel myself," and we have already noted that her striking word-finding problems, a new Self 2 attribute caused by AD along with the negative belief she harbored about her not having "any good way of talking," gave her reason to feel this way. We can hear also in her words that follow, another reason for her to react this way. This reason, however, is intimately connected with issues surrounding her loss of the Self 3 of "teacher-guide":

SRS: I think that makes a lot of sense. I wonder if, when you're taking a walk, you have fewer problems finding words.
Dr. M: Yes, probably. But, well you see, I, I'm the teacher, not the, the thing, and uh, uh, being a teacher uh, wasn't, isn't something very – I can see the flower. It's not, I'm not, that I understand all the flowers and all the other things, it's just I guess what it is, and I have the role of a person who, and maybe I'm losing some of that too. I guess so. I guess you're right. I had, wouldn't, didn't think of it.
SRS: So when we were taking a walk you had a different role in the sense that you were leading,
Dr. M: Um hum.
SRS: guiding, showing,
Dr. M: And I, and I've, don't have very much of that now.

For most of her vocational life, Dr. M was an academic person, a professor, whose job it was to teach students, and the Self 3 of "teacher-guide-professor" was a source of great pride and an avenue through which she derived a great deal of self-worth. Of course, the manifestation of this Self 3 was also a means by which she maintained a place of honor, a moral career, in society. Although she retired from her academic position to pursue another moral career as a psychotherapist, the onset of AD prevented her from realizing that goal. Still, she clearly missed being in a position wherein she could be the "teacher" or "guide," as she commented in the extract above.

In addition, she expressed quite clearly her antipathy to being positioned primarily as an AD sufferer, when she commented that, "Sure, I can handle myself when I try not to let myself be presented as, as an Alcazheimer's, I'm very different." Her comment not only indexes (through her use of first-person pronouns), as her own, her commitment to self-management and her refusal to be positioned as a helpless victim of disease, but also her awareness of the effect of being positioned as such, with all the defects that such an identity would connote and emphasize. Thus she refused to cooperate with others who would attempt to position her in such a way. Refusing to be negatively positioned by others may not be an option common to many AD sufferers who then suffer harsh consequences in the absence of healthy others who are sensitive to the effects of such positioning.

On the other hand, Dr. M revelled in the fruits of my cooperating with her so that she could manifest the Self 3 of "Professor/Social Worker." In our discussions of the social dynamics of her support group, we touched upon the reactions and behavior of other group members as well as her own in a variety of situations that arose in meetings. After we went through one rather long discussion of the reactions of one of the group members, the following interchange occurred:

SRS: But at first I think he was feeling very uncomfortable because he didn't understand and maybe he was blaming himself for not understanding.

Dr. M: It seems to me uh, that that's int, interesting and I just *love* going through things like that and what it seems like and when and it uh, it's very, I like to do it. And I like to do it with you.

SRS: Oh, well thank you! It's mutual.

In these conversations, as with my interactions with Dr. B, I was determined to recognize her academic achievements and what they meant to her, and emphasized those Self 2 attributes in which she took pride. As a result, there was the opportunity for her at the present time to bring to bear the many skills she had developed throughout her life. Her ability to manifest a worthy Self 3 was clearly a source of great satisfaction to her, and the antithesis of her reaction to being positioned as an AD sufferer. Her plight as an AD sufferer was poignantly clear in her observation referring to me, "Ya, but there aren't very many yous, and many people that I would uh, free myself to put, uh, the way we were talking." Here she expresses the essence of the problem facing the AD sufferer's ability to manifest worthy Self 3 personae: the afflicted person desperately needs the cooperation of others and often finds it difficult to meet others who fulfill that need.

In another example of the construction of a valued Self 3, that of "academic-colleague," Dr. M encouraged me to use what I had learned as a result of my experiences with her support group:

> Dr. M: I knew that! *I knew that, I knew that it gives you just what you're looking for. So uh, and I think it gives, gives the group some.* You repeated, I mean I repeated what you had said in a sense.
> SRS: Yes indeed! I think we learn more about what people *can* do (when we observe them) in very rich social settings.
> Dr. M: Um hum, *and you can have it for the next uh . . . paper.*
> SRS: That's right!

Here, she is, in a real sense, acting as would a senior colleague or mentor, first in recognizing with great enthusiasm the connection between what the support group interactions yielded and the perspective I was taking as a researcher; and secondly, in encouraging me to use that information in my "next paper," or journal article.

It is of note, I think, that in the first of the above points she expressed her thoughts with great enthusiasm, for her tone of voice, facial expressions and other extra-linguistic forms of communication are hardly captured in transcribed words on a page. The sheer delight which she demonstrated in this situation seemed to be related not only to the benefits I derived from her having brought me into the support group meetings, but also to her being able to function in a way that was coeval with a highly valued, long-standing Self 3 which she was able to construct with my cooperation. In these situations, she was very much "herself" in ways that coincided with her own valued Self 2 attributes and beliefs.

In attempting to come to grips with the daunting problems that AD can cause for the persons afflicted and caregivers alike, it is of utmost importance that we recognize and find ways of supporting the afflicted person's selfhood. Toward that end, let us consider the following:

1   At the very least, it is crucial to recognize the significance of afflicted person's ability to index via first person pronouns, as his or her own, the experience of a singular point of view in the world, along with the feelings, beliefs, and desires which inhere in that viewpoint, for this is evidence of the AD sufferer's intact personal identity.

2   To ignore or to downplay the existence and significance of such an ability is to ignore or to downplay the afflicted person's sense and experience of personal identity and this, in turn, would mean ignoring or downplaying a fundamental aspect of his or her humanity. It would be naive to assume that treating the person wth AD in such a way would have little to no effect upon him or her. It would be similarly naive to describe the behavior of the afflicted person in response to such treatment as symptomatic of the disease and its neuropathology alone.

3   Despite the ravages of the disease in the moderate to severe stages, the afflicted person still retains a host of attributes, beliefs, and beliefs about those attributes (Self 2). Some attributes extending back to healthier days, remain intact and may be highly valued by the afflicted person. Others, including the very fact of being diagnosed and the weakening effect of the disease on some formerly healthy, valued attributes, are anathema to the AD sufferer and can be sources of great embarrassment, humiliation, and sadness. To emphasize, or to call attention to, mainly the latter set of attributes is to place the afflicted person in a very vulnerable and demeaning position which itself can result in depression and withdrawal. To assume that the afflicted person has no need to maintain dignity and honor is to strip the person of an attribute which may be intact still, and such an assumption would not only affect

the way in which the healthy treat the afflicted, but also the way in which the afflicted respond.

4   To position the afflicted person, even innocently, as "the demented patient" is to create a self-fulfilling prophesy in relation to the AD sufferer's ability to construct valued and meaningful social (Self 3) personae. This sort of positioning erases the possibility of providing the afflicted person with the kind of cooperation he or she needs in order to construct and manifest valued, honorable, positive, Self 3 personae. To assume that the afflicted person's social self is immune to the effects of how he or she is positioned by others would be to make a potentially grievous error and such an error would, in turn, make the process of caregiving far more difficult for everyone concerned.

5   On the other hand, to cooperate with the afflicted in constructing valued social personae would mean, in principle, an easing of social isolation, the ability to continue and even develop rewarding personal relationships, and providing the AD sufferer with a measure of honor that his or her lifetime of living deserves. In this way, the afflicted person's confinement would be determined more by the boundaries of neuropathology and less by the social misunderstanding which derives from innocently misguided positioning.

Paying heed to the many ways in which the selfhood of the AD sufferer still exists as well as to the ways in which it still can exist and be maintained, can bring the afflicted person some measure of satisfaction. In so doing, caregivers may aid the afflicted person as well as themselves in finding islands of meaningful calm while trying to navigate seas of torment and despair.

Chapter 8

The Tangled Veil is also a Mirror

"Before I turned on night lights at night, she used to see 'children hanging off the wall.' That was her expression. I don't understand children hanging off the wall, but I understand her saying it, on a certain level, because I realize that is her reality, even though it is not rational to me."

Mr. F talking about his wife

Mrs. F, whom you met in Chapter 2, had been diagnosed with probable AD three years prior to my association with her, but had experienced problems with her memory, with right-left discrimination and with organizing bodily movement for approximately five years before the diagnosis was made. We can hear in the comments of her loving husband, how the social dynamics of their relationship changed as a result of AD, especially in terms of Self 2 attributes and Self 3 personae. Speaking of why he married her,

Mr. F: I married her for two reasons. One is that I fell head over heels in love with her. That has not changed. My feelings toward her in that regard are the same as they were before. Put it this way – I still have a crush on her [*begins to cry*]. The other thing was, I saw in her someone who would fill in what I needed. She's very forthright, she has a lot of competence, she has a lot of confidence. She is a person who will take over things and get things done. Whereas, uh, I'm an intensely introverted person. I'm not outgoing and I don't hammer things home. I felt that for a partner, she would fill in the things that I needed and this turned out to be true. We have six children and she raised them all to be good people.

SRS: I guess you did too.

Mr. F: Well, the mother does most of the raising in families, and in our family . . . She was in community theater, she acted, was active in the choir as a singer and as an organist, she started a bell choir and wrote a book on handbell ringing . . . she trained bell ringers and was the head of the bell choir at church. So that was one of the little things she tossed off the little finger of her left hand.

SRS: While she was doing sixty other things?

Mr. F: While she was doing sixty other things. She ran a business giving piano lessons at home, made the contacts, handmade the ads and posted them in stores when she needed more publicity and she kept the books and when tax time came, she was able to provide all the information that I needed . . . she was the kind of person who could assert herself . . . that's who I married, this is what I expected to get and got in spades . . . she made a lot of the decisions, but now I'm making decisions.

SRS: This is a big shift.

Mr. F: This is a big shift and it's harder in a couple of ways. One, is uh, I'm now having to become assertive. I'm now having to try to become the person in the marriage that she was – the person who runs things, the person who decides things, so it's forcing me to be a different person than I was, a different person than I think I can be, and it's hard for Mrs. F, because . . . things are turned around for us.

Thus, Mr. F, who described himself as having been "intensely introverted" for most of his adult life and less involved in decision-making in the family, now has been forced to become more outgoing, more decisive (new Self 2 attributes and Self 3 personae), and he recognizes that this change is difficult not only for him, but also for his wife. Mrs. F's understanding of and reaction to the weakening of some of her valued Self 2 attributes as well as of the Self 3 social personae which she manifested in family, work, and community life, can be encapsulated in her comment to her husband, "I'm no good for you."

SRS: She senses that she isn't the partner now that she was before. Before the AD began, she was perfect for you.

Mr. F: As, as close as you could get, on this earth. You're not reasonably inclined to hope for more than I got.

SRS: Right. So she's operating from the point of view that she, at some level – I don't know that she verbalizes this, but she can look back and say, "I did this, this, this, this, and this, and I was perfect for him, and we worked together. And now, I can't do that stuff anymore. Therefore, I'm, I can't be any good for him."

Mr. F: Certainly, she never verbalizes all of that. If she did, if she had, if she could come up with that degree of understanding, we'd have a way to, to communicate.

SRS: Well, what I, what I'm suggesting to you is that – that she might have the feelings that would be describable in those words . . . and what I am suggesting to you is that you might want to say to her, "hey look – I have a crush on you and I've had it forever and that hasn't stopped" . . . it might be good for you to express that stuff to her.

Mr. F: Yeah, yeah, I like that.

Let us take together,

- Mr. F's comment, with which this chapter began, in which he recognizes that his wife's reality may in some ways be quite different from his own,
- that she might very well be feeling that she is "no good" for him because she is unable to do all that she used to do and which he valued so much in their relationship (her Self 2 attributes and Self 3 personae), and
- even though she doesn't express her reasons for feeling that she is "no good" for him in coherent, syntactically correct ways,
- she may still have those reasons and may be unable to express them linguistically due to the AD related problems she has, and thus
- it still may mean a great deal to her if he would continue to express to her the truth of his abiding feeling for her – that he still loves her and has a crush on her as he always did, going back to the beginning of their relationship.

If we take all this into consideration, we begin to touch upon something of great consequence regarding the reality of the afflicted and

311

the extremely positive as well as negative effects the behavior of healthy others may have on the experience and behavioral abilities of the AD sufferer. Let us delve more deeply into these matters by examining some of the contributions of the twentieth-century psychiatrist, R.D. Laing.

R.D. Laing and Existential Phenomenology

In his book about schizophrenic people, *The Divided Self* (1965), Laing explored some issues which are intimately related to many of those which I have addressed in the preceding chapters, including the subjectivity of experience and the problems of adopting a Classical Science approach to understanding that experience. In Laing's book and in the pages you have read herein, an attempt has been made to understand what we might call, "otherness." In Laing's work, "otherness" is exemplified by schizophrenic persons, and in this book, by persons afflicted with AD. In both cases, "otherness" results from the many stark behavioral differences between afflicted persons and those deemed to be healthy. In both cases, the "other" can be, and often is, analyzed in biochemical and neuropathological terms and in terms of "signs and symptoms" of disease, all of which are approaches drawn from the tradition of Classical Science, and more specifically from the realm of medicine.

For example, in his 1838/1845 work, *Des Maladies Mentales*, Esquirol wrote of his patients who suffered from dementia:

> What is passing around them, no longer awakens interest; and the events of life are of little account, because they can connect themselves with no remembrances, nor any hope. Indifferent to everything, nothing affects them ... Notwithstanding, they are irascible, like all feeble beings, and those whose intellectual faculties are weak or limited. Their anger, however, is only of a moment's duration ...
>
> Almost all who have fallen in a state of dementia, have *some sort of ridiculous habit or passion* [Esquirol's italics]. Some are constantly walking about, as if seeking something they do not find ... This one is constantly writing, but his sentiments have no connection or coherency. Words succeed words ...
>
> To this disturbance of the soundness of the understanding, are united the following symptoms. The face is pale, the eyes dull, and moistened

312

with tears, the pupils dilated, the look uncertain, the physiognomy without expression . . . He who is in a state of dementia imagines not, nor indulges in thought. He has few or no ideas. He neither wills nor determines, but yields; the brain being in a weakened state. (J.E.D. Esquirol, *Mental Maladies: A Treatise on Insanity*, traus. from French by E.K. Hunt, New York, Hafner Publishing Co., 1845/1965, pp. 418–19.)

For Esquirol, the dementia sufferer is hardly a person at all. He or she has no thoughts, no imaginings, "few or no ideas." Such beliefs can lead easily to behavior which constitutes malignant social psychology, and the afflicted person's subsequent behavior could be seen as a form of a self fulfilling prophesy and, in many respects, instances of excess disability. Yet, if one believed that the behavior of the afflicted was being driven by disease alone and not a whit by his or her ability to respond to the meaning of situations, such an insight would be lost.

Are the eyes "moistened with tears" a simple physiological symptom and nothing more, or an outward expression of the sufferer's grief and torment? On what basis can Esquirol possibly assert that the dementia sufferer "imagines not, nor indulges in thought . . . has few or no ideas"? Furthermore, would this assumption itself be confirmed by the way in which Esquirol interacted with his patients?

Laing, on the other hand, asserts that the practice of referring to persons in defectological ways, that is, in terms of their losses, failures, and mal-adaptations, constitutes a "vocabulary of denigration" in that ". . . it implies a certain standard way of being human to which the psychotic cannot measure up" (1965, p. 27). In many instances, with only slight alteration, the same can be said of the defectological approach which has been employed so often with regard to AD sufferers. As an alternative, Laing proposes that we adopt what he calls "existential phenomenology" whose task it is ". . . to articulate what the other's 'world' is and his way of being in it" (p. 25), and that ". . . one has to be able to orientate oneself as a person in the other's scheme of things rather than only to see the other as an object in one's own world . . . without prejudging who is right and who is wrong" (p. 26).

A further consequence of taking such an approach is that one recognizes that what Laing calls "relatedness" is of utmost importance – in other words, the tendency and need for each person to live in

313

some sort of relationship with others is something that Laing sees as being a key to psychotherapy:

> Psychotherapy is an activity in which that aspect of the patient's being, his relatedness to others, is used for therapeutic ends. The therapist acts on the principle that, since relatedness is potentially present in everyone, then he may not be wasting his time in sitting for hours with a silent catatonic who gives every evidence that he does not recognize his existence. (p. 26.)

That relatedness was indeed present in those AD sufferers whom you have met in these pages is demonstrated by their ability to construct valued Self 3 personae when given appropriate cooperation, to engage in meaning-driven behavior, their expressed desire for genuine relationships with others, and by their need for and ability to achieve some measure of self-esteem, all the while engaging others in the process.

Conversely, we see in the effects of malignant social psychology and specifically in its creation of excess disability, another outcome of the relatedness which is present in the person with AD. If there were no capacity for relatedness, if the person with AD were completely impervious to the ways in which he or she was treated by others, excess disability would not exist; there would be no striking, reliable differences in behavior from one social setting to another.

We could easily substitute "caregiver" for "therapist" and AD sufferer for "silent catatonic" in Laing's assertion and do no violence to the underlying point about the basis upon which one must engage the afflicted. In other words, since relatedness is potentially present in people with AD, caregivers of all kinds (relatives, physicians, nurses, social workers, psychologists, day care center and nursing home staff members) may not be wasting their time by treating the afflicted person with the same deference, concern, politeness, warmth, and interest as they would extend to any person who was not afflicted with AD. Indeed, as McCurdy (1998) has offered, the need and capacity for relationship to "whatever or whoever gives meaning, purpose, and direction to our lives" is coeval with "spirituality" – which is, in this light, "integral to the humanity – or personhood – not only of dementia sufferers, but also of those who are in relationship with them" (p. 82).

Although there are abundant differences between an AD sufferer and a schizophrenic, both people have a desperate need to be understood on their own terms. In the case of Mrs. F, it was clear that she understood that AD had weakened many of the Self 2 attributes which she and her husband valued, that as a result she thought of herself as being "no good" for him, and experienced great agony and anxiety (Mr. F reported that he could see her hyperventilate), and that she was in dire need of reassurance. The fact that the deterioration in her expressive linguistic skills prevented her from communicating in a coherent way exactly why she felt that she was "no good" for her husband did not in any way mean that she lacked reasons for feeling that way and that she did not need to be told by her husband how much he loved her still. Unfortunately, we have no way of knowing the extent to which the use of facilitative efforts such as indirect repair (Chapter 2) might have helped Mrs. F articulate her reasons for feeling as she did. Still, even if she had been given such facilitative support, and had she responded in kind, her need for loving reassurance still would have remained. That she was quite aware of and reactive to the ways in which other people behaved toward her was clear in her emotional reactions to some of the day care center staff members and volunteers (Sabat and Cagigas, 1997).

It is precisely these sorts of interpersonal dynamics and experiences that are illuminated by Romantic Science – of which Existential Phenomenology is an example – for it is in the nature of such approaches to delve deeply into the world of the "other" in ways that Classical Science's methods cannot. No battery of standard objective neuropsychological tests and resulting numerical scores, no matter how extensive, can open the door to the AD sufferer's interpersonal, social world, and to the reality of the afflicted person's psychological experience in that world. Personal experience and interpersonal interactions are not objective, but subjective. Laing was quite blunt in this regard:

> If it is held that to be unbiased one should be "objective" in the sense of depersonalizing the person who is the "object" of study, any temptation to do this under the impression that one is thereby being scientific must be rigorously resisted . . . it is unfortunate that personal and subjective are words so abused as to have no power to convey any genuine act of seeing the other as person . . . one frequently encounters

315

"merely" before subjective whereas it is almost inconceivable to speak
of anyone being "merely" objective. (pp. 24–5.)

In speaking of his wife, Mr. F poignantly acknowledged the existence of "her reality" as being different from his own. In so doing,
he granted her something which is all too often taken away from
the person with AD. When one describes him or her as having
"hallucinations" and "delusions," and as being "disoriented to time and
place," it is all too often the case that caregivers of various stripes
view the afflicted person as being "divorced from reality." Implicit in
such an interpretation is that there is one and only one "reality"
which is known by the healthy speaker and not by the person with
AD. In this way of thinking, it is assumed that what the afflicted
experiences is, by definition, not based in reality. Interestingly, in
many day care centers and nursing homes, the afflicted are given
what is called "reality orientation," which consists of noting the day
of the week, the date, the month, the season, the year. If one is not
able to retrieve those pieces of information by recall, one is, by definition, disoriented and divorced from reality. Of course, to a person
living in a nursing home, it may mean absolutely nothing of any value
to know the day of the week, the date, the month, the season, and so
forth.

To refer to someone as being "divorced from reality" is itself an act
that has far-reaching consequences in terms of how one then treats
that person, and can often constitute a violation of the "incorrigible"
nature of a person's subjective experience. It is one thing to say that
a person is seeing things that no one else sees (visual hallucination),
but it is quite another to deny that person's experience itself and
whatever meaning that person may attach to that experience. For
example, Mr. D commented that the maid "overindulges" his wife by
giving Mrs. D an afghan when Mrs. D complains of feeling cold.
Because Mr. D did not himself feel cold at those times, he interpreted
his wife's report of her subjective experience as being caused by AD
and thus not "real." Therefore, he would not take action to ease her
reported discomfort and viewed the maid's behavior as "overindul-
gent." It was precisely Laing's point that no one can deny the reality
of another person's private subjective experience. Imagine for a
moment how it would feel to tell a loved one, "I feel cold" or "I feel
ignored" and then be told in words or in actions, "No, you don't."

Let us take this storyline a step further, in the form of a "thought experiment." Suppose, after not having been "overindulged" by her husband in a variety of such instances, Mrs. D accuses her husband of not caring about her, of deliberately ignoring her needs, of treating her with disdain, and the like. Upon hearing this, Mr. D then argues that his spouse is not being truthful – that she is being paranoid in making such irrational accusations. After all, he loves her very much, is doing everything around the house, drives her here and there, and so on. According to Reisberg et al. (1987) paranoia is a symptom of AD. The simple act of denying the reality of Mrs. D's subjective feeling of being cold has now led to her being labelled as "paranoid." Suppose further that she becomes angry in the face of continuing treatment of this kind. She is then labelled as exhibiting irrational hostility which is another symptom of AD. And now, after such treatment has become chronic, she will, from time to time, be observed crying convulsively "for no apparent reason." She is, as a result, labelled "emotionally labile," which is still another symptom of AD.

We can view the same series of reactions as being reflective of Mrs. D's deep frustration about and objection to being treated in an unacceptable way. She was, despite all her efforts, not being heard or taken seriously by her husband. She still felt cold and he was taking no action to help her feel more comfortable. What was she to conclude from his behavior, other than that he was ignoring her complaints and needs, that he was not caring about her well-being? At the root of the foregoing seems to be the way in which the "healthy" among us interpret and respond to the behavior and experience of the afflicted. As long as the afflicted person is understood primarily as being "diseased," much about that person's experience and needs will be obscured, or not taken seriously, which is what Kitwood was referring to as part of the process of "labelling." In Laing's words, "If we look at [his or her] actions as 'signs' of a 'disease', we are already imposing our categories of thought on to the patient . . . [and] it is hardly possible at the same time to understand what (he or she) may be trying to communicate to us" (p. 33).

Laing's comment is exemplified yet again in the following interchange wherein I asked Dr. B about an incident at the day care center in which he experienced frustration at being unable to obtain the attention he wanted from the director:

317

SRS: The other day you mentioned that you had some problem with
      (name of program director). Does that strike any familiar notes?
Dr. B: Every so often I, I get uh, frustrated with him.
SRS: This is [name] – with the mustache?
Dr. B: Yeah, yeah. I like him very much. I like him very much.
      Um, he, he goes to a, let's see how could I do it? I'm certy not
      nasty with him at all whatsoever, and *but uh, every so often, uh,*
      uh, the uh, Barnum and Bailey – it's the Barnum and Bailey that
      I don't like.
SRS: You mean it's like a circus around here?
Dr. B: Oh yeah. It's a big, tremendously big circus . . .
SRS: All of the chaos becomes very difficult for you to deal with?
Dr. B: Yeah . . .

If one viewed Dr. B solely as an instantiation of AD, focusing upon
symptoms of linguistic difficulty, one might well look upon his use of
"the Barnum and Bailey" as evidence of such difficulty, and perhaps
even go so far as to characterize him as "responding in a way that is
unrelated to the question asked."

Yet, if one assumed from the outset that the speaker was trying to
communicate something meaningful, a different course of interpretation and action would unfold. To wit, one would try to understand
what the speaker was attempting to communicate, by probing further
and engaging the speaker as a person. By engaging the afflicted person in this manner, one discovers that Dr. B had been upset by the
circus-like chaos at the day care center which prevented him from
getting the director's attention. As it happened, at the time Dr. B
wanted to speak with the director, a number of emergency situations
had occurred and the director could not take the time to speak with
Dr. B. So, the situation was, in fact, chaotic, almost circus-like, with
many things happening simultaneously, and Dr. B's comment was
hardly unrelated to the question asked. In fact, his description of the
situation was quite accurate.

Similar examples of the effect of simply searching for meaning in
the behavior of afflicted persons are well documented in these pages
and elsewhere (see Kitwood, 1997; 1998, for example). The process
of trying to understand another person's comments is hardly unfamiliar to any of us. Yet looking at a person primarily in terms of his or
her symptoms immediately alters one's initial interpretation of what

318

has been said. This can easily subvert exactly the kind of behavior which is common to polite interaction between interlocutors, thereby rendering the AD sufferer isolated, and perhaps even feeling unworthy of others' interest. Perhaps such feelings were behind Dr. B's question to me: "What keeps you going about me?", which I understood to mean, "Why do you keep working with me?"

One can know just about everything that can be known about the pathology of AD without being able to understand one individual Alzheimer's sufferer because, to paraphrase Laing on the issue of schizophrenia, to look and listen to a patient and see the signs and symptoms of Alzheimer's disease and to look at and listen to him or her as a human being "are to see and to hear in . . . radically different ways" (p. 33). This is not to say that there is something inherently wrong with or malevolent about describing signs and symptoms. Rather, it is to say that an exhaustive catalogue of such descriptors will not, in and of itself, shed light on the totality of that which is experienced by the person who "the disease has," because to observe the behavior of a person and to see signs and symptoms of a disease is not to see neutrally, not to see objectively. This is the case because what is involved here is interpretation which, itself, is based upon the type of relationship we have with the person in the first place.

So, when Mr. F recognized that his wife's reality included seeing "children hanging off the wall," he was able to recognize that her resulting feeling of terror was also something that was real to her and that she needed him to comfort and reassure her. This, despite the fact that he did not share her visual experience. The fact that some of our experiences are not shared by others does not render those experiences less real or unreal to us. Many of our own hopes, loves, dreams, and fears are not necessarily shared by any other person, but they are still quite real to us. This is not to say that hallucinations are normal, but only that one cannot deny the reality of the experience and its meaning to the person who sees or hears them on the basis of the fact the others do not. Unfortunately, because of the diagnosis, other aspects of the afflicted person's experience, such as Mrs. D's report of feeling cold, can be interpreted as hallucinatory and, as a result, not taken seriously. As Kitwood (1990) states,

> In order to feel alive, grounded, in touch, we need our experience –
> especially our emotions and feelings – to be understood, accepted by

319

another. We also need the kind of response that takes our experience into account. All this may be described as the validation – the making real or valid – of our subjectivity. Invalidation occurs when the subjectivity of the dementia sufferer is ignored or overlooked. (p. 183.)

To view the AD sufferer as a human being as opposed to viewing him or her mainly in terms of signs and symptoms of disease affects the ways in which one positions and responds to him or her, which in turn can have a profound effect on the ability of the AD sufferer to construct Self 3 personae other than that of "The Burdensome, Confused Patient." We see, then, that the rather simple act of honoring the reality of the "other's" subjective experience entails viewing the "other" as a person as opposed to a "patient" and can have profoundly positive effects upon the social dynamics between the healthy and the afflicted such that malignant social psychology and excess disability may be minimized.

Honoring the afflicted individual's subjective reality and treating him or her as a person entails accepting the idea that the weakening of certain Self 2 attributes does not detract from the AD sufferer's status as a human being. The impact of the AD sufferer's relatively poor performance on neuropsychological tests and well-documented behavioral difficulties has, unfortunately, led some to question the personhood of the afflicted, and it is to this issue that I will now turn briefly.

The Impact of a "Hypercognitive Culture"

Stephen G. Post (1995, 1998) has written compellingly against the inclination of what he calls a "hypercognitive culture" to "exclude the deeply forgetful by reducing their moral status or by neglecting the emotional, relational, aesthetic, and spiritual aspects of well being that are open to them, even in the advanced stage of the disease" (1998, p. 72). Post's comments are made in reaction to what are called "personhood" theories of ethics which confer the status of moral agents on those who are cognitively intact and remove that status from the cognitively impaired, rendering them "nonpersons" in this sense. As Smith (1992) points out, even the more "inclusive" among personhood theorists (such as Engelhart, 1996) who consider

320

AD sufferers as non-persons in the sense of moral agents, while still conferring personhood in a "social sense," nonetheless leave room for viewing the afflicted as counting less than do those who are healthy.

The "hypercognitive culture" of which Post speaks is reflected in the use of, and power assumed to reside in, tools which are purported to measure cognitive function objectively: standard psychometric measures such as neuropsychological test batteries. Such tests, as has been pointed out in the cases of AD sufferers whom you have met in the preceding pages, fail to sample a host of significant cognitive functions which remain intact in the afflicted despite their poor performance on the tests themselves. The discrepancy exists, in part, for three reasons:

1 The tests measure individual functions one at a time, in situations which are removed from the typical social situations in which we live our lives, whereas in natural social situations those functions are brought into play simultaneously in combination.
2 There is a great deal of information in social situations which the afflicted can use to their benefit but which is excluded from the testing situation.
3 The afflicted can and often do react with anxiety to the testing situations and to their failures therein, thereby having a potentially negative impact on performance. It is not uncommon for AD sufferers to begin to cry in the face of their repeated failures on tests, only to have their behavior interpreted as still another symptom, called a "catastrophic reaction."

Post (1998) asserts that personhood theories which characterize AD sufferers as non-persons are to be rejected because such theories fail to take into account the capacities which remain intact among the afflicted. Interestingly, those capacities which remain intact and which are excluded by the "hypercognitive culture" are the very capacities which are not measured by standard objective tests; perhaps they cannot be measured this way. The following constitutes a short list of some of those remaining capacities:

- the capacity for experiencing shame and embarrassment
- the capacity for experiencing pride and maintaining dignity
- the capacity for feeling concern for the well-being of others

- the capacity to formulate goals of the autotelic and heterotelic variety (e.g. Stern)
- the ability to use extra-linguistic forms of communication to compensate for linguistic impairment
- the ability to communicate effectively with the help of an interlocutor's use of indirect repair
- the capacity to manifest and experience selfhood in a variety of ways
- the capacity to manifest indicators of relative well-being as defined by Kitwood
- the capacity to experience, and the ability to work effectively at maintaining, feelings of self-esteem
- the capacity to manifest spiritual awareness and expression (McCurdy, 1998).

It is ironic that although many of these capacities are highly valued by the human community, they remain unexamined and unaccounted for in assessments of cognitive function. In this sense, the term "hypercognitive" may be something of a misnomer in that the means by which cognition is typically measured are themselves quite limited to bare elements of cognitive life. Because the domain of cognitive abilities extends well beyond that which is sampled by standardized tests, a notion of "human worth" could hardly be based upon such a skeletal sample of mental abilities.

Viewed in this way, the "hypercognitive culture" is one which places a great deal of value on a rather small sample of objectively measured elements of cognitive life while ignoring other significant aspects of the individual's cognitive ability. Indeed, from this perspective, what Post refers to as the emotional, relational, aesthetic, and spiritual aspects of life are very much a part of cognitive functioning and most certainly should be taken into account especially by a "hypercognitive culture." The idea that emotion and cognition are intimately intertwined psychologically as well as neuroanatomically and neurophysiologically has been supported by the work of Parrott and Schulkin (1993). Brains, human understanding, and everyday life are not organized so as to correspond to the separate chapter headings of Introductory Psychology textbooks.

The choice to confer great importance on a rather restricted sample of the facets of human understanding in determining one's status as a person is clearly arbitrary. For example, as Post (1998) points out, in Chinese society, the so-called cognitive domain is not understood as being equivalent to the sum total of a person (Ikels, 1998) so that the afflicted individual is still "there" despite certain losses in that restrictive list of cognitive function. This issue of choosing the cognitive functions which define persons as beings who enjoy the rights and privileges customarily granted to adults is one which extends into homes and courts wherein issues of competency are taken up, and it is to this issue that we shall now turn.

Competency and the Person with Alzheimer's Disease

As a result of the progressive nature of Alzheimer's disease and its inexorable weakening of the afflicted person's ability to meet the demands of various aspects of everyday life, caregivers must find ways to compensate for what the afflicted can no longer do for him or herself. Decisions concerning such things as medical treatment, independent living, living with relatives, how to provide optimal care, the handling of finances, are among the issues which are typically faced. Can the afflicted person make decisions about such matters? If not, some sort of guardianship is usually established. But how do we determine what the afflicted person can decide independently, and how can we measure the extent to which he or she can do so as the disease progresses? These questions are important not only for judges, caregivers, and assessors, for the answers will have a tremendous impact as well on the afflicted person's life as an autonomous being.

The fact that the AD sufferer is potentially among the most vulnerable among us does not, *ipso facto*, licence a completely paternalistic stance that ignores his or her wishes, much as a parent often makes decisions for a child. There is a tremendous difference between the child and the AD sufferer, who has lived decades of independent adult life which can be understood as existing in his or her "personal present" (Chapter 6). Therefore, any abridgment of his or her role in decision-making will have quite a different effect than it does on young children who have never ever known life as independent beings. Self 2 attributes such as the memory (be it explicit memory or implicit memory) of having the ability and right to decide one's own

323

life course do not disappear even in the moderate to severe stages of the disease. Likewise, the capacity for embarrassment and humiliation, along with the sense of pride and need for feelings of self-worth still exist. Thus, any action which might be contemplated with regard to assuming the power of decision-making must take into account the effects such actions might well have on the afflicted person's psychological well-being.

For example, Mrs. T, having been diagnosed with probable AD, was living alone in her long-time home in a midwestern city. Although two of her adult male children lived in the same area, neither was involved in providing anything but the most cursory support for her. As time passed, she was less and less able to manage the house on her own. As a result of her daughter's concern, she moved to the east to live with the daughter, son-in-law, and their two young children. A few pieces of her furniture were brought along, but most of her household belongings stayed behind and her house was sold. The adult daughter approached me at a caregiver's education program, asking for help because, she explained, her mother's AD was creating problems in the family, especially with regard to the children.

Upon visiting the home, I first met with Mrs. T, her daughter, and her son-in-law. We had a very pleasant conversation, and although Mrs. T exhibited some word-finding and other recall memory problems, she was polite, warm, able to engage in conversation, and comported herself with evident charm. Among the problems that Mrs. T reported was the fact that the children often climbed on her furniture, which was in the family's living room, even though she objected to them doing so. These were the few vestiges of her own home and the life she left behind and, as such, were very precious to her. When the two young boys (aged 10 and 8 approximately) appeared, they immediately began throwing rolled up pieces of paper at their grandmother, some of which hit her, and they continued to do so despite their parents' instruction to cease. Mrs. T soon became upset, angry at the disrespect being shown to her. Eventually, the father took the boys out of the room.

I wondered about what the daughter had said to me initially – that her mother's AD was causing problems in the home. Was it the Alzheimer's disease? Or was it that the children were out of control which, in turn, provoked quite rational anger on the part of their grandmother? I could only speculate as to how Mrs. T must have been feeling day after day, having left her home and moved to an unfamiliar place, and now being treated disrespectfully by her grand-children. It seemed to me that the daughter's initial complaint was the product of the stigma attached to the diagnosis of AD. Although Mrs. T was unable to take care of her home as she had in years past, she was still able to understand the meaning of, and react appropri-ately to, being treated disrespectfully whether that treatment involved throwing paper at her or ignoring her wishes to have her belongings treated with care. In this situation, we can appreciate a number of issues which arise in a family's attempts to cope with the effects of AD by making decisions with, for, and about the afflicted person.

What makes an AD sufferer competent or incompetent to make decisions concerning his or her life, place of residence, finances, and the like? The issue of competency is a particularly vexing one for a variety of reasons. Although I make no pretense to provide an ex-haustive analysis of this issue herein, I will try to highlight some of the problems surrounding the matter of determining the competency of the AD sufferer:

(1) The existence of problems such as mental illness do not neces-sarily lead, in lock-step ways, to decisions about legal competency or incompetency. For example, Appelbaum and Grisso (1995 a, b, c) found that more than 50 percent of schizophrenics and more than 75 percent of people considered to be clinically depressed were judged to be legally competent to make decisions about hypothetical treat-ments. Yet, in what is called the "causal link" approach to determin-ing legal competency, a mental or physical condition is linked to a general incapacity for self-care. As a result, Tor and Sales (1996) point out that it is often the case that guardians are appointed solely on the basis of a diagnosis rendered by a family physician, and that judges rely on such diagnostic opinions rather than on behavioral evidence even when the statute calls for specific evidence of incapa-city. Causal link statutes, because of their rather vague standards for incompetency, provide judges with wide discretion over admissible evidence. In such cases, a person may fit into the statutory category while still having the ability to maintain some degree of self-care, and thereby might still be forced into Plenary Guardianship (in which authority to make decisions and take action on all matters relating to a person is granted to another person). Guardians have complete

authority over the individual and his or her estate, thus stripping the person of most of his or her rights.

Courts place a great deal of confidence in undocumented opinions rendered by physicians and as a result most proposed wards, especially if they are elderly, may be perceived as being incompetent in advance of the hearings themselves (Sales and Kahle, 1980). This, in turn can lead to ". . . a relaxation of important procedural rights, including the right to notice, an indigent's right to appointed legal counsel, and the right to be present at one's hearing to confront the allegations of incompetency" (Tor and Sales, 1996, p. 82), all of which might be understood as constituting assaults on due process guarantees. It must be remembered that the diagnosis of probable AD is made by exclusion, and thus requires the administration of a plethora of tests which rule out other possible causes for the behavioral problems in question. Therefore, the diagnosis cannot be made on the basis of an office visit to a family physician, but instead requires substantial supporting evidence.

(2) The Uniform Probate Code (1993) was established to avoid the problems of stigmatization found in the causal link approaches, by defining incapacity as the "lack of sufficient understanding or capacity to make or communicate responsible decisions" (Alabama Code, 1991). As pointed out by Tor and Sales (1996), however, the terms of the definition are still quite vague as they do not require sufficient information to make an objective determination about the conduct of the person in question. The lack of specificity regarding the criteria for competency or incompetency puts the defendant in a guardianship hearing at a great disadvantage by leaving the court in a quandary about how to make the level of guardianship match the proposed ward's functional disabilities.

(3) The legal definitions that surround implementation of guardianship do not correspond to the ways in which psychologists define and measure competency (Krauss and Sales, 1997) and the majority of neuropsychological tests were not created to address legal questions (Grisso, 1986). This is the case, Grisso argues, because legal decisions involve judgments of value by the court whereas the results of neuropsychological tests do not enter into the realm of values whatsoever. Although the results of such tests may be used to inform the

court, they do not constitute, and should not be portrayed as providing, scientific answers to questions which are legal and value-laden at their foundation (Krauss and Sales, 1997).

(4) Assessments of capacity or incapacity require the examiner to make predictions about future abilities or disabilities based upon a snapshot's worth of behavioral evidence (Krauss and Sales, 1997). In the case of AD, however, the behavioral effects can vary from individual to individual, from time to time within an individual (the person might be able to perform a task correctly at one point during the day, but not at another), and in their progression over the course of time. As a result, evidence gleaned from tests administered on a particular day may not provide an accurate portrayal of the afflicted person's abilities in question. This problem takes on great significance when what is at issue is the potential suspension of a person's rights.

(5) Coupled with this, there is the matter of who is making the assessment. Often, caregivers are interviewed to gain information concerning the afflicted person's ability to manage activities of daily living. As we have seen in Chapter 3, however, there are cases of excess disability wherein the afflicted can perform certain tasks in a day care center even though caregivers report they "cannot" do so at home. As a result, the testimony of family members may reflect something other than the actual ability of the afflicted person. Likewise, it is also clear that performance on standard tests may not reflect the afflicted person's cognitive function in the familiar environment of the home or day care center where they are not being "tested."

(6) In an attempt to address some of these issues, Grisso (1986) proposed a framework by which to analyze guardianship, in which he focused on five areas: (a) *functional impairment* as defined in terms of observable and measurable behaviors which the individual can and cannot engage in successfully; (b) *context*: the specific situations in which the behaviors must be performed; (c) *causal link*: the origins, stability, and probability of remediation of deficits; (d) *interaction*: the discrepancy between functional abilities and environmental demands; and (e) *judgment*: the legal decision when the discrepancy between environmental demands and functional abilities is great enough to warrant action. As Krauss and Sales (1997) point out,

however, it is not likely that one hearing would be sufficient to determine the need for guardianship when addressing all of these factors. This point is even more significant in the case of AD sufferers because, as already noted, brain injury creates increased variability in behavior, so that there may be incapacity on one occasion but not on another, and functional abilities may be intact in one environment but not in another.

(7)   In spite of the stigmatizing effects of the diagnosis of probable AD, the presence of the disease alone is not sufficient to show a lack of decision-making capacity *per se*. As Buchanan and Brock (1989) assert, a person's ability to make particular decisions can be closely related to the type of decision in question, and individuals can vary in the degree to which they can recognize and articulate their own values in making a deliberative choice. As we have seen in the cases of the AD sufferers whom you have met in this book, however, the way in which the afflicted person is approached and whether or not he or she is given facilitative support (such as by using indirect repair in conversation as seen in Chapter 2, for example) can have a powerful effect on the afflicted person's ability to articulate his or her thoughts. Approaching the afflicted person in an adversarial manner, such as that of a cross-examination, or even in a manner perceived to be adversarial, may lead to the incorrect belief that the afflicted person cannot understand and articulate his or her values with regard to a particular issue. The use of "standard questions" which allow for no variation may also compromise the position of the afflicted person because AD does have an effect on one's ability to maintain vigilant attention – which in turn may require that questions be restated, restated in other ways, or restated slowly, in order to assess the afflicted person's ability accurately.

(8)   In addition to issues involving legal definitions of competency and the problems of assessment, there are ethical issues involved as well. For example, in the case of persons with AD losing control over where they live, Lavin and Sales (1998) point out that the assumption, by a gerontological psychologist, that a person might do better in a different setting, is not enough to justify such a severe reduction in self-determination because this type of reduction can result in harm, despite all good intentions.

328

(9) The most recent innovation in standards for guardianship is called the Functional Approach (Nolan, 1984; Tor and Sales, 1996) in which the court is required to examine objective behavioral evidence of functional limitations in the afflicted person's daily activities such as securing food, clothing, and health care for him or herself. In this approach, there is the possibility of providing Limited Guardianship, which would apply only to those areas in which incapacity was demonstrated. Another virtue of the Functional Approach is that it employs the term "incapacity" instead of "incompetency," thereby attempting to avoid the stigma associated with being called "incompetent." Some (Tor, 1993) have argued that statutes of this kind should require pre-hearing standardized functional evaluations detailing the nature and extent of the afflicted person's deficits prior to a hearing. Here again, however, we must be cognizant of the possibilities of excess disability, of caregivers doing for the afflicted what they can still do for themselves, the variability in behavior which brain injury can produce, the limitations of one "snapshot" standard approach to evaluation, the well known potential effect of the evaluator's behavior on the subsequent performance of the afflicted person, and that standardized tests may not reveal a host of intact abilities.

Interim Summary, Analysis, and Further Challenges

At this point it should be clear that there is no uniform definition of incompetence and no general agreement as to how it can and should be measured (Rosoff and Gottlieb, 1987). As a result, there exists the distinct possibility that AD sufferers can be even more vulnerable to having further losses of autonomy imposed upon them unjustly. In an attempt to make some progress toward rectifying these problems, the authors make the refreshing proposals that (a) there is a need for multiple examinations for alleged AD sufferers, (b) the court should require "clear and unequivocal demonstration" of the afflicted person's deficits before entering a ruling of incapacity, and (c) in evaluations of competency, there is a need to test for retained abilities in individual cases. Although there is much to be said for these proposals, in order for them to be fulfilled in practice there are many related issues which desperately need attention and careful analysis. For example, the exact meaning of the "clear and unequivocal demonstration" of deficits must be adduced, as must the definition and range of relevant "remaining abilities" and the means by which they are to be measured.

It would seem, given what has been shown about excess disability (Chapter 3), that the afflicted person's remaining abilities would have to be determined by observing him or her in different environments (home and day care center, for example); that the remaining abilities sampled should include the ability to communicate effectively when given facilitative support (Chapter 2), the need and ability to maintain self-esteem and avoid humiliation (Chapter 4), the ability to behave in ways which are guided by the meaning of situations (Chapter 5), the ability to formulate and act to achieve goals (Chapter 6), and to experience and express selfhood in a variety of ways (Chapter 7). Even in the case of the promising Functional Approach, the functions enumerated are quite confined to a particularly limited set of activities of daily living. The ability to care for oneself and the like are important. But not being able to use eating utensils, a stove or a laundry machine, or not being able to perform simple calculations or clean efficiently or recall the day of the week, the date, and so on, may have little to no bearing whatsoever on a person's ability to decide against moving and having to live with a particular relative, or the ability to make other decisions which are consistent with long-held values and concerns.

For example, in a case cited by Rosoff and Gottlieb (1987), Mrs. F made errors in serial seven subtraction from one hundred, could not name the hospital at which her evaluation was taking place, could not state the day of the week and date, nor could she recall the names of three objects one minute after having been presented with and repeating their names. These errors, however, had little to no relationship with or bearing upon her ability to decide against having a colostomy – a decision which was consistent with her longheld desire to be "left in the same shape she started off in" as well as with her memories of an aunt who had herself undergone a colostomy. Mrs. F "stated categorically that she would prefer death to this potential deformity."

In this case, due to her daughters' prior concerns about Mrs. F's ability to manage her finances, plenary guardianship had already been granted to her longtime accountant who could have acted against her wishes and forced her to undergo the operation. Fortunately, her guardian did not exercise the ability to override her desire to refuse the operation. There is no reason to believe that other guardians would act in the same manner, and this case thereby serves as a valuable example in support of the Functional Approach and limited guardianship.

The stigmatizing effect of her diagnosis, however, was revealed rather innocently in the same case report and this is an issue that bears careful scrutiny not only in the determination of legal competency, but also in the manner in which AD sufferers are treated outside the court of law. Because Mrs. F protested vigorously against having the colostomy performed, her guardian asked a psychiatrist to evaluate her and to advise him about her ability to understand the nature and potential outcomes of her decision. Part of the report indicated that, "She stated perseveratively that she wanted help in proving to her daughters and her doctors that she 'could decide for herself.'" The use of the term, "perseveratively" is itself an example of a medical approach to interpreting her behavior as a symptom of illness. That is, the objective fact that she *repeatedly* expressed her desire to prove to her daughters that she was able to decide this health-related issue independently was presented in the report as a symptom of pathology, as revealed by the use of the term, "perseveratively." In the testing situation, one is "supposed" to answer questions in a particular way. Often, deviations from the standard, "correct," answers are interpreted in terms of pathology, even though further analysis can reveal that the behavior in question is not, in fact, pathological. This tendency is exacerbated when there is already a diagnosis of probable AD on record, for the expectations of the observer can have a profound effect upon how the observer then characterizes the afflicted person's behavior.

If one were to adopt a different approach, however, such as Laing's Existential Phenomenology, a very different interpretation would logically follow, because this approach constitutes an attempt to understand the person and his or her subjective experience of the situation at hand. Mrs. F had already lost control over managing her finances, had already endured the weakening of some of her abilities (Self 2 attributes), and now was facing what, to her, was a personally abhorrent, and potentially terrifying, situation. That is, one could just as easily recognize that Mrs. F was extremely upset and anxiety-ridden about the prospect of being forced to undergo an operation whose

331

effects she did not want to endure, that she deeply feared the possibility that she would lose this control over her life, and that this issue was, therefore, of paramount concern to her.

Given her situation there would seem to be no reason, other than the stigmatizing fact of her diagnosis, to use the term, "perseveratively," which connotes defective behavior, as opposed to the word "repeatedly," which more accurately and objectively describes the behavior in question. Her behavior reflected what was important to her, and what is important to the person being tested is not necessarily what is important to the evaluator in such situations. There is nothing amiss about there being a difference in what two people deem important in a situation, *per se*. However, in this case, Mrs. F's point of view was not being represented accurately by those who performed the evaluation and therein interpreted her behavior as a species of perseveration. The reality and meaning of her subjective experience are diminished, perhaps even obscured, when the repeated expression of her urgent concern is characterized by language which connotes a "symptom" of AD. What Mrs. F was evincing was the rational, perhaps desperate, behavior of a person who was logically experiencing great anxiety.

It is also unclear that her failures on the items mentioned were related solely to AD. For example, was her inability to mention the name of the hospital due to a failure of recall? Could she have correctly identified the name from a list of names? Was she ever told the name of the hospital by those who took her there – that is, was there reason to believe that she knew the name of the hospital in the first place? To what extent was her performance affected by her great anxiety about the possibility of losing her right to refuse surgery? Issues such as these must be addressed in the process of administering evaluations and interpreting the results thereof, for to ignore them can have profound effects on the afflicted person's course of life.

Preliminary Recommendations

Judges who must decide on the issue of guardianship, be it Limited or Plenary, must be in possession of all relevant facts in order to render a decision regarding the potential abridgement of a human being's rights. Judges are not necessarily conversant with the argot of physicians, neuropsychologists, and other professionals, and therefore must be given information which is understandable, accurate, and pertinent. Let us put ourselves in the position of such a judge for a moment. We are told that Mrs. F could not state the name of the hospital in which her evaluation was carried out, could not perform serial subtractions of seven from one hundred, could not state the day of the week, the date, could not recall the names of three objects one minute after having been told those names and repeating them. And now, on the heels of all these things which she cannot do, we are told that she "perseveratively stated. . . ."

It would be quite natural for us to assume that the last statement was a statement of fact as opposed to an interpretation which is itself open to challenge, and to assume that her behavior was somehow pathological as were the previous behaviors. We are not told exactly how these specific pieces of information pertain to Mrs. F's ability to make a medical decision for herself. We are told that, "her intellectual disability differentially impaired her short-term memory and recall while preserving her personality, values, and substantial long-term memory," but we are not informed as to how these conclusions were reached. There are no objective litmus tests for personality and values.

This case illustrates that when a person's competency or, perhaps more accurately, capacity to manifest a particular functional ability or abilities is at issue, relevant information given to a judge should include, in addition to what Rosoff and Gottlieb (1987) propose:

1 Documented evidence which is specifically related to the status of the person's ability in question;
2 The presentation of such evidence in objective behavioral terms when at all possible, indicating exactly how the evidence was gathered, and how it is logically related to, or reflects, the specific ability in question;
3 Instances in which interpretations are made by an evaluator (such as "perseveratively" as opposed to "repeatedly") being presented clearly as such and not as objective facts;
4 Detailed qualitative documentation of the significant issues surrounding the person's present situation including his or her subjective experience, remaining cognitive abilities, and abiding values

and beliefs. Such documentation should include the afflicted person's discourse which reflects his or her values and beliefs, and how they relate to the specific issues at hand;

5   Details of how the circumstances of the person's present situation may have affected his or her performance on whatever tests were administered as part of the evaluation procedure.

As Rosoff and Gottlieb (1987) aptly point out, "Making good, comprehensive functional evaluations requires a mixture of art and science and the input of substantial amounts of time by qualified health professionals" (p. 44).

As we have seen in the pages of this book, AD can produce varying degrees of loss in some abilities while leaving others intact even in the moderate to severe stages of the disease. It would stand to reason that the afflicted person's functional ability to engage in particular types of behavior and to make particular decisions is likewise not an all-or-nothing matter which can be assessed solely on the basis of an existing diagnosis or standard tests of cognitive function. Moody (1992) and Lyman (1998) likewise observe that in the realm of independent decision-making, mental abilities are not to be understood in global terms, but in terms which are specific to the issues at hand. The Functional Approach and limited guardianship would seem to hold the greatest possibility for the court to make decisions which are fair, relentlessly and properly respectful of the afflicted person's rights and abilities, and helpful to the afflicted person and his or her loved ones. The means by which we evaluate, and arrive at our conclusions about, the afflicted person's competency may well ultimately be a test of our own competency as thoughtful, judicious, humane human beings.

Incompetency as Stigma

The use of the term "incapacity" in the Functional Approach statutes, instead of "incompetency" as is used in the Uniform Probate Code and the Causal Link approaches, indicates a clear sensitivity to the stigmatizing effects which can follow in the wake of describing a person as being "incompetent." The fact of being diagnosed with probable AD can itself carry a significant stigma which colors caregivers' interpretations of the afflicted person's behavior and the treatment accorded to the AD sufferer (forms of malignant social psychology as discussed in Chapter 3). The additional application of the term, "incompetent" can create still other stigmatic burdens for the AD sufferer to bear.

Lay persons are not necessarily conversant with the meaning of legal competence. Yet it is among lay persons that the AD sufferer dwells for most of his or her days. When the judgment of legal incompetence filters down to nursing home or day care center administrators and staff members, to family members, and to friends, the connotation of incompetence may carry meaning far beyond the confines of the strict legal definition. Where an AD sufferer may be declared incompetent on the basis of his or her inability to manage finances, and where plenary guardianship is granted, what may be lost on lay persons is the fact that the AD sufferer was judged to be incapacitated with regard to a specific functional ability and that the incapacitation is not a "general mental condition." Where plenary guardianship is granted in such a situation, the afflicted person can easily lose the ability to exercise a variety of rights which themselves have no connection to the lack of functional ability which formed the basis for granting guardianship in the first place. Additionally, in the absence of a guardian as caring and conscientious as was Mrs. F's accountant in the case described by Rosoff and Gottlieb (1987), the afflicted person can become even more vulnerable to mistreatment and great psychological distress.

Under such circumstances, the person with AD may become exposed to further instances of malignant social psychology, suffer further indignities, and sink even more deeply into an environmentally caused helpless and depressed state in which his or her remaining abilities, selfhood, and humanity are obscured even further. Such a situation would be tragic not only for the AD sufferer, but also for the society in which he or she lives. The financial and psychological burdens which accrue from caring for brain-injured people are directly related to the degree of independence which the afflicted person can exercise. If "we," the healthy, fall prey to social stigmata, and fail to extend to the "others" in our community the type of understanding and humane treatment they deserve, and which is incumbent upon us to give, we will have failed not only the afflicted but ourselves as well.

"Their" Tangled Veil is "Our" Mirror

The plaques and tangles in the brains of AD sufferers are thought to be major neuropathological signs of the disease. It is through, and in spite of, these plaques and tangles that the AD sufferer interacts with the world. Environmental events make their impressions on the afflicted and he or she acts on the world through the ever enlarging confines of that veil. Yet, there is more meaning in this tangled veil than neuropathology and behavioral dysfunction, even more meaning than the afflicted person's valiant efforts to persist.

In an old Hassidic tale, we are told of a middle-aged man whose father is dying. The man informs his young son that it is time to take Grandpa up to the top of the mountain to die. Father and son then seat the old man in a wheelchair and take him to the mountain top, where they will push him over the edge so that he can speedily meet his death.

Just as the boy's father is about to push his own father over the precipice, the young boy urgently says to his father, "Don't let go of the wheelchair when you push Grandpa over the edge." The boy's father is stupefied for a moment and then asks his son, "Why?" The young boy responds by saying, "Because we're going to need it for you someday."

The young boy's wisdom is as telling as it is limited. He clearly sees the utility of retaining the wheelchair so that it can be used again for his own father when the time arrives. His message is also pregnant with the dictum that one should treat others as one would want to be treated, that one day the middle-aged man will be an old man who will be brought to the mountain top just as he has brought his own father. In that momentary exchange with his young son, the middle-aged man is brought face to face with his own destiny. Such messages can and should give one pause. What the boy does not see through his young eyes, however, is that this entire approach to dealing with the elderly and infirm is itself questionable; that there may be another way, a better way.

Five weeks before he entered a nursing home, four months before he died, Dr. B and I had a conversation which began with him asking about my daughter. I told him that she was just beginning a new school year (she was then entering the sixth grade), that she was excited about many things regarding her return to school, but there was one exception. Inevitably, there are those aspects of life which we would rather not have to endure, but which we must face nonetheless:

SRS: But then there's all the schoolwork to do.
Dr. B: Yeah, sooner or later the hammer comes down.

In the absence of a way to curtail the progression of Alzheimer's disease or even prevent its occurrence, its incidence in the population will triple in the coming decades in North America alone as the "Baby Boom" generation enters into senior citizenship. At the present time, the annual cost of "managing" AD sufferers in nursing homes is already staggering, and the process of "managing patients" is quite different from that of interacting with persons. Even if interventions are developed to delay or halt the progression of the disease, there will still be millions of AD sufferers in our community, each trying, along with their caregivers, to cope with the effects of varying degrees of brain damage. Hence the lurking, approaching "tidal wave" of which I spoke at the beginning of this book.

At present, we are hardly prepared to care for and support the humanity of the millions who are afflicted. For those millions who will become afflicted in the coming years, the outlook is bleak at best. This is the case in part because the flashlight of our understanding regarding the abilities and needs of the afflicted is just beginning to illuminate wider vistas, and in part because the significant resources required to support those abilities and needs in the future are hardly being planned for and readied at present. Indeed, the approaching "tidal wave" is not even a blip on the radar screen of most of those elected to formulate national and state policy. As Rosoff and Gottlieb commented about what would be required just to make comprehensive functional evaluations, "There is ample cause to be concerned that the public will to address these problems is not yet sufficiently great to bring about the allocation of resources needed to make the crucial difference. When necessary forces do combine to bring about change, the outlook for the mentally impaired elderly will be a good deal brighter" (1987, p. 44). What will be the circumstances when those of us who read and write books such as this are among the elders of our community? How would we wish to be treated and what will be required to make that type of treatment a reality?

337

In his extraordinary book, *Dementia Reconsidered: The Person Comes First* (1997), Tom Kitwood presents a situation which he encountered when he visited a nursing home in the US not long ago. Although Kitwood is quick to inform us that the staff member was "acting under instruction" and doing so in the kindest way he knew how, that there was nothing necessarily malevolent about the use of bean-bag chairs as an alternative to physical restraints, that such treatment is probably the standard, "improved" form of care for dementia sufferers in nursing homes, the stark reality of the situation screams out:

> The scene is the "Alzheimer's Unit" of an American nursing home. A young male care assistant is pushing a woman of about 75 years old across the room. She is protesting and resisting, but without words. Gradually he manoeuvres her towards a bean-bag chair, and manages to get her down into it. The chair is very low to the floor; it supports her back, but provides no way in which she can rest her head. She has not got the strength to get up out of it. She looks up at me, and suddenly expresses herself with perfect clarity: "It's cruel mental torture. They're doing it to me all the time." (p. 47.)

All too often, it is the case that AD and other dementia sufferers are given what has come to be called, "palliative care" which amounts to keeping the "patient" physically comfortable and little else. In the foregoing vignette, what was palliative care to the staff was "cruel mental torture" to the recipient. As Kitwood observed, she was a victim of "depersonalization" – being treated as though she was not "fully a person," much in the same manner as Mrs. L (beginning of Chapter 3) was treated when a staff member abruptly wheeled her away from her interlocutor while Mrs. L was in the midst of conversing. Perhaps it is the specter of such treatment day after day that moves many to assert that they would prefer to die rather than to live out their days in an Alzheimer's Unit or nursing home which offers such palliative care. Of course, there are exceptions to such situations, but they are just that – exceptions.

That there are so few exceptions has been underscored in many conversations I have had with caregivers. This issue arose in an especially poignant way when, some years ago, I was trying to administer a neuropsychological test of language function to a man who was in the "end stage" of AD. In 20 minutes, he was able to say only five coherent words through the muscular rigidity that had grown ever more severe. It was clear that he would not be able to respond to any of the test items. Uttered with what seemed to have been a herculean effort, the five words were "Welder" and "She's knocking herself out," and they had nothing whatsoever to do with the test items. In fact, however, the man had worked as a welder in a shipyard for decades, and he was living at home with his wife who truly was "knocking herself out" in the process of caring for him. He was telling me something significant about himself and about his wife and their situation at home.

When his wife was asked by a physician and a nurse if she had considered having her husband admitted to a nursing home, she replied, "No, because he still knows things." In effect, because he still knew things, she could not in good conscience place him in a situation in which he would receive "palliative care" or be "managed." In her view, such an action would cause him further torment and, therefore, harm. Whatever "things" he knew were not measurable by standard neuropsychological tests. Perhaps the idea that "he still knows things" would be more saliently stated in terms such as "someone who knows is there still." What evidence must be summoned to convince us of that presence? Might our own behavior have a part to play in what can be evoked in another? What claim, other than the fact that one simply "is," must one have to make in order to secure humane treatment?

When we realize that, at present, providing even "palliative care" comes at a staggering price, the cost of providing what is truly humane treatment is almost beyond imagining save for the assumption that it will be available only to the extraordinarily wealthy. That need not, however, be the case any more than pushing the old man off the mountain top had to be the way for him to die.

Yet, in the coming decades, the number of AD and other dementia sufferers will likely triple, and the percentage of elderly in our community will increase tremendously. In other words, "Sooner or later, the hammer comes down." In the not-too-distant future, it will come down on us just as it has already come down on people like Mrs. L, and the woman seated in the bean-bag chair, and the old man in the Hassidic story who was about to be pushed over the edge of the mountain. In these people, and in the faces of millions of AD sufferers, we are seeing our own fate or the fate of our loved ones. That fate will remain as such until we as a people come to the conclusion that we as people deserve better and thereupon summon the will to achieve what is better.

Creating what is better for future generations begins with improving the treatment given to those now suffering from Alzheimer's disease. What is required to make those improvements involves a journey far beyond the goal of palliative care, a journey in which caregivers of all types seek out and support the sundry aspects of Alzheimer's sufferers' remaining abilities – indeed, their very humanity. This, in turn, requires what Post (1995) has aptly called, "moral solidarity" between the afflicted and the healthy, which has at its foundation the recognition of our mutually shared humanity. This rather "simple" recognition changes the social dynamics because in order to support and sustain the humanity of the afflicted, caregivers must delve more deeply into and develop further their own humanity. This is, in part, what McCurdy (1998) refers to when he says that, "... the awareness of a deeply shared humanity ... might permit caregiver and [nursing home] resident to become 'means of grace' [Niebuhr, 1963] to each other."

Already there has been too much talk of "them," those who are afflicted with Alzheimer's, and "us," those who are deemed unimpaired. I apologize for my use of these nouns and pronouns, for such unfortunate distinctions blur the formidable and distinct reality that this book is about all of us as human beings. To paraphrase Lewis Mumford (1970), like Brahma, we are the slayer and the slain, those who are afflicted with AD and those who give care, whether they be physicians, psychologists, nurses, social workers, lawyers, judges, day care center or nursing home staff members, relatives, or friends. Our treatment of people with Alzheimer's disease speaks of who and what we are, and so the tangled veil is truly a mirror. The challenge to all of us is outlined in the reflection.

References

Alabama Code 26-2A-20 (1991).

Albert, M.S., Naeser, M.A., Levine, H.L., and Garvey, J. 1984. Ventricular size in patients with presenile dementia of the Alzheimer's type. *Archives of Neurology, 41*, 1258–63.

Allender, J. and Kaszniak, A.W. 1989. Processing of emotional cues in patients with dementia of the Alzheimer's type. *International Journal of Neuroscience, 46*, 147–55.

American Psychiatric Association. 1994. *Diagnostic and Statistical Manual of Mental Disorders.* Washington, D.C.: APA.

Appelbaum, P. and Grisso, T. 1995a. The MacArthur treatment study I. *Law and Human Behavior, 19*, 105–26.

Appelbaum, P. and Grisso, T. 1995b. The MacArthur treatment study II. *Law and Human Behavior, 19*, 127–48.

Appelbaum, P. and Grisso, T. 1995c. The MacArthur treatment study III. *Law and Human Behavior, 19*, 148–74.

Appell, J., Kertesz, A., and Fisman, M. 1982. A study of language functioning in Alzheimer patients. *Brain and Language, 17*, 73–91.

Aronson, E. 1980. *The Social Animal.* San Francisco: W.H. Freeman and Co.

Austin, J.L. 1961. *How to Do Things with Words.* Oxford: Clarendon Press.

Bayles, K.A. 1979. Communication Profiles in a Geriatric Population. Unpublished Ph.D. dissertation.

Bayles, K.A. 1982. Language function in senile dementia. *Brain and Language, 16*, 265–80.

Berger, E.Y. 1980. A system for rating the severity of senility. *Journal of the American Geriatrics Society, 28*, 234–6.

Bird, J.M., Levy, R., and Jacoby, R.J. 1986. Computed tomography in the elderly: Changes over time in a normal population. *British Journal of Psychiatry, 148*, 80–5.

Blessed, G., Tomlinson, B.E., and Roth, M. 1968. The association between quantitative measures of dementia and of senile change in the cerebral grey matter of elderly subjects. *British Journal of Psychiatry, 114,* 797–811.

Boschen, K. 1996. Correlates of life satisfaction, residential satisfaction, and locus of control among adults with spinal cord injuries. *Rehabilitation Counseling Bulletin, 39,* 230–43.

Bowen, M. 1990. *Family Therapy in Clinical Practice.* Northvale, NJ: Jason Aronson, Inc.

Bozzola, F., Gorelick, P., and Freels, S. 1992. Personality changes in Alzheimer's disease. *Archives of Neurology, 49,* 297–300.

Breteler, M.M.B., Claus, J.J., Van Duijn, C.M., Launer, L.J., and Hofman, A. 1992. Epidemiology of Alzheimer's disease. *Epidemiology Reviews, 14,* 59–82.

Brody, E. 1971. Excess disabilities of mentally impaired aged: Impact of individualized treatment. *Gerontologist, 25,* 124–33.

Brun, A. 1983. An overview of light and electron microscopic changes. In B. Reisberg (ed.), *Alzheimer's Disease.* New York: The Free Press.

Buchanan, A.E. and Brock, D.W. 1989. *Deciding for Others: The Ethics of Surrogate Decision Making.* New York: Cambridge University Press.

Carlsson, A. 1983. Changes in neurotransmitter systems in the aging brain and in Alzheimer's disease. In B. Reisberg (ed.), *Alzheimer's Disease.* New York: Free Press.

Chatterjee, A., Strauss, M., Smyth, K., and Whitehouse, P.J. 1992. Personality changes in Alzheimer's disease. *Archives of Neurology, 49,* 486–91.

Cohen, D. and Eisdorfer, C. 1986. *The Loss of Self.* New York: Norton.

Collerton, D. and Fairbairn, A. 1985. Alzheimer's disease and the hippocampus. *Lancet,* 2 February, 278–9.

Coulter, J. 1981. *The Social Construction of Mind.* London: Macmillan.

Coupland, N., and Coupland, J. 1999. Ageing, ageism, and anti-agism. In H. Hamilton (ed.), *Language and Communication in Old Age: Multidisciplinary Perspectives.* New York: Garland.

Coupland, N., Coupland, J., and Giles, H. 1991. *Language, Society, and the Elderly: Discourse, Identity, and Ageing.* Oxford: Blackwell.

Coulter, J. 1981. *The Social Construction of Mind.* London: Macmillan.

Critchley, M. 1953. *The Parietal Lobes.* London: Edward Arnold.

Dawson, R., Kline, K., Wianko, D.C., and Wells, D. 1986. Preventing excess disability in patients with Alzheimer's disease. *Geriatric Nursing, 7,* 298–301.

De Bleser, R. and H. Weisman. 1986. The communicative impact of non-fluent aphasia on the dialogue behavior of linguistically unimpaired partners. In F. Lowenthal and F. Vandamme (eds.), *Pragmatics and Education.* New York: Plenum Press.

Dennett, D.C. 1990. An instrumentalist theory. In W.G. Lycan (ed.), *Mind and Cognition.* Oxford: Blackwell.

342

References

Engelhart, H.T. 1996. *The Foundations of Bioethics*, 2nd edition. New York: Oxford University Press.

Esquirol, E. (1838/1845). *Mental Maladies: A Treatise on Insanity.* Translated from the French by E.K. Hunt. Philadelphia: Lea and Blanchard.

Evans, D.A., Funkenstein, H., Albert, M.S., Sherr, P.A., Cook, N.R., Chown, N.J., Hebert, L.E., Hennekens, C.H., and Taylor, J.O. 1989. Prevalence of Alzheimer's disease in a community population of older persons. *Journal of the American Medical Association, 262,* 2551–6.

Feil, N. 1982. *Validation: The Feil Method.* Cleveland, Ohio: Edward Feil Productions.

Flicker, C., Ferris, S.H., Crook, T., and Bartus, R.T. 1987. Implications of memory and language dysfunction in the naming deficit of senile dementia. *Brain and Language, 31,* 187–200.

Folstein, M., Folstein, S., and McHugh, P.R. 1975. Mini-Mental State: A practical method for grading the cognitive state of patients for the clinician. *Journal of Psychiatric Research, 12,* 189–98.

Freed, D.M., Corkin, S., Growdon, J.H., and Nissen, M.J. 1989. Selective attention in Alzheimer's disease: Characterizing subgroups of patients. *Neuropsychologia, 27,* 325–39.

Fuster, J. 1995. Memory and planning: Two temporal perspectives of frontal lobe function. In H.H. Jasper, S. Riggio, P.S. Goldman-Rakic (eds.), *Epilepsy and the Functional Anatomy of the Frontal Lobe.* New York: Raven Press, pp. 9–20.

Gardner, H. 1974. *The Shattered Mind: The Person After Brain Damage.* New York: Random House.

Geertz, C. 1973. *The Interpretation of Cultures.* New York: Basic.

Goffman, E. 1969. *Stigma.* Harmondsworth: Penguin Books.

Goodwin, C. 1980. Processes of mutual monitoring implicated in the production of descriptive sequences. *Sociological Inquiry, 50,* 303–17.

Goodwin, C. and Heritage, J. 1990. Conversation analysis. *Annual Review of Anthropology, 19,* 283–307.

Graf, P., Mandler, G., and Squire, L.R. 1984. The information that amnesic patients don't forget. *Journal of Experimental Psychology: Learning, Memory, and Cognition, 10,* 164–78.

Grisso, T. 1986. *Evaluating Competencies, Forensic Assessments and Instruments.* New York: Plenum Press.

Gurland, B., Copeland, J., Kuriansky, J., Kellever, M., Sharpe, L., and Dean, L.L. 1983. *The Mind and Mood of Aging.* Beckenham: Croom Helm.

Hamel, M., Pushkar, D., Andres, D., Reis, M., Dastoor, D., Grauer, H., and Bergman, H. 1990. Predictors and consequences of aggressive behavior by community-based dementia patients. *Gerontologist, 30,* 206–11.

Harré, R. 1983. *Personal Being.* Oxford: Blackwell.

Harré, R. 1991. The discursive production of selves. *Theory and Psychology*, *1*, 51–63.

Harré, R. and van Langenhove, L. (eds.) 1999. *Positioning Theory*. Oxford: Blackwell.

Heindel, W.C., Salmon, D.P., Shults, C.W., Walicke, P.A., and Butters, N. 1989. Neuropsychological evidence for multiple implicit memory systems: A comparision of Alzheimer's, Huntington's, and Parkinson's disease. *Neuroscience*, *9*, 582–7.

Heschel, A.J. 1965. *Who Is Man?* Stanford, California: Stanford University Press.

Hier, D.B., Hagenlocker, K., and Shindler, A.G. 1985. Language disintegration in dementia: effects of etiology and severity. *Brain and Language*, *25*, 117–33.

Huff, F.J., Corkin, S., and Growdon, J.H. 1986. Semantic impairment and anomia in Alzheimer's disease. *Brain and Language*, *28*, 235–49.

Huff, F.J., Mack, L., Mahlmann, J., and Greenberg, S. 1988. A Comparison of lexical-semantic impairments in left hemisphere stroke and Alzheimer's disease. *Brain and Language*, *34*, 262–78.

Hutchinson, J.M. and Jensen, M. 1980. A pragmatic evaluation of discourse communication in normal and senile elderly in a nursing home. In L. Obler and M. Albert (eds.), *Language and Communication in the Elderly*. Lexington Books: Lexington, MA.

Ikels, C. 1998. The experience of dementia in China. *Culture, Medicine, and Psychiatry*, *22*, 257–283.

Irigaray, L. 1973. *Le Langage des Dements*. Mouton, The Hague.

James, W. 1983. *The Principles of Psychology*. Harvard University Press: Cambridge MA. (original work published in 1890.)

Kempler, D. 1984. Syntactic and Symbolic Abilities in Alzheimer's Disease. Unpublished Ph.D. dissertation.

Kitwood, T. 1988. The technical, the personal, and the framing of dementia. *Social Behaviour*, *3*, 161–79.

Kitwood, T. 1990. The dialectics of dementia: With particular reference to Alzheimer's disease. *Ageing and Society*, *10*, 177–96.

Kitwood, T. 1997. *Dementia Reconsidered: The Person Comes First*. Philadelphia: Open University Press.

Kitwood, T. 1998. Toward a theory of dementia care: Ethics and interaction. *Journal of Clinical Ethics*, *9*, 23–34.

Kitwood, T. and Bredin, K. 1992. Towards a theory of dementia care: Personhood and well-being. *Ageing and Society*, *12*, 269–87.

Krauss, D.A. and Sales, B.D. 1997. Guardianship and the elderly. In P.D. Nussbaum (ed.), *Handbook of Neuropsychology and Aging*. New York: Plenum.

Laing, R.D. 1965. *The Divided Self*. Baltimore, Maryland: Penguin Books.

References

Lamiell, J.T. 1996. William Stern: More Than "The IQ Guy." In G.A. Kimble, C.A. Boneau, and M. Wertheimer (eds.), *Portraits of Pioneers in Psychology*, Vol.II, pp. 73–85. APA Books/Lawrence Erlbaum Assoc.

Lamiell, J.T. and Deutsch, W. 1999. Introduction to Stern, C. and Stern, W. 1909/1999, *Recollection, Testimony, and Lying in Early Childhood*. English translation by J.T. Lamiell. Washington, D.C.: APA Books.

Lamiell, J.T. and Durbeck, P.K. 1987. Whence cognitive prototypes in impression formation? Some empirical evidence for dialectical reasoning as a generative process. *Journal of Mind and Behavior, 8*, 223–44.

Langer, E.J. and Rodin, J. 1976. The effects of choice and enhanced personal responsibility for the aged: A field experiment in an institutional setting. *Journal of Personality and Social Psychology, 34*, 191–8.

Lavin, M. and Sales, B.D. 1998. Moral and ethical considerations in Geropsychology. In M. Hersen and V.B. Van Hasselt (eds.), *Handbook of Geropsychology*. New York: Plenum.

Lipowski, Z.J. 1969. Psychosocial aspects of disease. *Annals of Internal Medicine, 71*, 1197–1206.

Luria, A.R. 1987a. *The Man With a Shattered World*. Cambridge, Massachusetts: Harvard University Press, x.

Luria, A.R. 1987b. *The Mind of a Mnemonist*. Cambridge, Massachusetts: Harvard University Press, xii.

Lyman, K.A. 1998. Living with Alzheimer's disease: The creation of meaning among persons with dementia. *Journal of Clinical Ethics, 9*, 49–57.

McCurdy, D.B. 1998. Personhood, spirituality, and hope in the care of human beings with dementia. *Journal of Clinical Ethics, 9*, 81–91.

McKhann, G., Drachman, D., Folstein, M., Katzman, R., Price, D., and Stadlan, E.M. 1984. Clinical diagnosis of Alzheimer's disease: Report of the NINCDS-ADRDA work group under the auspices of the Department of Health and Human Services task force on Alzheimer's disease. *Neurology, 34*, 939–44.

MacNalty, A.S. (ed.) 1963. *The British Medical Dictionary*. Philadelphia: J.B. Lippincott.

Martin, A. and Fedio, P. 1983. Word production and comprehension in Alzheimer's disease: The breakdown of semantic knowledge. *Brain and Language, 19*, 124–41.

Mead, G.H. 1934. *Mind, Self, and Society*. Chicago: University of Chicago Press.

Milner, B. 1995. Aspects of human frontal lobe function. In H.H. Jasper, S. Riggio and P.S. Goldman-Rakic (eds.), *Epilepsy and the Functional Anatomy of the Frontal Lobe*. New York: Raven Press, pp. 67–84.

Moody, H.R. 1992. *Ethics in an Aging Society*. New York: Springer.

Mulhausler, P. and Harré, R. 1993. *Pronouns and People*. Oxford: Blackwell.

Mumford, L. 1970. *The Conduct of Life*. New York: Harcourt Brace Jovanovich.

Murdoch, B.E., Chenery, H.J., Wilks, V., and Boyle, R.S. 1987. Language disorders in dementia of the Alzheimer type. *Brain and Language, 31*, 122–37.

Nebes, R.D., Martin, D.C., and Horn, L.C. 1984. Sparing of semantic memory in Alzheimer's disease. *Journal of Abnormal Psychology, 93*, 321–30.

Neville, H.J. and Folstein, M.F. 1979. Performance on three cognitive tasks by patients with dementia, depression, or Korsakoff's syndrome. *Gerontology, 25*, 285–90.

Niebuhr, H.R. 1963. *The Responsible Self: An Essay in Christian Moral Philosophy*. New York: Harper and Row.

Nolan, B.S. 1984. Functional evaluation of the elderly in guardianship proceedings. *Law, Medicine, and Health Care, 12*, 210–18.

Obler, L. 1981. Review of "Le Langage des Dements" by L. Irigaray. *Brain and Language, 12*, 375–86.

O'Connell, D.C., Kowal, S., and Kaltenbacher, E. 1990. Turn-taking: A critical analysis of the research tradition. *Journal of Psycholinguistic Research, 19*, 345–73.

Ogden, J.A. 1996. *Fractured Minds: A Case Study Approach to Clinical Neuropsychology*. New York: Oxford University Press.

Parrott, W.G. and Schulkin, J. 1993. Psychophysiology and the cognitive nature of the emotions. *Journal of Cognition and Emotion, 7*, 43–59.

Post, S.G. 1995. *The Moral Challenge of Alzheimer's Disease*. Baltimore, Maryland: Johns Hopkins University Press.

Post, S.G. 1998. The fear of forgetfulness: A grassroots approach to an ethics of Alzheimer's disease. *Journal of Clinical Ethics, 9*, 71–80.

Pribram, K.H. 1971. *Languages of the Brain*. Englewood Cliffs, NJ: Prentice Hall.

Reisberg, B., Ferris, S., de Leon, M., and Crook, T. 1982. The global deterioration scale for the assessment of primary degenerative dementia. *American Journal of Psychiatry, 139* (9), 1136–9.

Reisberg, B., Borenstein, J., Salob, S., and Ferris, S. 1987. Behavioral symptoms in Alzheimer's disease: Phenomenology and treatment. *Journal of Clinical Psychiatry, 48* (Suppl.), 9–15.

Rodin, J. 1986. Aging and health: Effects of the sense of control. *Science, 233*, 1271–6.

Rommetveit, R. 1974. *On Message Structure: A Framework for the Study of Language and Communication*. London: Wiley.

Rosoff, A.J. and Gottlieb, G.L. 1987. Preserving personal autonomy for the elderly. Competency, guardianship, and Alzheimer's disease. *Journal of Legal Medicine, 8*, 1–47.

References

Rothschild, D. and Sharpe, M.L. 1941. The origin of senile psychoses: Neuro-pathological factors and factors of a more personal nature. *Diseases of the Nervous System*, 2, 49–54.

Sabat, S.R. 1991a. Facilitating conversation via indirect repair: A case study of Alzheimer's disease. *Georgetown Journal of Languages and Linguistics*, 2, 284–96.

Sabat, S.R. 1991b. Turn-taking, turn-giving, and Alzheimer's disease: A case study of conversation. *Georgetown Journal of Languages and Linguistics*, 2, 167–81.

Sabat, S.R. 1994a. Language function in Alzheimer's disease: A critical review of selected literature. *Language and Communication*, 14, 331–51.

Sabat, S.R. 1994b. Excess disability and malignant social psychology: A case study of Alzheimer's disease. *Journal of Community and Applied Social Psychology*, 4, 157–66.

Sabat, S.R. 1994c. Recognizing and working with remaining abilities: Toward improving the care of Alzheimer's disease sufferers. *American Journal of Alzheimer's Disease*, 9, 8–16.

Sabat, S.R. 1999. Facilitating conversation with an Alzheimer's disease sufferer through the use of indirect repair. In H. Hamilton (ed.), *Language and Communication in Old Age: Multidisciplinary Perspectives*. New York: Garland Publishing, Inc., pp. 115–31.

Sabat, S.R. and Cagigas, X.E. 1997. Extralinguistic communication compensates for the loss of verbal fluency: A case study of Alzheimer's disease. *Language and Communication*, 17, 341–51.

Sabat, S.R., Fath, H., Moghaddam, F.M., and Harré, R. 1999. The maintenance of self-esteem: Lessons from the culture of Alzheimer's sufferers. *Culture and Psychology*, 5, 5–31.

Sabat, S.R. and Harré, R. 1992. The construction and deconstruction of self in Alzheimer's disease. *Ageing and Society*, 12, 443–61.

Sabat, S.R. and Harré, R. 1994. The Alzheimer's disease sufferer as a semiotic subject. *Philosophy, Psychiatry, Psychology*, 1, 145–60.

Sabat, S.R., Wiggs, C., and Pinizzotto, A.J. 1984. Alzheimer's disease: Clinical vs. observational studies of cognitive ability. *Journal of Clinical and Experimental Gerontology*, 6, 337–59.

Sacks, H., Schegloff, E.A., and Jefferson, G. A. 1974. A simplest systematics for the organization of turn-taking for conversation. *Language*, 50, 696–735; reprinted in a variant version (1978) in J. Schenkhein (ed.), *Studies in the Organization of Conversational Interaction*. New York: Academic Press, pp. 7–55.

Sacks, O. 1985. *The Man Who Mistook His Wife for a Hat*. New York: HarperCollins.

References

Sales, B.D. and Kahle, L.R. 1980. Law and attitudes toward the mentally ill. *Journal of Law and Psychiatry*, 3, 391–403.

Schacter, D.L. 1996. *Searching for Memory: The Brain, The Mind, and the Past*. New York: Basic Books.

Schwartz, M., Marin, O., and Saffran, E. 1979. Dissociations of language function in dementia: A case study. *Brain and Language*, 7, 277–306.

Scrutton, J. 1990. Ageism: The foundation of age discrimination. In E. McEwen (ed.), *Age: The Unrecognized Discrimination*. London: Age Concern England.

Seligman, M. 1975. *Helplessness: On Depression, Development, and Death*. San Francisco: Freeman.

Shotter, J. and Newson, J. 1974. How babies communicate. *New Society*, 29, 345–7.

Shuttleworth, E.C. and Huber, S.J. 1988. The naming disorder of dementia of Alzheimer type. *Brain and Language*, 34, 222–34.

Shweder, R. 1983. Beyond self-constructed knowledge: The study of culture and morality. *Merrill-Palmer Quarterly*, 28, 41–69.

Shweder, R.A. and Sullivan, M. 1989. The semiotic subject of cultural psychology. In L. Previn (ed.), *Handbook of Personality Theory and Research*. New York: Guilford.

Smith, D.H. 1992. Seeing and knowing dementia. In R.H. Binstock, S.G. Post, and P.J. Whitehouse (eds.), *Dementia and Aging: Ethics, Values, and Policy*. Baltimore, Maryland: Johns Hopkins University Press.

Squire, L.R. 1986. Mechanisms of memory. *Science*, 232, 1612–19.

Stern, W. 1917. *Die Psychologie und der Personalismus* (Psychology and Personalism). Leipzig, Germany: Barth.

Stern, W. 1921. Richtlinien fur die methodik der psychologischen praxis (Guidelines for the Method of Psychological Praxis). *Beihefte zur Zeitschrift fur angewandte Psychologic*, 29, 1–16.

Stern, W. 1923. *Person und Sache. System des kritischen Personalismus. Band 2: Die menschliche Personlichkeit* (Person and Thing: System of Critical Personalism. Volume 2: The Human Personality), 3rd unrevised ed. Leipzig, Germany: Barth.

Stern, W. 1929. Personlichkeitsforschung und testmethode (Personality Research and Testing Methods). *Jahrbuch der Charakterologie*, 6, 63–72.

Stern, W. 1938. *General Psychology from the Personalistic Standpoint*. Translated from the German by H.D. Spoerl, New York: Macmillan. (Original work published 1935.)

Stuss, D.T. and Benson, D.F. 1984. Neurological studies of the frontal lobes. *Psychological Bulletin*, 95, 3–28.

References

Tajfel, H. 1978. Social categorization, social identity, and social comparison. In H. Tajfel (ed.), *Differentiation Between Social Groups* (pp. 61–76). London and New York: Academic Press.

Tannen, D. 1984. *Conversational Style*. Norwood, NJ: Ablex.

Tanner, W.P., Jr. and Swets, J.A. 1954. A decision-making theory of visual detection. *Psychological Review, 61*, 401–9.

Temple, V., Sabat, S.R., and Kroger, R. 1999. Intact use of politeness strategies in the discourse of Alzheimer's disease sufferers. *Language and Communication, 19* (2), 163–180.

Tomlinson, B.E., Blessed, G., and Roth. M. 1968. Observations on the brains of non-demented old people. *Journal of Neurological Science, 7*, 331–6.

Tomlinson, B.E., Blessed, G., and Roth, M. 1970. Observations on the brains of demented old people. *Journal of Neurological Science, 11*, 205–42.

Tor, P.B. 1993. Finding incompetency in guardianship: Standardizing the process. *Arizona Law Review, 35*, 739–64.

Tor, P.B. and Sales, B.D. 1996. Research on the law and practice of guardianship. In B. Sales and S. Shah (eds.), *Law and Mental Health: Research, Policy, and Services*. Durham, North Carolina: Carolina Academic Press.

Urban, G. 1989. The "I" of Discourse. In B. Lee and G. Urban (eds.), *Semiotics, Self, and Society*. Berlin and New York: Mouton de Guyter, 27–52.

Vygotsky, L. 1965. *Thought and Language*. Cambridge, Massachusetts: MIT Press.

Wittgenstein, L. 1953. *Philosophical Investigations*. Oxford: Blackwell.

Index

351